w.bma.org

D0321649

Suicide

Among Racial and Ethnic Minority Groups

The Series in Death, Dying, and Bereavement
Consulting Editor, Robert A. Neimeyer

Beder—*Voices of Bereavement: A Casebook for Grief Counselors*
Berge—*Music of the Soul: Composing Life Out of Loss*
Davies—*Shadows in the Sun: The Experiences of Sibling Bereavement in Childhood*
Harvey—*Perspectives on Loss: A Sourcebook*
Katz & Johnson—*When Professionals Weep: Emotional and Countertransference Responses in End-of-Life Care*
Klass—*The Spiritual Lives of Bereaved Parents*
Jeffreys—*Helping Grieving People—When Tears Are Not Enough: A Handbook for Care Providers*
Leenaars—*Lives and Deaths: Selections from the Works of Edwin S. Shneidman*
Leong & Leach—*Suicide among Racial and Ethnic Minority Groups: Theory, Research, and Practice*
Lester—*Katie's Diary: Unlocking the Mystery of a Suicide*
Martin, Doka—*Men Don't Cry ... Women Do: Transcending Gender Stereotypes of Grief*
Nord—*Multiple AIDS-Related Loss: A Handbook for Understanding and Surviving a Perpetual Fall*
Roos—*Chronic Sorrow: A Living Loss*
Rogers—*The Art of Grief: The Use of Expressive Arts in a Grief Support Group*
Rosenblatt—*Parent Grief: Narratives of Loss and Relationship*
Rosenblatt & Wallace—*African-American Grief*
Tedeschi & Calhoun—*Helping Bereaved Parents: A Clinician's Guide*
Silverman—*Widow to Widow, Second Edition*
Werth—*Contemporary Perspectives on Rational Suicide*

Formerly The Series in Death Education, Aging, and Health Care
Hannelore Wass, Consulting Editor

Bard—*Medical Ethics in Practice*
Benoliel—*Death Education for the Health Professional*
Bertman—*Facing Death: Images, Insights, and Interventions*
Brammer—*How to Cope with Life Transitions: The Challenge of Personal Change*
Cleiren—*Bereavement and Adaptation: A Comparative Study of the Aftermath of Death*
Corless, Pittman-Lindeman—*AIDS: Principles, Practices, and Politics,* Abridged Edition
Corless, Pittman-Lindeman—*AIDS: Principles, Practices, and Politics,* Reference Edition
Curran—*Adolescent Suicidal Behavior*
Davidson—*The Hospice: Development and Administration. Second Edition*
Davidson, Linnolla—*Risk Factors in Youth Suicide*
Degner, Beaton—*Life-Death Decisions in Health Care*
Doka—*AIDS, Fear, and Society: Challenging the Dreaded Disease*
Doty—*Communication and Assertion Skills for Older Persons*

Epting, Neimeyer—*Personal Meanings of Death: Applications for Personal Construct Theory to Clinical Practice*
Haber—*Health Care for an Aging Society: Cost-Conscious Community Care and Self-Care Approaches*
Hughes—*Bereavement and Support: Healing in a Group Environment*
Irish, Lundquist, Nelsen—*Ethnic Variations in Dying, Death, and Grief: Diversity in Universality*
Klass, Silverman, Nickman—*Continuing Bonds: New Understanding of Grief*
Lair—*Counseling the Terminally Ill: Sharing the Journey*
Leenaars, Maltsberger, Neimeyer—*Treatment of Suicidal People*
Leenaars, Wenckstern—*Suicide Prevention in Schools*
Leng—*Psychological Care in Old Age*
Leviton—*Horrendous Death, Health, and Well-Being*
Leviton—*Horrendous Death and Health: Toward Action*
Lindeman, Corby, Downing, Sanborn—*Alzheimer's Day Care: A Basic Guide*
Lund—*Older Bereaved Spouses: Research with Practical Applications*
Neimeyer—*Death Anxiety Handbook: Research, Instrumentation, and Application*
Papadatou, Papadatos—*Children and Death*
Prunkl, Berry—*Death Week: Exploring the Dying Process*
Ricker, Myers—*Retirement Counseling: A Practical Guide for Action*
Samarel—*Caring for Life and Death*
Sherron, Lumsden—*Introduction to Educational Gerontology. Third Edition*
Stillion—*Death and Sexes: An Examination of Differential Longevity Attitudes, Behaviors, and Coping Skills*
Stillion, McDowell, May—*Suicide Across the Life Span—Premature Exits*
Vachon—*Occupational Stress in the Care of the Critically Ill, the Dying, and the Bereaved*
Wass, Corr—*Childhood and Death*
Wass, Corr—*Helping Children Cope with Death: Guidelines and Resource. Second Edition*
Wass, Corr, Pacholski, Forfar—*Death Education II: An Annotated Resource Guide*
Wass, Neimeyer—*Dying: Facing the Facts.* Third Edition
Weenolsen—*Transcendence of Loss over the Life Span*
Werth—*Rational Suicide? Implications for Mental Health Professionals*

Suicide
Among Racial and Ethnic Minority Groups

Theory, Research, and Practice

Edited by

Frederick T.L. Leong • Mark M. Leach

Routledge
Taylor & Francis Group
270 Madison Avenue
New York, NY 10016

Routledge
Taylor & Francis Group
2 Park Square
Milton Park, Abingdon
Oxon OX14 4RN

Routledge is an imprint of Taylor & Francis Group, an Informa business

Printed in the United States of America on acid-free paper
10 9 8 7 6 5 4 3 2

International Standard Book Number-13: 978-0-415-95532-4 (Hardcover)

Library of Congress Cataloging-in-Publication Data

Suicide among racial and ethnic minority groups : theory, research, and practice / [edited by] Frederick T.L. Leong and Mark M. Leach.
p. cm. -- (The series in death, dying, and bereavement ; 17)
Includes bibliographical references and index.
ISBN-13: 978-0-415-95532-4 (hardcover)
1. Minorities--Suicidal behavior--United States. I. Leong, Frederick T. L. II. Leach, Mark M.

HV6545.5.S845 2007
362.28089'00973--dc22 2007024895

Visit the Taylor & Francis Web site at
http://www.taylorandfrancis.com

and the Routledge Web site at
http://www.routledge.com

CONTENTS

SERIES EDITOR'S FOREWORD

Although White middle-income people constitute only 5% of the world's population, nearly all approaches to suicide assessment and intervention derive from the assumptions of, and research upon, this restricted segment of humanity. The result has been an unintentional abetting of ethnic disparities in healthcare, as racial and cultural issues (and sometimes populations) have been marginalized or rendered invisible by dominant frameworks of suicidology. The thoughtful contributions to *Suicide among Racial and Ethnic Minority Groups* take a long step in the direction of rectifying this imbalance.

Beyond a general advocacy for multicultural sensitivity, what do the 13 chapters that constitute this volume add to our efforts to extend ethically appropriate, enthnologically informed and evidence-based attention to the suicide patterns and processes of American minorities? In a phrase, the answer is "a great deal." In response to the overly generalized depiction of "non-White" suicide statistics and deficit-based models of risk that characterized the early literature, Leong and Leach have assembled an impressive panel of experts—themselves diverse in race and ethnicity—to integrate and present the lessons of an evolving literature that is far more nuanced, and that attends to cultural factors that are protective against suicide, as well as contributory to it.

Some sense of the scope of this effort is provided by a quick perusal of the book's Table of Contents, which addresses classic suicide theories, and then stretches these through a close consideration of data on African American, Latino and Latina, Asian American, Pacific-Island, and Native American populations. The results of this careful sifting of hundreds of studies are always revealing and sometimes surprising, identifying unique risk factors associated with migration to the United States, acculturation struggles, and generational conflicts that increase the risk of suicide for both younger and older members of some ethnic communities. The reader frequently encounters evidence that distinguishes between various minority group members and the European American clients whose risk profiles may be more familiar, such as the discovery that self-destructiveness in African Americans is less likely to be associated with alcohol abuse at the time of an attempt, or cultural injunctions against communicating suicidal thoughts that create a group of "hidden ideators." Still more subtly, contributors probe the dimensions of "diversity within diversity" by decomposing large racial categories (e.g., Native Americans, Hispanics, Pacific Islanders) into their constituent subgroups in order to examine the sometimes surprisingly different rates of self-harm that characterize communities distinguished by language, social class, education, country of origin, and place of residence. Explanations for these differences are found in sources as varied as their distinct histories of colonization, experiences of racism, and patterns of immigration on the one hand, and distinctive social structures and patterns of language use on the other. To choose but a single example, native Hawaiians and Micronesians tend to use the word "anger" to describe experiences that normative (White) discourse would describe as "depression." Thus, beyond providing the best-available summary of epidemiological data on suicide risk for various groups and subgroups, the authors offer "news you can use" as a practicing clinician to function with greater cultural competence in serving diverse communities.

Although the authors are appropriately humble in acknowledging the need for better outcome research on suicide interventions with different cultural groups, they nevertheless offer a plethora of diversity-sensitive guidelines for improving both research and practice. Among these are suggestions for customizing assessment instruments and protocols to the needs of different minorities, the importance of partnering with community resource systems (e.g., churches) and influential members (e.g., elders) in the design and implementation of culturally adapted prevention programs, and the utilization of culture-specific protective factors, such as racial pride and spirituality to inform intervention. At its most ambitious, this effort transcends the overly individualized focus of most psychotherapy to encompass a transactional–ecological perspective that avoids "victim-blaming," instead situating therapy in a realistic understanding of suicide as a response to destructive social forces outside of persons, as well as psychological forces within them. I am therefore appreciative that Leong and Leach have orchestrated this major contribution to the Routledge *Series on Death, Dying, and Bereavement*, and that the series can play a role in bringing it to the attention of a broad community of researchers and practitioners who will benefit greatly from the counsel it has to offer.

Robert A. Neimeyer, PhD., Series Editor

July, 2007

ABOUT THE EDITORS

Frederick T. L. Leong is professor of psychology at Michigan State University in the Industrial/Organizational and Clinical Psychology programs. He has authored or co-authored more than 100 articles in various counseling and psychology journals and 60 book chapters. He has also edited or co-edited 10 books. He is editor-in-chief of the *Encyclopedia of counseling* (Sage Publications, in preparation). Dr. Leong is a Fellow of the APA, APS, Asian American Psychological Association and the International Academy for Intercultural Research. His major research interests center around culture and mental health, cross-cultural psychotherapy (especially with Asians and Asian Americans), cultural and personality factors related to career choice and work adjustment. He is the current president of APA's Division 45 (Society for the Psychological Study of Ethnic Minority Issues) and also serves on their Board of Scientific Affairs, the Minority Fellowship Program Advisory Committee and the Commission on Ethnic Minority Recruitment, Retention, and Training (CEMRRAT2) Task Force.

Mark M. Leach is director of training of the Counseling Psychology Program in the Department of Psychology at the University of Southern Mississippi. He recently published *Cultural diversity and suicide: Ethnic, religious, gender, and sexual orientation perspectives* (Haworth Press) and co-edited a recent special issue in *Death Studies* with Dr. Leong on ethnicity and suicide. He is on the Executive Committees of Division 36 (Psychology of Religion) of the American Psychological Association and Division 16 (Counseling Psychology) of the International Association of Applied Psychology. He has published in numerous areas, all with diversity as a foundation. Dr. Leach is on the editorial board of three journals, has been a member on others, and is an ad hoc reviewer for multiple psychology journals. He has three other books under contract in the areas of spirituality, culture, and counseling psychology.

CONTRIBUTORS

Carmela Alcántara, MA, is a doctoral candidate in clinical psychology at the University of Michigan in Ann Arbor. Her research interests include cultural psychology and mental health, specifically, the use of mixed methods to explore the interrelationships among culture, language, thought, and the phenomenology of psychopathology in ethnic minority communities. Other research interests include anxiety disorders, acculturation, immigration, and mental health service delivery.

Naleen N. Andrade is a professor and chair of the Department of Psychiatry at the John A. Burns School of Medicine, University of Hawai'i at Mānoa. She is the director of the National Center for Indigenous Hawaiian Behavioral Health and served as PI of a minority infrastructure grant from the National Institute of Mental health. Dr. Andrade received her MD from the John A. Burns School of Medicine and received post-doctoral public health–executive training at the Harvard School of Public Health. She was a Ginsberg Fellow for the group for the Advancement of Psychiatry and a Fellow and Regent of the American College of Psychiatrists. She is currently the director of the American Board of Psychiatry and Neurology and the chair of the Board of Trustees for the Queen's Medical Center. Dr. Andrade's research interests include indigenous health disparities and the role of Hawaiian culture in mental health and well-being.

David Dei Asiamah is a graduate student in the clinical-community program in the Department of Psychology at the University of South Carolina. He completed his BA in psychology with a minor in French at Morehouse College. David's primary research focus is minority mental health, including risk and protective factors for optimal well-being.

Guillermo Bernal is professor of psychology and director of the University Center for Psychological Services and Research at the University of Puerto Rico-UPR, Río Piedras. He is a Fellow of APA (Divisions 45,

12, & 27). His work has focused on training, research, and the development of mental health treatments responsive to ethnic minorities. He has published over 100 journal articles and chapters and six books. His current work is in the efficacy of parent interventions in the treatment of depression in adolescents (funded by NIMH). His most recent books are *Theory and practice of psychotherapy in Puerto Rico* (2005) and the *Handbook of racial and ethnic minority psychology* (2003). He is the associate editor for research of *Family Process.*

Yovanska M. Duarté-Vélez received her PhD (2007) in clinical psychology from the University of Puerto Rico. She was awarded an individual predoctoral fellowship from NMIH to study suicide risk in Puerto Rican adolescents. Her work has focused on assessment and treatment of depressed and suicidal Latino adolescents and their families. Her research interests are on evidence-based treatments for suicidal and depressed Latino adolescents, ethnic and sexual minority issues in mental health, gender roles, and family relationships.

Iwalani R. N. Else is an assistant professor with the Department of Psychiatry at the John A. Burns School of Medicine, University of Hawai'i at Mānoa, and serves as the associate director of the National Center for Indigenous Hawaiian Behavioral Health. Dr. Else is a NIH Health Disparities Scholar through the loan repayment program in Health Disparities Research and is a former Fellow of the American Sociological Association's Minority Fellowship Program in Mental Health. Dr. Else received a Ph.D. in Sociology from the University of Hawai'i at Mānoa. Her research interests include Native Hawaiian and Pacific Islander health disparities, the link between mental health and medical conditions, and culturally and socially responsive community-based behavioral health services.

Joseph P. Gone is assistant professor in the Department of Psychology (Clinical Area) and the Program in American Culture (Native American Studies) at the University of Michigan in Ann Arbor. As a cultural psychologist, Gone addresses in his research the key dilemma confronting mental health professionals who serve Native American communities, namely how to provide culturally appropriate helping services that avoid the neocolonial subversion of local thought and practice. He has published articles and chapters concerning the ethnopsychological investigation of self, identity, personhood, and social relations in American Indian cultural contexts vis-à-vis the mental health professions.

Jay M. Greenfeld is currently a doctoral student in the Counseling Psychology Program at The University of Iowa. He received his master's in counseling psychology from New York University in 2005. He is a student affiliate of Division 17 and Division 51 of the American Psychological Association. His major area of research is in social class, men and masculinity, and motivation, especially older adolescents and college students.

Arpana Gupta, MEd, is a fourth-year doctoral-level student in the Counseling Psychology program at the University of Tennessee, Knoxville. Her research interests include cultural/racial identity issues, the process of acculturation, stereotype threat, and discrimination experienced by Asian Americans, mental health problems specifically related to suicide in Asian Americans, Asian American public policy and quantitative research methods such as meta-analyses and structural equation modeling. She is active in Divisions 17 and 45 of the American Psychological Association and serves as the Division 45 student representative, the regional diversity coordinator for APAGS-CEMA and the Student Board representative for the Asian American Psychological Association (AAPA).

Joshua N. Hook, MS, is a doctoral candidate in counseling psychology at Virginia Commonwealth University, Richmond, Virginia. He is a student member of the American Psychological Association, the Eastern Psychological Association, and the Christian Association for Psychological Studies. His research interests include marriage therapy and enrichment, religion and spirituality, forgiveness, religiously tailored counseling, and cultural issues.

Julie Jenks Kettmann received her Master of Education degree in community counseling from Loyola University Chicago. She is currently a fifth-year Ph.D. student in counseling psychology at The University of Iowa and is completing an APA-approved predoctoral internship. Her research and practice interests include suicide prevention, college student mental health, and adults with learning disabilities or ADHD.

Antoon A. Leenaars, PhD, CPsych, CPQ, is a psychologist in private practice in mental health and public health and has been or is affiliated with or has consulted with international academic or government institutions and the WHO. He is a past president of the American Association of Suicidology (AAS). He has published over 150 professional articles, chapters, or books with colleagues in more than 30 nations on violence, suicide, suicide notes, genocide, gun control, and prevention/psychotherapy. His publication *Psychotherapy with suicidal people* (2004) is one of the first evidence-based books on the treatment of suicidality, with cultural sensitivity. He is internationally recognized for his efforts in suicide prevention and research/collaborations with indigenous people.

David Lester has PhD degrees from Cambridge University (in social and political science) and from Brandeis University (in psychology). He has served as president of the International Association for Suicide Prevention and written extensively on suicide, murder, and other topics in thanatology. He is presently professor of psychology at the Richard Stockton College of New Jersey.

Samantha Matlin is in the doctoral program in clinical/community psychology at the George Washington University in Washington, DC. She is currently a predoctoral fellow at the Yale University School of Medicine Department of Psychiatry, Connecticut Mental Health Center/The Consultation Center. She earned her B.A. in psychology from the University of Pennsylvania. In general, her research interests have focused on community-based prevention/intervention programs among ethnic minority adolescents targeting depression/suicide. Clinically, she enjoys working with adolescents, families, and adults from diverse backgrounds.

Sherry Davis Molock is an associate professor of psychology at George Washington University in Washington, DC and conducts research on depression and suicidal behaviors in the African American community with an emphasis on developing suicide-prevention programs in African American churches. She serves on the Board of Directors of the National Organization of People of Color against Suicide (NOPCAS), the National Scientific Advisory Committee of SPAN-USA and on NIMH's Interventions Committee for Disorders Involving Children and Their Families. She is a consulting editor for *Suicide and Life Threatening Behavior, Cultural Diversity and Ethnic Minority Psychology,* and the *Journal of Black Psychology.*

Henry Prempeh is currently a doctoral student in the Clinical/Community Psychology program at George Washington University in Washington, DC. He earned a BA degree in psychology from Georgetown University and an MA in clinical psychology from Pepperdine University. His research interests include mood disorders, suicidality among African American adolescents, and developing suicide prevention programs through African-American churches.

Lillian Range received a PhD in psychology (clinical) from Georgia State University. She is professor at Our Lady of Holy Cross College and professor emeritus of The University of Southern Mississippi. She is a fellow of Division 12 of the American Psychological Association and associate editor of *Death Studies.*

James R. Rogers received his PhD from the University of Akron in 1993 where he is currently a professor in the Collaborative Program in

Counseling Psychology. His research interests are in the areas of suicide, trauma and growth, disaster mental health response, and psychometrics.

Pia Stanard is a graduate student in counseling psychology at Virginia Commonwealth University (VCU) in Richmond, Virginia. She recently completed her Master of Science degree and is currently pursuing a doctorate with a sub-specialization in community psychology. She received her Bachelor of Arts in psychology and French language & literature from Loyola College in Maryland in 2003. Currently, she works as a research assistant and study coordinator at VCU's Literacy Institute. Her current research involves African American youth and academic outcomes. She is interested in the promotion of resilience and positive life outcomes among African American youth and plans to pursue a career in program development.

Gregory E. Townley is a graduate student in clinical-community psychology at the University of South Carolina. He received his baccalaureate degrees in psychology and Africana studies at North Carolina State University. His primary research foci are community integration of persons with serious mental illnesses, cross-cultural determinants of mental health, and neighborhood and community contexts as they relate to well-being. He has presented at numerous conferences, including the Society for Community Research and Action, and has four scholarly publications published or under review. He is poised to pursue an academic career and a program of community-based research among diverse cultural groups.

Shawn O. Utsey is an associate professor of counseling psychology in the Department of Psychology at Virginia Commonwealth University. He received his doctorate in counseling psychology from Fordham University in New York City. He is currently the editor-in-chief for the *Journal of Black Psychology* (*JBP*) and has served in this capacity since 2001. More recently, Dr. Utsey has examined the influence of African American culture (e.g., collective social orientation, spiritual centeredness, verve, etc.) on indicators of health and well-being. In addition, he is a leading scholar in the area of race and racism and, along with Joseph Ponterotto and Paul Pedersen, recently released the book *Preventing prejudice*, a second edition of a previous Sage Publications Multicultural Series bestseller. Dr. Utsey is the 2004 recipient of the Emerging Professional Award from Division 45 of the American Psychological Association and the 2004 Kenneth and Mamie Clark Mentoring Award from APAGS, the student division of the American Psychological Association.

Rheeda L. Walker, Ph.D., is an assistant professor in the Department of Psychology at Southern Illinois University (SIU) and a licensed clinical psychologist. Dr. Walker is a former visiting research scientist at the Center for the Study and Prevention of Suicide at the University of Rochester Medical Center's Department of Psychiatry. Her primary research foci are in sociocultural determinants of suicide risk and African American mental health processes. Dr. Walker has written or co-authored 16 peer-reviewed manuscripts in journals such as *Suicide and Life-Threatening Behavior, Cultural Diversity and Ethnic Minority Psychology,* and the *Journal of Black Psychology.*

John S. Westefeld is a professor in the Counseling Psychology Program at The University of Iowa. He received his PhD in counseling psychology from the University of North Carolina-Chapel Hill in 1978. He is a diplomate in counseling psychology and a Fellow of Division 17 of the American Psychological Association. His major area of research is suicide, focusing in particular on college student suicide.

Devon E. Whitehead is a doctoral student in counseling psychology at the University of Akron. Prior to entering her doctoral studies, she completed her master's degree in clinical psychology at the University of Northern Iowa, where her thesis focused on the refinement of a measure of suicide resilience. Her current research interests include suicide and post-traumatic growth.

Suicide Among Racial and Ethnic Minority Groups

An Introduction

Frederick T. Leong and Mark M. Leach

Most of what is known about suicidal behaviors is derived from the dominant culture, for a number of reasons. First, the majority of persons attempting and completing suicide are European American if one were to assess sheer numbers. Approximately 30,000 people kill themselves each year in the United States, with almost 90% being White. Second, until less than 40 years ago, suicides were tabled as "White" or "Non-White." Ethnic differences were nonexistent and there was little interest in determining culturally specific reasons for "Non-White" suicides. Third, the majority of suicidologists are European American and may consider groups of color but have not made them a focus of their research program. In essence, culture is considered a secondary factor instead of a primary factor. Fourth, although there is little literature assessing cultural issues relevant to ethnic suicide, there is an emerging amount. Finally, there has never been a call to the profession to begin to consider suicide from multiple worldviews. Leach (2006) was the first to compile much of the ethnic suicide literature, and this book is the second. The editors and authors of this text challenge researchers and clinicians to begin to consider suicide from a variety of cultural perspectives. Only through the addition of this knowledge will our understanding of suicide become more robust.

Because suicide is a major public health problem in the United States and much of our knowledge base of suicide is Eurocentric (i.e., based on the dominant European American culture), it is imperative that we begin to correct this oversight as another track within the scientific community's attempt to address the problem ethnic disparities in health. Therefore, the primary purpose of this book is to address the question of how the complex nature and manifestation of culture, race, and ethnicity may influence suicide among the various cultural groups within the United States. We have sought to compile and integrate this limited knowledge base with the goal of providing some guidance to clinicians, educators, and researchers who are faced with the challenge of understanding, preventing, and intervening to reduce suicide among racial and ethnic minority groups in this country.

To achieve this purpose, the volume is divided into three sections, the first being Theoretical Inclusion of Multicultural Issues, the second Specific Racial and Ethnic Groups, and the third Prevention, Assessment, Treatment, Training, and Research Recommendations. In Chapters 2 and 3 of Section I, Leenaars and Lester introduce readers to the notion that suicide is multidimensional, and that the ecological model has recently gained attention as a framework from which to conceptualize ethnicity and suicide. This model states that different levels (e.g., individual, social, cultural) interact to contribute to suicidal behaviors. Drawing from their work examining suicide from a cross-cultural perspective, the authors attempt to translate current cultural manifestations of suicide into a U.S. ethnic perspective. Unfortunately, though accurately, they acknowledge the dearth of existing theories that take ethnicity into account, and also indicate that further theory development is needed. More questions are offered than answers, reinforcing the original intent of chapters' inclusion: that suicide theoreticians should begin focusing their efforts on groups of color.

Leenaars mentions the need for an increased use of suicide-note investigations to further theory development. He then offers readers eight templates or patterns from which to understand suicide. Ethnicity and culture could seemingly be introduced into each one. Lester argues that we need to consider the linguistics of suicide, alluding to the fact that more research in the interpretation and expression of suicide with persons of color is needed. He also discusses the erroneous assumption that there is ethnic invariability in suicide, followed by international studies suggesting otherwise. Both Leenaars and Lester suggest that we begin to examine more closely our understanding of suicide internationally in order to glean ideas for theory development in the U.S. It is a place to begin discussions, although international research often comprises broad, almost categorical data. What is clear is that the authors are hopeful that theory development that includes more cultural data is possible, though fundamental questions surrounding suicide will have to be revisited or initially addressed.

In Section II, we invited leading scholars to critically review the literature with regards to suicide among racial and ethnic minority groups. In

Chapter 4, which is concerned with African Americans, Utsey, Hook, and Stanard discuss the risk and protective factors related to African American suicide and highlight the pattern of males and adolescents as being the most likely to complete suicidal acts within that community. Although suicide rates have fluctuated in an unpredictable fashion over the past 40 years in comparison with other ethnic groups, surprisingly little is known about the reasons underlying these trends. These authors go on to propose and investigate cultural models that explain the lower rates of suicide in African Americans from various perspectives: sociological, psychological, and ecological. In addition, strength-based protective factors are examined that help buffer African Americans from high suicide rates. Examples of these factors include religious and spiritual strength, cohesive family relationships, close friendships, supportive social networks, lower rates of drug and alcohol consumption, and Black consciousness—better known as racial pride. At the same time, these authors identify certain sociocultural risk factors that do contribute to increased rates of suicide among African Americans. These include psychological distress, substance abuse and illicit drug use, the availability of lethal means, social isolation, family dysfunction, impaired interpersonal functioning, maladaptive coping skills, exposure to racial inequality, prior history of suicide attempts, or social stigma associated with mental distress. All of these factors are discussed within the cultural context of the African American community and with an eye to future research directions and implications for clinical practice and public policy.

Chapter 5 is concerned with Hispanics. In this chapter, Duarte-Velez and Bernal examine the conceptual methodological contextual and developmental issues related to suicide among Hispanic youth, as suicide is the third leading cause of death among this population. Youths are known to have the highest suicide rates within the Hispanic population and have the highest suicide risk behaviors in comparison with other ethnic groups. Due to both the large amount of diversity and the similarities found within the subgroups of this ethnic group, the authors suggest that considerations be given to conceptual factors such as ethnicity, ethnic identity, race, and context. Within-group diversity can be investigated using nation of origin, generational status in the U.S., and language use. These factors are also linked to methodological issues and will determine study design, sampling, recruitment, measurement, and sample retention. The bottom line is that careful, thoughtful, and culturally sensitive approaches need to be applied to these analytical issues when researching this topic within this ethnic group. The authors also discuss other sociocultural and environmental factors that are important to the development of identity and in turn affect suicidal behavior(s). Some examples include concepts such as *familismo, machismo,* and acculturation. The authors highlight studies where Latino youngsters who had attempted suicide were experiencing significantly more school, personality, behavioral, and family stressors than the matched-pair control groups. The main drawback discussed was how researchers use the term "Hispanic" for all subgroups without any further differentiation of these subgroups within the larger population.

In a review of existing studies related to suicide behavior among Hispanic youth, the authors first summarize comparative population-based studies of suicide behavior among adolescents, and concluded that the evidence is suggestive of differential rates by ethnicity for suicide ideation, attempts, lethal attempts, and suicide. The authors also note that the differences in the use of definitions and temporal frames have made it difficult to reach specific conclusions. Then, within-group studies focusing on Hispanics are reviewed that allow a more critical evaluation of research findings and the formulation of more specific conclusions. The authors underscore the significant relationship of social and psychological variables to suicide behavior in Hispanic groups, as well as the lack of a theory to inform the findings. Finally, the authors examined evidence-based treatment for suicidal Hispanic adolescents, and stressed the urgent need for well controlled trials and outcome studies, as well as the need to document results and findings.

In Chapter 6, Leong, Leach, and Gupta review the literature on suicide among Asian Americans and recommend directions for future research to fill in the current gaps. A case study is described and discussed with reference to the culture-specific factors associated with suicide among Asian Americans. Asian Americans are a heterogeneous group and at first glance it appears that there is not enough information regarding suicide among the various subgroups or among the Asian American ethnic group as a whole. Recently, there has been an increased interest and effort to fill in the gaps in the current research, most of which has been done among the university student population and has focused on completed suicides versus suicidal attempts or ideations.

The chapter introduces and highlights cultural factors characteristic of suicide among Asian Americans. Some of these factors have been investigated in depth and have undergone rigorous empirical testing, while some of these other factors have not yet been investigated. The five main areas discussed in this chapter are: Age and Gender; Religious and Spiritual Issues; Acculturation and Social Support; Familial and Social Integration; and Gay/Lesbian/Bisexual issues. Other contributing factors shared by other ethnic groups include depression and hopelessness, job loss, death in the family, relationship breakups, and perfectionism. All these factors are important for counselors and researchers to consider when determining suicide risk. These factors also have important policy implications. Future directions for research are discussed and provide a foundation for future efforts in areas of research, clinical practice, and public policy.

Studies on suicide and suicide behaviors or issues among Pacific Islanders are fairly rare. Else and Andrade present a comprehensive review of some of the pressing factors associated with suicide among this group in Chapter 7. Specifically, sociocultural information about suicide among Hawaiians, Samoans, and Micronesians is presented within a historical context. Pacific Islanders have traditionally been included in the more general category of "Asian Americans" or "Asian Americans and Pacific Islanders." This grouping fails to take into account important differences in suicide rates, behaviors, and patterns among the various Asian subgroups. The important fact to highlight is that Pacific Islanders are not Asians and therefore factors associated with one group need to be delineated from the other. Contrary to popular belief, Pacific Islanders are not immigrants or descendants of American immigrants. Pacific Islanders are indigenous peoples and, similar to the suicide patterns displayed by Native Americans and Alaskan Natives, demonstrate the highest completed suicide rates in the world, especially for males between the ages of 15 and 25.

Pacific Islanders have been shown to display a preference for militaristic altruistic suicides, which, unlike terrorism suicide, are infused with a notion of nobility to carry out messages of resistance against enemies that cannot be defeated physically. Thus, the altruistic suicide offers an option to strive for metaphysical victory. Suicide in this framework gives it cultural meaning and relevance, especially with regard to group norms, conformity, and cohesion. Culture is extremely important in understanding, defining, investigating, and intervening with suicidality issues among Pacific Islanders. Chapter 7 also offers discussions of the influence of role norms and generational issues, traditions, and disparities between ideal, internalized ethnocultural identity and external persona in suicide among Pacific Islanders.

In Chapter 8, Alcantara and Gone discuss risk and protective factors for suicide within the Native American community using a transactional-ecological framework. They argue that it is important to realize that suicide is not only an individual and familial issue but a community and public concern, especially within smaller, tight-knit communities such as Native American communities. Suicide rates among Native Americans are proportionally almost twice as high as the national rate, with the majority being adolescent males, resulting in a great need to continue investigating causes and prevention efforts of suicide. The transactional-ecological framework is a developmental, preventive approach that focuses on the interactions between individuals and their environments, given that evidence indicates that local culture is influential with suicide ideation, attempts, and completions. The authors maintain that it is critically important to understand the trajectories that lead to intermediate negative outcomes that increase suicide risk but de-emphasize the individual and a particular disorder, and emphasize context. Restoring normative trajectories becomes the focus of intervention rather than an emphasis on an individual, disease model of treatment.

The third section of this volume is concerned with Prevention, Assessment, Treatment, Training, and Research aspects of suicide among racial and ethnic minority groups. This section begin with Chapter 9 by Walker, Townley, and Asiamah, who discuss the limited empirical information on suicide prevention efforts among ethnic minority groups. They initially make some interesting statements that raise even more interesting questions. For example, if suicide has different cultural meanings across ethnocultural groups, how can we adequately devise culturally inclusive prevention programs? Should we continue to use some existing prevention programs if they have not been adequately evaluated? The authors even report the question asked by Mishara (2006), president of the International Association for Suicide Prevention, when he asked how much of suicide is universal and how much of the etiology is culture-specific. It is good to know that prominent suicidologists are asking these questions, although due to the literature's infancy, our current knowledge does not transfer easily into prevention efforts.

Walker et al. then summarize selected pieces of the ethnic suicide literature, though interested readers should be referred back to earlier chapters that expand on the summary. The authors highlight the few existing ethnic suicide prevention programs, focusing their efforts on American Indian suicide, because multiple, though largely unsystematic, programs have been developed and implemented. To increase research into prevention programs the authors propose three key domains for persons of color, including a "(1) accurate assessment and treatment of psychiatric symptoms, which include (2) the impact of race-related stressors and acculturative vulnerability, and (3) ethnocultural resilience." They argue that ethnocultural perspectives may be most beneficial and systematic prevention models should be customized for specific ethnic groups. Walker et al. offer suggestions to begin to create these programs and cultural factors to consider. Multiple research questions follow to accelerate prevention research and program development.

In Chapter 10, Westefeld, Range, Greenfeld, and Kettman introduce readers to the paucity of literature and complexity involved with culturally sensitive suicide assessment. They indicate that inclusion of culture in risk assessment involves at least four facets: (1) ethnic minority inclusion in assessment instrument standardization, (2) awareness of disclosure differences, (3) knowledge of different ethnic groups, and (4) increased attention to cultural issues when assessing suicidal thoughts and actions. Currently, the few researchers who have considered ethnicity when developing risk assessment instruments do not use a multicultural framework as their theoretical foundation. Westefeld et al. summarize nicely the most widely used instruments, including their attention to ethnic issues. They argue for increased attention to broader segments of society when developing instruments to determine both reliability and validity with groups of color. Due to different definitions, perceptions, understanding, acceptability, and language associated with suicide, most current instruments have questionable utility. The authors' views of language differences are consistent with views of other authors in this text. Suicide terminology differs among ethnic groups whether English is the first language or not, and it would benefit the field to continue to examine the role of language on suicide.

Assessment includes disclosure of potential lethality. The authors report literature indicating that ethnic minority individuals are reluctant to open up to European American counselors, although they may also be reluctant regardless of counselor ethnicity. Westefeld et al. mention that persons of color are less likely to disclose suicide ideation on intake forms, and highlight that racial identity and previous discrimination may be important suicide assessment factors to consider. Assessment of these and other cultural variables becomes especially important during less structured, face-to-face interviews, as it is unlikely that structured interviews and instruments can tap these cultural nuances. The authors then briefly summarize the literature on assessment with the four broad ethnic groups in the U.S., followed by the application of the Multicultural Assessment Procedure (MAP) (Ridley, Li, & Hill, 1998) to suicide assessment. The model is a generic, culturally sensitive approach to assessment and Westefeld et al. introduce the four-phase model and apply it to suicide assessment.

In Chapter 11, Rogers and Whitehead continue to delve into new territory along with the rest of the book's authors by focusing on interventions and treatments from a culturally sensitive perspective. They acknowledge the limited literature regarding ethnic issues in treatment and indicate that the lack of specificity mirrors that of general suicide interventions. Their criticism of the "one size fits all" model is consistent with the intent of this text, as approaches to suicide interventions can be modified based on contextual relevance.

The authors begin with the crisis intervention approach to treatment and draw attention to Thomas and Leitner's (2005) three response styles of suicide intervention. The "ideal" response is one most consistent with the values associated with a culturally sensitive approach espoused by authors of this book. Rogers and Whitehead then discuss suicide questions for counselors to consider within a cultural framework, followed by areas for clinicians and researchers to consider such as language, respect for diversity, counselor–client suicide belief compatibility, and both general and causative client beliefs about suicide.

Their chapter ends with an introduction to the Collaborative Assessment and Management (CAMS) (Jobes, 2006) model of suicide, which is well-suited for a culturally sensitive approach to treatment. This model allows for increased shared understanding between client and clinician on the individual factors associated with suicide. It allows for greater client input and promotes a collaborative therapeutic relationship, unlike other models that emphasize counselor control or detachment. Though research incorporating cultural components of suicide into the CAMS model is sorely needed, it does offer promise as an initial framework from which to approach suicidal clients.

In Chapter 12, Molock, Matlin, and Prempeh focus on current suicide training in graduate programs and indicate that training varies greatly depending on program type and model considered. After reviewing the literature they conclude that no research has investigated the role of ethnicity on suicide training, which has relevance to the American Psychological Association's call for cultural competence training. They include barriers to addressing ethnicity in suicide training, including the difficulty involved for some trainers to examine their own ethnic identity; ignoring heterogeneity within ethnic groups, bringing culture from unconsciousness to consciousness, and measurement issues. The authors provide some solutions to these barriers including using ecological frameworks, providing safe training environments, identifying practicum and course experiences that integrate suicide and ethnic minority groups, incorporating spirituality into treatment, and building relationships with community leaders and psychologists.

Molock et al. then call on trainers to teach students to conduct multicultural research on suicide, with their earlier guidelines being directly applicable to research. They mention that it is perfectly acceptable to study suicide within a particular ethnic group so as to avoid assumptions that all ethnic groups and individuals will respond similarly. Culturally related values need to be incorporated into the research through relationship-building and language use. The authors also highlight the need for increased contextual studies aimed at prevention, multiple methodologies, and understanding of research biases.

In Chapter 13, Leach and Leong highlight some of the research questions posed by the authors of each chapter, as well as questions from Leach (2006). Consistent with the structure of the text the authors begin with Section I questions surrounding whether theories that embrace cultural components can be constructed. They move to Section II of the text on specific ethnic groups. All authors in this text discussed the paucity of literature on ethnicity and suicide and the need for greater research efforts. Thus, research questions are numerous, yet also brief because of the overwhelming possibilities, and Leach and Leong propose that readers carefully review individual chapters in addition to their own chapter for research ideas. Each of the authors of the five ethnic-group chapters stress the need for studies assessing within-group variation from multiple levels. For example, on an ethnic level, rather than simply examining Asian Americans, it is time that we begin to further consider Japanese Americans, Cambodian Americans, Malaysian Americans, and Chinese Americans, among others. The same could be said of most other groups. On an identity level it would be beneficial for extended research in areas such as racial identity, acculturation, sexual identity, community identity, and religious identity, for example. In essence, the field needs to move beyond ethnic generalizations to an exacting and meaningful understanding of the cultural nuances among ethnic subgroups.

Leach and Leong highlight areas of needed research from Section III chapters on prevention, assessment, intervention and treatment, and training. Given the current state of the field it is no wonder these areas are in need also. Consistent with the chapter authors, Leach and Leong call for more specific prevention research, being mindful of within-group differences. They also highlight questions needing answers surrounding our current methods of assessment, the effectiveness of some interventions to address concerns among some suicidal individuals of color, and areas of suicide training that could be tackled.

The intent of this book is to stimulate ideas and the field to address suicidal behaviors among individuals of color. Which components of suicide are universal and which are culture-specific? Overall, there is such a paucity of available research information that researchers, clinicians, and ultimately, clients, benefit from greater interest and resources. It is the hope of the editors and each of the authors that we will begin to reconsider, re-conceptualize, and offer a more robust understanding of suicide in order to ultimately offer the best care possible for those in need.

☐ References

Jobes, D.A. (2006). *Managing suicidal risk: A collaborative approach.* New York: Guilford.

Leach, M.M. (2006). *Cultural diversity and suicide: Ethnic, religious, gender, and sexual orientation perspectives.* Binghamton, NY: Haworth Press.

Mishara, B.L. (2006). Cultural specificity and the universality of suicide. *Crisis, 27,* 1–3.

Ridley, C.R., Li, L.C., & Hill, C.L. (1998). Multicultural assessment: Reexamination, reconceptualization, and practical application. *Counseling Psychologist, 26,* 827–910.

Thomas, J.C., & Leitner, L.M. (2005). Styles of suicide intervention: Professionals' responses and clients' preferences. *The Humanistic Psychologist, 33,* 145–165.

Theories and Models

Suicide

A Cross-Cultural Theory

Antoon A. Leenaars

No one really knows why human beings die by suicide.

One of the most frequent questions asked about suicide in all countries is, "Why do people kill themselves?" Or, more specifically, "Why did that person die by suicide?" People are perplexed, stressed, confused, and even overwhelmed when they are confronted with suicide. Indeed, at the moment of decision, the person who takes his/her own life may be the least aware of the essence of the reasons for doing so. Understanding suicide, like understanding any complicated human act, is a complex endeavor involving knowledge and insight drawn from many points of view. This is true for all people studying, working in and surviving suicidology. My goal here is to provide a point of view on the questions, based on my international studies of suicide in different cultures over the years. In keeping with the aim of this book, my hope is that the perspective will be useful whether one is a Russian American, (East) Indian American, Mexican American, or of any other ethnicity.*

Most frequently, people identify external causes (e.g., ill health, being abandoned by a lover, losing one's income) as to why a person killed him/herself. This pervasive view in almost all cultural and ethnic groups is too simple, although often the suicidal person holds the same perspective.

* I wish that I could focus on some other predominant cultural groups in the United States (US), such as African American, Native American, and Asian American; however, although I have worked with people in more than 35 countries, my studies to date, as you will read, do not allow me to do so. I want to be empirical. Yet, I hope that my research and thoughts will be helpful to many ethnic groups in the US.

This is not to suggest that a recent traumatic event (e.g., a drop in income, an unacceptable sin, a change in work, a divorce, a failing grade) cannot be identified in many suicides. However, although there are situational considerations in every suicidal act, they are only one aspect of the complexity.

Suicide is a multidimensional malaise (Shneidman, 1985). Suicide is not a sin, although many ethnic and religious groups treat it as such. Suicide is not a crime, although there are a few cultural groups or countries in which this is still so. It is, rather, an interplay of individual, relationship, social, cultural, and environmental factors. This interplay is sometimes called the ecological model (Bronfenbrenner, 1979; Dahlberg & Krey, 2002; Jenkins & Singh, 2000). First applied to child abuse (Garbarino & Crouter, 1978), the model has been applied to a vast array of behaviors, most recently violence, including self-directed violence, i.e., suicide (WHO, 2002) (see Figure 2.1). The model simply suggests that there are different levels (i.e. individual, relationship(s), community, and societal) that influence suicide and thus, by implication, one can understand behavior at various levels. Cultural/ethnic approaches target the factors beyond the individual. They are primarily focused on the community and societal levels, but may also be at the relationship level (e.g., family members, relations with peers).

Although there has been increasing study at the individual level, such as biological, intrapsychic, logical/cognitive (conscious, unconscious), and interpersonal, there has been a lack of study at the community and societal levels. Culture, especially as this volume shows, has been neglected (Leach, 2006). The empirical literature of cultural or ethnic factors in suicide, beyond the most basic information on geographic regions and rates, has been sparse, but within an ecological model, such data would be essential and life saving. It thus seems reasonable that we, regardless of cultural or ethnic group in America, would be perplexed and bewildered about answering the question, "Why?"

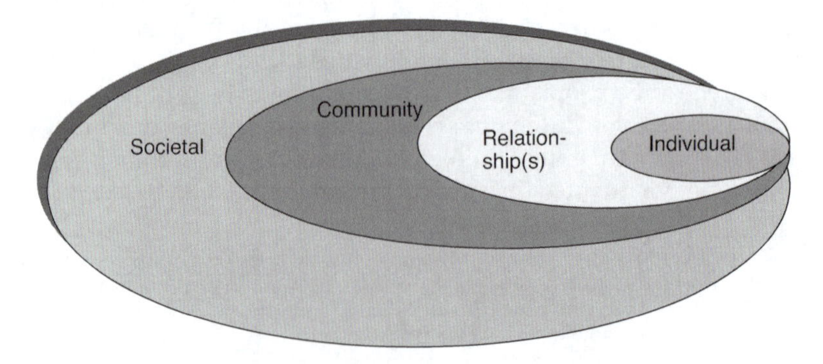

FIGURE 2.1 The ecological model for understanding suicide.

Any element of the malaise is, of course, a legitimate avenue to understanding suicide. Studies of serotonin have a place. Studies of the effect of gun control have a place. Studies of cultural diversity equally have a place (Leach, 2006; Leenaars, Maris, & Takahashi, 1997). In fact, I oppose any reductionistic model in understanding suicide. Many would argue that the study of culture—never mind beyond the individual, as some espouse just genetics—has no place. In such a model, only genetics will explain suicide (Stoff & Mann, 1997). On the other hand, I would agree with Shneidman (2001) that this is the biologizing of suicide; an integral part of reductionistic medicalization of what is essentially a complex event. Besides, even the respected researchers on the biology of suicide, such as Marie Asberg, Alec Roy, and Herman van Praag, would disagree with Stoff and Mann and go so far as to suggest that genes cannot be solely causative. Furthermore, the research to date suggests that "the reductionistic biological analyses do not provide the lubricating fluids for the essences of suicide" (Shneidman, 2001, p. 73). The answers, in fact, will never be found largely in the brain (although in some individuals they are). Suicide is a multifaceted event that is open to study from multiple points of view. In this chapter, I offer a psychological/psychiatric perspective with diverse ethnic and racial applications. I do so because I agree with Shneidman (1985) that the psychological dimensions of suicide are the "trunk" of suicide. This is true regardless of the culture. Shneidman (1985), using an arboreal image, wrote:

> An individual's biochemical states, for instance, are the roots. An individual's method of suicide, the contents of the suicide note, the calculated effects on the survivors and so on, are the branching limbs, the flawed fruit, and the camouflaging leaves. But the psychological component, the problem solving choice, the best solution of the perceived problem, is the main "trunk" (pp. 202–203).

Regarding the "trunk," I would like to offer a few observations on the question of "why." These ideas are not exhaustive, but are ideas gleaned from significant suicidologists in our psychological history that have some empirical support. Specifically, the clinicians are the following: Alfred Adler, Ludwig Binswanger, Sigmund Freud, Carl G. Jung, Karl A. Menninger, George Kelly, Henry A. Murray, Edwin S. Shneidman, Harry Stack Sullivan, and Gregory Zilboorg. However, there may well be other perspectives from various cultures or countries not represented by these views.

□ Cross-Cultural: A Few Opening Questions

Before turning to questions of theory, I want to raise some *a priori* cross-cultural questions. First, what is it that we are talking about? What do we mean by the word "culture" (or ethnic) group? This is the very first step, what are we studying in this volume. The *Oxford English Dictionary* (OED) defines culture as:

(1) The cultivation or development of the mind, manners, etc.; improvement by education and training.
(2) Refinement of mind, tastes, and manners; artistic and intellectual development; the artistic and intellectual side of civilization.
(3) A particular form, stage, or type of intellectual development or civilization in a society; a society or group characterized by its distinctive customs, achievements, products, outlook, etc.
(4) The distinctive customs, achievements, products, outlook, etc., of a society or group; the way of life of a society or group.

Although these definitions fall short, they provide at least a first attempt at definition. They suggest that this cultivation results in a community or society having shared skills and knowledge, shared ways of doing things—even in suicide. Culture is a collective meaning: to allow people to know who they are, where they come from and where they are going, again, even in suicide. This is entirely consistent with Leong and Leach's definition in the introductory chapter of culture as worldview. One of the best definitions of culture I have ever read is from The Royal Commission on Aboriginal Peoples (1995) in Canada:

> Culture is the whole complex of relationships, knowledge, languages, social institutions, beliefs, values and ethical rules that bind a people together and give a collective and its individual members a sense of who they are and where they belong. (p. 25)

Culture is rooted in one's land, whether from India or Russia or Canada or the U.S. The associated word, ethnic, according to the OED, refers to a population or group sharing a distinctive cultural tradition—such as ethnic Russian. It pertains to race. Ethnic is peculiar to a race or nation. Thus, an ethnic or racial group shares a culture, a worldview. Culture is one's heritage. It is one's meaning, even in death (Leach 2006; Leenaars, Maris & Takahashi, 1997). As I stated in the Preface to my own volume on culture and suicide: "The individual, such as John—is among other things a social being. Individuals live in a meaningful world. Culture may well give us meaning in the world. It may well give the world its theories/perspectives" (Leenaars, Maris, Takahashi, 1997, p. 2).

Although I do not think that culture will ever be clearly and distinctly defined, the definitions offered at least allow us to know better what we are talking about. This means that by the very fact of being from different communities, societies or nations, we are different. We are our community. We are our culture. We transpose that culture when we move to a new country such as the U.S. This raises a number of questions on our topic of suicide (or any topic): Is suicide the same for all groups? Or is it different? What is cultural suicide? Or ethnic suicide? Are people in the U.S. who have immigrated from say, Russia, so different from other Americans? Are there commonalities? Or are there factors or aspects that are different? How can we study suicide in different communities or societies or nations? Can I apply my understanding of suicide to all people? To all cultural or ethnic groups? If I need to change my theory with culturally different people, what do I need to change? Do I need to change at the individual, or relationship(s) or community or society levels? What are they? Can being a member of a cultural group contribute to suicide? Do we need culturally sensitive theory(ies)? What factors must we consider in the theory(ies)? What might it take to create such a theory(ies)? And, after we have answered these questions, there are many more, not only in study but in praxis. How can I study suicide? And, once we know, what do we need to do to help suicidal people from different groups? Are there commonalities in, for example, psychotherapy? And are there cultural barriers in psychotherapy? Etc.

Having raised some questions, and they are only a first step in theory development, I offer some beginning empirical answers to the questions. Theory, I believe, will guide us.

□ Theory and Suicide

As a crucial final point of introduction, there are, of course, views that theory should not play a role in understanding suicide; suicidology should only be tabular and statistical. I believe, however, that theory, explicit and implicit, plays a key role in understanding any behavior (regardless of the racial or ethnic group). Theory is the foundation in science (Kuhn, 1962). Newton, Einstein, and all great scientists are great because they were theorists. It is only through theory, as Edwin Shneidman (1985) once noted to me, that we will sort out the booming buzzing mess of experience (James, 1890). In fact, it can be argued, "sciences have achieved their deepest and most far reaching insights by descending below the level of familiar empirical phenomena" (Hempel, 1966, p. 77). Theory may well be in the eye of the beholder

(Kuhn, 1962), but it is pivotal in scientific understanding whether one is a researcher, survivor, crisis worker or clinician. There is nothing as useful as good theory, wherever one lives. And I would go further: I believe that we can only have our understanding (theory) of a person, whether the person is suicidal or not. People must make formulations (theories) about things to understand them (Husserl, 1907/1973). Thus, it would be wise to borrow the ideas of some of our leading theorists to answer the question "why."

☐ Suicide Notes

How can we answer our initial questions? How do we study suicide? Our answers, whether theoretical or not, should be based on logical and empirical fact (Ayer, 1959). Shneidman and Farberow (1957), Stengel (1964), Maris (1981) and others have suggested the following alternatives for scientifically answering these questions: statistics, third-party interviews (often called psychological autopsies), nonfatal suicide-attempter studies and personal documents (including suicide notes, poems, therapy protocols). Of course, there is the problem of obtaining any of these data. The database for potential explanations of suicide is conspicuously absent. Maris (1981), points out that this is because "most researchers have been trapped by either the Scylla of official or 'vital' statistics or the Charybdis of individual case histories."

A related (if not embedded) problem is the one that is the ubiquitous issue of mental health itself: the mind–body problem; or, the admissibility of introspective accounts as opposed to objective reports. This resonates to Windelband's (1904) division of two possible approaches to knowledge between the nomothetic and the idiographic. The nomothetic tabular, statistical, arithmetic, and demographic approach deals with generalizations, whereas the idiographic approach involves the intense study of individuals—the clinical methods, history, biography. In this latter approach, personal documents are frequently utilized—personal documents such as letters, poems, e-mails, memoirs, diaries, autobiographies, or suicide notes. Before addressing the topic at hand, let us explore the views on the idiographic approach in more detail; the other, the nomothetic approach, is well ingrained in psychology and science in general.

Allport (1942) has provided us with a classic statement on the advantages of the idiographic approach, noting that personal documents have a significant place in psychological research. Shneidman (1980, xii), in *Voices of Death* (a book about letters, diaries, notes, and other personal documents relating to death), has stated that such "documents contain special revelations of the human mind and that there is much one can learn from them." Although Allport (1942) cites some shortcomings in the use of personal documents in psychological science, unrepresentativeness of sample, self-deception, blindness to motives, and errors of memory, he makes a clear case for the use of personal documents, including the following: learning about the person, advancing both nomothetic and idiographic research, and aiding in the aims of science—understanding, prediction, and control. As an interesting footnote to his trailblazing work (Shneidman, 1980), Allport wrote about diaries, memoirs, logs, letters, and autobiographies, but it did not occur to his capacious mind to think of perhaps the most personal document of all: suicide notes.

As an aside, I recall being introduced to Aaron T. Beck's *Cognitive Therapy and the Emotional Disorders* (Beck, 1976), as a graduate student. I remember reading and rereading this book. What struck me at that time was Beck's ability to provide an aspiring clinician with the actual protocols of patients met in our offices. I learned how the patients' "pain" is embodied in their language and how we can use these protocols, regardless of racial or ethnic group, to understand them from a cognitive view. Even if one does not adhere to Beck's view, his perspective has provided many of us with a sound clinical view of people's cognitions/protocols. Using extensive personal documents (Allport, 1942), Beck and associates have developed our understanding of people through their own words, regardless of the ethnic group.

My study of suicide is equally not defensive about the use of the occasional admissibility of personal documents, whether the person's own words, narratives, or otherwise. On the contrary, it emphasizes their special virtues and their special power in doing the main business of psychology—the intensive study of the person.

Suicide notes are ultrapersonal documents. They are the unsolicited productions of the suicidal person, usually written minutes before the suicidal death. They are an invaluable starting point for comprehending the suicidal act and for understanding the special features of the people who actually commit suicide and what they share in common with the rest of us who can only imagine it. This is true whether the person speaks or writes a note in India, Russia, the United Kingdom or the U.S. (or whether one is an ethnic Russian writing a suicide note in the U.S.).

Early research (e.g., de Boismont, 1856; Wolff, 1931) on suicide notes largely utilized an anecdotal approach that incorporated descriptive information. Subsequent methods of study have primarily included classification analysis and content analysis. Only a very few studies, however, have utilized a theoretical-conceptual analysis, despite the assertion in the first formal study of suicide notes (Shneidman & Farberow, 1957) and in ongoing discussion (Diamond, More, Hawkins & Soucar, 1995) that such an approach offers much promise. To address this lack, I applied a logical, empirical analysis to suicide notes more than 30 years ago. The method permits a theoretical analysis of suicide notes, augments the effectiveness of controls, and allows us to develop some theoretical insight into the vexing problem of suicide that may have cross-cultural application.

The method has been previously described in detail (Leenaars, 1988; 2004). It treats suicide notes as an archival source. This source is subjected to the scrutiny of control hypotheses, following an *ex post facto* research design (Kerlinger, 1964). The major problem with the current type of research is the lack of control over extraneous variables and the large number of potentially important antecedent variables, and thus there is the danger of misinterpreting relationships. Kerlinger (1964) suggested that these problems could be largely overcome by explicitly formulating not just a single hypothesis, but several "control" hypotheses as well. This would call for suicide protocol, such as notes to be recast in different theoretical contexts (hypotheses, theories, models) for which lines of evidence of each of these positions can then be pursued in the data. Carnap's logical and empirical procedures (1931/1959) can be utilized for such investigations. To date, the theories of 10 suicidologists, as noted earlier, have been investigated: Adler, Binswanger, Freud, Jung, Menninger, Kelly, Murray, Shneidman, Sullivan and Zilboorg. Carnap's positivistic procedure (1931/1959) calls for the translating of theoretical formulations into observable (specific) protocol sentences in order to test the formulations.

Essentially, the positivistic empirical approach calls for theory to be tested (Ayer, 1959). Researchers translate abstract ideas/theory into observable implications ("protocol sentences"), compare these protocol sentences with observable data (such as surveillance data, interviews with survivors, suicide notes), and then, on the basis of this comparison, make decisions about the validity of the theory—the ideas, models, views—that you started with. For example, a core aspect of the theories of the 10 suicidologists is that the stimulus for suicide is unbearable pain; thus, a protocol sentence under this rubric would be as follows: "Suicide has adjustive value and is functional because it stops painful tension and provides relief from intolerable psychological pain." In the method, the protocol sentence is compared with actual data such as suicide notes. This approach is the very basics of science. Next, one introduces the method of induction from the available verified protocol for the discovery of general (sameness) insights and to allow further theory building to occur. One should have an empirically based understanding and, by implication, treatment of the suicidal person, whether one is in the United Kingdom, Canada or Germany.

To summarize from a series of empirical studies (e.g., age, sex, method used, nation) of the theories of the 10 suicidologists, a number of theoretical propositions/implications (or protocol sentences) have been identified to be observable in various samples of notes, the very words of a suicidal person (much like our patient's in the psychotherapy room). A cluster analysis was undertaken to reduce the protocol sentences to a meaningful empirical schema. The analysis produced a classification of eight discrete clusters identified by a word or short phrase are as follows:

I. Unbearable Psychological Pain
II. Cognitive Constriction
III. Indirect Expressions
IV. Inability to Adjust
V. Ego
VI. Interpersonal Relations
VII. Rejection-Aggression
VIII. Identification-Egression.

From a series of studies, Leenaars (1988, 1996) proposed a meta-frame to organize the clusters into intrapsychic and interpersonal elements. (Table 2.1 presents the protocol sentences organized in clusters.) Suicide can be theoretically understood from the proposed theory (templates, constructs, and frames) outlined next in detail. First, just one final philosophical point on theory.

Theory gives us patterns or templates. Plato called it forms; Plotnius, a seal; Jung, archetypes; Murray, unity thema; and Shneidman, commonalities. A philosophical question for millennia has been: How can we have patterns, templates, seals, commonalities, or whatever we call "it"? Or to

TABLE 2.1 The Protocol Sentences Organized in Clusters on Intrapsychic and Interpersonal Aspects

Intrapsychic

I. **Unbearable Psychological Pain**

1. Suicide has adjustive value and is functional because it stops painful tension and provides relief from intolerable psychological pain.
2. In suicide, the psychological or environmental traumas, among many other factors, may include: incurable disease, threat of senility, fear of becoming hopelessly dependent, feelings of inadequacy, humiliation. Although the solution of suicide is not caused by one thing, or motive, suicide is a flight from these specters.
3. In the suicidal drama, certain emotional states are present, including pitiful forlornness, emotional deprivation, distress, or grief.
4. S* appears to have arrived at the end of an interest to endure and sees suicide as a solution for some urgent problem(s) or injustices of life.
5. There is a conflict between life's demands for adaptation and S's inability or unwillingness to meet the challenge.
6. S is in a state of heightened disturbance (perturbation) and feels boxed in, harassed, especially hopeless and helpless.

*S represents an unnamed person.

(continued)

TABLE 2.1 (CONTINUED) The Protocol Sentences Organized in Clusters on Intrapsychic and Interpersonal Aspects

II. **Cognitive Constriction**

7. S reports a history of trauma (e.g., poor health, rejection by significant other, a competitive spouse).
8. Figuratively speaking, S appears to be "intoxicated" by overpowering emotions. Concomitantly, there is a constricted logic and perception.
9. There is poverty of thought, exhibited by focusing only on permutations and combinations of grief and grief-provoking topics.

III. **Indirect Expressions**

10. S reports ambivalence; e.g., complications, concomitant contradictory feelings, attitudes or thrusts.
11. S's aggression has been turned inward; e.g., humility, submission and devotion, subordination, flagellation, and masochism, are evident.
12. Unconscious dynamics can be concluded. There are likely more reasons to the suicide than the person is consciously aware of.

IV. **Inability to Adjust**

13. S considers him/herself too weak to overcome personal difficulties and, therefore, rejects everything, wanting to escape painful life events.
14 Although S passionately argues that there is no justification for living on, S's state of mind is incompatible with an accurate assessment/perception of what is going on.
15. S exhibits a serious disorder in adjustment.
    (a) S's reports are consistent with a manic-depressive disorder such as the down-phase; e.g., all-embracing negative statements, severe mood disturbances causing marked impairment.
    (b) S's reports are consistent with schizophrenia; e.g., delusional thought, paranoid ideation.
    (c) S's reports are consistent with anxiety disorder (such as obsessive-compulsive, post traumatic stress); e.g., feeling of losing control; recurrent and persistent thoughts, impulses or images.
    (d) S's reports are consistent with antisocial personality (or conduct) disorder; e.g., deceitfulness, conning others.
    (e) S's reports are consistent with borderline personality; e.g., frantic efforts to avoid real or imagined abandonment, unstable relationships.
    (f) S's reports are consistent with depression; e.g., depressed mood, diminished interest, insomnia.
    (g) S's reports are consistent with a disorder (or dysfunction) not otherwise specified. S is so paralyzed by pain that life, future, etc. is colourless and unattractive.

V. **Ego**

16. There is a relative weakness in S's capacity for developing constructive tendencies (e.g., attachment, love).
17. There are unresolved problems ("a complex" or weakened ego) in the individual; e.g., symptoms or ideas that are discordant, unassimilated, or antagonistic.

(continued)

TABLE 2.1 (CONTINUED) The Protocol Sentences Organized in Clusters on Intrapsychic and Interpersonal Aspects

18. S reports that the suicide is related to a harsh conscience; i.e., a fulfilment of punishment (or self–punishment).

Interpersonal

VI. **Interpersonal Relations**

19. S's problem(s) appears to be determined by his or her history and the present interpersonal situation.
20. S reports being weakened or defeated by unresolved problems in the interpersonal field (or some other ideal such as health, perfection).
21. S's suicide appears related to unsatisfied or frustrated needs; e.g., attachment, perfection, achievement, autonomy, control.
22. S's frustration in the interpersonal field is exceedingly stressful and persisting to a traumatic degree.
23. A positive development in the disturbed relationship was seen as the only possible way to go on living, but such development was seen as not forthcoming.
24. S's relationships (attachments) were too unhealthy or too intimate (regressive, "primitive"), keeping him/her under constant strain of stimulation and frustration.

VII. **Rejection–Aggression**

25. S reports a traumatic event or hurt or injury (e.g., unrequited love, a failing marriage, disgust with one's work).
26. S, whose personality (ego) is not adequately developed (weakened), appears to have suffered a narcissistic injury.
27. S is preoccupied with an event or injury, namely a person who has been lost or rejecting (i.e., abandonment).
28. S feels quite ambivalent, i.e., both affectionate and hostile toward the same (lost or rejecting) person.
29. S reports feelings or ideas of aggression and vengefulness toward him/herself although S appears to be actually angry at someone else.
30. S turns upon the self those murderous impulses that had previously been directed against someone else.
31. Although maybe not reported directly, S may have calculated the self-destructiveness to have a negative effect on someone else (e.g., a lost or rejecting person).
32. S's self-destructiveness appears to be an act of aggression, attack, /or revenge toward someone else who has hurt or injured him/her.

VIII. **Identification–Egression**

33. S reports in some direct or indirect fashion an identification (i.e., attachment) with a lost or rejecting person (or with any lost ideal [e.g., health, freedom, employment, all grades of A]).
34. An unwillingness to accept the pain of losing an ideal (e.g., abandonment, sickness, old age), allows S to choose, even seek to escape from life and accept death.
35. S wants to egress (i.e., to escape, to depart, to flee, to be gone) to relieve the unbearable psychological pain.

restate the question from a clinical view: If Jennifer and Jeff are suicidal, how are they really the same … or, scientifically stated, alike and different? What is his or her suicidal nature? Does the nature differ in India or Canada or the U.S.? Does it differ in different cultural (ethnic) groups in the United States? Are there predictive clues or patterns regardless of cultural or racial or ethnic group, and if so, what are they? Without the "sameness," there can be no seals or patterns or templates for understanding, prediction and control. We need to know, not necessarily the universal, but, at least, what is most common, the same—despite the ever flowing buzzing of life (James, 1890), i.e., flux, change, difference, and so on.

□ A Theory of Suicide

Theory must begin with definition. Thus, to begin, let me offer Shneidman's (1985) formal definition of suicide:

> Currently in the Western world, suicide is a conscious act of self-induced annihilation, best understood as a multidimensional malaise in a needful individual who defines an issue for which suicide is perceived as the best solution (p. 203).

Suicide is not simply a disease; it is not a psychopathological entity in the DSM-IV (American Psychiatric Association, 1994). I also do not agree with those who point to an external stress as the sole cause of suicide. I, as noted earlier, tend to place the emphasis on its multideterminant nature. Suicide is intrapsychic. It is stress and pain, but not simply the stress or even the pain, but the person's inability to cope with the event or pain. There is desperation (Hendin et al., 2004). The issue of any schema about human personality, i.e., personology (Murray, 1938), is one that makes an individual unique. This is true for any cultural group. It should be the study of the whole organism, not only the stress or pain. People do not simply commit suicide because of pain, but because it is unbearable; they are mentally constricted; they have a mental/emotional disorder; they cannot cope, etc.

However, from a psychological view, suicide is not only intrapsychic, it is also interpersonal (or stated differently, it is all levels in the ecological model). The suicidal individual is not only depressed, mentally constricted and so on, but he or she is also cut off from relationships, or even the community or the society. The suicidal person is painfully estranged—he/she is estranged from his/her culture. The ethnic group is lost. I disagree with those who point only to some intrapsychic aspects such as anger turned inward or primitive narcissism to explain suicide. Suicide occurs in a person and between people (or some other ideal; e.g., health, ethnicity). This is not a Descartesian dichotomy; it is rather a dynamic interactional system. Yet, the intrapsychic world is figural. Suicide occurs as a solution in a mind. The mentalistic processes are the foreground (such as the pain or depression). This is an important difference. It is in the inner world that a person makes the decision to jump, shoot, etc. It is here that he or she decides, "This is the best solution." It is the intersection between the different levels in the ecological model that is essential to understand in suicide. It is, for example, not simply unemployment on the stage, but how the person's drama unfolds on this very personal, individual stage. Metaphorically speaking, suicide is an intrapsychic drama on an interpersonal stage.

Although space is limited here, the theory needs to be made more explicit for the reader. Suicide can be clinically understood from at least the following templates or patterns (Leenaars, 1988, 1996, 2004).

☐ Intrapsychic Drama

1. Unbearable Psychological Pain

The common stimulus in suicide is unendurable psychological pain (Shneidman, 1985, 1993). The pain is unbearable. The suicidal person is in a heightened state of perturbation, an intense mental anguish. The author of the famed *Sophie's Choice*, William Styron (1990) called the pain, "A veritable howling tempest in the brain (p. 38)." It is the pain of feeling pain. Although, as Menninger (1938) noted, other motives (elements, wishes) are evident, the person primarily wants to flee from pain experienced in a trauma, a catastrophe. The fear is that the trauma, the crisis, is bottomless—an eternal suffering. The person may feel any number of emotions such as boxed in, rejected, deprived, forlorn, distressed, and especially hopeless and helpless. It is the emotion of impotence, the feeling of being hopeless/helpless that is so painful for many suicidal people. The situation is unbearable and the person desperately wants a way out of it. The suicide, as Murray (1967) noted, is functional because it abolishes painful tension for the individual. It provides escape from intolerable suffering—pain beyond pain.

2. Cognitive Constriction

The common cognitive state in suicide is mental constriction (Shneidman, 1985). Constriction, i.e., rigidity in thinking, narrowing of focus, tunnel vision, concreteness, etc., is the major component of the cognitive state in suicide. The person is figuratively "intoxicated" or "drugged" by the constriction; the intoxication can be seen in emotions, logic, and perception. In his/her thoughts and communications the suicidal person exhibits at the moment before his/her death only permutations and combinations of a trauma (e.g., marital problems, political scandal, poor health, and rejection by spouse). The person frequently uses words like "only," "always," "never," "no one," and so on. The suicidal mind is in a special state of relatively fixed purpose and of relative constriction. In the face of the painful trauma, a possible solution becomes the solution. Suicide is the only choice. This constriction is one of the most dangerous aspects of the suicidal mind.

3. Indirect Expressions

Ambivalence, complications, redirected aggression, unconscious implications, and related indirect expressions (or phenomena) are often evident in suicide. The suicidal person is ambivalent. There are complications, concomitant contradictory feelings, attitudes, or thrusts, often toward a person and even toward life. Not only is it love and hate but it may also be a conflict between survival and unbearable pain. The person experiences humility, submission, devotion, subordination, flagellation, and sometimes even masochism. And there is much more. What the person is conscious of is only a fragment of the suicidal mind (Freud, 1917a/1974). There are more reasons to the act than the suicidal person is consciously aware of when making the final decision (Freud, 1917a/1974; Freud, 1917b/1974; Leenaars, 1988, 1993). The driving force may well be unconscious processes.

4. Inability to Adjust (or Psychopathology)

People with all types of pains, problems, disorders, etc., are at risk for suicide. Psychological autopsy studies suggest that as many as 90% of people who kill themselves have some symptoms of psychopathology or problems in adjustment but that figure may be lower in some countries such as China and India (Hawton & van Heeringen, 2000; Philips, Liu, & Zhang, 1999; Vijayakumar & Rajkumar, 1999; Wasserman, 2001). In those studies, up to 60% of suicides appear to be related to mood disorders (although likely even fewer, about 40%, in teens). Although the majority of suicides may best fit into mood nosological classifications, (e.g., depressive or bipolar disorders), other emotional/mental disorders have been identified. For example, anxiety disorders, schizophrenic disorders (especially paranoid type), panic disorders, borderline disorders, and antisocial disorders, have been related to suicides (Sullivan, 1962, 1964; Leenaars, 1988). Schizophrenics have a very high rate (about 5%—not the often cited 10%) (Palmer, Pankratz, & Bostwick, 2005). In addition, there are other disorders not specified that may result in risk. From the autopsy data, it is learned that at least as many as 10% may have no disorder identifiable in DSM-IV (or some other classification scheme). The person may be simply paralyzed by pain that life, a future, and so on are colorless and unattractive.

Mood disorders, in their varieties, are, thus, the most frequent disorders in people who die by suicide. It must, however, be understood that not all suicidal people are depressed, and that not all depressed people are suicidal. It is often cited that 15% of people who develop depression ultimately kill themselves. Bostwick (2000) has, however, clearly demonstrated in a meta-analysis of the research that this is a myth. It may well, in fact, be as low as 2%. Most important, it should be remembered that suicidal people experience unbearable pain, not always depression, and even if they do experience depression, the critical stimulus is the "unbearable" nature of the depression. Anxiety may well be as important a pain as depression (Fawcett, 1997). Suicidal people see themselves as being in unendurable pain and unable to adjust. The individual's state of mind is, however, incompatible with accurate discernment of what is going on. Having the belief that they are too weak to overcome difficulties, these people reject everything except death; they do not survive life's difficulties.

5. Ego

The ego, with its enormous complexity (Murray, 1938), is an essential factor in the suicidal scenario. The OED defines ego as "the part of the mind that reacts to reality and has a sense of individuality." Ego strength is a protective factor against suicide. The biological perspective has equally argued this conclusion; van Praag (1997) has, for example, clearly documented a biological aspect to suicidal people: increased susceptibility to stressors, labile anxiety, and aggression regulation. Suicidal people frequently exhibit a relative weakness in their capacity to develop constructive tendencies and to overcome their personal difficulties (Zilboorg, 1936). The person's ego has likely been weakened by a steady toll of traumatic life events (e.g., loss, rejection, abuse, failure). This implies that a history of traumatic disruptions and pain placed the person at risk for suicide; it likely mentally or emotionally handicapped the person's ability to develop mechanisms (or ego functions) to cope. There is, to put it in one simple word, vulnerability. A weakened ego, thus, correlates positively with suicide risk.

□ Interpersonal Stage

6. Interpersonal Relations

The suicidal person has problems establishing or maintaining relationships (object relations). There frequently is a disturbed, unbearable, interpersonal situation. A calamity prevailed. A positive development may have been seen as the only possible way to go on living, but such a development did not appear to be forthcoming. The person's psychological needs are frustrated (Murray, 1938). Suicide appears to be related to an unsatisfied or frustrated attachment need, although other needs, often more intrapsychic, may be equally evident, e.g., achievement, autonomy, dominance, honor. Suicide is committed because of thwarted or unfulfilled needs, needs that are often frustrated interpersonally.

7. Rejection–Aggression

Wilhelm Stekel first documented the rejection–aggression hypothesis in the famous 1910 meeting of the Psychoanalytic Society in Freud's home in Vienna (Friedman, 1910/1967). Adler, Jung, Freud, Sullivan, and Zilboorg have all expounded variations of this hypothesis. Loss is central to suicide; it is, in fact, often a rejection that is experienced as abandonment. It is an unbearable narcissistic injury. This injury is part of a traumatic event that leads to pain and, in some, self-directed aggression. In the first controlled study of suicide notes, Shneidman and Farberow (1957) reported, for example, that hate directed toward others and self-blame are both evident in notes. The suicidal person is deeply ambivalent and, within the context of this ambivalence, suicide may become the turning back upon oneself of murderous impulses (wishes, needs) that had previously been directed against a traumatic event, most frequently someone who had rejected that individual. Biological research in the field has demonstrated a neurobiological link between aggression and suicide. Despite a minimizing of this fact by some (e.g., Shneidman, 1985), aggression, whether other- or self directed, has for example, an association to serotonin dysfunction (Asberg et al, 1976). Freud's hypothesis appears to have a biological basis, within the biopsychosocial (i.e., ecological) view of suicide. Aggression is, in fact, a common emotional state in suicide. Suicide may be veiled aggression, it may be murder in the 180th degree (Shneidman, 1985).

8. Identification–Egression

Freud (1917a/1974, 1920/1974, 1921/1974) hypothesized that intense identification with a lost or rejecting person or, as Zilboorg (1936) showed, with any lost ideal (e.g., health, youth, employment, freedom, ethnicity) is crucial in understanding the suicidal person. Identification is defined as an attachment (bond) based on an important emotional tie with another person (object) (Freud, 1920/1974) or any ideal. If this emotional need is not met, the suicidal person experiences a deep pain (discomfort). There is an intense desperation and the person wants to egress, i.e., to escape. Something must be done to stop the anguish. The suicidal person wants to leave, to exit, to get out, to get away, to be gone, to be elsewhere ... not to be ... to be dead. Suicide becomes the only solution and the person plunges into the abyss.

This theory is only one point of view. Yet its elements have utility in understanding suicide, not only in America, but, elsewhere also. These common dimensions (or sameness) are what suicide is. Not necessarily the universal, but certainly the most frequent or common characteristics provide us with a meaningful conceptualization of suicide. This is an attempt to outline an empirically supported theory. There are few empirical theories tested in more than one culture. The question raised remains: Does this theory apply to different cultural groups in the U.S.? Are there commonalities? Or are there differences?

Independent research on suicide notes (O'Connor, Sheeby, & O'Connor, 1999) and biographical studies of suicides (Lester, 1994) have supported, for example, the utility of the approach to a note or any narrative analysis. In-depth studies of inter-judge reliability (for example, O'Connor et al, 1999) and over three decades of study by the author show that, indeed, the percentage of inter-judge agreement has been satisfactory (>85%; see Shaughnessy, Zechmeister, & Zechmeister, 2000). Reliability and validity have also been established in different countries. I will next highlight those studies.

□ Cross-Culture

Are our theories or models applicable to different cultural or ethnic groups? Much of our understanding of suicide may, in fact, be culture specific. Thus, caution is needed in the field. We simply do not know whether the protocol (data) of a suicidal person, such as suicide notes, is applicable in the U.S. and to India and vice versa. Shneidman (1985) noted that when making "cross-cultural comparisons, do not make the error of assuming that a suicide is a suicide" (p. 203).

Studies of suicide in different cultures and nations suggest that there may be (empirical) differences. For example, a study by Rao and Mehendran (1989), shows that Western theories of suicide may not be sufficient to explain the marital and interpersonal problems presented in so many (East) Indian people (and by implication, in many (East) Indian American people) who kill themselves. These are aspects of relationship(s), community, and society levels that differ within and among the many ethnic groups in the U.S. This is true not only in East Indian American but in many ethnic groups in the U.S. It has been documented in African Americans (Gibbs, 1997), Mexican Americans (Hovey & King, 1997), Asian Americans (Shiang, Blinn, Bongar et al, 1997), Native Americans (Echo-Hawk, 1997), and so on. Suicide may have different meanings for different people. Culture is an especially powerful vehicle for meaning. Insensitivity to this fact will likely result in problems in our understanding of why people kill themselves. Despite this, extensive cultural (or even international) research is only a little more than a decade old, being spurred on by the World Heath Organization (Leenaars, DeLeo, Diekstra et al., 1997).

There are only a few studies, for example, on suicide in different cultural groups in the U.S. (Leach, 2006), never mind from different countries. (Besides my own, the works of George Domino [see 2005] and David Lester (Lester & Yang, 2005) are the only other exceptions that I know of). Because this is so, how can we understand suicide in different cultural or ethnic or racial groups in the U.S.? Indeed, should we even attempt to do so? There are many limits. Perhaps we should abandon our *a priori* questions and just accept that we do not know. Perhaps we should be just tabular. My own opinion on these pessimistic views is that we should not. This volume does, in fact, begin to offer a a lifesaving answer to how culture affects suicide. This book may just be a beginning, but the reader will also better understand the suicidal individual—whether Russian American, East Indian American, Indian American, or Mexican American—and once the reader knows the individual and his/her diversity better, the more effective his/her treatment will be, whether through psychotherapy or psychopharmacology or otherwise.

We are, however, left with a problem in my current topic: There is no research on suicide notes from different cultural or ethnic groups in the U.S. How do we then develop a cross-cultural theory for the present? I hereby offer some speculations. It is a truism that people in different countries have different rates of suicide. It is also a fact that when people emigrate from one country to another they bring their rate of suicide with them, not only the overall rate, but also the incidence for age, sex, and even preferred method (Lester, 1972; Sainsbury & Barraclough, 1968). Thus, they transpose their culture, at least the rate and pattern of suicide, and if that is so, do they transpose the meaning and the interpersonal (relationship), community, and societal impact? Does the study of suicide notes in different countries allow us to say something about cross-cultural suicide or about suicide in different cultural or ethnic groups in the U.S.? I believe that the answer is yes. Thus, I offer some beginning considerations: there is, in fact, research on suicide notes, and by implication, suicide from different countries, that allow us to do so. Leenaars (1992), noting that Canada has a higher rate of suicide than the U.S. (Leenaars & Lester, 1992), in the first cross-cultural study of suicide notes, examined fifty-six suicide notes from Canada and the U.S. whose writers were matched for age and sex. None of the intrapsychic or interpersonal aspects (protocol sentences) differed. Leenaars, Lester, Wenckstern and Heim (1994) examined 70 suicide notes from Germany and the U.S. whose writers were matched for age and sex. None of the variables reached significance. Subsequently, studies from the U.K. (O'Connor & Leenaars, 2004), Hungary (Leenaars, Fekete, Wenckstern, & Osvath, 1998), Russia (Leenaars, Lester, Lopatin, et al, 2002), Australia (Leenaars, Haines, Wenckstern, et al., 2003) and India (Leenaars, Girdhar, Dogra & Leenaars, 2007) supported this observation, but not always. (We are currently doing cross-cultural research in Lithuania (the country with the highest rate of suicide and thus, probably the ethic group in the U.S. with a similar rate), Mexico, and Turkey).

Primarily, differences observed to date were within the interpersonal realm or stage, although rarely. To provide an example, Russians (and ethnic Russians in the U.S.) in their suicide notes, and by implication, their suicides, more frequently identify external causes (such as injuries, losses, rejections in their relationships) as the reason for their deaths, having been overly attached to some person (or other ideal) and steadfastly unwilling to accept the loss. Ethnic Russians are often prone to aggression; there are murderous impulses against the offending person and they even calculate the suicide to be revenge, an attack (see protocol sentences 26, 30–35 in Table 2.1). People from India also express considerable aggression, as do people from Hungary, but less so. This raises a significant empirical question, are interpersonal aspects more affected by culture? Are the relationship(s), community, or societal elements more affected by culture? Sainsbury and Barraclough's (1968) and Lester's (1972) studies would suggest that is so. My own cross-cultural studies would suggest the same. Yet, at this time, this is theoretical conjecture. Perhaps by the very fact that we are human, regardless of cultural or ethnic group in the U.S., this is true. Pain is pain. Mental disorder is mental disorder. Still, there are differences. Cultures are different; people are different.

This raises more questions: Because suicide is often determined by an individual's history and the present interpersonal situation (see protocol sentence 19 in Table 2.1), can this be associated to community or social hurts or injuries? Can unresolved problems in the interpersonal field be due to social pressure due to being African American or Native American? Interpersonally, in every suicide—well almost every—there are unsatisfied and frustrated needs (see protocol sentence 21 in Table 2.1); can this be due to inequitable social factors, such as power, bias, or stigma? Suicidal people often have attachments that are too unhealthy and regressive (see protocol sentence 24 in Table 2.1); can this be due to belonging to an ethnic group? Similarly, suicide is associated in a direct or indirect fashion to identification(s) (see protocol sentence 33 in Table 2.1); can the loss be due to the loss of identification with one's ethnic group (acculturation issues)? And what about extreme traumatization—for example, it is well documented that the high risk of suicide in indigenous peoples in the U.S. and around the world is associated to colonization and its associated genocide (Leenaars, EchoHawk, Lester, Leenaars, & Haramic, 2006). Suicide is egression (see protocol sentence 35 in Table 2.1); can suicide be an escape from "the enormous social and cultural turmoil created by the policies of colonialism and the difficulties ever since faced by indigenous peoples in adjusting and integrating into modern-day societies" (WHO, 2002, p. 190)?

I believe that the answer to all these new questions is probably yes. At this time, we do not have the answer, but we do have some beginning understanding. I wish that I could empirically offer more. There is, however, hope of a scientific theory. Indeed, from what I have seen in this volume, we do not have to speculate as much. We can understand culture and suicide better. You will, I predict, not be disappointed. We have answered at least some preliminary questions. For example, on the question, "Can being a member of a cultural group contribute to suicide?" the answer is yes. And, other questions are answered. Interpersonally, the cultural stage does indeed contribute and affect suicide.

The empirical facts reported are, therefore, entirely consistent with the WHO's ecological model of understanding suicide and violence in general (Leenaars, 2005; WHO, 2002). Figure 2.1 illustrates the ecological model. Suicide notes, and by implication, the intrapsychic dimensions of suicide, may be more similar than different in ethnic Canadians, ethnic Germans, and ethnic Arabs in the U.S. Maybe unbearable pain is unbearable pain, depression is depression, but interpersonal dimensions differ. Maybe culture affects these aspects more than issues of pain, mental blindness, psychopathology, and so on, but is this always the case? Are there ethnic groups where intrapsychic factors differ too? Probably.

Cross-cultural research allows us to cautiously assume that the multidimensional theory is applicable to different cultures in the U.S. There is some cross-cultural reliability and validity; this is rare in suicidology. Questions remain about how different ethnic Canadians or ethnic Germans in the U.S. are compared with cultural differences with, for example, ethnic (East) Indians or ethnic Mexicans or ethnic Turks, cultural groups who are much different from the predominant White Christian groups (from developed nations) studied to date. For example, we simply do not know enough about whether the suicide of the ethnic (East) Indian is the same as or different from other ethnic or racial Americans. This is the purpose, of course, of this whole volume, to understand suicidal people from different racial and ethnic groups better. Suicide, as defined, is a cultural event. Yet, I believe that understanding the common psychological factors of the "trunk" has equal value. This does not mean that I am not a wholehearted participant in this volume largely devoted to the study of ethnic and racial differences. The American, Russian, Canadian, and (East) Indian are, of course, different, but, paradoxically, by the virtue of our human quality, are also the same. This is may be my main contribution to this volume: there are, despite differences, commonalities in cultural groups.

□ Concluding Thoughts

The findings from diverse countries around the world, and by implication, diverse ethnic groups in the U.S., provide support for the multidimensional model, both interpersonal and intrapsychic, proposed by ten leading suicidologists (Leenaars, 1996, 2004). In fact, there is considerable evidence of both intrapsychic and interpersonal psychological correlates of suicide. This is, for example, as true in India as in the U.S. Despite cross-cultural differences, there seem to be commonalities among suicides by the ethnic Russian or ethnic Canadian in the U.S. By virtue of our human quality, we have a number of important psychological characteristics in common. Pain is pain. Mental constriction is mental constriction. Psychopathology is psychopathology. The suicidal mind is the suicidal mind, whether in a Russian American or Mexican American or any cultural group in the U.S. However, differences emerge in cross-cultural studies. Thus, despite the value of looking at psychological commonalities, it is useful to group suicides under a cultural, ethnic, or racial rubric. Of course, (East) Indians, Americans, Russians, Australians, and so on die by suicide and it is useful to empirically examine such. In any analysis of suicide, it is useful to think of culture. The differences merit this whole volume. One cannot assume a suicide is a suicide.

Although the thesis of this volume is critical and lifesaving, my studies also suggest there may be few intrapsychic and interpersonal differences (although more so) in the suicidal mind; at least in the ethnic groups studied. This argues for commonalities in suicide. On a different note, but important to theory building, it may be cautiously assumed that the multidimensional model of suicide presented (Leenaars, 1996, 2004) is as applicable to a person from India as a person from Russia in America. Cross-cultural applications of the theory, and thus, racial and ethnic applications to diverse groups in the U.S. Of course, as a basic in science, further study is warranted. There is too little cultural (and international) study (WHO, 2002). We need to better understand the suicidal person and all suicidal people in the U.S.

□ References

Allport, G. (1942). *The use of personal documents in psychological science.* New York: Social Science Research Council.

American Psychiatric Association (1994). *Diagnostic and statistical manual of mental disorders,* (4th. ed.) (DSM-IV). Washington, DC: Author.

Asberg, M., Traskman, L., & Thorien, P. (1976). 5-H1AA in Cerebrospinal fluid: A biochemical suicide prediction? *Archives of General Psychiatry, 33,* 1193–1197.

Ayer, A. (Ed.) (1959). *Logical positivism.* New York: Free Press.

Beck, A. (1976). *Cognitive therapy and the emotional disorders.* New York: International Universities Press.

Bostwick, J. (2000). Affective disorders and suicide risk: A re-examination. *American Journal of Psychiatry,* 157, 1925–1932.

Bronfenbrenner, U. (1979). *The ecology of human development: Experts by nature and design.* Cambridge: Harvard University Press.

Carnap, R. (1959). Psychology in physical language. In A. Ayer (Ed.), *Logical positivism* (pp. 165–197). New York: Free Press (Original work published 1931).

Dahlberg, L. & Krey, E. (2002). Violence—a global public health problem. In World Health Organization (Ed.), *World report on violence and health* (pp. 3–21). Geneva: World Health Organization.

de Boismont, B., (1856). *Du suicide et de la folie suicide.* Paris: Germer Baillière.

Diamond, G., More, D., Hawkins, A., & Soucar, E. (1995). Comment on Black's (1993) article "Comparing genuine and simulated suicide notes: A new perspective." *Journal of Consulting and Clinical Psychology, 63,* 46–48.

Domino, G. (2005). Cross-cultural attitudes towards suicide: The SOQ and a personal odyssey. *Archives of Suicide Research,* 9, 107–122.

EchoHawk, M. (1997). Suicide: The scourge of Native American people. In Leenaars, A., Maris, R., & Takahashi, Y. (Eds.), *Suicide: Individual, cultural, international perspectives* (pp. 60–67). New York: Guilford Press.

Fawcett, J. (1997). The detection and consequences of anxiety in clinical depression. *Journal of Clinical Psychiatry, 58* (suppl. 8), 35–40.

Freud, S. (1974). Mourning and melancholia. In J. Strachey (Ed. & Trans.), *The standard edition of the complete psychological works of Sigmund Freud, Vol. XIV* (pp. 239–260). London: Hogarth. (Original work published 1917a.)

Freud, S. (1974). General theory of neurosis. In J. Strachey (Ed. & Trans.), *The standard edition of the complete psychological works of Sigmund Freud, Vol. XVI.* (pp. 243–483). London: Hogarth Press. (Original work published 1917b.)

Freud, S. (1974). A case of homosexuality in a woman. In J. Strachey (Ed. & Trans.), *The standard edition of the complete psychological works of Sigmund Freud, Vol. XVIII.* (pp. 147–172). London: Hogarth Press. (Original work published 1920.)

Freud, S. (1974). Group psychology and the analysis of the ego. In J. Strachey (Ed. & Trans.), *The standard edition of the complete psychological works of Sigmund Freud, Vol. XVIII* (pp. 67–147). London: Hogarth Press. (Original work published 1921.)

Friedman, P. (Ed.) (1967). *On suicide.* New York: International Universities Press. (Original work published 1910.)

Garbarino, J., & Crouter, A. (1978). Defining the community context for parent-child relations: The correlates of child maltreatment. *Child Development, 49,* 604–616.

Gibbs, J. (1997). African American suicide: A cultural paradox. In A. Leenaars et al. (Eds.), *Suicide: Individual, cultural, international perspectives* (pp. 68–79). New York: Guilford Press.

Hawton, K. & van Heeringen, C. (Eds.) (2000). *Suicide and attempted suicide.* Chichester: John Wiley & Sons.

Hempel, C. (1966). *Philosophy of natural sciences.* Englewood Cliffs, NJ: Prentice-Hall, Inc.

Hendin, H., Maltsberger, J., Pollinger Haas, A., Szanto, K., & Rubinowicz, H. (2004). Desperation and other affective states in suicidal patients. *Suicide and Life-Threatening Behavior,* 34, 386–394.

Hovey, D. & King, C. (1997). Suicidality among acculturating Mexican Americans: Current knowledge and directions for research. In A. Leenaars et al. (Eds.), *Suicide: Individual, cultural, international perspectives* (pp. 92–103). New York: Guilford Press.

Husserl, E. (1973). *The idea of phenomenology* (W. Alston & G. Nokhnikian, Trans.), The Hague: Martinus Nijhoff. (Original work published 1907.)

James, W. (1890). *The principles of psychology.* New York: Henry Holt & Co.

Jenkins, R. & Singh, B. (2000). General population strategies of suicide prevention. In K. Hawton & K. Heeringen (Eds.), *The international handbook of suicide and attempted suicide.* (pp. 598–615). Chichester, UK: Wiley & Sons, Inc.

Kerlinger, F. (1964). *Foundations of behavioral research.* New York: Holt, Rinehart and Winston, Inc.

Kuhn, T. (1962). *The structure of scientific revolutions.* Chicago: The University of Chicago Press.

Leach, M. (2006). *Cultural diversity and suicide: Ethnic, religious, gender, and sexual orientation perspectives.* New York: The Haworth Press.

Leenaars, A. (1988). *Suicides notes.* New York: Human Sciences Press.

Leenaars, A. (1992). Suicide notes from Canada and the United States. *Perceptual and Motor Skills, 74,* 278.

Leenaars, A. (1993). Unconscious processes. In A. Leenaars (Ed.), *Suicidology: Essays in honor of Edwin Shneidman* (pp. 127–147). Northvale, NJ: Aronson.

Leenaars, A. (1996). Suicide: A multidimensional malaise. *Suicide and Life-Threatening Behavior, 26,* 221–236.

Leenaars, A. (2004). *Psychotherapy with suicidal people.* Chichester, UK: John Wiley & Sons.

Leenaars, A. (2005). Effective public health strategies in suicide prevention are possible: A selective review of recent studies. *Clinical Neuroscience, 2,* 21–31.

Leenaars, A., De Leo, D., Diekstra, R. et al. (1997). Consultations for research in suicidology. *Archives of Suicide Research, 3,* 139–151.

Leenaars, A., EchoHawk, M., Lester, D., Leenaars, L., Haramic, E. (Eds.) (2006). Suicide among Indigenous Peoples: The research. (Special issue), *Archives of Suicide Research, 10*, 101–224.
Leenaars, A., Fekete, S., Wenckstern, S., & Osvath, P. (1998). Suicide notes from Hungary and the United States. *Psychiatrica Hungarica, 13*, 147–159. (In Hungarian.)
Leenaars, A., Girdhar, S., Dogra, T., Wenckstern, S., & Leenaars, L. (2007). *Suicide notes from India and the United States: A thematic comparison.* (in process).
Leenaars, A., Haines, J., Wenckstern, S., Williams, C., & Lester, D. (2003). Suicide notes from Australia and the United States. *Perceptual and Motor Skills, 92*, 1281–1282.
Leenaars, A. & Lester, D. (1992). A comparison of rates and patterns of suicide for Canada and the United States, 1960–1988. *Death Studies*, 16, 433–440.
Leenaars, A., Lester, D., Lopatin, A., Schustov, D., & Wenckstern, S. (2002). Suicide notes from Russia and the United States. *Social and General Psychiatry*, 12–3, 22–28. (In Russian.)
Leenaars, A., Lester, D., Wenckstern, S., & Heim, N. (1994). Suizid—abschiedsbriefe—Ein vergleich deutscher und amerikanischer abschiedbriefe von suizidenten. *Suizidprophylaxe*, 3, 99–101. (In German.)
Leenaars, A., Maris, R., & Takahashi, Y. (Eds.) (1997). *Suicide: Individual, cultural, international perspectives.* New York: Guilford.
Lester, D. (1972). Migration and suicide. *Medical Journal of Australia*, i, 941–942.
Lester, D. (1994). A comparison of fifteen theories of suicide. *Suicide and Life-Threatening Behavior, 24*, 80–88.
Lester D. & Yang, B. (2005). Regional and time-series studies of suicide in nations of the world. *Archives of Suicide Research, 9*, 123–133.
Maris, R. (1981). *Pathways to suicide.* Baltimore, MD: Johns Hopkins University Press.
Menninger, K. (1938). *Man against himself.* New York: Harcourt, Brace & Co.
Murray, H. (1938). *Explorations in personality.* New York: Oxford University Press.
Murray, H. (1967). Death to the world: The passions of Herman Melville. In E. Shneidman (Ed.), *Essays in self-destruction* (pp. 3–29). New York: Science House.
O'Connor, R. & Leenaars, A. (2004). A thematic comparison of suicide notes drawn from Northern Ireland and the United States. *Current Psychology, 22*, 339–347.
O'Connor, R., Sheeby, N. & O'Connor, D. (1999). A thematic analysis of suicide notes. *Crisis, 20*, 106–114.
Palmer, B., Pankratz, V., & Bostwick, J. (2005). The lifetime risk for schizophrenia: A reexamination. *Archives of General Psychiatry, 62*, 247–253.
Phillips, M., Liu, H., & Zhang, Y. (1999). Suicide and social change in China. *Culture, Medicine and Psychiatry, 22*, 368–370.
Rao, V. & Mahendran, N. (1989). One hundred female burn cases—a study in suicidology. *Indian Journal of Psychiatry, 31*, 43–50.
Royal Commission on Aboriginal Peoples (1995). *Choosing life: Special report on suicide among aboriginal people.* Ottawa: Ministry of Supply & Service, Canada.
Sainsbury, P. & Barraclough, B. (1968). Differences between suicide rates. *Nature, 220*, 1252.
Shaughnessy, J., Zechmeister, E., & Zechmeister, J. (2000). *Research methods in psychology.* New York: McGraw-Hill.

Shiang, J., Blinn, R., Bongar, B., Stephens, B., Allison, D., & Schatzberg, A. (1997). Suicide in San Francisco, CA: A comparison of Caucasian and Asian groups, 1987–1994. In A. Leenaars et al. (Eds), *Suicide: Individual, cultural, international perspectives* (pp 80–91). New York: Guilford Press.

Shneidman, E. (1980). *Voices of death*. New York: Harper & Row.

Shneidman, E. (1985). *Definition of suicide*. New York: Wiley.

Shneidman, E. (1993). *Suicide as psychache*. Northvale, N.J.: Aronson.

Shneidman, E. (2001). *Comprehending suicide: Landmarks in the 20th Century of suicidology*. Washington, DC: American Psychological Association.

Shneidman, E. & Farberow, N. (Eds.). (1957). *Clues to suicide*. New York: Harper & Row.

Stoff, D. & Mann, J. (Eds.) (1997). *The neurobiology of suicide: From the bench to the clinic*. New York: New York Academy of Sciences.

Stengel, E. (1964). *Suicide and attempted suicide*. Baltimore: Penguin Books.

Styron, W. (1990). *Darkness visible*. New York: Random House.

Sue, D. & Sue, D. (1990). *Counseling the culturally different*. New York: John Wiley & Sons.

Sullivan, H. (1962). Schizophrenia as a human process, In H. Perry, N. Gorvell & M. Gibbens (Eds.). *The collected works of Harry Stack Sullivan, Vol. II*, New York: W.W. Norton.

Sullivan, H. (1964). The fusion of psychiatry and social sciences. In H. Perry, N. Gorvell, & M. Gibbens (Eds.), *The collected works of Harry Stack Sullivan*. New York: W.W. Norton.

Van Praag, H. (1997). Some biological and psychological aspects of suicidal behavior: An attempt to bridge the gap. In A. Botsis, C. Soldatos, & C. Stefanis (Eds.), *Suicide: Biopsychosocial Approaches* (pp. 73–92). Amsterdam: Elsevier.

Vijayakumar, L. & Rajkumar, S. (1999). Are risk factors for suicide universal? A case-control study in India. *Acta Psychiatrica Scandinavica, 99*, 407–411.

Wasserman, D. (Ed.). (2001). *Suicide: An unnecessary death*. London: Martin Dunitz.

Windelband, W. (1904). *Geschichte und Naturwissenschaft*. (3rd ed.). Strassburg: Hertz.

Wolff, H. (1931). Suicide notes. *American Mercury, 24*, 264–272.

World Health Organization (WHO). (2002). *World report on violence and health*. Geneva: Author.

Zilboorg, G. (1936). Suicide among civilized and primitive races. *American Journal of Psychiatry, 92*, 1347–1369.

Theories of Suicide

David Lester

Culture and ethnicity can have an impact on both the phenomena of suicidal behavior and on theories of suicidal behavior, and even on the definition of what is viewed as suicide.

□ The Linguistics of Suicide

As Douglas (1967) pointed out, a shared linguistic terminology for suicidal behavior is associated with shared meanings of the behavior, and there are also shared associated terms and phrases, such as despair, hopelessness, and "life isn't worth living." Douglas emphasized that these terms are not the phenomenon itself but rather are adopted by members of the culture (or subculture) to construct meanings for suicidal behavior. However, because the terms are rarely clearly defined or detailed and because there is often disagreement among commentators on their meaning, it follows that the meaning of suicide is ambiguous. Furthermore, because these terms are used to construct meanings for suicidal behavior, then estimates of the incidence and circumstances of suicidal behavior are in part a social construction.

For example, according to the Mohave, a Native American tribe in the southwest of the U.S., a fetus that presents itself in the transverse position for birth, leading to its own death and that of its mother, is viewed as having intended to commit suicide and to murder its mother so that they can be together in the spirit world (Devereux, 1961). Medical examiners and coroners in the rest of the U.S. would not view such a stillborn infant as a suicide. A similar phenomenon is observable today in that many Muslims do not conceptualize "suicide bombers" as committing suicide—"martyrdom" is a preferred term (Abdel-Khalek, 2004).

Counts (1980), who has studied the suicidal behavior of women in the Kaliai district of Papua New Guinea, noted that in the past elderly widows sometimes immolated themselves on their husbands' funeral pyres. The German and Australian colonial governors considered this behavior to be a form of ritual murder rather than suicide, and they outlawed it. Counts, however, saw neither term (suicide and murder) as appropriate for this custom because the practice differed so much from what North Americans and Europeans regard as either suicide or murder. Neither term describes the behavior, the interpersonal relationships involved, or the attitudes toward the widow and those assisting in her death, nor do they predict how the community will respond to her death.

Some scholars, especially in Europe, have expressed doubts that people engaging in nonfatal suicidal behavior have self-destruction as their aim, and they have moved to calling the behavior "self-poisoning," "self-injury" or "deliberate self-harm" (e.g., Hawton, et al., 2006). The semantic implication is that nonfatal suicidal behavior is not "suicide." Because, in most cultures, women engage in more nonfatal suicidal actions than do men, this renaming of nonfatal suicidal behavior as self-injury makes "suicidal behavior" less common in women than it was hitherto.

Other suicidologists, on the other hand, include a wider range of behaviors under the rubric of "suicidal behavior." For example, Menninger (1938) classified behaviors such as alcoholism, drug abuse, and anorexia as *chronic suicide* because the individuals were shortening their lives by their behaviors. Menninger also classified behaviors such as polysurgery, self-castration, and self-mutilation as *focal suicide*, in which the self-destructive impulse is focused on one part of the body. These behaviors are often gender-linked. For example, anorexia is more common in women, whereas illicit drug abuse is more common in men. Canetto (1991) has speculated that adolescents may respond differently when under stress, with girls choosing nonfatal suicidal behavior more and boys choose drug abuse more. The use of Menninger's categories would change greatly the relative incidence of nonfatal suicidal behavior in women and men. The way in which "suicide" is defined will clearly impact the theories proposed to explain it.

☐ The Impact of Ethnicity and Culture on the Phenomenom of Suicide

Lester (1994a) examined the epidemiology of suicide in Chinese in Hong Kong, Singapore, Taiwan, and the U.S. The ratio of the male to female suicide rates in 1980 was 1.2 for Chinese Americans, 1.2 for Hong Kong residents, 1.2 for Singapore Chinese, and 1.2 for Taiwanese residents, identical gender ratios. Suicide rates peaked in the elderly in all the nations: for those 65 and older in Chinese Americans, 75 and older in Hong Kong and Taiwan and 70 and older in Singapore Chinese.*

However, the methods used for suicide differed for the different groups of Chinese: jumping was more common in Singapore and Hong Kong, hanging in Chinese Americans and poisons in Taiwan, probably a result of the difference between the nations in the availability of methods for suicide.** Furthermore, the suicide rates differed: in 1980 the suicide rates were 13.5 (per 100,000 per year) in Singapore and Hong Kong Chinese, 10.0 in Taiwan and 8.3 for Chinese Americans.

Thus, the gender and age patterns in Chinese suicide seem to be affected strongly by culture, while the absolute suicide rates and methods used are affected by the nation in which the Chinese dwell.

As noted above, the methods chosen for suicide often differ among cultures. DeCatanzaro (1981) documented culturally unique methods for suicide, such as hanging by tying a noose around one's neck and running to another part of the house in Tikopia in the British Solomon Islands. Suttee, or suicide by burning on the husband's funeral pyre, was once a common form in India, while seppuku, which is ritual disembowelment, was honored in feudal Japan. These well-known examples of cultural influences on suicide methods also have culturally determined motives (grief for suttee and shame for seppuku).

There are also cultural and ethnic influences on the motives for suicide, as demonstrated by Hendin's (1964) classic study of suicide in Scandinavian countries. In Denmark, Hendin noted that guilt arousal was the major disciplinary technique employed by Danish mothers to control aggression, resulting in strong dependency needs in their sons. This marked dependency was the root of depression and suicidality after adult experiences of loss or separation. Reunion fantasies with lost loved ones were common in those committing suicide.

In Sweden, a strong emphasis was placed by parents on performance and success, resulting in ambitious children for whom work was central

* The nations used different classifications by age.

** For example, Lester (1994b) showed that the use of jumping to one's death in Singapore was strongly associated with the development of high-rise apartments.

to their lives. Suicide typically followed failure in performance and the resulting damage to the men's self-esteem.

At the time Hendin conducted his study in Norway, the suicide rate was much lower than that found for Denmark. Although Hendin found sons' strong dependency on their mothers in both countries, Norwegian children were more aggressive than Danish children. Alcohol abuse was more common among the Norwegians, and Norwegian men were more open about their feelings—able to laugh at themselves and cry more openly. Norwegian boys strove to please their mothers by causing no trouble, and they did not worry unduly about failure, typically blaming others for their personal failures and retreating into alcohol abuse.

In her account of suicide among females in Papua-New Guinea, Counts (1988) has illustrated the ways in which a culture can determine the meaning of the suicidal act. In Papua-New Guinea, female suicide is a culturally recognized way of imposing social sanctions. Suicide also holds political implications for the surviving kin and for those held responsible for the events leading women to commit suicide. In one such instance, the suicide of a rejected fiancée led to sanctions being imposed on the family that had rejected her. Counts described this woman's suicide as a political act that symbolically transformed her from a position of powerlessness to one of power.

Cultures also differ in the degree to which suicide is condemned. It has been argued that one explanation for the low suicide rate in African Americans is that suicide is a less acceptable behavior than for European Americans (Early, 1992). Murder rates are much higher in African Americans, both as perpetrators and as victims, and a larger proportion of the murders involving African Americans are victim-precipitated, that is, the victims played some role, conscious or unconscious, in precipitating their own demise (Wolfgang, 1957). African American culture appears to view a victim-precipitated murder as a more acceptable method of dying than suicide (Gibbs, 1988).

☐ Ethnic and Cultural Differences Can Challenge Myths

Many theories of human behavior, including suicidal behavior, are based on physiological factors. Cultural anthropology helps challenge such theories by showing, for example, that behaviors that we consider gender-specific are not found in every culture. As we have noted above, in the U.S. and in European nations, nonfatal suicidal behavior appears to occur at a higher rate in women than in men; as a result it is has come to be viewed as a "feminine" behavior by the general public (Linehan, 1973) and by suicidologists as well. Other cultures, however, provide examples where nonfatal suicidal behavior, often carried out in front of others, is more common in men than in women. The Nahane (or Kaska), a Native Canadian tribe located in British Columbia and the Yukon, provide a good example of this.

> ... observations and communications agree that attempted suicide by men is of frequent occurrence and very likely to appear during intoxication. There is a general pattern for such attempted self-destruction. In the two cases of the sort observed during field work, the weapon selected was a rifle. As he brandishes the weapon the would be suicide announces his intention in an emotional outburst. This becomes the signal for interference to block the deed. One or more men leap forward to wrest the gun from the intended suicide's possession and toss it out of sight. The would be victim is now usually emotionally overwhelmed by his behavior. This pattern is illustrated by Louis Maza's behavior during intoxication. Several times during the afternoon, Louis had manifested aggression toward himself, crying: "I don't care if I'm killed. I don't care my life." After several hours of such emotional outbursts interspersed with quarreling and aggression toward his companions, he seized his large caliber rifle and threatened to kill himself. Old Man threw himself on the gun and as the two men grappled for the weapon, Louis succeeded in firing one wild shot. John Kean and the ethnographer ran to the camp and together wrenched the gun from the drunken man. John fired the shells in the chamber and Old Man tossed the gun half-way down the cutbank. No punishment or other discrimination is reserved for attempted suicides. The individual is comforted and in the future, while intoxicated, he is watched lest he repeat the attempt. (Honigmann, 1949, p. 204)

It seems, therefore, that nonfatal suicidal behavior is not always a "feminine" behavior.

□ The Assumption of Ethnic and Cultural Invariability of Research Findings

Investigators often assume that a research finding discovered in one culture will apply to other cultures. Therefore, to check on this assumption, it is important to replicate research findings in cultures other than the one in which the results were first obtained. For example, at the sociological level, Lester and Yang (1991) found that females in the labor force and the ratio of divorces to marriages predicted suicide rates in the U.S. and Australia from 1946 to 1984, but that the associations were in opposite directions for the two nations. While in the U.S. the ratio of divorces to marriages was positively associated with the suicide, the association was negative in Australia.

Stack (1992) found that divorce had a deleterious effect on the suicide rate in Sweden and Denmark, but not in Japan. Stack offered four possible reasons: the divorce rate may be too low in Japan to affect the suicide rate, Japanese family support may be strong enough to counteract the loss of a spouse, ties between couples may be weak in Japan, and the cultural emphasis on conformity in Japan may suppress suicidal behavior.

At the individual level, Lester, Castromayor and Icli (1991) found that an external locus of control was associated with a history of suicidal preoccupation in American, Philippine, and Turkish students, but that the association was no longer found for American students once the level of depression was controlled.

In a comparison of depression and suicide in mainland China and the U.S., Chiles et al. (1989) found that suicidal intent was predicted better by depression for Chinese psychiatric patients and better by hopelessness for American psychiatric patients.

De Man et al. (1987) have validated scales to assess suicidality in French-speaking Canadians, and Abdel-Khalek and Lester (e.g., Abdel-Khalek & Lester, 2002) have explored whether research findings are similar in Kuwait and in the U.S.*

It is important, therefore, for researchers to identify which findings have cross-cultural generality (and to which cultures) and which are specific to one culture.

□ Theories of Suicide

There is some evidence that theories of suicide proposed by Western scholars may not be applicable to other nations and cultures. For example, Lester (2005) studied 17 industralized nations and tried to predict their suicide rates using five variables derived from different theories of suicide.

* Abdel-Khalek, an Egyptian psychologist working in Kuwait, has also devised personality and psychopathology scales in Arabic as alternative measures to those devised by Americans and Europeans (e.g., Abdel-Khalek, 1998).

1. One possible explanation for differences in national suicide rates is that different nationalities differ in their *physiology*. For example, there are clear differences in the frequency of genes in the people from the different nations of Europe (Menozzi, Piazza & Cavalli-Sforza, 1978). Thus, different nations and cultures may differ in their genetic structure and physiology.

   One study has attempted to demonstrate an association between physiological factors and suicide rates at the cross-national level. Lester (1987) found that the suicide rates of nations were associated with the proportion of people with Types O, A, B and AB blood—the higher the proportion of people in the nation with Type O blood, the lower the suicide rate. However, few studies have explored the role of physiological differences in accounting for national differences in suicide rates.
2. The major *psychological* factors found to be associated with suicidal behavior are depression, especially hopelessness, and psychological disturbance such as neuroticism, anxiety, or emotional instability. Psychiatric disorder appears to increase the risk of suicide, with affective disorders and alcohol and drug abuse leading the list. Nations may differ in the prevalence of these conditions, and such differences could account for the differences in suicide rates. For example, nations certainly do differ in their consumption of alcohol (Adrian, 1984), as well as depression (Weissman and Klerman, 1977).
3. Moksony (1990) noted that one simple explanation of national differences in suicide rates is that the national populations differ in their *composition*, in particular the proportion of those at risk for suicide. For example, typically in developed nations, suicide rates are highest among the elderly, especially elderly males. Therefore, nations with a higher proportion of elderly males will have a higher suicide rate.
4. The most popular explanation of the variation in national suicide rates focuses on *social variables*. These can be viewed in two ways: (1) as direct causal agents of the suicidal behavior, or (2) as indices of broad social characteristics which differ between nations.

Durkheim (1897) hypothesized that the suicide rate is related to the level of social integration (the degree to which the people are bound together in social networks) and the level of social regulation (the degree to which people's desires and emotions are regulated by societal norms and customs). According to Durkheim, *egoistic* and *anomic* suicides result from too little social integration and social regulation, respectively, while *altruistic* and *fatalistic* suicides result from too much social integration and social regulation, respectively. Later sociologists have argued that altruistic and fatalistic suicide are rare in modern societies. Therefore, suicide rarely results from excessive social integration or regulation. As a result, suicide in modern societies seems to increase as social integration and regulation *decrease* (e.g., Johnson, 1965).

Studies of samples of nations have found that suicide rates are associated with such variables as low church attendance, the amount of immigration and interregional migration, and divorce (e.g., Stack, 1983). Some investigators view these associations as suggesting a positive relationship between broken relationships and suicidal behavior. For example, divorce may be associated with suicide at the societal level because divorced people have a higher suicide rate than those with other marital statuses.

A major issue here has been raised by Moksony (1990) and Taylor (1990) concerning whether *specific* social variables are directly related to social suicide rates or whether these specific social variables are measures of more basic, abstract, and broad social characteristics that determine social suicide rates. Lester (2004) proposed that the strong associations among social variables argue for the importance of basic broad social characteristics. For example, in the U.S., interstate migration, divorce, church nonattendance and alcohol consumption all intercorrelate highly, supporting the importance of a broad social characteristic, perhaps best called *social disorganization*, as a determinant of societal suicide rates. In this case, regions with high rates of divorce would not simply have high rates of suicide among the divorced, but among the never-married, married, and widowed too. This is found for the U.S. where states with higher divorce rates have higher suicide rates among the single, the married, and the widowed as well as among the divorced (Lester, 1995a).

Lester (2005) found that the percentage of the population with Type O blood, the per capita consumption of alcohol, the percentage of the population 65 years of age and older, and the divorce and birth rates predicted the suicide rate of the 17 industrialized nations very well—the multiple R was 0.85. The regression equation that he derived also predicted the suicide rates in seven other European nations not in the original sample (e.g., Bulgaria and Greece)—the Spearman correlation between predicted and actual suicide rates was 0.89.

But the regression equation failed miserably in predicting the suicide rates of Egypt, El Salvador, Mexico, Sri Lanka, Thailand, Trinidad and Tobago, and Venezuela. The Spearman correlation between predicted and actual suicide rates was 0.00. Thus, there is some evidence that Western theories of suicide do not apply to nonWestern cultures. Given that theories are culturally based, it could be argued that theory development among other cultural groups is needed.

□ An Anthropological Theory of Suicide

One theory of suicide, proposed by Naroll (1962, 1963, 1969), was based on a study of nonliterate societies and tested using data from those societies rather than data from European nations, which were the basis for Durkheim's (1897) theory of suicide. Naroll proposed that suicide occurred in those who were *socially disoriented*, that is, in those who lack or lose basic social ties. But because all of those who are in this condition do not commit suicide, there must also be a psychological factor involved, that is, the individual's reaction to *thwarting disorientation contexts*.

Thwarting disorientation contexts are those in which the individual's social ties are broken or weakened and those in which another person thwarts the individual and prevents him or her from achieving desired and expected satisfactions or in which frustration is experienced. This thwarting must be interpersonal and not impersonal. Storm damage to one's dwelling is not thwarting, but when another person sets fire to it and destroys it, that is thwarting. The widow is not thwarted, but the divorced wife is thwarted. Under the conditions of thwarting disorientation, individuals are more prone to commit suicide in such a way that it comes to public notice, that is, *protest suicide*. Naroll believed that this theory, better than others, explained suicide committed by indigenous peoples.* In his critique of Naroll's theory of suicide, Lester (1995b) noted that it adds a dynamic dimension to the standard Durkheimian concepts of social integration and social regulation. It generates new hypotheses, and Naroll also speculated provocatively that the suicide rate of a society was a measure of its mental health.

Jeffreys (1952) believed that Durkheim's (1897) categories of suicide, based on the concepts of social integration and social regulation, were not sufficient to explain cases of suicide he found in African tribes. He described suicide committed in order to revenge oneself on those one is angry at—a type of suicide he called "Samsonic suicide" after the story of Samson in the Bible.

Revenge can be obtained in two ways. In some societies, the belief is that one's ghost can return and harm those at whom one is angry, as among the Herero of South West Africa (Vedder, 1928). Alternatively, the societal laws demand that those who provoked a suicide must pay some penalty, usually a fine, and in some societies, death. The payment of a heavy fine by the person who provoked a suicide is customary, for example, among the Bavenda (Stayt, 1931) and the Kassena (Cardinall, 1920).

* Lester (1995b) has compared and contrasted Naroll's theory with those of Durkheim (1897) and Henry and Short (1954).

New Theories

It is often proposed that we need theories of suicide from a feminist, ethnic or cultural perspective, but rarely is a new theory actually proposed. Lester (1997b) noted that the Mohave have a clearly specified theory of suicide, namely that it is increasingly due to a breakdown in ties to the community and to the tribe as a whole, and to an increasing dependence on a primary relationship with a lover or spouse. Lester (1997b) tested this hypothesis by exploring whether suicide would be common in nations with higher levels of individualism, and the results confirmed the hypothesis.

It can be seen that examples of suicide behaviors, customs, and attitudes in indigenous peoples can challenge traditional Western theories of suicide, although theories similar to the Mohave theory have been proposed also by Western suicidologists (e.g., Lester, 1997a; Masaryk, 1881).

The Future

There are no new theories of suicide based on cultures or ethnicities other than White, middle-class ones. What must be done to remedy this? Schuuster and Van Dyne (1985) discussed how a discipline might be transformed from a feminist perspective, and Lester (1989) applied this to suicidology.

The first two steps in such a transformation is that scholars discuss the "invisible women" and "search for missing women." In suicidology, for example, who are the women who were writing about suicide in the 1800s along with people like Enrico Morselli and Emile Durkheim? Lester (1989) cited the work of Ruth Shonle Cavan (1928) and drew attention to the writings of Lauretta Bender (Bender & Schilder, 1937), Marguerite Hertz (1948) and Meliita Schmideberg (1948) on suicide. The next two steps are "women as disadvantaged" and "women studied on their own terms." Nowadays, the problem of suicide in women is clearly perceived as a topic worthy of study (e.g., Canetto & Lester, 1995). It is the final two steps that are problematic: (1) women as a challenge to disciplines and (2) transformation of the field. Lester (1989) found very little scholarship on suicide that achieved these two steps.

Let us apply these steps to theories of suicide from an ethnic (e.g., African American) or cultural (e.g., Islam) perspective. The first four steps are easily accomplished. Certainly, suicide as a problem in African Americans, particularly young men (Lester, 1998) and in Muslims (Lester, 2006) has received a great deal of attention.

It is again steps 5 and 6 that raise a problem. Has any scholar yet proposed a way of transforming the discipline (and, in particular, the theories) of suicidology by taking an African American or an Islamic perspective? It is difficult, if not impossible, to find examples here. This is the challenge for the next generation of suicidologists.

□ Multiculturalism and Suicide

Many, if not most nations, are multicultural. Although countries such as Australia and the U.S., with their many immigrants from every nation of the world, are the best examples of multicultural societies, many other nations are also multicultural. Belgium contains two major groups, the Flemish and the Walloons. The United Kingdom comprises Welsh, Scots, and Irish citizens as well as smaller groups such as the Cornish. Most African nations, whose boundaries were determined by the colonial rulers in the past, contain several ethnic groups who are often in conflict. Nigeria, for example, contains three major ethnic groups (the Hausa, the Yoruba, and the Ibo) in addition to many smaller groups. Many nations of the world, including Australia, Japan, New Zealand, Taiwan, and all the Central and South American countries, also have aboriginal groups.

This raises many questions. Are the standard theories of suicide applicable to the different ethnic groups in, for example, the U.S. (African Americans, Asian Americans, Hispanic Americans, etc.)? Which factors are unique to suicide among these ethnic groups that might lead to new ideas in the field of suicidology? Which culturally specific ethnic variables have been overlooked that might be important?

Other chapters in this book examine the epidemiology of and some of the research into suicide in different ethnic groups in the U.S. and clear differences have emerged, such as the low rate of suicide among African Americans. There are several issues here.

First, in their discussion of African American suicide, Utsey, Hook, and Stanard (Chapter 4) talk of resiliency and protective factors, such as religiosity, for African Americans. Do protective factors really exist that differ from risk factors? There are, for example, separate psychological tests of optimism and pessimism. A pessimistic outlook on life may be labeled a risk factor in contrast to the protective factor of an optimistic outlook, but they are opposite sides of the same coin. If a high score on a single measure of hopelessness is a risk factor for suicide, then a low score is a protective factor.

A further question here is whether a factor such as religiosity is a "protective" factor only for African Americans or whether it reduces the risk of suicide in all ethnic groups in the society. At the cross-cultural level of analysis, Abdel-Khalek and Lester (2007) found that religiosity was negatively associated with suicidal ideation in both Kuwaiti (Muslim) respondents and American (Christian) respondents. It may be that the similarities in the causes and the predictors of suicide for different ethnic groups in a multicultural society far outweigh the differences. The conclusion may be that the weighting of the causes and correlates of suicide may differ in different ethnic groups, but that the set of correlates and predictors remains the same.

On the one hand, minority ethnic groups clearly have to deal with culture conflict in a way that the majority ethnic groups do not. The study of culture conflict and acculturation have appeared only in studies of suicide among ethnic groups such as Native Americans, African Americans, and Hispanic Americans. Psychologists appear to have missed an opportunity here by relying on simple single-measure scales rather than conducting a zone analysis based on the coping strategies possible for the nondominant culture: integration (maintain relations with the dominant culture and maintaining cultural identity), assimilation (maintaining relations and losing cultural identity), separation (maintaining cultural identity but breaking relations), and marginalization (losing cultural identity and breaking relations) (Berry, 1990). It would be interesting to explore the different patterns of suicide in these four different coping strategies.

An intriguing situation arises when one factor that is a "risk" factor for one group is a "protective" factor for another group. There is some evidence, for example, that assimilation reduces the risk of suicide for Native Americans (because suicide rates are higher for Native Americans who remain on reservations than for those who move into the larger society [Lester, 1997c]), but increases the risk of suicide for African Americans (whose suicide rate appears to increase as they move from the lower classes into the middle classes [Lester, 1998]).

But what of "new" theories? Are new theories possible by taking a multicultural perspective (or, for that matter, a feminist, transgendered, or class perspective)? None have appeared so far. Indeed, it may be easier to generate new theories of suicide by borrowing ideas from other disciplines than by taking a multicultural perspective. Lester (1990) reviewed the major theories of crime and proposed parallel theories of suicide. For many of these theories, there was no empirical evidence to support or refute at that time, and so important areas of future research were suggested. For example, a major theory of criminal behavior is that labeling offenders as delinquents by the criminal justice system is the single most important factor in leading an individual into a criminal career. There is no research on whether labeling plays any role in leading an individual into a suicidal career.

Conclusions

There are large ethnic and cultural differences in the incidence of suicidal behavior. Culture also influences the methods used for committing suicide and the reasons for doing so. It should be noted that, in societies that are culturally heterogeneous, such as the U.S., Canada, and Australia, it cannot be assumed that suicides from the different cultural groups are similar in rate, method, motive, and precipitating factors. Those working to prevent suicide in such societies must take these cultural influences into account (Leach, 2006; Sue & Sue, 1990; Zimmerman & Zayas 1993).

Yet more work needs to be done on taking the ideas about suicide held in nonWestern societies and exploring whether new and different hypotheses, and even comprehensive theories of suicide, can be developed from them.

References

Abdel-Khalek, A. M. (1998). The development and validation of the Arabic Obsessive Compulsive Scale. *European Journal of Psychological Assessment, 14,* 146–158.

Abdel-Khalek, A. M. (2004). Neither altruistic suicide, not terrorism but martyrdom. *Archives of Suicide Research, 9,* 99–113.

Abdel-Khalek, A. & Lester, D. (2002). Can personality predict suicidality? *International Journal of Social Psychiatry 48,* 231–239.

Abdel-Khalek, A. & Lester, D. (2007). Religiosity, health, and psychopathology in two cultures. *Mental Health, Religion and Culture, 10,* 537–550.

Adrian, M. (1984). International trends in alcohol production, trade and consumption, and their relationship to alcohol-related problems, 1970 to 1977. *Journal of Public Health Policy, 5,* 344–367.

Bender, L. & Schilder, P. (1937). Suicidal preoccupations and attempts in children. *American Journal of Orthopsychiatry, 7,* 225–234.

Berry, J. W. (1990). Acculturation and adaptation. *Arctic Medical Research, 49,* 142–150.

Canetto, S. S. (1991). Gender roles, suicide attempts, and substance abuse. *Journal of Psychology, 125,* 605–620.

Canetto, S. S. & Lester, D. (1995). *Women and suicidal behavior.* New York: Springer.

Cardinall, A. W. (1920). *Natives of the northern Territories of the Gold Coast.* London: G. Routledge & Sons.

Cavan, R. S. (1925). *Suicide.* Chicago: University of Chicago.

Chiles, J. A., Strosahl, K., Ping, Z. Y., Clark, M., Hall, K., Jemelka, R., Senn, B., & Reto, C. (1989). Depression, hopelessness and suicidal behavior in Chinese and American psychiatric patients. *American Journal of Psychiatry, 146,* 339–344.

Counts, D. A. (1980). Fighting back is not the way: Suicide and the women of Kaliai. *American Ethnologist, 7,* 332–351.

Counts, D. A. (1988). Ambiguity in the interpretation of suicide. In D. Lester (Ed.) *Why women kill themselves*. (pp. 87–109). Springfield, IL: Charles Thomas.
De Man, A. F., Balkou, S., & Iglesias, R. I. (1987). A French-Canadian adaptation of the scale for suicide ideation. *Canadian Journal of Behavioural Science, 19*, 50–55.
DeCatanzaro, D. (1981). *Suicide and self-damaging behavior*. New York: Academic Press.
Devereux, G. (1961). *Mohave ethnopsychiatry*. Washington, DC: Smithsonian Institution.
Douglas, J. D. (1967). *The social meanings of suicide*. Princeton, NJ: Princeton University Press.
Durkheim, E, (1897). *Le suicide*. Paris: Felix Alcan.
Early, K. E. (1992). *Religion and suicide in the African-American community*. Westport, CT: Greenwood.
Gibbs, J., (1988). Conceptual, methodological, and sociocultural issues in black youth suicide. *Suicide & Life-Threatening Behavior, 18*, 73–89.
Hawton, K., Bale, L., Casey, D., Shepherd, A., Simkin, S., & Harriss, L. (2006). Monitoring deliberate self-harm presentations to general hospitals. *Crisis, 27*, 157–163.
Hendin, H. (1964). *Suicide and Scandinavia*. New York: Grune & Stratton.
Henry, A. F. & Short, J. F., (1954). *Suicide and homicide*. New York: Free Press.
Hertz, M. R. (1948). Suicidal configurations in Rorschach records. *Rorschach Research Exchange, 12*, 1–56.
Honigmann, J. J. (1949). *Culture and ethos of Kaska society*. New Haven, CT: Yale University Press.
Jeffreys, M. D. W. (1952). Samsonic suicide or suicide of revenge among Africans. *African Studies, 11*, 118–122.
Johnson, B. D. (1965). Durkheim's one cause of suicide. *American Sociological Review, 30*, 875–886.
Leach, M. M. (2006). Cultural *diversity and suicide: Ethnic, religious, gender and sexual orientation perspectives*. Binghamton, NY: Haworth Press.
Lester, D. (1987). National distribution of blood groups, personal violence (suicide and homicide), and national character. *Personality & Individual Differences, 8*, 575–576.
Lester, D. (1989). The study of suicide from a feminist perspective. *Crisis, 11*, 38–43.
Lester, D. (1990). *Understanding and preventing suicide: New perspectives*. Springfield, IL: Charles Thomas.
Lester, D. (1997). The epidemiology of suicide in Chinese populations in six regions of the world. *Chinese Journal of Mental Health, 7*, 21–24.
Lester, D. (1994). Suicide by jumping in Singapore as a function of high-rise apartment availability. *Perceptual and Motor Skills, 79*, 74.
Lester, D. (1995). Explaining the regional variation of suicide and homicide. *Archives of Suicide Research, 1*, 159–174.
Lester, D. (1995). Thwarting disorientation and suicide. *Cross-Cultural Research, 29*, 14–26.
Lester, D. (1995). An empirical examination of Thomas Masaryk's theory of suicide. *Archives of Suicide Research, 3*, 125–131.
Lester, D. (1997). Note on a Mohave theory of suicide. *Cross-Cultural Research, 31*, 268–272.

Lester, D. (1997). *Suicide in American Indians.* Commack, New York: Nova Science.

Lester, D. (1998). *Suicide in African Americans.* Commack, New York: Nova Science.

Lester, D. (2004). *Thinking about suicide.* Hauppauge, NY: Nova Science.

Lester, D. (2005). Predicting suicide in nations. *Archives of Suicide Research, 9,* 219–223.

Lester, D. (2006). Suicide and Islam. *Archives of Suicide Research, 10,* 77–97.

Lester, D., Castromayor, I. J., & Icli, T. (1991). Locus of control, depression, and suicidal ideation among American, Philippine, and Turkish students. *Journal of Social Psychology, 131,* 447–449.

Lester, D. & Yang, B. (1991). The relationship between divorce, unemployment and female participation in the labour force and suicide rates in Australia and America. *Australian & New Zealand Journal of Psychiatry, 25,* 519–513.

Linehan, M. (1973). Suicide and attempted suicide. *Perceptual and Motor Skills, 37,* 31–34.

Masaryk, T. (1881). *Der Selbstmord als sociale Massenerscheinung der modernen Civilisation.* Vienna: Konegen.

Menninger, K. (1938). *Man against himself.* New York: Harcourt, Brace & World.

Menozzi, P., Piazza, A. & Cavalli-Sforza, L. (1978). Synthetic maps of human gene frequencies in Europeans, *Science, 201,* 786–792.

Moksony, F. (1990). Ecological analysis of suicide. In D. Lester (Ed.) *Current concepts of suicide* (pp. 121–138). Philadelphia: Charles Press.

Naroll, R. (1962). *Data quality control.* New York: Free Press.

Naroll, R. (1963). Thwarting disorientation and suicide. Unpublished discussion paper, Northwestern University.

Naroll, R. (1969). Cultural determinants and the concept of the sick society. In S. C. Plog & R. B. Edgerton (Eds.) *Changing perspectives in mental illness* (pp. 128–155). New York: Holt, Rinehart and Winston.

Schmideberg, M. (1948) A note on suicide. *Psychoanalytic Review, 35,* 181–182.

Schuster, M. R. & Van Dyne, S. R. (1985). *Women's place in the academy.* Totowa, NJ: Rowman & Allanheld.

Stack, S. (1983). The effect of religious commitment on suicide. *Journal of Health & Social Behavior, 24,* 362–374.

Stack, S. (1992). The effect of divorce of suicide in Japan. *Journal of Marriage and the Family, 54,* 327–334.

Stayt, H. A. (1931). *The Bavenda.* Oxford: Oxford University Press.

Taylor, S. (1990). Suicide, Durkheim, and sociology. In D. Lester (Ed.) *Current concepts of suicide* (pp. 225–236). Philadelphia: Charles Press.

Vedder, H. (1928). The Herero. In C. H. L. Hahn (Ed.) *The native tribes of South West Africa* (pp. 135–211). Cape Town, South Africa: *Cape Times.*

Weissman, M. M. & Klerman, G. L. (1977). Sex differences and the epidemiology of depression. *Archives of General Psychiatry, 34,* 98–111.

Wolfgang, M. E. (1957). Victim-precipitated criminal homicide. *Journal of Criminal Law, Criminology & Police Science, 48,* 1–11.

Research on Racial and Ethnic Cultures

Understanding the Role of Cultural Factors in Relation to Suicide Among African Americans

Implications for Research and Practice

Shawn O. Utsey, Pia Stanard, and Joshua N. Hook

In the tradition of the Eugenics Movement of the early 20th century, the study of African American suicide had a nefarious beginning. For example, the first known major work in this area, published by Charles Prudhomme in 1938, characterized the "American Negro" as too ignorant to consider suicide. According to Prudhomme, "The Negro of uneducated ancestry, who has become a scholar by severe study, is less liable to suicide dependent upon education than the white man whose ancestors have felt the effect of education for generations" (p. 373). Prudhomme asserted that, besides lacking in intelligence, the Negro's religious nature predisposed him to increased agitation, greater physical expressions of emotion, and consequently, a reduced tendency toward suicide. Other scholars have attributed the low suicide rate among African Americans to the lack of high educational and occupational aspirations (Breed, 1966; Hendin, 1969; Swanson & Breed, 1976). They reasoned that because African Americans had been conditioned over time to accept their inferior status in society, suicide risk resulting from goal frustration would be reduced. Most psychologists now agree that deficit models of African American mental health, like those proposed by Prudhomme and Hendin, have outlived their theoretical and conceptual usefulness.

Moving from this deficit model, contemporary researchers have begun to examine strength-based protective factors that buffer African

Americans from suicide risk. For example, a number of researchers have examined religious and spiritual protective factors in this regard (e.g., Anglin, Gabriel, & Kaslow, 2005; Barnes & Bell, 2003; Burr, Hartman, & Matteson, 1999; Kaslow, et al., 2004; Marion & Range, 2003; Stack & Wasserman, 1995; Walker, Utsey, Bolden, & Williams, 2005). Furthermore, research links cohesive family relationships, close friendships, and supportive social networks to reduced suicide risk among African Americans (Marion & Range, 2003; Nisbet, 1996; Stack, 1996; Willis, Coombs, Drentea, & Cockerham, 2003). For example, a study by Palmer (2001) found that social support, including family, friends, and significant others, buffered African Americans from suicide risk. Mollock, Kimbrough, Lacy, McClure, & Williams (1994) attributed the lower suicide rates among African American adolescents to lower rates of drug and alcohol consumption. Drug and alcohol use is a major contributing factor in the suicide rates of White adolescents (Berman, 1990). Kirk and Zucker (1979) found that racial pride was inversely correlated with suicide risk in African Americans. Individuals higher in black consciousness (racial pride) were less likely to attempt suicide.

While such research represents an example of significant progress in the right direction, we need broader and more accurate conceptualizations of the cultural protective factors that buffer African Americans from suicide risk. Much of the current literature that examines the role of cultural factors in reducing the risk of suicide among African Americans focuses on religion, spirituality, familial variables, social support, and prosocial behavior (e.g., absence of substance abuse). However, religiosity, spirituality, family cohesiveness, social support, and prosocial behaviors may not constitute a cultural orientation or worldview that is unique to African Americans. Furthermore, other aspects of the African American cultural orientation may be important as well. For example, Boykin (1983) observed that the cultural orientation and worldview of African Americans were characterized by a rhythmic and social time-orientation, verve (high expressive energy), emphasis on affect, collective or communal orientation, orality, and a person-to-person social orientation. We need conceptual clarity of African American cultural behaviors if we are to advance our understanding of the cultural protective factors that buffer against suicide risk in this population.

This chapter examines the research literature on the risk and protective factors related to African American suicide. In the context of these findings, we discuss the implications for suicide assessment and clinical interventions with this population. First, we provide a historical context, some background on the suicide rates among African Americans noting past and present trends, and introduce several traditional theories of suicide and discuss if and how they are applicable to African Americans. The two subsequent sections discuss risk and protective factors associated with

African American suicide. Next, we discuss some of the conceptual and methodological limitations inherent in previous research and make recommendations for future research with this population. We conclude by discussing implications for assessment and clinical practice. Included in this section is a case study example to illuminate many of the points made regarding the importance of cultural factors in considering suicide risk in African Americans.

□ Background and Overview of African American Suicide

According to the American Association of Suicidology (2004), African Americans, as a group, completed 1,939 suicides in 2002. Eighty-four percent of suicide completers were male; this constitutes a suicide rate of 9.1 per 100,000. African American females, though attempting suicide more often, had a lower rate of completion (1.6 per 100,000). In fact, African American females have the lowest suicide rate of all U.S. racial/ethnic groups. However, increases in recent suicide rates among African American youth ages 15 to 24 have been alarming. From 1990 to 1995, the suicide rate for males between ages 15 and 24 was 11.3 per 100,000, which is more than six times higher than for females (1.7 per 100,000). Similarly, the overall suicide rate for African Americans between ages 25 and 34 was 24 per 100,000 (Goldsmith, Pellmar, Kleinman, & Bunney, 2002). For African American youth, suicide is the third leading cause of death after homicides and accidents (American Association of Suicidology, 2004). In spite of these numbers, the suicide rate for African Americans as a group remains significantly lower than the suicide rate for White Americans. Note, however, that African American suicide rates have fluctuated considerably over the past 40 years, peaking and declining in an unpredictable fashion.

Historically, African Americans have had the lowest suicide rate among all U.S. racial/ethnic groups (Barnes & Bell, 2003; Joe & Kaplan, 2001; Kaslow et al., 2004; Lester, 1998). However, beginning in the late 1980s there was a dramatic increase in African American suicide rates, especially among youth. Prior to 1965, suicide rates for African Americans were a quarter of the suicide rates for White Americans. By 1975 there was a dramatic increase, and African Americans were now committing suicide at half the rate of White Americans (Barnes & Bell, 2003). From 1981 to 1994, the suicide rate for African American males ages 15–24 increased 83%; there was a 10% increase for females (American Association of Suicidology, 2004). According to Barnes & Bell (2003), an even more dramatic increase in suicide rates occurred during the same time period for African American males between ages 10–19 (114% increase) and 10–14 (233% increase). However, beginning in 1993 and continuing to 2002, the suicide rates for all African Americans showed a steady decline from 6.9 per 100,000 (in 1993) to 5.2 per 100,000 (in 2002). The biggest decline occurred among African American youth, whose suicide rates went from 11.48 per 100,000 in 1994 to 6.5 per 100,000 in 2002. Note that the suicide rates for White Americans for the same time period also declined, but beginning in 1999, have slightly increased (American Association of Suicidology, 2004). Little is known about why we see these patterns of fluctuations in suicidal behavior among African Americans.

Conceptually, several theoretical frameworks have been used to explain suicide among African Americans. According to Gibbs (1988), the three major theories that have been used to explain it are the sociological perspective, the psychological perspective, and the ecological perspective. The sociological perspective, first proposed by Emile Durkheim (1951), posits that suicide is a function of a lack of fit between a person and society. Given the long history of exposure to chronic racism and other forms of oppression experienced by African Americans, this theory has enjoyed a great deal of popularity in the suicide literature. The psychological perspective, which suggests that suicide is a function of anger turned inward toward oneself, has occasionally been used to explain the low suicide rates among African Americans. It is asserted that instead of internalizing feelings of hopelessness, depression, and anger, African Americans turn these feelings outward in expressions of interpersonal violence (Willis, Coombs, Drentea, & Cockerham, 2003). The ecological perspective posits that an increasing competition for scarce resources results in the loss of self-esteem and a sense of failure, which increases the risk for suicide (Gibbs, 1988). This theory may be particularly relevant to African Americans living in urban settings where poverty, crime, unemployment, and social and economic despair are rampant. All of the above theories point to specific factors that place some African Americans at increased risk for suicide.

□ Risk Factors and African American Suicide

Risk factors are characteristics or conditions that have been shown to increase the likelihood that an individual will develop a disorder or experience an adverse outcome (Kaplan, Turner, Norman, & Stillson, 1996). In the case of African American suicide, known risk factors include psychological distress (e.g., depression, hopelessness, trauma, and psychotic symptoms), substance abuse, access to a firearm, social isolation, family dysfunction, impaired interpersonal functioning, maladaptive coping skills, exposure to racial inequality, and a prior history of suicide attempts (Anglin et al., 2005; Burr et al., 1999; Durant et al., 2006; Gibbs, 1988; Kaslow et al., 2004; Palmer, 2001; Stack, 1996; Vega, Gil, & Warheit, 1993; Willis et al., 2003). Moreover, according to the National Institute of Health (2001) there is evidence that African Americans may have a genetic predisposition for lower levels of serotonin, which is a biological risk factor for suicide.

African Americans as a group have been found to use mental health services inconsistently (Thompson, Bazile, & Akbar, 2004). Several factors have been posited to explain this inconsistent use including reduced access to services due to residential location or lack of insurance coverage (Willis et al., 2003), mistrust of medical professionals (Terrell & Terrell, 1984; Nickerson, Helms, & Terrell, 1994), poor service quality (Willis et al., 2003), and stigma toward individuals with mental illness (Walker, Lester, & Joe, 2006). This reduced use of mental health services by African Americans may exacerbate the risk of suicide from factors such as psychological distress and substance abuse in African Americans, because they are less likely to seek professional help to alleviate their symptoms.

In addition to having negative attitudes toward people with mental illness, there may be social stigma among African Americans for verbalizing suicidal ideation (Willis et al., 2003). Although few studies have examined the role of stigma in suicidal behaviors within this group (Walker et al., 2006), the belief that they do not commit suicide is prevalent in American society, even among African Americans (Early, 1992; Early & Akers, 1993). Furthermore, African Americans often have negative attitudes toward suicide (Early, 1992). Thus, it is possible that an African American who verbalizes suicidal thoughts or intentions may not be taken seriously (Willis et al., 2003).

Studies on SES as a risk factor have produced conflicted findings. A review of the literature by Rehkopf and Buka (2006) found that lower SES (e.g., higher poverty, deprivation of resources, and higher unemployment) was associated with greater suicide risk. The two periods in which suicide rates were highest for young and elderly African Americans overlap with two peaks in national unemployment rates, 1981–1985 and 1991–1993, with the highest rates reaching almost 10% from 1982–1983 (U.S. Bureau of Labor Statistics, 2002). According to Joe (2006), the simultaneous increase in suicide rates in both young and elderly African Americans from 1983–1986 is a phenomenon commonly seen in less developed countries. In addition to higher unemployment rates, there was a marked reduction in the availability of social services during the mid to late 1980s. These conditions would have been difficult for both the young and elderly, as the latter rely on social services for support and the former have not yet established the resources to weather such difficult economic challenges (Joe & Kaplan, 2001).

In contrast to the studies that link SES to suicide incidence among African Americans, other researchers have found the reverse to be true. For example, both Lester (1996) and Burr et al. (1999) found that where racial disparities in economic resources were the greatest, African American suicide rates were lowest. Moreover, an earlier study by Lester (1993) found that unlike European Americans, there was no relationship between social disintegration, unemployment, and suicidality among African Americans. There is credible evidence that African Americans at the higher end of the education and income spectrum are at greater risk for suicide (Burr et al., 1999; Lester, 1993). Some scholars have suggested this phenomenon is related to acculturative stress in African Americans (Walker, Utsey, Bolden, & Williams, 2005).

If past trends are any indicator, current U.S. economic conditions suggest the potential for a shift in suicide trends among African Americans. According to a recent National Public Radio (NPR) news report (see http://www.npr.org/templates/story/story.php?storyId=7272202), the unemployment rate among African American adults went from 8.4% in December 2006 to 8% in January 2007. Unemployment among African American teenagers remains at a staggering 29%, six times the national rate. There were 1.2 million Black-owned businesses in 2002, a 45% increase from 1997 (U.S. Census Bureau, 2006). In addition, the number of African Americans enrolled in college doubled over the last 15 years, going from 624,000 in 1994 to 1.1 million in 2004 (U.S. Census Bureau). These are just a few indicators of the current economic well-being of Black America. Based on the work of Burr et al. (1999) and Lester (1993), these economic indicators might signal an impending increase in the suicide rates among African Americans. On the other hand, the review by Rehkopf and Buka (2006) would suggest the opposite—that based on the current economic conditions, suicide rates among African Americans are likely to continue to decline. Based on the equivocal findings regarding the relationship between SES conditions and suicide risk among African Americans, predicting future trends with any degree of accuracy is likely impossible.

Differences in risk factors and the availability of resources may account for some of the gender differences in African American suicide rates. Gender differences in suicide behavior among this populatioin generally parallel findings from other racial groups: Males complete suicide more often whereas women are more likely to think about suicide and attempt suicide (Willis et al., 2003). For example, African American men are more likely to use more lethal means in their suicide attempts than African American women (Joe & Kaplan, 2001). Important to our review, however, research has also shown that African American women utilize certain protective factors more often than African American men, which may also contribute to differences in suicide rates. For example, the women often have large social support networks and fill several social roles (Nisbet, 1996).

African American men, on the other hand, have or create fewer social roles into which to integrate themselves (Willis, Coombs, Cockerham, & Frison, 2002). Similarly, African American women report much higher levels of religiosity, religious affiliation, and church attendance, and are more likely to believe that the church can improve their lives (Griffin-Fennell & Williams, 2006).

Another potential suicide risk factor somewhat specific to African Americans is chronic exposure to invidious racism (Jones, 1997; Outlaw, 1993). The stress associated with chronic exposure to racism has been linked to a number of mental health problems, including depression (Fernando, 1984; Noh, Beiser, Kaspar, Hou, & Rummens, 1999), increased hostility (Utsey, 1997), lowered life satisfaction and self-esteem (Broman, 1997), and feelings of trauma, loss, and helplessness (Clark, Anderson, Clark, & Williams, 1999; Thompson & Neville, 1999). In addition, chronic exposure to racism has been linked to the onset of cardiovascular disease (Brondolo, Rieppi, Kelly, & Gerin, 2003; Merrit, Bennett, Williams, Edwards, & Sollers, 2006).

Brown et al. (1996) suggested that any deleterious consequences resulting from daily encounters with racism was primarily the result of inadequate coping resources. A number of researchers have examined the relation between the strategies used by African Americans to cope with race-related stress and their psychological and somatic health outcomes (Bowen-Reid & Harrell, 2002; Krieger & Sidney, 1996; Plummer & Slane, 1996; Utsey, Ponterotto, Reynolds, & Cancelli, 2000). There is agreement among researchers that the coping resources and protective factors that buffer individuals from the deleterious effects of chronic exposure to racism are essential to the healthy psychological and emotional well-being of African Americans (Daly, Jennings, Beckett, & Leashore, 1995; Plummer & Slane, 1996; Utsey et al., 2000). Although there is no empirical evidence linking chronic exposure to racism to suicide risk, it is clear that general life stress, which for African Americans includes racism-related stress, is a risk factor.

Although the literature related to the role of coping resources and protective factors that buffer against suicide risk is extensive, many of the identified protective factors are not unique to African Americans. Indeed, excluding cursory references to religion and spirituality, the role of culture and worldview has not been adequately examined in relation to African American suicide risk. Therefore, in the following section, we define the African American cultural worldview and review specific literature that examines the effects of these specific cultural protective factors on suicide risk among African Americans.

Cultural Protective Factors and African American Suicide

Culture and worldview are two related, but somewhat distinct constructs that provide a framework for living and relating to others (Hall, 2005). Although culture has been defined in many ways, there is agreement that culture consists of shared elements that provide the standard for perceiving, believing, evaluating, communicating, and acting (Triandis, 1996). Worldview, according to Sue & Sue (1999), is the psychological orientation that determines what people think and how they behave, make decisions, and define events. A number of scholars have proposed a cultural orientation and worldview to describe the ways in which African Americans interpret reality and experience the world (e.g., Boykin, 1983; Grills, 2002; Jones, 2003; Nobles, 2004).

The cultural reality and worldview of African Americans is grounded in a strong religious belief system, a collective social orientation, strong family/kinship bonds, communalism, cognitive flexibility, affective expressiveness, and present time orientation (Grills, 2002; Hill, 1999; Holloway, 1990; Jones, 2003; Nobles, 2004; Taylor, Chatters, & Levin, 2004). These cultural values yield culture-based strengths such as spiritually based coping, broad social support networks, flexible family roles, strong kinship bonds, positive ethnic group identity, and a high level of psychological and emotional hardiness (Harvey & Hill, 2004; Majors & Billson, 1992; Mattis, 2004; Miller, 1999; Miller & MacIntosh, 1999; Nobles, 2004; Utsey, Adams, & Bolden, 2000). Denby (1996) noted that, among African Americans, spiritually based cultural protective factors "can be manifested in a belief structure of perpetual optimism and the ability to recover from adversity" (p. 153). Jones (2003), in his TRIOS model of culture and psyche, proposed that present-time orientation, rhythm, improvisation, orality, and spirituality each moderated or mediated important behavioral outcomes in African Americans. The role of culture in the mental health functioning of African Americans is undeniably critical, and as recommended by the U.S. Surgeon General (2001), warrants further study by psychologists and other social scientists.

The protective function of African American culture has been empirically established. For example, Utsey, Hook, and Standard (2006) found that cultural factors (time orientation, racial pride, and religiosity) moderated the relationship between race-related stress and psychological distress in a sample of African American college students. Similarly, a study conducted by Utsey, Bolden, Lanier, and Williams (2006) with a community sample of African Americans found that, in addition to social support and family cohesiveness, collective and spiritual coping were significant predictors of quality of life. Johnson (1995) found that spirituality, rituals, extended family, elder advice, and family cohesion/structure predicted positive outcomes in a sample of African American families. Harvey and Hill (2004) evaluated the efficacy of an Africentric rites-of-passage program for at-risk youth and found that Africentric cultural values correlated with resilient outcomes for the study's participants. Bowman (1990) found that extended family systems, strong spiritual beliefs, and ethnic pride served as a resource for African Americans dealing with adversity. A number of studies have found that racial pride and racial identity function as a protective factor (Fischer & Shaw, 1999; Miller & MacIntosh, 1999; Sellers & Shelton, 2003).

Not surprisingly, cultural factors have been found to buffer African Americans against suicide risk. Kaslow et al. (2004) found that religious involvement and spiritual well-being reduced the risk of suicide attempts in a clinical sample of African Americans. Likewise, Anglin et al. (2005) found that religious well-being was inversely related to suicide attempts in a sample of low-income African Americans. Walker et al. (2005) found that religious well-being moderated the relationship between acculturation and suicidality in a community sample of African Americans. A previous review of the literature on African American suicide led Gibbs (1988) to conclude that family cohesiveness, extended family and kinship networks, the African American church, fraternal and social organizations, and social support networks all served to promote a sense of belonging that diminished suicide risk in African Americans. Kirk and Zucker (1979) found that Black consciousness reduced suicide risk in the group. As noted earlier, whether these factors (e.g., religiosity, spirituality, family support, social support, etc.) are uniquely African American is debatable.

Although investigators have recently begun to examine the role of culture as a protective factor in relation to African American suicide, the exact mechanisms by which culture protects African Americans from suicide risk have not been established. However, by examining the cultural orientation and worldview of African Americans we might uncover the protective features of the beliefs, behaviors, and practices that reduce suicide risk in this population. This may also lead to an understanding of the erratic and unpredictable fluctuations in the suicide rates of African Americans over time.

□ Implications for Suicide Assessment and Intervention

We now briefly explore several implications for suicide assessment and intervention in clinical practice.

Suicide Assessment

Based on our review of the literature of cultural factors that affect African American suicide, we offer several guidelines for clinicians to accurately assess suicide risk in African American clients. First, because African Americans have lower suicide rates than members of other racial/ethnic groups, clinicians should guard against underestimating the risk of suicide in this population. It is easy to focus on between-group differences and ignore important within-group differences in specific clients. Although African Americans as a group may have a reduced risk for suicide, clinicians are urged to focus on and evaluate the risk with each individual client.

Factors other than low base rates may contribute to underestimating the risk of suicide for an African American client. For example, he or she may be less likely to use drugs during a suicide crisis, and also express little suicide intent or depressive symptoms during that time (Luoma, Pearson, & Martin, 2002). In other words, the typical behaviors observed in a client at high risk for suicide may not be as obvious for an African American. This may be due to the stigma surrounding suicide in African American communities. Clinicians working with African Americans are encouraged to take overt suicide behavior or expressions seriously, but also to probe or explore possible suicide ideation that is more covert.

Second, clinicians are encouraged to familiarize themselves with the suicide risk factors that are more common among African Americans. Reviewed above, these include psychological distress, substance abuse, lethal means, social isolation, family dysfunction, impaired interpersonal relationships, maladaptive coping skills, and exposure to racial inequality. While many of these risk factors are common to all racial/ethnic groups (e.g., psychological distress), others are not (e.g., exposure to racial inequality). Indeed, the stress associated with chronic exposure to racism (race-related stress), as noted earlier, has been linked to a number of mental health problems (Broman, 1997; Clark et al., 1999; Noh, Beiser, Kaspar, Hou, & Rummens, 1999; Utsey, 1997). To the extent that an individual has been consistently exposed to race-related stress, he or she may be at an increased risk for suicide. Brief assessments are available to measure a client's level of perceived race-related stress (e.g., IRRS-B, Utsey, 1999).

Third, clinicians are encouraged to assess a client's access to and use of cultural protective factors that may lessen his or her risk for suicide. Reviewed above, these protective factors include religiosity and spirituality, strong family and communal bonds, and feelings of racial or cultural pride. Clinicians are encouraged to ask whether religion or spirituality is a part of a client's worldview. Brief assessments are available to measure a client's level of religious commitment (e.g., RCI-10; Worthington et al., 2003). If a client is highly religious, using religion may be a helpful avenue for intervention. If a client is involved in a church, this also usually indicates the presence of a supportive group. Clinicians are also encouraged to inquire about a client's familial experiences and level of family support. Again, brief assessments are available to measure the level of functioning of a family system (e.g., FACES II; Olson, Portner, & Bell, 1982). The client may have additional strong bonds with others besides his or her family, such as a school, club, work group, or support group. It may be useful to assess the level of connectedness the client feels with others. Greater feelings of connectedness may indicate lower risk of suicide as well as tools for suicide intervention. Brief assessments are available to measure the level of connectedness a client feels to others (e.g., SCS; Singelis et al., 1994). Finally, the clinician might assess a client's level of pride in his or her racial group. High racial pride is associated with lower suicide risk (Kaslow et al., 2004), and can be a springboard for discussing positive aspects about a client's life. A brief assessment such as the African American Acculturation Scale (Snowden & Hines, 1999) may be given.

Clinicians are encouraged to explore other state-of-the-art assessment techniques that have been underutilized with African American populations. For example, the psychological autopsy has found utility in the posthumous examination of suicide risk factors. However, there is little research that examines that psychological autopsy as a reliable and valid method of assessment for African American populations. Given the racial/ethnic differences in the expression of suicide risk, an examination of the utility of psychological autopsies as a viable assessment tool for use with African Americans is warranted.

Psychological Autopsy

A psychological autopsy (PA) is a data-gathering technique designed to assess the thoughts, feelings, behaviors, and relationships of the deceased suicide victim (Ebert, 1987). Traditionally, the PA is used to analyze non-equivocal suicides. It is a posthumous assessment of the psychological, social, and environmental factors that may have influenced the suicide victim's decision to act (Ebert, 1987). Most importantly, because the PA is an instrument that enables clinicians and researchers to investigate the lives of suicide victims, it has the potential to reduce the risk of suicide among individuals with similar psychological, social, and environmental profiles. In an effort to illustrate the role of cultural factors in the clinical assessment of suicide risk, and their potential for formulating intervention strategies, we present a case study of a psychological autopsy.

Case Study

Malik was a 32-year-old African American male who committed suicide via a self-inflicted gunshot wound to the head. He was found in his bedroom by his wife, Khayla, a 30-year-old African American female who was interviewed for the purpose of constructing this psychological autopsy. As she talks about her husband's death, it becomes clear to the interviewer that her husband lacked many of the protective factors believed to buffer African Americans from suicide. Helping Khayla reconstruct her husband's life may provide insight into some of the psychological, social, and environmental factors that may have influenced his decision to end his life. Moreover, we will be able to assess the degree to which her husband had access to cultural protective factors that might have reduced his risk for suicide completion.

Malik and Khayla had been married for 11 years when she found his body in their bedroom. They grew up in the same neighborhood of a major metropolitan city and met through mutual friends when she was 13 years old. She reports being attracted to his intelligence and describes his personality as "quiet," "reserved," and "well-mannered." They began dating in high school. After high school, he joined the military and she enrolled in a four-year college. They married two years after high school, when she was 19 years old. Soon after their marriage, he received military assignment to be stationed on the west coast and left to continue his military training. She left college less than a year later to be with him. During their fifth year of marriage, they returned to the east coast and had their first child shortly thereafter.

Khayla described these first five years of their marriage as "amazing." She stated that she waited to have children because she wanted to spend her time enjoying Malik and getting closer to him. She reported that he was fun, responsible, and a good provider. She felt secure.

Malik had a difficult upbringing. His family lacked structure, cohesion, and warmth. Khayla shared what she knew of his family life:

> "Malik's family was poor. We both were. That was why I liked him. I felt we could relate to each other. But as I got to know his family, I learned they were very different from us. I mean, it's like his family had no family values. My family had better values. He had no boundaries. He was never told "no." He was never disciplined; he was kicked or had things thrown at him when they were angry or something, you know, but never spanked like us—never disciplined. He had no time for dinner, no time to come home—he could stay out all night. No one cared when he came home. …
>
> When he was little, he thought his mom was his sister. She had him at 14. I guess, because back then, having a kid that young was

> disgraceful, so her mother [who is his grandmother] raised him. Actually, she only raised him because his great-grandmother died at 6 or 7. He was attached to [his great grandmother]. That was tough for him. She cared for him since he was born. When she died, he moved to live with his mother and grandmother. He wasn't treated well. His mother would go away for weekends at a time. He saw her in and out of the house; she never made it through high school. His grandmother drank. So did his grandfather. They treated him mean. He never got Christmas gifts. When we were younger, I asked him what he got for Christmas, he said, "Nothing, I never get gifts." You know, I think he missed a lot of his childhood because he grew up fast.

Khayla reported that Malik had often mentioned that she was the only constant in his life and the only person he could trust. Although he had a number of close friends, it was difficult for him to feel comfortable turning to others. The trauma he experienced as a child negatively affected his emotional expressiveness. Khayla reported wondering if he was "holding it all in," and she now regrets not asking more about his trauma.

Despite Khayla's assertion that Malik was involved in church, she admitted that she was "not really sure about how spiritual he was. I mean I don't know if he read the Bible or anything like that. I can't remember him praying, or talking about praying.... I feel like he turned to drugs, not God, when things got rough. Khayla believes that drugs made Malik's problems unbearable. She elaborates, "Things were tough, yeah, but things were always tough for Malik. He could have managed them sober—always had. Once he started using heavily, he changed. The drugs changed his mind. I truly believe he wasn't in his right mind when he did it. I don't know if he was high or not, but he hadn't been in his right mind since he started using."

During the interview Khayla stated that there might have been something she could have done or something that she should have noticed that could have prevented his downfall. As we explored some of the challenges in Malik's life, she explained that he was using marijuana socially in high school. She reported that she didn't know exactly when he started using heavier stuff, but that she thinks he got into PCP and some crack cocaine about the time of his death. ... she thinks he started using drugs because it was socially accepted in his peer group. She said, "He could feel casual and comfortable around friends—entertain, you know. He was quiet, remember, but when he was using he was different."

She explained that he began using drugs more heavily after the birth of their first child. He had gotten a better job and expressed beginning to feel pressured by the expectation of having to be a good father and a responsible family man. Family dysfunction and childhood trauma were now coupled with feelings of inadequacy and depression. Unable to vocalize his distress, he became more violent and agitated. According to Khayla, Malik acknowledged that he was having problems, and he promised to seek help. However, he couldn't bring himself to see anyone professionally about his problems and decided to handle them alone.

This case study illustrates several important issues regarding suicide assessment in African American populations. First, we note that typical expressions of suicide risk are initially absent from Malik's profile. For example, there are no signs of depressed mood, hopelessness, despair, or previous attempts. He does not exhibit any of the typical presuicidal behaviors, including giving away valued belongings, contacting people he hadn't spoken with for some time, or talking about death and dying. We do observe, however, that Malik's family history would suggest that he was at increased risk for suicide. Poverty, violence, alcoholism, substance abuse, and familial dysfunction are all factors that place individuals at increased risk for suicide (Joe & Kaplan, 2001). Moreover, those cultural protective factors that are typically associated with low suicide risk were not available to Malik. For example, Khayla reported that Malik was not active in church, lacked close familial ties, had few reliable social networks, and was unable to experience a sense of community integration (communalism).

The question is—given what we now know about Malik's level of risk—what interventions might have reduced his risk for suicide completion? As noted, the psychological autopsy is intended to provide insight into the thoughts, feelings, behaviors, social relationships, and environment of the victim. To this end, the information gathered as a result of the psychological autopsy can be used to develop effective suicide interventions for those individuals recognized to be at increased risk for suicide. Below we discuss the development of culture-specific interventions for reducing suicide risk among African Americans.

□ Recommendations for Clinical Interventions

A good place to begin this discussion is with interventions for individuals who are acutely suicidal. For the individual who has a plan, intent, and the necessary lethal means, the appropriate intervention is hospitalization. Individuals who have a plan and the intent, but lack the lethal means to follow through can be monitored in an outpatient setting. Depressive symptoms can be managed with pharmacotherapy. Crisis counseling interventions might include encouraging individuals to express their feelings and offering support. Be sure to avoid judgmental statements, giving advice, debating with the person, or being sworn to secrecy. If an individual's level of risk is high it will be important to stay with him or her until the level decreases. The immediate goal is to reduce risk until the individual can receive follow-up or longer-term care. *No-harm contracts* are commonly used to further reduce the risk of an actively suicidal person. No-harm contracts are short-term agreements between the individual and a trusted family member, friend, therapist, or other mental health personnel, where the individual agrees not to harm him or herself for a specified period of time. In addition, the contract should provide the names and phone numbers of persons to contact in the event of a crisis. Furthermore, efforts should be made to remove any weapons, drugs, or other potentially lethal objects/substances from the person's home environment.

As it regards intervention strategies that are specific to the social and cultural ethos of African Americans, we recommend that clinicians involve the family, social networks, community supports, and possibly the church (i.e., cleric or congregants). The decision as to whom to involve, or to what degree they should be involved, is made in consultation with the client. Given what we know about the protective function of religiosity and spirituality in relation to suicide risk, it is recommended that the client be encouraged to avail those religious or spiritual resources available. Be careful not to use religion in a judgmental way that castigates the individual for thoughts and feelings. Religious and spiritual resources are best used as mechanisms of support and affirmation. To summarize, clinicians are advised to consider cultural protective factors in developing interventions for African Americans who are suicidal. These culture-specific interventions are intended to augment traditional intervention strategies to reduce suicide risk among African Americans in acute or long-term crisis.

☐ Future Directions for African American Suicide Research

A recent special issue of the *Journal of Black Psychology* (JBP, 2006; volume 32, number 5) was dedicated exclusively to the examination of African American suicide. Included was a mix of theoretical and empirical articles on various topics related to suicide behaviors among African Americans. The breadth and depth of coverage given to the various topics covered in this special issue were noteworthy and may be an indication of the direction research in this area is moving toward.

The issue begins with an article by Crosby and Molock (2006) identifying a variety of risk and protective factors related to African American suicide. The authors go on to critique the current state of theory and research related to suicide within this population. Next, Joe and Kaplan (2006) provided an in-depth analysis of the changing patterns of suicide behavior among African Americans. He identified a pattern of birth-cohort effects whereby younger generations were found to be at greatest risk for suicide behavior (i.e., ideation, attempts, and completions). Joe and Kaplan suggested that the cohort effects for younger generations, if continued into later life, may reverse the recent decline in African American suicide rates. A study by Kaslow, Jacobs, Young, and Cook (2006) examined suicidal behaviors among low-income African American women. Specifically, they were interested in psychological and historical factors that differed between first-time and repeat attempters. Their findings indicated that compared with first-time attempters, repeat attempters demonstrated higher levels of intent, planning, and perceived lethality. Moreover, repeat attempters had higher levels of psychological distress, hopelessness, substance abuse, and childhood trauma.

Durant et al. (2006) conducted a case-control study to examine whether racial difference existed for level of hopelessness in a sample of African American and European American nearly lethal attempters. They found that hopelessness was strongly associated with suicide attempts for both groups, but that the odds were greater for African Americans than for European Americans.

Just one qualitative study appeared among the articles published in the special issue of the *Journal of Black Psychology*. To examine how African American families respond in the aftermath of a suicide, this study used semi-structured interviews with 19 African American families who had lost a loved one to suicide. Durant et al.'s findings indicated that African American families often experienced isolation and had to endure the grieving process alone. Furthermore, some respondents thought that when they did receive support (primarily from the church), it was unhelpful. Barnes et al. (2003) concluded that negative attitudes from the larger community as well as from family members made it more difficult to cope.

Surprisingly, only two studies published in the *JBP* special issue examined the role of cultural beliefs and behaviors as risk or protective factors related to suicide among African Americans. The first study, conducted by Molock Puri, Matlin, & Barksdale (2006), investigated the relationship between religious coping and suicidal behaviors among African Americans. This study was significant in that it targeted high school students, a population considered most at increased risk for suicide behavior. The investigators found that religious coping was significantly related to suicidal behaviors in the sample. A study by Walker, Lester, and Joe (2006) examined culturally relevant suicide beliefs and attributions among African Americans. They compared a sample of African Americans with a sample of European Americans and found that the former were less likely to attribute suicide to interpersonal problems. Moreover, African Americans were significantly more likely than European Americans to report that God is responsible for life. Taken together, these studies illustrate the importance of considering cultural factors in examining suicide risk and protective factors among African Americans.

In spite of the important contributions of the *JBP* special issue, the existing body of research on culture, risk, and protective factors and African American suicide remains limited in several ways. First, there is disagreement among researchers as to whether the cultural protective factors that buffer against suicide risk in African Americans are distinctive to African American culture. Moreover, a majority of research on African American suicide is based on cross-sectional correlational designs. More sophisticated methodologies such as longitudinal designs or autopsy studies have generally not been used.

Generally speaking, the scope of research on the protective and risk factors for suicide among African Americans should be expanded across the developmental life span (e.g., children, adolescents, and the elderly). Research among these populations is vital for clinicians, who need culturally appropriate therapies for the individuals they treat. In addition, research comparing less vulnerable populations (e.g., African American women) with higher risk populations (e.g., African American men) may provide information that improves treatment of the higher risk groups. For example, since religiosity is a factor primarily seen among African American females, studies may reveal that clinicians who encourage the exploration of religiosity or an equivalent protective factor may render African American males less likely to consider or attempt suicide.

Moreover, there is a need for more sophisticated and exact methodologies for conducting suicide research. For example, future research should focus more on individual differences between suicide attempters and suicide completers. Valid and reliable conclusions cannot always be drawn about one group (e.g., completers) through the study of another (e.g., attempters). Methods that study actual suicide completers, such as the psychological autopsy (e.g., Moskos, Olson, & Halbern, 2005; Preville, Hebert, & Boyer, 2005), may be applied to African American populations. Furthermore, a shift from the use of cross-sectional correlational research designs to longitudinal studies is needed to expose patterns of suicidal behavior and offer valuable information regarding the likelihood of future suicide completion. Experimental designs and longitudinal studies are just two examples of methodologies that hold promise in uncovering the complexities associated with suicide in African American populations.

□ Summary/Conclusion

Historically, African Americans have had a lower risk of suicide than other ethnic groups, but as rates have fluctuated, the changes reflect important differences in the African American community today. A better understanding of suicide among African Americans not only seeks to ascertain what is undermining the mental health of this group, but provides valuable information about the cultural climate of African Americans in the U.S. today.

Because African Americans have lower suicide rates than members of other ethnic groups, clinicians should guard against underestimating the suicide risk for a specific African American client. This is particularly true given that African Americans are less likely to use drugs during a suicide crisis, and also express little suicide intent or depressive symptoms during that time (Luoma, Pearson, & Martin, 2002).

Suicide assessment for African Americans should begin with an increased awareness of cultural differences in the expression of suicidal behaviors. A crucial step in assessing suicide risk among African Americans is to evaluate a client's access to cultural protective factors. Clients with fewer cultural protective factors may be at greater risk for suicide.

Regarding clinical implications, the importance of cultural factors in relation to the mental health functioning of African Americans cannot be overestimated. Counselors are encouraged to consider how racial pride, religiosity, and social networks can facilitate positive outcomes among their African American clients. Religious or spiritual approaches can be incorporated into individual and group psychotherapy by counselors in most clinical settings. In fact, a number of clinician's guides incorporate religiosity and spirituality into counseling (e.g., Faiver, Ingersoll, O'Brien, & McNally, 2001; Wiggins Frame, 2003).

An important implication of our examination of the literature on African American suicide and cultural protective factors is that there is a need for more culturally relevant research and programming. Given the relation between African American suicide and family issues, local and national government officials should seek to fund programs that promote a sense of community in neighborhoods and support cohesiveness among African American families, particularly during difficult times. In addition, African American communities may benefit from programs administered through faith- or community-based organizations. Psycho-educational programs can be used to alert the community to prevalence rates, survival rates and risk, and effects on family, friends and the community, as well as to offer a familiar setting for obtaining resources. These types of programs may aid in dispelling condemnatory attitudes, which may prevent help-seeking behavior. Moreover, given the need for research in this area, current efforts to stimulate awareness may need support from government and institutional funding sources in order to attract novice scholars and suicidologists experienced in working with other populations.

References

American Association of Suicidology (2004). *African American suicide fact sheet.* Retrieved from www.cdc.gov/ncipc/wisqars/default.htm. April, 15 2006.

Anglin, D.M., Gabriel, K.O.S., & Kaslow, N.J. (2005). Suicide acceptability and religious well-being: A comparative analysis in African American suicide attempters and non-attempters. *Journal of Psychology and Theology, 33,* 140–150.

Barnes, D.H., & Bell, C.C. (2003). Paradoxes of Black Suicide. *The National Journal,* January.

Berman, A.L. (1990). Clinical issues: Treating the difficult patient. *Suicide and Life-Threatening Behavior, 20,* 267–274.

Boykin, A.W. (1983). The triple quandary and the schooling of Afro American children. In E. Neisser (Ed.), *The school achievement of minority children* (pp. 57–92). Hillside, NJ: Lawrence Erlbaum Associates.

Bowman, P. (1990). Coping with provider role strain: Adaptive cultural resources among Black husband-fathers. *Journal of Black Psychology, 16,* 1–21.

Bowen-Reid, T.L., & Harrell, J.P. (2002). Racist experiences and health outcomes: An examination of spirituality as a buffer. *Journal of Black Psychology, 28,* 18–36.

Breed, W. (1966). Suicide, migration, and race: A study of cases in New Orleans. *Journal of Social Issues, 22,* 30–43.

Brondolo, E., Rieppi, R., Kelly, K.P., & Gerin, W. (2003). Perceived racism and blood pressure: A review of the literature and conceptual and methodological critique. *Annals of Behavioral Medicine, 25,* 55–65.

Broman, C.L. (1997). Race-related factors and life satisfaction among African Americans. *Journal of Black Psychology, 23,* 36–49.

Burr, J.A., Hartman, J.T., & Matteson, D. W. (1999). Black suicide in U. S. metropolitan areas: An examination of the racial inequality and social integration-regulation hypotheses. *Social Forces, 77,* 1049–1080.

Clark, R., Anderson, N.B., Clark, V.R., & Williams, D.R. (1999). Racism as a stressor for African Americans: A biopsychosocial model. *American Psychologist, 54,* 805–816.

Daly, A., Jennings, J., Beckett, J.O., & Leashore, B.R. (1995). Effective coping strategies of African Americans. *Social Work, 40,* 240–248.

Denby, R.W. (1996). Resiliency and the African American family: A model of family preservation. In S.L. Logan (Ed.), *The Black family: Strengths, self-help, and positive change* (pp. 144–163). Boulder, CO: Westview Press, Inc.

Durant, T., Mercy, J., Kresnow, M., Simon, T., Potter, L., & Hammond, W.R. (2006). Racial differences in hopelessness as a risk factor for a nearly lethal suicide attempt. *Journal of Black Psychology, 32,* 285–302.

Durkheim, E. (1951). *Suicide.* New York, NY: Free Press.

Early, K. (1992). *Religion and suicide in the African American community.* New York: Free Press.

Early, K.E., & Akers, R.L. (1993). "It's a white thing": An exploration of beliefs about suicide in the African American community. *Deviant Behavior, 14,* 277–296.

Ebert, B.W. (1987). Guide to conducting a psychological autopsy. *Professional Psychology: Research and Practice, 11,* 52–56.

Fernando, S. (1984). Racism as a cause of depression. *International Journal of Social Psychiatry, 30,* 41–49.

Gibbs, J.T. (1988). Conceptual, methodological, and sociocultural issues in Black youth suicide: Implications for assessment and early intervention. *Suicide and Life Threatening Behavior, 18,* 73–89.

Goldsmith, S.K., Pellmar, T.C., Kleinman, A.M., & Bunney, W.E. (Eds.). (2002). *Reducing suicide: A national imperative.* Washington, D. C.: National Academies Press.

Griffin-Fennell, F., & Williams, M. (2006). Examining the complexities of suicidal behavior in the African American community. *Journal of Black Psychology, 32,* 1–17.

Grills, C. (2002). African-centered psychology: Basic principles. In T.A. Parham (Ed.), *Counseling persons of African descent: Raising the bar of practitioner competence* (pp. 10–21). Thousand Oaks, CA: Sage Publications.

Hall, G.C.N. (2005). Introduction to the special section on multicultural and community psychology: Clinical psychology in context. *Journal of Consulting and Clinical Psychology, 73,* 787–789.

Harvey, A.R. & Hill, R.B. (2004). Africentric youth and family rites of passage program: Promoting resilience among at-risk African American youths. *Social Work, 49,* 65–77.

Hill, R. (1999). *The strengths of African American families: Twenty-five years later.* Lanham, MD: University Press of America

Hendin, H. (1969). Black suicide. *Archives of General Psychiatry, 210,* 407–422.

Holloway, J.E. (1990). The origins of African American culture. In J.E. Holloway (Ed.), *Africanisms in American culture* (pp. 1–18). Bloomington, IN: Indiana University Press.

Joe, S. & Kaplan, M.S. (2001). Suicide among African American men. *Suicide and Life-Threatening Behavior, 31,* 106–121.

Johnson, A.C. (1995). Resiliency mechanisms in culturally diverse families. *Family Journal: Counseling and Therapy for Couples and Families, 3,* 316–324.

Jones, J.M. (1997). *Prejudice and Racism (2nd ed.).* New York: McGraw-Hill.

Jones, J.M. (2003). TRIOS: A psychological theory of the African American legacy in American culture. *Journal of Social Issues, 59,* 217–242.

Kaplan, C., Turner, S., Norman, E., & Stillson, K. (1996). Promoting resilience strategies: A modified consultation model. *Social Work in Education, 18,* 158–168.

Kaslow, N.J., Jacobs, C.H., Young, S.L., & Cook, S. (2006). Suicidal behavior among low-income African American women: A comparison of first-time and repeat suicide attempters. *Journal of Black Psychology, 32,* 1–17.

Kaslow, N. J., Price, A.B., Wycoff, S., Grall, M.B., Sherry, A., Young, S., Scholl, L., Upshaw, V.M., Rashid, A., Jackson, E.B., & Bethea, K. (2004). Person factors associated with suicidal behavior among African American women and men. *Cultural Diversity and Ethnic Minority Psychology, 10,* 5–22.

Kaslow, N.J., Thompson, M.P., Okun, A., Price, A., Young, S., Bender, M., Wyckoff, S., Twomey, H., & Goldin, J. (2002). Risk and protective factors for suicidal behavior in abused African American women. *Journal of Consulting and Clinical Psychology, 70,* 311–319.

Kirk, A.R., & Zucker, R.A. (1979). Some sociopsychological factors in attempted suicide among urban Black males. *Suicide and Life Threatening Behavior, 9,* 76–86.

Krieger, N., & Sidney, S. (1996). Racial discrimination and blood pressure: The CARDIA study of young Black and White adults. *American Journal of Public Health, 86,* 1370–1378.

Lester, D. (1993). Economic status of African Americans and suicide rates. *Perceptual and Motor Skills, 77,* 1150.

Lester, D. (1996). Inequality of income and rates of violence in Caucasian and Black groups. *Psychological Reports, 79,* 979–998.

Lester, D. (1998). *Suicide in African Americans.* Commack, New York: Nova Science Publishers.

Lester, D. (1999). Suicide and homicide in Caribbean nations. *Perceptual and Motor Skills, 88,* 1350.

Luoma, J.B., Pearson, J.L., & Martin, C.E. (2002). Contact with mental health and primary care prior to suicide: A review of the evidence. *American Journal of Psychiatry, 159,* 909–916.

Majors, R. & Billson, J.M. (1992). *Cool pose: The dilemmas of Black manhood in America.* New York, NY: Touchstone

Marion, M.S. & Range, L.M. (2003). African American college women's suicide buffers. *Suicide and Life-Threatening Behavior, 33,* 33–43.

Mattis, J. (2004). Spirituality and religion in African American life. In R.L. Jones (Ed.) *Black psychology (4th Ed.)* (pp. 93–115). Hampton, VA: Cobb & Henry Publishers.

Merritt, M.M., Bennett, G.G., Williams, R.B., Edwards, C.L., & Sollers, J.J. (2006). Perceived racism and cardiovascular reactivity and recovery to personally relevant stress. *Health Psychology, 25,* 364–369.

Miller, D.B. (1999). Racial socialization and racial identity: Can they promote resiliency for African American adolescents? *Adolescence, 34,* 493–501.

Miller, D.B., & MacIntosh, R. (1999). Promoting resilience in urban African American adolescents: Racial socialization and identity as protective factors. *Social Work Research, 23,* 159–169.

Mollock, S.D., Kimbrough, R., Lacy, M.B., McClure, K.P., & Williams, S. (1994). Suicidal behavior among African American College Students: A preliminary study. *Journal of Black Psychology, 20,* 234–251.

Mollock, S.D., Puri, R., Matlin, S., & Barksdale, C. (2006). Relationship between religious coping and suicidal behavior among African American adolescents. *Journal of Black Psychology, 32.*

Moskos, M., Olson, L., & Halbern, S. (2005). Utah youth suicide study: Psychological autopsy. *Suicide and Life-Threatening Behavior, 35,* 536–546.

Nickerson, K., Helms, J., & Terrell, F. (1994). Cultural mistrust, opinions about mental illness, and Black students' attitudes toward seeking psychological help from White counselors. *Journal of Counseling Psychology, 41,* 378–385.

Nisbet, P.A. (1996). Protective factors for suicidal Black females. *Suicide and Life-Threatening Behavior, 26,* 325–341.

Nobles, W. (2004). African philosophy: Foundation for Black psychology. In R. Jones (Ed.*), Black Psychology (4th Ed.)* (pp. 57–72). Hampton, VA: Cobb & Henry Publishers.

Noh, S., Beiser, M., Kaspar, V., Hou, F., & Rummens, J. (1999). Perceived racial discrimination, depression, and coping: A study of Southeast Asian refugees in Canada. *Journal of Health and Social Behavior, 40,* 193–207.

Olson, D.H., Portner, J., & Bell, R.Q. (1982). *FACES II: Family adaptability and cohesion evaluation scales.* St Paul, MN: Family Social Science, University of Minnesota.

Outlaw, F.H. (1993). Stress and coping: The influence of racism on the cognitive appraisal processing of African–Americans. *Issues in Mental Health Nursing, 14,* 399–409.

Palmer, C. (2001). African Americans, depression, and suicide risk. *Journal of Black Psychology, 27,* 110–111.

Plummer, D.L., & Slane, S. (1996). Patterns of coping in racially stressful situations. *Journal of Black Psychology, 22,* 302–315.

Preville, M., Hebert, R., & Boyer, R. (2005). Physical health and mental disorder in elderly suicide: A case-control study. *Aging and Mental Health, 9,* 576–584.

Prudhomme, C. (1938). The problem of suicide in the American Negro. *Psychoanalytic Review, 25,* 187–204; 372–391.

Rehkopf, D.H. & Buka, S.L. (2006). The association between suicide and the socioeconomic characteristics of geographical areas: A systematic review. *Psychological Medicine, 36,* 145–157.

Sellers, R.M., & Shelton, J.N. (2003). The role of racial identity in perceived discrimination. *Journal of Personality and Social Psychology, 84,* 1079–1092.

Singelis, T.M. (1994). The measurement of independent and interdependent self-construals. *Personalilty and Social Psychology Bulletin, 20,* 580–591.

Snowden, L.R., & Hines, A.M. (1999). A scale to assess African American acculturation. *Journal of Black Psychology, 25,* 36–47.

Stack, S. (1996). The effect of marital integration on African American Suicide. *Suicide and Life-Threatening Behaviors, 26,* 405–414.

Stack, S., & Wasserman, I. (1995). The effect of marriage, family, and religious ties on African American suicide ideology. *Journal of Marriage and the Family, 57,* 215–223.

Sue, D.W., & Sue, D. (1999). Counseling the culturally different: Theory and practice (3rd ed.). New York: John Wiley.

Swanson, W., & Breed, W. (1976). Black suicide in New Orleans. In E. Schneidma (Ed.), *Suicidology: Contemporary developments* (pp. 103–128). Grune and Stratton.

Taylor, R.J., Chatters, L.M., & Levin, J. (2004). Religion in the lives of African Americans: Social, psychological, and health perspectives. Thousand Oaks, CA: Sage Publications.

Terrell, F., & Terrell, S. (1984). Race of counselor, client, sex, cultural mistrust level and premature termination from counseling among Black clients. *Journal of Counseling Psychology, 31,* 371–375.

Thompson, V.L.S., Bazile, A., & Akbar, M. (2004). African Americans' perceptions of psychotherapy and psychotherapists. *Professional Psychology: Research and Practice, 35,* 19–26.

Thompson, C.E., & Neville, H.A. (1999). Racism, mental health, and mental health practice. *Counseling Psychologist, 27,* 155–223.

Triandis, H.C. (1996). The psychological measurement of cultural syndromes. *American Psychologist, 51,* 407–415.

U.S. Department of Labor (2002). Overview of BLS statistics on employment and unemployment. A report of the Bureau of Labor Statistics. Washington, DC.

U.S. Department of Health and Human Services (2001). Mental health: Culture, race, and ethnicity—A supplement to mental health: A report of the surgeon general. Rockville, MD: U.S. Department of Health and Human Services, Public health services, Office of the surgeon general.

Utsey, S.O. (1997). Racism and the psychological well-being of African American men. *Journal of African American Men, 3*, 69–87.

Utsey, S.O. (1999). Development and validation of a short form of the Index of Race-Related Stress—Brief Version. *Measurement and Evaluation in Counseling and Development, 32*, 149–166.

Utsey, S.O., Adams, E.P. & Bolden, M.A. (2000). Development and initial validation of the Africultural Coping Systems Inventory. *Journal of Black Psychology, 26*, 194–215.

Utsey, S.O., Bolden, M.A., Lanier, Y., & Williams, O. (2006). Examining the role of culture as a protective factor in the resilience of African Americans. Unpublished manuscript, Virginia Commonwealth University.

Utsey, S.O., Hook, J.N., & Stanard, P. (2006). Psychological, physiological, and cultural factors that moderate the relationship between race-related stress and psychological functioning in African Americans. Unpublished manuscript, Virginia Commonwealth University.

Utsey, S.O., Ponterotto, J., Reynolds, A., & Cancelli, A. (2000). Racial discrimination, coping, life satisfaction, and self-esteem among African Americans. *Journal of Counseling and Development, 78*, 1, 72–80.

Vega, W.A., Gil, A.G., & Warheit, G.J. (1993). The relationship of drug use to suicide ideation and attempts among African American, Hispanic, and White non-Hispanic male adolescents. *Suicide and Life-Threatening Behavior*, 23, 110–119.

Walker, R.L., Lester, D., & Joe, S. (2006). Lay theories of suicide: An examination of culturally relevant suicide beliefs and attributions. *Journal of Black Psychology,32,*

Walker, R.L., Utsey, S.O., Bolden, M.A., & Williams, O., III. (2005). Do sociocultural factors predict suicidality among persons of African descent living in the U.S.? *Archives of Suicide Research, 9*, 203–217.

Wiggins Frame, M. (2003). Integrating religion and spirituality into counseling: A comprehensive approach. Belmont, CA: Wadsworth.

Willis, L.A., Coombs, D., Cockerham, W.C., & Frison, S.L. (2002). Ready to die: A postmodern interpretation of the increase of African American adolescent male suicide. *Social Science and Medicine, 55*, 907–920.

Willis, L.A., Coombs, D.W., Drentea, P., & Cockerham, W.C. (2003). Uncovering the mystery: Factors of African American suicide. *Suicide and Life Threatening Behavior, 33*, 412–429.

Suicide Risk in Latino and Latina Adolescents

Yovanska M. Duarté-Vélez and Guillermo Bernal*

Latinos and Latinas are the fastest growing ethnic minority in United States. Hispanics represent 14.1% (40.5 million persons) of the U.S. population and surpass all other racial/ethnic minority populations in size (U.S. Bureau of the Census, 2004). Hispanic youth are at a greater risk for suicide ideation and attempts and there are serious disparities in the delivery of mental health services to this population. Hispanics have less access to mental health services than do Whites and are less likely to receive needed care. Further, when they do access care it is frequently of poor quality (U.S. Department of Health and Human Services, 2001).

For the general population, young people are at an increasingly high risk for suicide, which is the cause of 11.7% of all deaths among youth and young adults aged 10 to 24 years in the U.S. (Grunbaum et al., 2004). Among Latinos and Latinas, the largest proportion of suicides occurs among the young. In fact, suicide is the third leading cause of death for young Hispanics (aged 10 to 24 years) and the seventh leading cause of years of potential life lost before age 75 (Center for Disease Control and Prevention, 2004). Also, Hispanic youth are at a greater risk of suicide behavior than other ethnic groups (Canino & Roberts, 2001).

This chapter expands on a previous review in the scientific literature related to suicide behavior among Hispanic adolescents (Duarté-Vélez & Bernal, 2007). Conceptual and methodological issues in research are examined and the role of contextual and developmental factors on suicide

* Work on this article was supported in part by grants from the National Institute on Mental Health (R24-MH49368) and (RO1-MH67893).

behavior is discussed. The empirical findings of comparative ethnic minority studies, studies focused on Hispanic youth, and within-group studies are reviewed, as is the role of contextual and developmental factors, and the status of evidence-based treatment for suicidal Hispanic adolescents. Finally, implications for future research are presented.

Studies were identified through a comprehensive search of online databases (e.g., Psych Info, Medline) that were published from 1990 to 2006. Studies were selected based on the following criteria: (1) inclusion of outcomes directly related to suicide behavior, such as suicide ideation, suicide attempts, and completed suicide; and (2) reporting Hispanic ethnicity as a research variable (not just as a sample description). Samples were middle or high school students or adolescents 12 to 20 years old.*

□ Epidemiology of Suicide Behavior

Suicide is the third leading cause of death among young people 15 to 24 years of age, following unintentional injuries and homicide (National Institute of Mental Health, 2001). Also, suicide is the fourth leading cause of death for children aged 10 to 14, with a gender ratio of 3:1 (males:females). Approximately 8.3% to 8.7% of all high school students attempt suicide one or more times each year in the U.S. (Eaton et al., 2006; Grunbaum et al., 2004; Grunbaum et al., 2002; Kann et al., 2000; Kann et al., 1998; Kann et al., 1996). Females consistently demonstrate a higher prevalence of depression, suicide ideation, and suicide attempts than males, even though males are more apt to actually kill themselves. Hispanic adolescents have shown a tendency to be at a greater risk for depressive symptoms, suicide ideation, and suicide attempts than other groups of adolescents in the U.S. (Canino & Roberts, 2001; Hovey & King, 1997; Zayas, Lester, Cabassa, & Fortuna, 2005).

□ Diversity among Hispanics in the U.S.

Hispanics are a large and heterogeneous group of people who share some common characteristics but differ from one another in many aspects (McGoldrick, Giordano, & Garcia-Preto, 2005). The Census Bureau's code list contains more than 30 Hispanic or Latino subgroups. The largest group is Mexican Americans (64%); next are Puerto Ricans (9.57%),**

* Two studies included a sample up to age 30.

** The U.S. citizens who live on the island of Puerto Rico (3.8 millions) are not included on these estimates.

followed by Cubans (3.55%), Dominicans (2.59%), and Central and South Americans (12.6%), with another 7.6% from Spain and some who did not identify their country of origin (4.9%) (U.S. Census Bureau, 2004). Key differences among Hispanics are related to the varied circumstances leading to their migration (U.S. Department of Health and Human Services, 2001). The historical context greatly influences the experience of given population in the U.S. (Saez-Santiago & Bernal, 2003). Hispanic subgroups also differ in terms of their geographic location in the U.S., their knowledge of English, and other demographic and socioeconomic characteristics such as education level and family income (Ungemack & Guarnaccia, 1998). Yet, Hispanics share a common language and for many, the experience of migration from their country of origin, acculturation process, racism, and discrimination (McGoldrick, Giordano, & Garcia-Preto, 2005).

□ Conceptual and Methodological Issues in Hispanic Research

Conceptual and methodological issues are almost inseparable in research. The conceptual part of a study entails the basis for structuring the "what, when, and how" of research. The worldview of an investigator is at the core of the concepts that will inform the methods (Marín & Marín, 1991). For example, if an investigator assumes a worldview based on universalism (Norenzayan & Heine, 2005), little consideration will be given to ethnic-minority issues and concepts. Alternatively, if a cultural or multicultural perspective is assumed, the place of culture, ethnicity, and context will more likely play a prominent role in the primary research question (Burlew, 2003; Marín & Marín, 1991; Potts & Watts, 2003; Rogler, 1999).

The use of ethnicity and race as independent variables in research assumes that persons belonging to such groups share some common psychological characteristics (related to personality or psychopathology) associated with culture (Okazaki & Sue, 1998). Theories about which psychological variables associated with culture to explain ethnic group differences in suicide behavior should guide comparative approach. Also, explanatory variables in specific population studies should be specified and directly measured (Okazaki & Sue, 1998).

Does the fact that there are similarities among Latino subgroups justify placing them in one broad category, such as "Hispanic," for comparative studies addressing adolescent suicide behavior? Do differences among Latino subgroups justify specific population studies (for example, focusing only on Puerto Ricans), or within-group studies (Puerto Ricans vs. Mexicans vs. Cubans) to address adolescent suicide behavior? Answers to these questions depend on the research question and the theory investigators may have on the relationship between historical background and contextual factors to explain ethnic differences among Hispanic adolescents.

Conceptual considerations on the nature of ethnicity, ethnic identity, race, and context should be reflected in the methodology. Methodological issues, such as study design, sampling, recruitment, retention, accounting for within-group diversity (such as national origin, generational status in the U.S.), measurement (which variables are included and how these are measured), language use, and culturally sensitive aspects of analytical issues require thoughtful and careful consideration in ethnic-minority research (Bernal & Sharron-del-Rio, 2001). Indeed, as Rogler (1999) recommended, culture should be an integral part of the research enterprise. This "effort should span the entire research process, from planning and pre-testing to instrumentation, to translation of instruments and collection of data, to data analyses and interpretation of findings" (Rogler, 1999, p. 430). Confidence in the findings will depend on the investigators' sensitivity to ethnic and cultural aspects at both the conceptual and methodological level.

□ Role of Contextual and Developmental Factors on Hispanic Adolescent Suicide Behavior

Sociocultural and environmental processes are central to the development of an individual's identity, ability to function in everyday life, and perception of mental illness and mental health (Basic Behavioral Science Task Force of the National Advisory Mental Health Council, 1998). Social context and experiences, combined with biological and psychological characteristics, influence individual psychological strength and vulnerability. Within each culture, nation, and society there are particular histories, legacies, worldviews, opportunities, challenges, and stresses that constitute the framework for individual and group identity (Dana, 1998). Historical experiences of migration and the context of how the different groups of Hispanics were received in the U.S. play an important role in ethnic identity and current health status (Bernal, Trimble, Burlew, & Leong, 2003).

Common threads of the Latino identity are Spanish language, physical features (predominantly heterogeneous racially, due to the mixing of races), spirituality, common values and beliefs rooted in a history of conquest and colonization, and *familismo* (Garcia-Preto, 2005). Familismo is described as a core system of values centered on the family. Indeed, there is evidence of a strong link between parental/family variables and adolescent depression (Bernal, Cumba, & Saez-Santiago, 2006).

Familismo values of collectivism and interdependence interact and compete with dominant Euro American values of autonomy and individuality (Oyserman, Coon, & Kemmelmeier, 2002), creating issues of intergenerational tension between parents and their children, depending on their varying levels of acculturation. At the microsystem level, familismo reinforces deference to parents, restrictions on adolescent female autonomy, and family unity, while at the mesosystem level, U.S. cultural norms result in increased adolescent autonomy and sexuality (Zayas, Lester, Cabassa, & Fortuna, 2005). Zayas (2005) theorizes that migration, acculturative stress, discrepant levels of acculturation, Hispanic sociocultural factors, socioeconomic disadvantage, traditional gender role socialization, ethnic identity, and adolescent–parental conflict (influenced by family functioning) are all factors that can lead to suicide attempts.

From a developmental perspective, Hispanic adolescents seem to be more deeply troubled by such questions as: "Who am I? Who do I want to be?" than by "Who does my family want me to be?" than do their peers of other ethnic backgrounds. This is a common dilemma during adolescence, which seems to be intensified in this group due to the two contradicting cultural traditions surrounding them (i.e., the American mainstream individualism versus the Hispanic culture's collectivism and familismo).

Due to the Latino cultural value known as *machismo,* boys and girls experience different processes of gender role socialization (Beck & Bargman, 1993; Chavez, Edwards, & Oetting, 1989; Garcia-Preto, 2005; Scott, Shifman, Orr, Owen, & Fawcett, 1988; Tamez, 1981). Divergent expectations, rules, and roles are inculcated into each gender during adolescence. Furthermore, acculturation processes and stress may impact boys and girls in different ways. For example, within machismo's traditional values some aspects of autonomy and sexuality are encouraged for men but not for women (Scott, Shifman, Orr, Owen, & Fawcett, 1988; Tamez, 1981). Further research is required into the different processes of socialization by gender that could suggest distinct pathways to suicidality for Latinas and Latinos living in the U.S.

Despite the fact that acculturating stress may be experienced differently between boys and girls, at some time during development Hispanic adolescents inevitably face the realization that they belong to a minority group. Adolescence is characterized by a search of individual identity, but minority Hispanic adolescents have the additional challenge of defining and integrating their ethnic identity within Euro American society, usually in the face of acculturative stress, racism, discrimination, and oppression (Phinney, 1998; Trimble, Helms, & Root, 2003). Numerous research findings indicate that racism and discrimination result in stress that adversely affects physical and mental health (U.S. Department of Human Services, 2001).

To summarize, a developmental perspective in the study of Hispanic adolescent suicide behavior places identity, and in particular ethnic identity, at center stage in relation to other important variables such as acculturation, acculturative stress, and other family variables. Alternatively, an ecological perspective highlights the interaction of the social and historical influences (the mesosystem) with the family environment (the microsystem). Furthermore, a gender perspective acknowledges the different socialization of boys and girls that could lead to identifying distinct pathways to suicide behavior. An eco-developmental gender-specific perspective seems to integrate milestones for the understanding of suicide behavior in Hispanic adolescents.

□ Latino Culture, Sexual-Minority Youth, and Suicidality

Latino culture has been characterized in terms of values related to spirituality, collectivism, and machismo among other characteristics (Garcia-Preto, 2005; Nagayama Hall, 2001). Within the Latino culture, Judeo-Christian values are the predominant moral parameters that represent a continuum of very conservative-traditional to liberal values. Within the conservative-traditional values, a prevalent point of view considers non-heterosexual relationships sinful.

Sexuality is a fundamental aspect of human existence. Sexual identity is a milestone of human development. Adolescents within the Judeo-Christian tradition that experiment with same-sex attraction are challenged to integrate their sexuality to an apparent ideological contradiction (Ransom, 2004). In this sense, to identify as gay, lesbian, or bisexual (GLB) compromises the incorporation of two opposite parts of the adolescent's identity. This conflict could result in distress not only because of the internal difficulties to conciliate these two fundamental aspects of his/her identity (spirituality and sexuality), but also because of the social implications of assuming a non-heterosexual identity (Ransom, 2004). In the worst scenario, family, religious community, and school peers will show disapproval (rejection, humiliation, criticism) to a non-traditional course of sexual development (Savin-Williams, 2004). One example concerning this internal struggle was captured in the phrase of one Puerto Rican Christian girl in the clinical practice as: "Not being able to express myself is like being dead."

Meyer (2003) argues that the concept of minority stress is an elaboration of the social stress theory that "distinguishes the excess stress to which individuals from stigmatized social categories are exposed as a result of their social, often minority position" (p. 675). This concept refers to the enduring and persistent stress that crystallizes in the form of prejudice and rejection and is in turn mediated by particular social circumstances (e.g,. as job discrimination, bullying by peers) quite different from the circumstantial stress that most would experience.

If minority stress and identity issues are taken into consideration, it is understandable why adolescents who self-identify as gay show more suicidality, depression, and hopelessness than their counterparts (Safren & Heimberg, 1999). These authors compared 56 GLB youth with 48 heterosexual youth and found that the differences in suicidality, depression, and hopelessness (significantly higher in GLB youth) were consequential to the effect of stress, social support, and coping through acceptance. GLBN orientation (gay, lesbian, bisexual, or not sure) and same-gender sex were identified as risk factors for suicide ideation and attempts among one population-based study (Garafalo, Wolf, et al., 1999) and one large sample of adolescents (O'Donnell, O'Donell, Wardlaw, & Stueve, 2004; O'Donnell, Stueve, Wardlaw, & O'Donell, 2003). Also, Hispanic ethnicity was a risk factor among these samples, but the combined effect of being Hispanic and non-heterosexual was not explored. Some scholars suggest that persons belonging to diverse minority groups have to deal with the integration of diverse identities, and to manage minority stress of different kinds depending on the social context results in a greater challenge (Meyer, 2003). Also, we argue that the Hispanic's cultural values of spirituality, collectivism, and machismo may result in a more difficult scenario for adolescent development toward a GLB orientation.

In conclusion, the integration of GLB sexuality as part of a developing identity represents a set of tasks that increase in complexity given the multiple identities that may be involved (e.g., racial, ethnic, gender, spiritual, and sexual orientation). Indeed, the acceptance and support expected from family members, the religious community, and peers is challenged when an adolescent is moving toward a non-heterosexual development of sexuality. Being part of both a sexual and an ethnic minority group increases by far the stress experienced, especially when the adolescent's spiritual ideology is in opposition to the expression of a GLB orientation, which could result in increased vulnerability to high-risk behavior such as suicidality. Sexual orientation, as well as ethnicity and race, should be explored in any research related to suicide behavior in adolescents. Also, the impact of religious affiliation or spirituality in dealing with internalized homophobia and minority stress needs to be considered.

Suicide Behavior Prevalence and Risk Factors among Hispanic Youth

Comparative Studies with Representative Sample

Table 5.1 presents the comparative population-based studies of suicide behavior among Hispanic adolescents in terms of study source, nature of sample, predictive variables, outcomes, and results. We summarize these studies next.

Population-based samples of middle and high school adolescents in the U.S. reflect that being female (Blum et al., 2000; Garofalo, Wolf, Wissow, Woods, & Goodman, 1999; Grunbaum, Basen-Engquist, & Pandey, 1998; Guiao & Thompson, 2004; Hallfors et al., 2004) and suffering from depression were significantly and strongly related to suicide ideation and suicide attempts. The Youth Risk Behavior Survey (YRBS) reports suggest that being Hispanic constitutes a risk factor for depression, suicide ideation, and suicide attempts, with Hispanic females at the highest risk (Grunbaum et al., 2004; Grunbaum et al., 2002; Kann et al., 2000; Kann et al., 1998; Kann et al., 1996). Different results were found in the National Longitudinal Study of Adolescent Health studies (NLSAH). No significant differences were found for Hispanic ethnicity in suicide behavior (Blum et al., 2000; Guiao & Thompson, 2004; Hallfors et al., 2004). However, among females, Latinas reported significantly higher risk for depression than their Euro American peers (Guiao & Thompson, 2004).

Blum et al. (2000) examined the unique and combined contributions of race/ethnicity, income, and family structure to some risky behaviors, including suicidal thoughts or attempts. Those three demographic variables taken together explained less than .5% of the variance in suicide attempts in middle and high school students. The authors concluded that knowing race/ethnicity, income, and family structure provides little predictive power at the individual level and suggest further studies of the more proximal social contexts of young people, including families and communities, in order to better understand what predisposes some young people to increased suicide risk.

Comparative Studies with Large and Small Samples

Another set of studies are comparative studies with large and small samples of suicide behavior among Hispanic adolescents. Table 5.2 and Table 5.3 present these studies organized by study source, sample, predictive variables, outcomes, and results.

In school-based surveys with 6th to 8th graders, Mexican Americans reported a higher prevalence of suicide ideation than their Anglo peers (Olvera, 2001; Roberts, Chen, & Roberts, 1997; Roberts & Chen, 1995; Tortolero & Roberts, 2001). Risk for suicide ideation remained significant among Mexican Americans even after adjusting for other important psychological and sociodemographic variables in a large sample (N = 3,442) from New Mexico and Texas (Tortolero & Roberts, 2001). Mexican American females reported the highest prevalence of suicide ideation (Olvera, 2001; Roberts, Chen, & Roberts, 1997; Roberts & Chen, 1995; Tortolero & Roberts, 2001).

Four studies compared Hispanics with African Americans in suicide behavior, three with high school students (Lester & Anderson, 1992; O'Donnell, O'Donnell, Wardlaw, & Stueve, 2004; O'Donnell, Stueve, Wardlaw, & O'Donnell, 2003) and one with middle school students (Walter et al., 1995). Suicide ideation in high school students was more frequent in Hispanics. In Walter et al. study (1995) with middle school students evaluating lifetime involvement in suicide intentions/attempts no difference by race/ethnicity group were found.

In O'Donnell's sample, suicide attempt was more strongly related to Hispanic ethnicity than suicide ideation. In this study, race/ethnicity was measured by asking the participants, "Are you Black/African American, Hispanic/Latino, Black and Hispanic, Black and white, or other?" Responses were coded into either Hispanic or non-Hispanic. Students that identified as "Black and Hispanic" were labeled as non-Hispanic in the first study (O'Donnell, Stueve, Wardlaw, O'Donnell, 2003). In an effort to differentiate ethnic and racial groups, O'Donnell, O'Donnell, Wardlaw, and Stueve (2004) reanalyzed the O'Donnell et al. (2003) data. Hispanic remained as one category, but non-Hispanic was separated into Black/African American, Black and Hispanic, and Other. Those who reported suicide attempts were 17.9% of Hispanics, 16.9% of those who identified as "other," 10% of Black and Hispanic, and 8.1% of Black/African Americans.

Some studies focused on suicide behavior in high school students or older adolescents, comparing Whites, Blacks, and Hispanic Americans. In a large sample from Connecticut, researchers Rew, Thomas et al. (2001) found that the percentage of suicide attempts was significantly higher among Latina girls than in any other ethnic-gender group. Even in a sample of homeless adolescents (aged 12 to 22), significantly more Hispanics (57%) than Whites (31.7%) reported having considered suicide (Rew, Taylor-Seehafer, & Fitzgerald, 2001)

Suicidal ideation has also been studied as a common experience in adolescent development in response to normal developmental crisis (Marcenko, Fishman, & Friedman, 1999). The main hypothesis was that if attitudes toward suicide were controlled, ideation would not vary significantly by ethnicity, gender, or psychosocial variables usually associated

TABLE 5.1 Comparative Population-Based Studies of Suicide Behavior among Latino and Latina Adolescents: Study (Source), Sample, Predictive Variables, Outcomes, and Results

Study (Source)	Sample	Predictive Variables	Outcome	Results
NLSAH database In-home interview; Blum, Beuhringn, Shew, Beuringer, Sieving, and Resnick (2000)	N = 10,803 White, non-Hispanic = 7,684 (71.1%); Hispanic = 1,355 (12.6%); Black, non-Hispanic = 1,734 (16.3%)	race/ethnicity, income, family structure	Suicidal thoughts or attempts during the past year (ordinally scaled composite measures with no report of specific items used)	No significant racial/ethnic differences in suicidal thoughts or attempts were found for younger teens (7th to 9th graders). High school White (14%) and Hispanic youth (13.4%) were more at risk for suicidal thoughts or attempts than Blacks (10.7%). No differences in prevalence were found between Hispanic and White youths. Being female was associated with a greater risk for suicidal thoughts or attempts.
NLSAH databaseWave I, In-home interview; Hallford, Waller, Ford, Halper, Brodish, and Iritani (2004)	N = 18,924 Race: White = 12,429; Black = 4,247; Other = 2,248 (mostly Asian); Ethnicity: Hispanic = 3,230; Non-Hispanic = 15,635	adolescent sex and drug behavior	Lifetime suicide ideation (ever think about committing suicide? Yes/No) Lifetime suicide attempt (ever actually attempt? Never/one or more times)	No differences were found for "Hispanic ethnicity" and "race/ethnicity" when controlling for SES. Major depression was a strong predictor for suicide ideation and attempt, as was female gender. Increase in risky behavior (sex and drugs) increased the risk for depression, suicide ideation, and suicide attempts.
NLSAH database Wave I; Guiao and Thompson (2004)	N= 3,310 females Euro Americans 57.7%; African Americans 24.9%; Latinas 11.6%; Asian Americans 3.8%; Native Americans 2%	ethnicity	Suicide behavior during past year: composite measure of 3 items (suicide thoughts, number of suicide attempts, and need for treatment following an attempt)	No significant ethnic differences in suicidal behavior were found. Latinas reported significantly higher risk for depression than did their Euro American peers, and higher risk for alcohol use than did African- and Asian Americans.

YRBS 1992 Southeast Texas; Grunbaum, Basen-Engquist, and Pandey (1998)	N = 1,786 Mexican American 65%; non-Hispanic White 26%; unknown 9%; Analyses compared Mexican Americans vs. non-Hispanic White	ethnicity, gender, and substance use	Planned suicide and attempted suicide during past year	No ethnic difference within gender category in prevalence of planned or attempted suicide. 15% of males and over 20% of females planned suicide. Attempted suicide was two times greater among females. Use of alcohol, marijuana, and steroids all increased the risk of suicide plans and attempts among Mexican American females.
YRBS 1995 Massachusetts; Garofalo, Wolf, et al. (1999)	N = 3,365	sexual orientation, drug use, sexual behavior, and violence/ victimization	Planned suicide and attempted suicide during past year	Female gender, GLBN orientation (gay, lesbian, bisexual, or not sure), Hispanic ethnicity, higher levels of violence/ victimization, and more drug use were independent predictors of suicide attempt ($P<.001$). Gender-specific analyses for predicting suicide attempts revealed that among males the odds ratios for GLBN orientation increased, while among females GLBN orientation was not a significant predictor.

TABLE 5.2 Comparative Studies with Large Samples of Suicide Behavior among Latino and Latina Adolescents: Study (Source), Sample, Predictive Variables, Outcomes, and Results

Study (Source)	Sample	Predictive Variables	Outcome	Results
Roberts and Chen (1995)	N = 2,614 (6th to 8th graders) three largest middle schools form Las Cruces, New Mexico Anglo = 924; Mexican American = 1,354, 49% families below poverty level	ethnicity, gender, age, loneliness, depression, and other socio-demographic variables	Suicide ideation during past week: composite measure of 4 items (thoughts about death, family and friends would be better off if I were dead, thoughts about killing self, felt that would kill self if knew a way)	Adolescents of Mexican origin reported more thoughts of suicide than their Anglo counterparts (approximately 50% more). Females reported more ideation than males, with the most dramatic differences occurring among Mexican American females. Rates were much higher for those 14 years of age and older. Adjusted odds ratios for suicide ideation indicate that depression is the most significant correlate, followed by loneliness, then ethnic status (1.6), living in other than a two-parent household and English use.
Sorenson and Shen (1996)	32,928 California death certificates from 1970 to 1992 of 15- to 34-year-olds (Hispanics, mostly Mexican Americans)	ethnicity, nativity (US born vs. born elsewhere)	Suicide	Foreign-born Hispanics are at lower risk of suicide than their U.S.-born counterparts, especially in Mexican Americans. Even 15- to 34-year-olds who were born and remained in Mexico are at lower risk of suicide than those who moved to the U.S.
Tortolero and Roberts (2001)	N=3,442 Las Cruces, New Mexico n = 2,140 from 3 middle schools, Anglo 41%; Mexican American 59% Houston, Texas n = 1,302 from 5 middle schools, Anglo 53%; Mexican American 47%	ethnicity, gender	Suicide ideation during past week: composite measure of 4 items; New Mexico: same measure of Roberts & Chen (1995); Texas: (felt life was hopeless, thought about death or dying, wished were dead, suicide or killing self)	In both samples, Mexican American females had significantly higher prevalence of suicidal thinking, approximately twice the odds compared to European American females. Mexican American males had higher prevalence of suicide ideation; 60% more likely than European American males. The suicide ideation risk for Mexican Americans remained significant after adjusting for gender, age, family structure, depression, low social support, and low self-esteem.

Rew, Thomas, Horner, Resnick, and Beuhring (2001)	N = 8,806 (7th, 9th, and 11th graders) Connecticut African American = 932; Hispanic Latino = 717; Caucasian = 7,157	risk factors and protective resources by ethnic-gender group	Suicide attempts during past year, yes/no	Suicide attempts were significantly higher among Latina girls (19.3%), as suicide attempts by family and friends, than any other ethnic-gender group. Significant relationships were found between recent suicide attempts and: (a) family history of suicide attempt, (b) friend's history of suicide attempt, (c) history of sexual abuse, (d) history of physical abuse, and (e) environmental stress. The significant set of explanatory variables for recent suicide attempts for the three ethnic groups combined were stress, internalizing and externalizing behaviors, physical and sexual abuse, family and friend attempted suicide, social connectedness, and religious influence.
Reach for Health Study O'Donnell, Stueve, Wardlaw, and O'Donnell (2003)	N = 879 (11th graders) Brooklyn, New York; Hispanic 22.5% (145); Non-Hispanic 77.5% (734) (mostly African Americans)	socio-demographic characteristics, perceived adult support, family and formal network availability, and network activation	Suicide ideation during past year: composite measure of 4 items (seriously consider suicide, tell anyone, killing self will be a solution, make a plan; yes/no) Suicide attempts during past year (times actually attempt suicide)	Hispanic youth report significantly more attempts (17.9%) than non-Hispanics (9.1%). Females were 1.8 times more likely to report a suicide attempt; significant predictors of suicide ideation were low perceived support, being Hispanic, and same-gender sex. Among males, the pattern remained the same but family availability was added as a significant predictor in the unexpected direction: those with suicide ideation were more likely to say they will go to their family for support.
Reach for Health Study O'Donnell, O'Donnell, Wardlaw, and Stueve (2004)	N = 879 (11th graders) Brooklyn, New York;Hispanic =145; African American = 603; Black and Hispanic = 60; Other = 71	Socio-demographic characteristics, potential risk and resiliency factors	Suicide ideation during past year: composite measure of 4 items (seriously consider suicide, tell anyone, killing self will be a solution, make a plan; yes/no) Suicide attempts during past year (times actually attempt suicide)	Those who reported suicide attempts were 17.9% Hispanic, 16.9% were in category "Other," 10% were Black and Hispanic, and 8.1% were Black/African Americans. Risk factors identified with suicide ideation were having basic needs unmet, same-gender sex (fourfold risk), and depression. Resiliency factors were living in the neighborhood for more than 5 years and family closeness. Being female, Hispanic, having basic needs unmet, same-gender sex, and depression are risk factors for suicide attempts, and family closeness is a protective factor.

TABLE 5.3 Comparative Studies with Small Samples of Suicide Behavior among Latino and Latina Adolescents: Study (Source), Sample, Predictive Variables, Outcomes, and Results

Study (Source)	Sample	Predictive Variables	Outcome	Results
Lester and Anderson (1992)	N = 63 high school students in New Jersey; M =16.6 (SD1.2) African American = 42; Hispanic American = 21	ethnicity	Beck Depression Inventory, Hopelessness Scale, and the measure for suicide ideation was not described	Hispanics obtained significantly higher scores on the Beck (M = 12.7, SD 12.6 vs. x = 7.9, SD 6.5) and were more likely to have serious suicidal ideation (19% vs. 2%).
Marcenko, Fishman, and Friedman (1999)	N=120 (16 years old; females 60, males 60) selected randomly from 3 high schools in low-income neighborhoods African American = 40; Hispanic = 40; white students = 40	attitudes toward suicide	Suicide ideators (thoughts about their own suicide) at least once during one's lifetime.	No significant differences were found by ethnicity. Females were more tolerant than males to suicide. Females, substance users, those with greater tolerance toward suicide, higher family coping, lower self-esteem, were more likely to report ideation. Differences were found in reporting ideation by gender for Blacks and Hispanics, and not for Whites. Seventy percent were classified as ideators, the average age of ideation was 13.3 (3 years ago), and two thirds (63%) just though about it, 28% thought about the means, 5% obtained the means, and 5% made attempts.

Olvera (2001)	N = 158 (6th to 8th graders), Texas Hispanic 56% (92% Mexican origin); Non-Hispanic White 21%; mixed-ancestry 14%; African American 1%	ethnicity, depression, coping strategies, family problems, acculturation	Suicide ideation (thoughts more than usual about death or dying, a wish of being dead, thoughts of suicide or of killing self) almost every day or often, to any of these items.	Suicide ideation was significantly higher for Hispanic adolescents (34.8%) and mixed-ancestry (45.5%) when compared to Anglo peers (14.7%). Hispanic students used less social coping than Anglo peers. Also, Hispanics used less humor and less active coping than mixed-ancestry peers. Acculturation was related to an increased risk for suicidal ideation. A hierarchical regression model for suicide ideation identified Hispanic ancestry, elevated depression scores, family problems, and lack of social coping as significant factors.
Rew , Taylor-Seehafer, and Fitzgerald (2001)	N = 96 homeless youth (ages 12–22 years; M = 17.9) from a street outreach program in a southern state; Whites 65.6%; Hispanics 21.9%; Blacks 3.1%; American Indians 5.2%; Asians 2.1%; and other = 1	ethnicity, gender	Suicide behavior during past 12 months: seriously considered attempting suicide, have made a plan, times actually attempted suicide, attempted suicide had to be treated by a doctor or nurse: yes/no, number of attempts	Significantly more Hispanics (57%) than Whites (31.7%) had considered suicide. Not quite significant (p = .054), there were ethnic differences between those who planned suicide (33.3% Hispanics vs. 12.5% Whites). Hispanics report significantly greater percentage of sexual abuse than Whites (71% compare to 54%). Females, more often than males, indicated that their attempts required medical treatment.

with ideation. No significant differences were found for ethnicity. In general, females were more tolerant and supporting than males in issues related to suicide. Marcenko, Fishman, and Friedman (1999) suggest cultural factors in attitudes toward admitting suicide ideation. Ideators (70%) were those who admit they had thought about their own suicide at least once in their lives. This is an extremely broad definition of suicide ideation, compared with phrases used in other studies, such as "I have thought about killing myself" or "I have felt I would kill myself," in the time frame of "past week."

In a study of suicide rates by ethnicity, 32,928 California death certificates of 15- to 34-year-olds (from 1970 to 1992) were reviewed to compare foreign-born versus U.S.-born circumstances (Sorenson & Shen, 1996). Foreign-born Hispanics (mostly Mexican Americans) were found to be at a lower risk of suicide than their U.S.-born counterparts. Even those 15- to 34-year-olds who were born and remained in Mexico were at lower risk of suicide than those who moved to the U.S., suggesting that acculturation plays an important role in suicide behavior.

Comparative Studies Focus on within-Group Diversity

We identified three studies that addressed within-group diversity among Hispanic adolescents, but also included White non-Hispanics and African Americans (Roberts, Chen, & Roberts, 1997; Vega, Gil, Warheit, Apospori, & Zimmerman, 1993; Vega, Gil, Zimmerman, & Warheit, 1993). We did not find a single within-group study conducted with Hispanic adolescents only (see Table 5.4).

Roberts, Chen, and Roberts (1997) analyzed an ethnically diverse sample of middle school students of both genders (grades 6–8; n = 4,186) for ethnic differences in suicide behavior from a school district in the Houston metropolitan area. More than 20 distinct ethnic groups were identified. The nine largest groups were used for the analyses. Central and Mexican Americans were two Hispanic groups analyzed separately. Comparing ethnic groups, Mexican Americans had a higher prevalence of recent suicide ideation, plans, and attempts. One unexpected finding was that Hispanics of Central American origin did not report higher rates of suicidal behavior.

A large sample of 6th- to 7th-grade boys was recruited for a longitudinal year-long study to examine suicide ideation and attempts by ethnicity among other variables (Vega, Gil, Warheit, Apospori, & Zimmerman, 1993; Vega, Gil, Zimmerman, & Warheit, 1993). Three groups of Hispanics were identified among the eight ethnic groups included in the

TABLE 5.4 Comparative Studies Focus on Within-Group Diversity; Suicide Behavior among Latino And Latina Adolescents: Study (Source), Sample, Predictive Variables, Outcomes, and Results

Authors	Sample	Predictive Variables	Outcome	Results
Vega, Gil, Zimmerman, and Warheit (1993)	Time IN = 6,760 boys (6th and 7th graders) from 48 middle schools in Miami, Florida Cuban Americans 25.8%; Nicaraguans 8.5%; Other Hispanics 29.2%; African Americans 14%; White non-Hispanics 13.3%; Haitians 2.9%; Caribbean Blacks 2.8%; Others 3.5%	ethnicity	Suicide ideation during last six months: thought about killing self, affirmative response were sometimes true and often true Suicide attempts: ever tried to kill self, yes/no; and number of attempts	African American boys had the highest level of suicide ideation (19.2%). Nicaraguans and other Hispanics had the highest levels of lifetime suicide attempts (7.8%). The highest percentage of attempts among boys with eight or more risk factors was among other Hispanics (56.9%), and the lowest percentage was among non-Hispanic White boys (21.7%). Predicting attempts for African Americans and Hispanics indicated that depressive symptoms, low self-esteem, and teacher and parent derogation were relatively higher. In predicting attempt for non-Hispanic Whites, deviancy/delinquency was relatively higher. High acculturation was associated with higher levels of suicide attempts in the three Hispanic subsamples ($P < .05$). The risk factor analyses indicated a differential distribution of risk factors by ethnicity. Cumulative risk factors were related to increased suicidal ideation and attempts.

(continued)

TABLE 5.4 (CONTINUED) Comparative Studies Focus on Within-Group Diversity; Suicide Behavior among Latino And Latina Adolescents: Study (Source), Sample, Predictive Variables, Outcomes, and Results

Authors	Sample	Predictive Variables	Outcome	Results
Vega, Gil, Warheit, Apospori, and Zimmerman (1993); longitudinal study of one year between Time I and Time 2	Time 1 was described in Vega, Gil et. al (1993)Time 2N = 6,010 Hispanics = 4,015 (66.8%); African Americans = 780 (13%); White non-Hispanics = 762 (12.7%); few were Haitians, Caribbean Blacks, and Others.	ethnicity, drug use, and acculturation stress	Suicide ideation during last six months: thought about killing self, affirmative responses were sometimes true and often true. Suicide attempts: ever tried to kill self, yes/no; and number of attempts	Lifetime suicide ideation was highest among African Americans (20.5%), Haitians (19.9%) and White Non-Hispanics (19.3%). Suicide attempts were highest among Haitians (11.4%), other Hispanics (9%), and Cuban Americans (8.5%). Analysis with Other Hispanics and Cuban Americans showed that the use of cocaine/crack, as well as psychoactive drugs, by respondents experiencing these acculturation stresses (language conflicts, acculturation conflicts, perceived discrimination, perceived poor life chances) creates a greater likelihood of attempts than use of drugs alone for Cubans and Other Hispanics. In time 1 predicting Time 2 report suicide attempts a significant interaction between language conflicts and cigarette use, and between acculturation conflicts and alcohol use in predicting suicide attempts was found among other Hispanics (not found among Cuban Americans).

Walter, Vaughan, Armstrong, Krakoff, Maldonado, Tiezzi, and McCarthy (1995)	N = 3,738 (6th to 8th graders) from four schools in one of New York City's most economically disadvantaged and medically under-served areas; Dominican 73.7%; other Hispanic 6.9%; African American 10.4%; born outside of the US 47%	demographic variables, psychosocial (adverse social circumstances, acculturation, depressive disorder, and social influence in involvement in sexual intercourse), and behavioral variables (academic problems and substance use)	Lifetime involvement in suicide intentions/ attempts: ever having intent to commit suicide or ever having attempted suicide	The primary risk factor for suicide intentions/attempts was symptoms of depression (7 times more likely), followed by adverse social circumstances (5 time more likely) and female gender (3 times more likely). Assaultive behavior, sexual intercourse, and academic problems increase risk two fold.
Roberts, Chen, and Roberts (1997)	N = 4,186 (6th to 8th graders) Houston metropolitan area; Nine largest groups were used for analyses: African-, Anglo-, Central-, Chinese-, Indian-, Mexican- Pakistani-, Vietnamese-, (all Americans), and Mixed Ancestry.	ethnicity, gender	Suicidal ideation during past 2 weeks: (Felt life was hopeless, thoughts about death or dying, wished were dead, suicide or killing self). 4 point likert answers; suicide plan (ever made a plan, ever tried to kill self, made a plan, tried to kill self) yes/no	Mexican Americans had higher prevalence of recent suicide ideation, plans, and attempts. Youth of mixed ancestry had a higher rate of suicide plans and Pakistani youths had a higher rate of suicide attempts. Hispanics of Central American origin did not report higher rates of suicidal behavior. Suicidal ideation and suicide plan were higher among female, older youths, and those whose socioeconomic circumstances were worse to much worse than their peers. The same pattern held for suicide attempts, with the exception that males report higher levels of attempts.

study: Cuban Americans, Nicaraguans, and Other Hispanics. Findings at Time 1 showed that lifetime suicide attempts were higher among Nicaraguans and Other Hispanics. At Time 2, suicide attempts were higher among Haitians, Other Hispanics, and Cuban Americans, in that order. The risk factor analysis indicated a differential distribution of risk factors by ethnic-racial subsamples. High acculturation was associated with higher levels of suicide attempts in the three Hispanic subsamples (Vega, Gil et al., 1993). But further analysis at Time 2 indicated a different pattern between acculturation stress and attempts between Other Hispanics and Cubans. Significant interactions were found for Other Hispanics, but not for Cubans.

The three studies of adolescents used large samples of middle school students. Each study indicated some differences between Latino subgroups in suicide behavior and related patterns. It is evident that more within-group studies are needed, and particularly with Hispanic older adolescents (high school students).

Conclusions about Comparative Studies

The diversity of how suicide behavior, especially suicide ideation, is conceptualized and operationalized makes it difficult if not impossible to arrive at specific conclusions in comparative studies. Some of the studies reviewed used broad definitions, others narrow ones, and one simply didn't report how the outcome variable had been measured. For example, suicide ideation was defined in some studies as a composite measure related to thoughts of dying and killing oneself within the last week, versus "Have you ever thought about committing suicide?" Some studies used composite measures of suicide behavior (with items related to ideation, attempts, and severity of attempts) while others focused only on one kind of behavior (suicide ideation, attempts, or suicide rates). Also, the temporal frame is another important concern, because some studies measured suicide behavior within the last year, others within the last month, and others within one's lifetime. It is essential to specify and describe which kind of suicide behavior is the focus of research in its temporal frame and how it is being measured. Despite some inconsistent findings, the evidence suggests differential rates by ethnicity for suicide ideation, attempts, lethal attempts, and suicide.

In two cases, investigators used different category systems for race and ethnicity with the same database, grouping and analyzing the same sample in various ways (Blum et al., 2000; Hallfors et al., 2004; O'Donnell, O'Donnell, Wardlaw, & Stueve, 2004; O'Donnell, Stueve, Wardlaw, & O'Donnell, 2003). A clear theoretical approach was missing from such groupings. Rather than a conceptual one, the approach appears to be guided more by a criterion of convenience, namely grouping certain ethnic and racial groups for comparative purposes. Thus, the relevance of the role of ethnicity or race in suicide behavior studies was not clear. The purpose or interest in the use of particular racial or ethnic categories was not well developed. Most studies lack of a clear theoretical framework to discuss and analyze their findings.

Unfortunately, most comparative studies, especially those with representative samples, do not account for within-group differences among Hispanics, nor do they report on psychological or social variables relevant to ethnic minority issues, such as acculturation, acculturating stress, perceived discrimination, ethnic identity, or possible barriers to physical- and mental-health services. In race comparison studies, the common practice is to compare one or more ethnic minority groups with Whites. Thus, Whites become the control group and too often the implied norm. The comparative approach has been criticized for reinforcing racial stereotypes, underestimating variations within ethnic groups, and supporting a viewpoint that mainstream behavior patterns are the standard, which result in the interpretation of non-White behavior as deviant or problematic (Burlew, 2003; Okazaki & Sue, 1998).

Overall, comparative studies that categorized participants as either "Latinos and Latinas" or "Hispanics" to compare with Whites, Blacks or Others did not identify differences between Hispanic subgroups. Such studies base their analysis on the assumption that similarities among Hispanic subgroups are greater than their differences. Within-group studies accounted for diversity not only because Hispanics are grouped by national origin, but also because the research question and analysis were formulated based on a culturally sensitive framework that allowed the evaluation of possible differences in suicide behavior and patterns.

Studies Focused on Hispanics

Few empirical studies have addressed suicide behavior exclusively among Hispanic adolescents or in a specific group of Latinos (Guiao & Esparza, 1995; Hovey, 1998, 1999a, 1999b; Hovey & King, 1996, 1997; Locke & Newcomb, 2005; Queralt, 1993; Razin et al., 1991; Swanson, Linskey, Quintero-Salinas, Pumariega, & Holzer, 1992). A qualitative study with structured interviews was conducted to understand suicide attempts in Hispanic adolescent girls (mostly Puerto Rican) in New York City (Razin et al., 1991). Thirty-three girls (12–17 years old) hospitalized for suicidal behavior, and 15 demographically identical non-suicidal subjects were interviewed, along with their mothers (more than 90% of both groups had Puerto Rican ancestry). Attempts were described generally as impulsive and nonlethal, but often with a stated wish to die. Most were overdoses precipitated by conflicts with a girl's mother or boyfriend. Attempters' families were more often characterized by medical, criminal, and psychiatric problems and were more likely to be receiving public assistance. Attempters had poorer school performance and had recently suffered more losses (particularly the loss or absence of the biological fathers). They were more likely to have boyfriends, and had begun sexual activity. Their mothers had fewer friends. Daughters were much more parentified (mothering their mothers) and relationships between them seemed more intense, desperate, and even violent. Attempters were more negatively described by themselves and by their mothers. Also, the modeling of suicide behavior was higher in the attempter's families. Most families were mobilized by the suicide attempt. These findings supports Zayas et al.'s thesis (2000, 2005) about Latinas and suicide attempts.

Mexican American adolescents (N = 50) living in southwestern cities (x = 16.5 13–19 years of age) were recruited to evaluate suicidality (Guiao & Esparza, 1995). Within the sample, 46% were born in the U.S. and the other 54% in Mexico. Life stress, coping mechanisms, depression, and family function were proposed as predictors. Suicidality was assessed using the Brief Suicidality Scale, a two-item scale that assesses current suicide ideation and past suicide attempts. A significant and positive relationship was found between depression and suicidality. A significant and negative relationship was found between suicidality and coping efficacy, and between suicidality and family cohesion. No relationship was established between suicidality and the following variables: life stress, coping frequency, and family adaptability.

Potential psychosocial risk factors associated with completed suicide were explored based on the cases of 14 Hispanic adolescents (11 males and 3 females) (Queralt, 1993). The adolescents committed suicide in Miami, Florida from January, 1988 to June, 1989. Five were born in the continental U.S., and the rest were born in Cuba, Puerto Rico, Nicaragua, the Dominican Republic, Spain, and Honduras. Victims of Puerto Rican origin were overrepresented (n = 5 [38%]; at that time Puerto Ricans constituted only 6% of Miami's Latino population). In contrast, suicide victims of Cuban origin were underrepresented (n = 2 [15%]; they represented 67% of the Latinos in Miami). Most were from lower- to lower-middle-class backgrounds. Data were obtained from victims and from an equal number of randomly selected Latino non-suicidal matched-pair controls. At the time of their deaths, these Latino youngsters were experiencing significantly more school, personality, behavioral, and family stressors than the matched-pair controls. Nearly half had given prior warnings through suicide ideation or attempt.

In an effort to determine the prevalence and demographic distribution of depressive symptoms, illicit drug use, and suicidality between Mexicans living in their country of origin and Mexican Americans in the U.S., secondary students (aged 11 to 19 years) from the U.S./Mexico border were recruited to participate in a cross-sectional study (Swanson, Linskey, Quintero-Salinas, Pumariega, & Holzer, 1992). There were 2,382 students from Mexican border towns and 1,175 from Texas border towns. Suicidality was defined as "I thought about killing myself for a period during at least 1 day of the preceding week." Findings indicated that Mexican Americans were more likely to report elevated scores for depression (48.08% vs. 39.41%), illicit drugs (21% vs. 4.9%), and suicide ideation (23.4% vs. 11.57%) than Mexicans. Drug use and depressive symptoms alone increased risk for suicidal ideation. A larger increase was associated with depressive symptoms, and the combination of both conditions corresponded to a higher risk than either one alone. Country (U.S.) and female gender were significantly associated with suicide ideation. Findings suggest that migration to the U.S. has a negative impact on Mexican adolescents.

A cross-sectional study was conducted to determine the relationships among suicidal ideation, depressive symptoms, and acculturative stress in a sample of 70 immigrant and second-generation Hispanic American adolescents (87% Mexican Americans) from a southern California public high school (Hovey and King, 1996). Seventy-five percent indicated low socioeconomic status. One fourth of the adolescents reported critical levels of depression and suicide ideation, which correlated positively with acculturative stress. Acculturative stress, depression, and suicide ideation were highly intercorrelated, and low levels of perceived family functioning were significantly correlated with high levels of depression. Depression, acculturative stress, and expectations for the future were all significant independent predictors of suicidal ideation, which when combined with family functioning, accounted for 36% of the variance in suicidal ideation.

Hovey (1998) presented an analysis of 54 immigrant Mexican American adolescents from a re-analysis of data from Hovey and King (1996). Subjects included 26% early immigrants (immigrating before the age of 12) and 74% late immigrants (immigrating after the age of 12). Acculturating stress scores were dichotomized into high and low score categories, using the mean as the cut-off point. Twenty-eight (52%) of the subjects fell into the low-stress category and twenty-six (48%) into the high-stress category. The results show significant main effects for acculturative stress on suicide ideation and depression. These studies (Hovey & King, 1996; Hovey, 1998) support the notion that Hispanic adolescents experiencing high levels of acculturating stress may be at an increased risk for depression and suicide ideation.

Risk and protective factors of suicidality were examined from an ecodevelopmental perspective in a community sample of 349 Latino adolescent males from the Los Angles area (Locke and Newcomb, 2005). This inner-city sample of young men (ranging from 13 to 30 years old) was primarily of Mexican American descent, and 79% were born in the U.S. The strongest predictor for suicidality was the external microsystem variable of emotional abuse. Other variables that predicted suicidality from the external microsystem domain were sexual abuse and having a mother with alcohol-related problems. The second strongest predictor was the internal microsystem domain of hard drug use. Three significant protective factors were found. These were problem-solving confidence from the internal microsystem domain, good relationships with parents from the external microsystem, and being law abiding, a mesosystemic variable from the domain of social conformity.

In sum, most studies focused on "Latinos and Latinas" or "Hispanics" described the sample in terms of country of origin, generational status in U.S., and contextual factors such as socioeconomic status. Such sample description allowed a more critical evaluation of research findings and the formulation of possible conclusions to specific groups rather than generalizing to all Hispanics. Most studies were with Mexican American adolescents. Also, variables relevant to ethnic minority issues were included such as acculturation and acculturative stress. Variables related to *familismo* were incorporated and found to be pertinent in the study of suicide behavior in Hispanic adolescents. Social and psychological variables were identified to be significantly related to suicide behavior in Latino groups but the lack of a theory to inform the findings was evident. One study (Locke and Newcomb, 2005) clearly formulated a theoretical framework to inform the results. Finally, only one qualitative study (Razin et al., 1991) was found.

Evidence-Based Treatment for Suicidal Hispanic Adolescents

Data on evidence-based treatments for suicidal Hispanic youth is quite limited. A report by the U.S. Surgeon General about Mental Health Care for Hispanic Americans (2001) recognized that Hispanic youths are at a greater risk for poor mental health outcomes, abandoning school, experiencing depression and anxiety, and considering suicide more than White youths. The report stated that prevention and treatment are needed to address this population's mental health problems and specified that these interventions could have major implications for the ongoing health of the nation's youths.

The American Psychological Association's Division 12 Task Force on Promotion and Dissemination of Psychological Procedures published its report on empirically validated treatments in 1995, which include a list of empirically support treatments (EST) (Chambless et al., 1996). This report, while highlighting the need for empirically supported psychological treatments with ethnic minorities, also generated controversies. One issue was the absence of information on the external validity of efficacious treatments and their generalizability to ethnic minorities (Bernal & Saez-Santiago, 2006; Bernal & Sharron-del-Rio, 2001; Miranda et al., 2005). Bernal & Sharrón-Del Río (2001) in a critical review of EST and ethnic minorities point out that "the external validity of EST is simply not known, and there is no scientific basis (contemporary or otherwise) for the application to other groups except on a faith, perhaps even blind, distorted view of empiricism (p. 339)." The Division 12 Task Force in an update on empirical supported therapies state that there is no psychotherapy treatment research demonstrated to be efficacious to minority populations (Chambless et al., 1998). The Surgeon General recognized efficacy studies include such a few minority participants that most studies do not have the power necessary to examine its impact on such minority groups (U.S. Department of Health and Human Services, 2001).

In 2006, the American Psychological Association (APA) Presidential Task Force on Evidence-Based Practice agreed on the following definition: Evidence-based practice in psychology (EBPP) is the integration of the best available research with clinical expertise in the context of patient characteristics, culture, and preferences. Psychological practice refers to all direct services, including treatment, but we will focus in this section exclusively on treatment and psychotherapies for suicidal Hispanic youths. APA Task Force (2006) delineated the difference between EST and EBPP. EST is defined as specific psychological treatments that have been shown to be efficacious in controlled clinical trials for a certain disorder or problem under specific circumstances, and EBPP starts with the patient and asks what research evidence will assist the psychologist in achieving the best outcome.

Weisz and Hawley (2002) reviewed studies of psychosocial treatments for adolescents that met methodological standards for acceptable research (referring to random assignment and at least one treatment and one control group) from 1963 to 2000. They found a disproportionate number of studies dedicated to adolescents, compared with adult and child populations in relation to the prevalence of psychopathology on this phase of life according to epidemiological data. They also indicated that few studies (12 out of 114 [10.5%]) addressed treatment for depression relative to the prevalence at this age level. None of these studies made any effort to address suicidality and four directly indicated that subjects who were suicidal were excluded. Only two studies that targeted suicidality were found to meet methodological criteria (Cotgrove, Zirinsky, Black, & Weston, 1995; Harrington et al., 1998) but neither involved treatment for depression, and neither study found a significant benefit over treatment as usual.

Two studies of psychosocial treatment using a randomized controlled design that measured outcomes of suicide ideation and attempts have been recently published (Huey et al., 2004; King et al., 2006). Huey et al. (2004) reports the efficacy of a multisystemic therapy (an intense family-based therapy) over psychiatric hospitalization in reducing self-harm behavior in youths (mostly African Americans [65%]). Both conditions were associated with decrease of symptoms over time, but no differences were found between treatment in ameliorating depressive affect, hopelessness, and suicidal ideation. Another study evaluated the effectiveness of a youth-nominated support team for suicidal adolescents (84.4% White) after discharge from psychiatric hospitalization. The authors reported a small to medium effect in the interaction of time x intervention interaction group for girls in comparison with treatment as usual (King et al. 2006).

Macgowan (2004) reviewed the psychosocial treatment of adolescent suicidality (10 to 17 years old) and found 10 studies (nonpharmacological treatments) up to December of 2002. Only studies that included outcomes directly related to suicidality (suicide ideation or suicide attempts) were included in the review, and the general parameters of the Division 12 Task Force were used to evaluate well-established treatments and probably efficacious treatments for suicidal adolescents. Results indicated that no studies of well established treatments were found and only two were probably efficacious with limitations, in terms of the poor outcomes obtained (Harrington et al., 1998; Wood, Rothwell, Moore, & Harrington, 2001). In general, the major concerns were a lack of rigorous design: half of the studies employed randomized designs and most samples did not have enough power to detect differences between groups (Macgowan, 2004). Yet, Macgowan (2004) noted that when using more flexible criteria, in pre- to post-treatment changes, to assess whether each treatment was successful in reducing suicidality, most studies obtained a significant reduction.

Of the 10 studies, two of these reported the inclusion of mostly Hispanics in their sample, but lacked a randomized design (Rathus & Miller, 2002; Rotheram-Borus, Piacentini, Cantwell, Belin, & Song, 2000; Rotheram-Borus et al., 1996). Even though neither treatment was considered probably efficacious, both used a quasi-experimental design and reported pre-post treatment changes that indicated reduction in outcome markers of suicide ideation, depression, and youth adherence to treatment, among other indirect markers of suicidality. Rathus and Miller (2002) used 12 weeks of twice weekly individual dialectical behavioral therapy and a multi-family skills training group. Sixty-eight percent out of 111 participants were Hispanic. Rotheram-Borus et al. (1996, 2000) delivered a specialized emergency room care and six sessions of family-based cognitive behavioral outpatient program called Successful Negotiation/Acting Positively (SNAP). Eighty-eight percent out of 140 female adolescent attempters and their mothers were of Hispanic origin. Both included elements of cognitive and behavioral therapy with the adolescent and integrated a family component.

Recently, a comprehensive review of the science on psychosocial intervention for ethnic minorities and mental health outcome of mental health care for children and youth was published (Miranda et al., 2005). The review documents the work conducted to treat diverse disorders such as depression, anxiety, attention deficit hyperactivity, and disruptive behavior in the Hispanic population. But no study that addressed suicidality was mentioned. Even using a more flexible definition of evidenced-based treatment to consider the available research, the evidence on the effectiveness of psychotherapy for suicidal Hispanic adolescents is scarce.

To achieve the best outcome with suicidal Hispanic adolescent and their families, according to EBPP, one should consider the clinical expertise in the context of patient characteristics, culture, and preferences. In this sense, the extensive literature dedicated to Hispanic adolescents and their families needs to be evaluated as a source of pertinent knowledge; some good examples are the work done by the Center for Family Studies in Miami (Muir, Schwartz, & Szapocznik, 2004), in the San Francisco General Hospital (Muñoz & Mendelson, 2005), and the work done by Rosselló and Bernal (1999) with depressed Puerto Rican adolescents. An extensive literature exists on the importance of developing culturally sensitive therapy for the delivery of mental health services to the Hispanic population (Bernal & Sáez-Santiago, 2006; Nagayama Hall, 2001), the need of cultural competency (Cauce et al., 2002; Douglas, Maldonado-Molina, Pantin, & Szapocznik, 2005; Sue, 2003), and how to adapt or develop treatment for minority groups (Bernal, Bonilla, & Bellido, 1995; Bernal & Sharron del-Rio, 2001; Domenech-Rodríguez & Wieling, 2004). Yet there is still a wide gap among scientific knowledge, treatment development, and strong evidence of psychological treatments that have been found efficacious for suicidal Hispanic adolescents.

In the general adolescent population, much work needs to be done in the area of ESTs and EBPPs for suicidality in terms of psychosocial treatments. Given the size and growth of the Hispanic population, the field is only now turning to an examination of ESTs and EBPPs among suicidal Hispanic adolescents. To date, no or very limited empirical support on the psychological treatment for Hispanic suicidal adolescents exists. In fact, there are no ESTs for suicidal adolescents in general (Macgowan, 2004; Weisz & Hawley, 2002). Certainly, there is an urgent need for well controlled trials of suicide ideation with Hispanic adolescent samples. Similarly, there is a pressing need for well designed outcome studies above and beyond the randomized controlled trials. Descriptive and qualitative studies of the treatment process, case studies that illustrate changes in suicidal Hispanic adolescents and that illustrate the management of issues such as acculturation, minority stress, spirituality, and family values, etc., in clinical practice need to be a priority in the field. Professionals with clinical and cultural expertise/competency who are working with suicidal Hispanic adolescents and have found good outcomes in their treatments need to document their results and communicate their findings. Also, more funding and resources are needed in order to move mental health services from poor- (U.S. Department of Health and Human Services, 2001) to high-quality services for populations at risk for suicide such as adolescents.

Conclusions

Research on suicide behavior and on the mental health outcome studies among Hispanic adolescents is scant. The majority of studies on suicide behavior among adolescents that includes Hispanics use a comparative research strategy, contrasting Whites, Hispanics, Blacks, and Other groups. There are few population-specific studies. Research focusing on within-group differences among Hispanics is rare. This review highlights the importance of more research focusing on within-group comparisons among Hispanics and the need for studies focusing only on specific Hispanic groups.

Unfortunately, most comparison research on adolescent suicide behavior uses the general term of "Hispanic" for all subgroups without any further differentiation of subgroups. Indeed, in any research with Hispanic populations a basic description of the sample should include gender, age, educational level, socioeconomic status, ancestry/country of origin, generational status, and acculturation level (Marín & Marín, 1991). Generalization based on studies that do not differentiate between Latino subgroups or with a poor sample description are bound to be limited (Hovey & King, 1997; Marín & Marín, 1991).

Varied rates of suicide behavior, as well as different correlates among factors related to suicide behavior between subgroups of Hispanic adolescents, suggest that assessment of risk and development of prevention and treatment efforts must be group-specific rather than generic for all Hispanics (Canino & Roberts, 2001; Ungemack and Guarnaccia, 1998). In fact, such generalizations could have negative implications on the understanding, identification, and prevention of suicide behavior in specific community settings. For example, based on the available evidence, a prevention strategy to impact suicide attempts in Puerto Rican girls may be directed to mother–daughter relationships. However, this might be a misguided approach with, for example, Cuban Americans girls, who demonstrate a lower suicide risk.

The evidence reviewed underscores that Hispanic adolescents (e.g., Mexican Americans) are at a greater risk for suicide behavior than the comparison groups, but few studies have attempted to understand why this is the case. Hispanic adolescent suicide behavior studies are primarily descriptive. For the most part, no explanatory variables were found that might account for these differences among groups or that help explain the meaning of the suicide behavior. Most studies were not guided by a theoretical framework. Yet there is a need to go beyond description and explore the causes that gives rise to such elevated rates, as well as the processes that should be informed by theory.

For the field to advance, research informed and guided by theory is needed. Models of suicide behavior that take into consideration culture and context in their full complexity and that propose particular processes with specific population groups are needed. In this effort, methodological strategies need to capture a more comprehensive view of the contextual environment and the meaning of behavior integrating both qualitative and quantitative strategies (Bernal & Sharron-del-Rio, 2001; Zayas, Lester, Cabassa, & Fortuna, 2005). Zayas el al. (2005) proposed using in-depth interviews from multiple informants (the adolescent and family) to gather personal narratives, family sociocultural environment, and family history of suicide behavior.

The individual and psychological variables are important but not enough to explain suicide behavior in Hispanic adolescents. A broader theoretical framework that includes social, cultural, and contextual factors is imperative. Gender was another relevant factor in suicide behavior among Hispanic adolescents. Almost all studies that included analysis by gender demonstrated significant differences. Developmental consideration is critical in understanding the stage of change and identity formation of adolescents. Also, sexual identity formation is a sensitive and critical aspect to explore, especially on a non-heterosexual development of sexuality, because a "double or triple" minority status should be handled. Thus, suicide behavior studies among Hispanic adolescents should move toward the incorporation of an ecological, developmental, and gender-specific perspective to move the field forward.

□ References

APA Presidential Task Force on Evidence-Based Practice. (2006). Evidence-Based practice in psychology. *American Psychologist*, 61, 271–285.

Basic Behavioral Science Task Force of the National Advisory Mental Health Council. (1998). Basic behavioral science research for mental health: Sociocultural and environmental process. In Readings in ethnic psychology (pp. 43–58). New York: Routledge.

Beck, K. H. & Bargman, C. J. (1993). Investigating Hispanic adolescent involvement with alcohol: a focus group interview approach. *Health Education Research, 8,* 151–158.

Bernal, G., Bonilla, J., & Bellido, C. (1995). Ecological validity and cultural sensitivity for outcome research: Issues for the cultural adaptation and development of psychosocial treatments with hispanics. *Journal of Abnormal Child Psychology, 23,* 67–82.

Bernal, G., Cumba, E., & Saez-Santiago, E. (2006). Relational process and depression in Latino adolescents. In S. Beach & N. Kaslow (Eds.), Relational processes and mental health. Washington, DC: American Psychiatric Press.

Bernal, G. & Saez-Santiago, E. (2006). *Culturally centered psychosocial interventions. Journal of Community Psychology, 34,* 121–132.

Bernal, G., & Sharron-del-Rio. (2001). Are empirically supported treatments valid for ethnic minorities? Toward an alternative approach for treatment research. *Cultural diversity & ethnic minority psychology, 7,* 328–342.

Bernal, G., Trimble, J. E., Burlew, A. K., & Leong, F. T. L. (2003). Introduction: The Psychology Study of Racial and Ethnic Minority Psychology. In *Handbook of racial and ethnic minority psychology* (pp. 1–12). Thousand Oaks, CA: Sage Publications.

Blum, R. W., Beuhring, T., Shew, M. L., Bearinger, L. H., Sieving, R. E., & Resnick, M. D. (2000). The effects of race/ethnicity, income, and family structure on adolescent risk behaviors. *American Journal of Public Health, 90,* 1879–1884.

Burlew, A. K. (2003). Research with ethnic minorities: Conceptual, methodological, and analytical issues. In G. Bernal, J. E. Trimble, A. K. Burlew, & F. T. L. Leong (Eds.), *Handbook of racial and ethnic minority psychology* (pp. 179–197). Thousand Oaks, CA: Sage Publications.

Canino, G., & Roberts, R. E. (2001). Suicidal behavior among Latino youth. *Suicide Life-Threatening Behavior, 31* Suppl, 122–131.

Cauce, A. M., Domenech-Rodríguez, M., Paradise, M., Cochran, B. N., Munyi Shea, J., Srebnik, D., et al. (2002). Cultural and contextual influences in mental health help seeking: A focus on ethnic minority youth. *Journal of Consulting and Clinical Psychology, 70,* 44–55.

Center for Disease Control and Prevention. (2004). Suicide among Hispanics—U.S., 1997–2001. *Morbidity and Mortality Weekly Report, 53,* 478–481.

Chambless, D. L., Baker, M. J., Baucom, D. H., Beutler, L. E., Calhoun, K. S., & Crits-Cristoph, P. (1998). Update on empirically validated therapies, II. *The Clinical Psychologist, 51,* 3–16.

Chambless, D. L., Sanderson, W. C., Shoham, V., Bennett Johnson, S., Pope, K. S., & Crits-Cristoph, P. (1996). An update on empirically validated therapies. *The Clinical Psychologist, 49,* 5–18.

Chavez, E. L., Edwards, R., & Oetting, E. R. (1989). Mexican American and white American school dropouts' drug use, health status, and involvement in violence. *Public Health Report, 104,* 594–604.

Cotgrove, A., Zirinsky, L., Black, D., & Weston, D. (1995). Secondary prevention of attempted suicide in adolescence. *Journal of Adolescence, 18,* 569–577.

Domenech-Rodríguez, M. & Wieling, E. (2004). Developing culturally appropriate, evidence-based treatments for interventions with ethnic minority populations. In Rastogn, M. & E. Weiling (Eds.), *Voices of color: First person accounts of ethnic minority therapists* (pp. 313–333). Thousand Oaks, CA: Sage Publications.

Douglas, J., Maldonado-Molina, M., Pantin, H., & Szapocznik, J. (2005). A person-centered and ecological investigation of acculturation strategies in hispanic immigrant youth. *Journal of Community Psychology, 33,* 157–174.

Duarté-Vélez, Y., & Bernal, G. (in press). Suicidal behavioral among Latino and Latina adolescents: Conceptual and methodological issues. Death Studies.

Eaton, D. K., Kann, L., Kinchen, S., Ross, J., Hawkins, J., Harris, W. A., et al. (2006). Youth risk behavior surveillance—U.S., 2005. *Morbidity and Mortality Weekly Report 55,* 1–108.

Garcia-Preto, N. (2005). Latino families: An overview. In M. McGoldrick, J. Giordano & N. Garcia-Preto (Eds.), *Ethnicity & Family Therapy* (3rd ed., pp. 153–165). New York: The Guilford Press.

Garofalo, R., Wolf, R. C., Wissow, L. S., Woods, E. R., & Goodman, E. (1999). Sexual orientation and risk of suicide attempts among a representative sample of youth. *Archive of Pediatric Adolescent Medicine, 153,* 487–493.

Grunbaum, J. A., Basen-Engquist, K., & Pandey, D. (1998). Association between violent behaviors and substance use among Mexican American and non-Hispanic white high school students. *Journal of Adolescent Health, 23,* 153–159.

Grunbaum, J. A., Kann, L., Kinchen, S., Ross, J., Hawkins, J., Lowry, R., et al. (2004). Youth risk behavior surveillance—U.S., 2003. *Morbidity and Mortality Weekly Report, 53,* 1–96.

Grunbaum, J. A., Kann, L., Kinchen, S. A., Williams, B., Ross, J. G., Lowry, R., et al. (2002). Youth risk behavior surveillance—U.S., 2001. *Morbidity and Mortality Weekly Report, 51,* 1–62.

Guiao, I. Z. & Esparza, D. (1995). Suicidality correlates in Mexican American teens. *Issues in Mental Health Nursing, 16,* 461–479.

Guiao, I. Z. & Thompson, E. A. (2004). Ethnicity and problem behaviors among adolescent females in the U.S. *Health Care for Women International, 25,* 296–310.

Hallfors, D. D., Waller, M. W., Ford, C. A., Halpern, C. T., Brodish, P. H., & Iritani, B. (2004). Adolescent depression and suicide risk: Association with *sex and drug behavior. American Journal of Preventive Medicine, 27,* 224–230.

Harrington, R., Kerfoot, M., Dyer, E., McNiven, F., Gill, J., & Harrington, V. (1998). Randomized trial of a home-based family intervention for children who have deliberately poisoned themselves. *Journal of the American Academy of Child and Adolescent Psychiatry, 37,* 512–518.

Hovey, J. D. (1998). Acculturative stress, depression, and suicidal ideation among Mexican American adolescents: Implications for the development of suicide prevention programs in schools. *Psychological Reports, 83,* 249–250.

Hovey, J. D. (1999a). Moderating influence of social support on suicidal ideation in a sample of Mexican immigrants. *Psychological Reports, 85,* 78–79.

Hovey, J. D. (1999b). Religion and suicidal ideation in a sample of Latin American immigrants. *Psychological Reports, 85,* 171–177.

Hovey, J. D. & King, C. A. (1996). Acculturative stress, depression, and suicidal ideation among immigrant and second-generation Latino adolescents. *Journal of American Academy of Child and Adolescent Psychiatry, 35,* 1183–1192.

Hovey, J. D. & King, C. A. (1997). Suicidality among acculturating Mexican Americans: current knowledge and directions for research. *Suicide Life-Threatening Behavior, 27,* 92–103.

Huey, S. J., Henggeler, S. W., Rowland, M., Halliday-Boykins, C., Cunningham, P. B., Pickrel, S., et al. (2004). Multisystemic therapy on attempted suicide by youths presenting psychiatric emergencies. *Journal of American Academy of Child and Adolescent Psychiatry, 43,* 183–190.

Kann, L., Kinchen, S. A., Williams, B. I., Ross, J. G., Lowry, R., Grunbaum, J. A., et al. (2000). Youth risk behavior surveillance—U.S., 1999. *Morbidity and Mortality Weekly Report, 49,* 1–32.

Kann, L., Kinchen, S. A., Williams, B. I., Ross, J. G., Lowry, R., Hill, C. V., et al. (1998). Youth risk behavior surveillance—U.S., 1997. *Morbidity and Mortality Weekly Report, 47,* 1–89.

Kann, L., Warren, C. W., Harris, W. A., Collins, J. L., Williams, B. I., Ross, J. G., et al. (1996). Youth risk behavior surveillance—U.S., 1995. *Morbidity and Mortality Weekly Report, 45,* 1–84.

King, C. A., Kramer, A., Preuss, L., Kerr, D. C., Weisse, L., & Venkataraman, S. (2006). Youth-nominated support team for suicidal adolescents (Version 1): A randomized controlled trial. *Journal of Consulting and Clinical Psychology, 74,* 199–206.

Lester, D. & Anderson, D. (1992). Depression and suicidal ideation in African American and Hispanic American high school students. *Psychological Reports, 71,* 618.

Locke, T. F. & Newcomb, M. D. (2005). Psychosocial predictors and correlates of suicidality in teenage latino males. *Hispanic Journal of Behavioral Sciences, 27,* 319–336.

Macgowan, M. J. (2004). Psychosocial treatment of youth suicide: A systematic review of the research. *Research of Social Work Practice,* 14, 147–162.

Marcenko, M. O., Fishman, G., & Friedman, J. (1999). Reexamining adolescent suicidal ideation: A developmental perspective applied to a diverse population. *Journal of Youth and Adolescence, 28,* 121–138.

Marín, G. & Marín, B. V. (1991). Research with hispanic populations (Vol. 23). Newbury Park: Sage Publications.

McGoldrick, M., Giordano, J., & Garcia-Preto, N. (2005). Latino families. In *Ethnicity & Family Therapy* (3rd ed., pp. 153–256). New York: The Guilford Press.

Meyer, I. (2003). Prejudice, social stress, and mental health in lesbian, gay and bisexual populations: Conceptual issues and research evidence. *Psychological Bulletin, 129,* 674–697.

Miranda, J., Bernal, G., Lau, A., Kohn, L., Hwang, W.-C., & LaFromboise, T. (2005). State of the science on psychosocial interventions for ethnic minorities. *Annual Review of Clinical Psychology,* 113–142.

Muir, J. A., Schwartz, S. J., & Szapocznik, J. (2004). A program of research with hispanic and African American families: Three decades of intervention development and testing influenced by the changing cultural context of Miami. *Journal of Marital Family Therapy, 30,* 285–303.

Muñoz, R. F., & Mendelson, T. (2005). Toward evidence-based interventions for diverse populations: The San Francisco General Hospital prevention and treatment manuals. *Journal of Consulting and Clinical Psychology, 73,* 790–799.

Nagayama Hall, G. (2001). Psychotherapy research with ethnic minorities: Empirical, ethical, and conceptual issues. *Journal of Consulting and Clinical Psychology, 69*, 502–510.

National Institute of Mental Health. (2001). Suicide Facts and Statistics. Retrieved January 10, 2005, from http://www.nimh.nih.gov/suicideprevention/suifact.cfm.

Norenzayan, A. & Heine, S. J. (2005). Psychological universals: What are they and how can we know? *Psychological Bulletin, 131*, 763–784.

O'Donnell, L., O'Donnell, C., Wardlaw, D. M., & Stueve, A. (2004). Risk and resiliency factors influencing suicidality among urban African American and Latino youth. *American Journal of Community Psychology, 33*, 37–49.

O'Donnell, L., Stueve, A., Wardlaw, D., & O'Donnell, C. (2003). Adolescent suicidality and adult support: The reach for health study of urban youth. *American Journal of Health Behavior, 27*, 633–644.

Okazaki, S. & Sue, S. (1998). Methodological issues in assessment research with ethnic minorities. In P. B. Organista, K. M. Chun & G. Marín (Eds.), Readings in ethnic psychology (pp. 26–40). New York: Routledge.

Olvera, R. L. (2001). Suicidal ideation in Hispanic and mixed-ancestry adolescents. *Suicide Life-Threatening Behavior, 31*, 416–427.

Oyserman, D., Coon, H. M., & Kemmelmeier, M. (2002). Rethinking individualism and collectivism: Evaluation of theoretical assumptions and meta-analyses. *Psychological Bulletin, 128*, 3–72.

Phinney, J. S. (1998). Ethnic identity in adolescents and adults. In P. B. Organista, K. M. Chun & G. Marín (Eds.), *Readings in ethnic psychology*. New York: Routledge.

Potts, R. & Watts, R. (2003). Conceptualization and models: The meaning(s) of difference in racial and ethnic minority psychology. In G. Bernal, J. E. Trimble, A. K. Burlew, & F. T. L. Leong (Eds.), *Handbook of racial and ethnic minority psychology* (pp. 65–75). Thousand Oaks, CA: Sage Publications.

Queralt, M. (1993). Risk factors associated with completed suicide in Latino adolescents. *Adolescence, 28*, 831–850.

Ransom, L. S. (2004). Navigating sex, sexuality, and Christian values. In M. S. Kimmel & R. F. Plante (Eds.), In *Sexualities: identities, behaviors, and society*. New York: Oxford University Press.

Rathus, J. H. & Miller, A. L. (2002). Dialectical behavioral therapy adapted for suicidal adolescents. *Suicide and Life-Threatening Behavior, 32*, 146–157.

Razin, A. M., O'Dowd, M. A., Nathan, A., Rodriguez, I., Goldfield, A., Martin, C., et al. (1991). Suicidal behavior among inner-city Hispanic adolescent females. *General Hospital Psychiatry, 13*, 45–58.

Rew, L., Taylor-Seehafer, M., & Fitzgerald, M. L. (2001). Sexual abuse, alcohol and other drug use, and suicidal behaviors in homeless adolescents. *Issues in Comprehensive Pediatric Nursing, 24*, 225–240.

Rew, L., Thomas, N., Horner, S. D., Resnick, M. D., & Beuhring, T. (2001). Correlates of recent suicide attempts in a triethnic group of adolescents. *Journal of Nursing Scholarship, 33*, 361–367.

Roberts, R. E., Chen, Y. R., & Roberts, C. R. (1997). Ethnocultural differences in prevalence of adolescent suicidal behaviors. *Suicide Life-Threatening Behavior, 27*, 208–217.

Roberts, R. E. & Chen, Y. W. (1995). Depressive symptoms and suicidal ideation among Mexican-origin and Anglo adolescents. *Journal of American Academy of Child and Adolescent Psychiatry, 34*, 81–90.

Rogler, L. (1999). Methodological sources of cultural insensitivity in mental health research. *American Psychologist, 54*, 424–433.

Rosselló, J. & Bernal, G. (1999). The efficacy of cognitive-behavioral and interpersonal treatments for depression in Puerto Rican adolescents. *Journal of Consulting and Clinical Psychology, 67*, 734–745.

Rotheram-Borus, M. J., Piacentini, J., Cantwell, C., Belin, T. R., & Song, J. (2000). The 18-month impact of an emergency room intervention for adolescent female suicide attempters. *Journal of Consulting and Clinical Psychology, 68*, 1081–1093.

Rotheram-Borus, M. J., Piacentini, J., Van Rossem, R., Graae, F., Cantwell, C., Castro-Blanco, D., et al. (1996). Enhancing treatment adherence with a specialized emergency room program for adolescent suicide attempters. *Journal of the American Academy of Child Adolescent Psychiatry, 35*, 654–663.

Saez-Santiago, E. & Bernal, G. (2003). Depression in ethnic minorities. In G. Bernal, J. E. Trimble, A. K. Burlew & F. T. L. Leong (Eds.), *Handbook of Racial Ethnic Minority Psychology* (pp. 401–428). Thousand Oaks, CA: Sage.

Safren, S. & Heimberg, R. (1999). Depression, hopelessness, suicidality, and related factors in sexual minority and heterosexual adolescents. *Journal of Consulting and Clinical Psychology, 67*, 859–866.

Savin-Williams, R. (2004). Dating and romantic relationships among gay, lesbian, and bisexual youths. In M. S. Kimmel & R. F. Plante (Eds.), *Sexualities: identities, behaviors, and society*. New York: Oxford University Press.

Scott, C. S., Shifman, L., Orr, L., Owen, R. G., & Fawcett, N. (1988). Hispanic and black American adolescents' beliefs relating to sexuality and contraception. *Adolescence, 23*, 667–688.

Sorenson, S. B. & Shen, H. (1996). Youth suicide trends in California: An examination of immigrant and ethnic group risk. *Suicide and Life-Threatening Behavior, 26*, 143–154.

Sue, S. (2003). In defense of cultural competency in psychotherapy and treatment. *American Psychologist*, 964–970.

Swanson, J. W., Linskey, A. O., Quintero-Salinas, R., Pumariega, A. J., & Holzer, C. E., 3rd. (1992). A binational school survey of depressive symptoms, drug use, and suicidal ideation. *Journal of American Academy of Child and Adolescent Psychiatry, 31*, 669–678.

Tamez, E. G. (1981). Familismo, machismo and child rearing practices among Mexican Americans. *Journal of Psychosocial Nursing Mental Health Services, 19*, 21–25.

Tortolero, S. R. & Roberts, R. E. (2001). Differences in nonfatal suicide behaviors among Mexican and European American middle school children. *Suicide Life-Threatening Behavior, 31*, 214–223.

Trimble, J. E., Helms, J. E., & Root, M. P. (2003). Social and psychological perspectives on ethnic and racial identity. In G. Bernal, J. E. Trimble, A. K. Burlew & F. T. L. Leong (Eds.), *Handbook of racial and ethnic minority psychology* (pp. 239–275). Thousand Oaks, CA: Sage Publications.

U.S. Census Bureau. (2004). American Community Survey 2004: Hispanic or Latino origin by specific origin—universe: Total population. Retrieved April 27, 2006, from www.census.gov/population/RaceandEthnicity/2004/HispanicorLatinobyOrigin.

Ungemack, J. A. & Guarnaccia, P. J. (1998). Suicidal ideation and suicide attempts among Mexican Americans, Puerto Ricans and Cuban Americans. *Transcultural Psychiatry, 35*, 307–327.

Vega, W. A., Gil, A., Warheit, G., Apospori, E., & Zimmerman, R. (1993). The relationship of drug use to suicide ideation and attempts among African American, Hispanic, and white non-Hispanic male adolescents. *Suicide Life-Threatening Behavior, 23*, 110–119.

Vega, W. A., Gil, A. G., Zimmerman, R. S., & Warheit, G. J. (1993). Risk factors for suicidal behavior among Hispanic, African American, and non-Hispanic white boys in early adolescence. *Ethnicity and Disease, 3*, 229–241.

Walter, H. J., Vaughan, R. D., Armstrong, B., Krakoff, R. Y., Maldonado, L. M., Tiezzi, L., et al. (1995). Sexual, assaultive, and suicidal behaviors among urban minority junior high school students. *Journal of American Academy of Child and Adolescent Psychiatry, 34*, 73–80.

Weisz, J. & Hawley, K. (2002). Developmental factors in the treatment of adolescents. *Journal of Consulting and Clinical Psychology, 70*, 21–43.

Wood, A., Rothwell, J., Moore, A., & Harrington, R. (2001). Randomized trial of group therapy for repeated deliberate self-harm in adolescents. *Journal of the American Academy of Child and Adolescent Psychiatry, 40*, 1246–1253.

Zayas, L. H., Lester, R. J., Cabassa, L. J., & Fortuna, L. R. (2005). Why do so many latina teens attempt suicide? A conceptual model for research. *American Journal of Orthopsychiatry, 75*, 275–287.

Suicide among Asian Americans

A Critical Review with Research Recommendations

Frederick T. L. Leong, Mark M. Leach, and Arpana Gupta

> Historian and human rights activist Iris Chang is dead. She was found Tuesday morning in her car in Santa Clara County California; apparently a suicide. Chang had reportedly suffered a breakdown and was hospitalized about five months ago while working on a new book. She is best known for 1997 book *The Rape of Nanking: The Forgotten Holocaust of WWII* about war crimes committed by the Japanese against Chinese civilians in 1937. She said she was inspired to write that book after learning that her grandparents had narrowly escaped the slaughter. Though Chang was only 36 when she died, she dedicated much of her career to telling the world about the Chinese and Chinese Americans.... Iris Chang was 36 years old. She died yesterday in California.
>
> **NPR** *Talk of the Nation*, November 11, 2004

□ An Overview of What We Know

The apparent suicide of Iris Chang, a highly gifted author and historian, was a severe shock to the Asian American community. It poignantly illustrates the tragic losses of suicide to families, friends, the community, and society at large. This chapter offers a critical review of the literature to identify key factors underlying antecedents, correlates, and consequences of suicide among Asian Americans.

Asian Americans are a diverse ethnic group with significant intra-group differences in culture, history, and customs. Even though Asian Americans make up only 2% of the general population in the United States, they consist of almost 50 distinct Asian American ethnic groups and speak 30 different languages (Baruth & Manning, 2003). This diversity is also evidenced in attitudes toward mental health issues, especially with regard to suicide. No significant amount of information on suicide among Asian Americans exists in the literature. Often, blanket statements are made about the rates of suicide among Asian Americans in comparison with European Americans or with other ethnic groups (McKenzie, Serfaty, & Crawford 2003). According to Leach (2006), this is misleading because Asian Americans display varying suicide rates and reasons for suicide, depending upon a variety of within-group factors such as age, acculturation, religious orientation, and sexual orientation.

McKenzie, Serfaty, & Crawford (2003) reported that in 2000, approximately 800,000 individuals died from suicide worldwide. These authors reported that suicide rates differ depending upon the ethnic group involved or the region being investigated. According to Beautrais (2006) a majority of the world's suicides can be attributed to those occurring in Asia, despite the fact that suicidal behaviors may well be underreported there (Lau, Jernewall, Zane, & Myers, 2002).

As with most other parts of the suicide literature, much of what we know about suicide among Asian Americans is founded on studies using university students as participants. These studies are valuable, as statistics show that a large proportion of deaths occur among 15–24- (and especially 20–24-) year-old Chinese and Japanese Americans, consistent with European Americans. Asian American college students are more likely than European Americans (Gregersen, Nebeke, Seely, & Lambert, 2004) to exhibit psychological issues that could benefit from treatment.

More concerning is that Asian American university students were found to be more likely to attempt suicide than European Americans (Kisch, Leino, & Silverman, 2005). In another study it was reported that ethnic minorities in general, in comparison with European Americans, were less likely to report or disclose suicidal ideation. This group is often referred to as the "hidden ideators" and consists of a majority (almost 90%) of students of color (Morrison & Downey, 2000). These ideators have direct implications for practitioners working with Asian Americans because this group is the least likely to seek out mental health services (Sue & Sue, 2003). By the time Asian Americans enter the mental health system they have already reached levels of intense distress, discomfort, and hopelessness (Kearney, Draper, & Baron, 2005; Paniagua, 2005), and the clinician may have to consider the first session as an emergency situation.

The limited information that does exist on Asian Americans and suicide is applicable only to those Asian groups that have been in the United States for a significant amount of time, such as the Chinese, Japanese, and Filipino Americans (Fugita, 1990). No firm empirical information on suicidal behaviors exists for recent Asian groups such as the Hmong and Laotians, as both of these groups have resided in the U.S. for only a few generations.

Comparative studies conducted over the past 40 years have shown that Japanese Americans have slightly higher completed suicide rates than Chinese Americans, whereas Filipino Americans have significantly lower suicide rates than either the Chinese or Japanese Americans (Kalish, 1968; Lester, 1994). Compared with other ethnic groups, both Japanese and Chinese Americans have higher suicide rates than African Americans but lower numbers than both American Indians and European Americans. These within-and between-group suicide rates can be attributed to certain cultural factors (Lester, 1994). For example, 30 years ago, Yamamoto (1976) demonstrated that Japanese Americans showed higher suicide rates than other Asian groups, as the Japanese have culturally and historically viewed suicide as an acceptable and honorable solution in dealing with stressful or distressful situations. Yamamoto also reported that less acculturated Japanese Americans turned to cutting as a suicide method, which is based upon their traditional samurai methods. These findings are limited, but they do draw our attention to important within-group differences among Asian American groups that need to be considered and evaluated further.

Grunbaum, Lowry, Kann & Pateman (2000) evaluated health risk behaviors, including suicide among Asian American/Pacific Islander high school students, and compared them with other ethnic groups such as European American, African American, and Hispanic students in the U.S. They reported that generally the health risk behaviors of Asian Americans/Pacific Islanders (AAPI) were slightly different from the other ethnic groups in that they were less likely to engage in drinking, smoking marijuana, premarital sexual intercourse or attempting suicide. However, a substantial number of AAPI students did engage in these risky behaviors and thus needed culturally sensitive prevention programs to help them improve their current and future health.

As with multiple other studies, alcohol has been known to contribute toward suicide indicators (i.e., suicide attempts, ideations, and actions) among Asian Americans. In a study investigating the effect of alcohol on suicidality in AAPI adolescents living in Hawaii, Nishimura, Goebert, Ramisetty-Mikler, & Caetano (2005) found that drinking patterns were the best predictors of suicidal behaviors and ideation. These authors also suggested using school- and community-based prevention programs to help increase students' awareness about alcohol use and in turn the prevention of suicide.

Assessing suicide becomes important and currently quite a few scales are presently being used to assess suicidal ideation. For example, the psychometric properties of the Positive and Negative Suicide Ideation (PANSI) inventory was evaluated with a diverse sample (Muehlenkamp et al. 2005). The researchers found that the two-factor structure and the internal consistency of the scale were upheld with the diverse ethnic minority sample. The authors also caution that differences in responses were present on the various subscales between the ethnic groups. This means that professionals need to be careful when assessing suicidal ideation and behaviors in diverse populations. Professionals and researchers also need to create separate ethnic/racial norms (Muehlenkamp, Gutierrez, Osman, & Barrios, 2005).

While common factors are associated with suicide regardless of ethnic background, other culturally relevant factors are introduced in this chapter for consideration. As indicated earlier, even a brief perusal of the literature suggests that more research is needed with Asian Americans. The factors mentioned here are not fully inclusive but will shed some light on the concept of suicide within the Asian American cultures. The purpose of this chapter is to introduce the various factors characteristic of suicide among Asian Americans, and those that have not yet been highlighted but could be considered important and deserving of more research merit. A brief overview of the literature on suicide among Asian Americans is provided within the context of five main areas: Age and Gender; Religious and Spiritual Issues; Acculturation and Social Support; Familial and Social Integration; and Gay/Lesbian/Bisexual issues. Readers interested in further information on these and additional factors can consult Leach (2006). Future directions for research are also discussed and a case study is introduced to illustrate some of the points in the literature.

□ Age, Gender and Culture

Age and gender are important contributing factors associated with suicide among Asian Americans, as the elderly and adolescent age groups are most likely to complete suicide. Most studies conducted have focused on Chinese, Japanese, and Filipino Asian groups, with an emphasis on the first two. For example, Shiang et al. (1997) investigated suicide rates in the Chinese subgroup from 1988 to 1994 in San Francisco and reported that these rates had not changed significantly over the past 40 years. The older Chinese Americans were more likely to complete suicide regardless of gender, especially when compared with other ethnic groups where suicide rates were found to decrease with age. Similarly, Bartels & Coakley (2002) found that older Asian American primary caregivers reported higher rates of suicide ideation in comparison with other ethnic groups. McKenzie, Serfaty, & Crawford (2003) found that East Asian women above 65 reported the highest proportional rate of suicide of all women residing in the United States. There has been some speculation and investigation into the reasons reported for these higher rates of suicide in elderly Chinese and Japanese Americans. For example, Diego, Yamamoto, Nguyen, & Hifumi (1994) determined that the higher suicide rates can be attributed to intergenerational conflict between these elderly individuals and their children; such conflicts often arise as a result of acculturation clashes. Acculturation results in a decrease in the traditional notion of filial piety, which potentially results in a change in individual and community identities, social isolation, and familial misunderstandings, all of which can lead to psychological distress and depression.

The Centers for Disease Control (2002) reported that, as with most ethnic groups, suicide is the third leading cause of death among adolescents and young adults (15–24-year-olds), placing adolescents in a high-risk category. However, culture is an important mediating variable and accounts for the varying suicide rates and level of acceptableness associated with suicide. Wyche & Rotheram-Borus (1990) in a study comparing adolescent suicide rates in ethnic groups with European Americans reported the following: (1) due to various cultural factors associated with suicide, ethnic minority youth experience greater distress than their White counterparts, which could contribute to increased suicide rates, (2) Acculturation is a deep and multidimensional phenomenon that adds complexity to the ethnic identity formation stage in adolescents, which further complicates and affects suicide rates in ethnic minority youth, and (3) in contrast, it may be that ethnic or cultural factors could work in the opposite direction to hinder suicidal behaviors.

Mayer & Ziaian (2002) investigated the effects of age and gender variations on suicide in India between the years 1991 and 1997. They reported that the rate of suicides in India is characteristically bimodal. This means that the rates were the highest for 30–44-year-olds, with this rate declining with age; this was true for both males and females. In comparison with developed countries, it was found that suicide rates were nearly equal for both sexes, which was different from the pattern found in the developed countries. In another study, Bhugra (2002) investigated the suicidal behavior of South Asians in the UK. Bhugra (2002) claims that South Asians, especially women, report higher rates of self-harm and suicidal behavior, especially those between the ages of 18 and 24. These high rates of self-harm and suicidal behavior are usually associated with factors such as cultural alienation and previous attempts (Bhugra, 2002). Burr (2002) suggests that the high rates of suicide and low rates of treated depression in South Asian women in the UK can be explained through stereotypes of these repressed South Asian cultures. These stereotypes are constructed on the supposition that Eastern cultures are inferior, repressed, and patriarchal in comparison with the ideal, superior Western culture. Burr (2002) points out that with time these stereotypes can be ingrained as fact, and eventually become a source for misdiagnosis and inappropriate treatment, which is why it is important that both professionals and the community be informed about these stereotypes and be shown ways to correct them.

Depression, of course, is a significant and common factor associated with suicide. For ethnic groups this becomes even more compounded, as there are many cultural variables that could contribute and increase the likelihood of depression. Professionals need to consider cultural motivating factors that may lead to depression. For example, ethnic minority adolescents experience added cultural stresses that compound the usual stresses associated with adolescent growth and development, and these can ultimately result in low self-esteem, self-dislike, self-blame, and self-criticism (Wyche & Rotheram-Borus, 1990). Asian Americans must often contend with the cultural stress associated with being a member of the myth known as the "model minority" that has made some Asian American adolescents scapegoats in the social system and has also pitted them against other minority groups. This means that their true mental and social problems can get trivialized (Liu, Yu, Chang, & Fernandez, 1990). As a result of being considered part of the model minority group some Asian American adolescents feel intense pressure to succeed in addition to being plagued by self-identity problems.

□ Religious and Spiritual Issues

The diversity of religious and spiritual beliefs and values within any ethnic group is large, and Asian Americans are no exception, given historical belief systems extending thousands of years. This variability and diversity means that certain practices and behaviors can have multiple etiologies and influences. Therefore, it is imperative that both clinicians and researchers consider addressing issues of religion and spirituality when working with Asian American suicidality.

Limited information links religion and spirituality with suicide among Asian Americans. What little information exists is presented within the framework of a collectivist culture, which arises from specific religious belief systems such as Buddhism, Confucianism, Taoism, and Hinduism. Most of the current information presented in the literature is done so from a Western, Christian perspective, and not from the Eastern faiths. Nonetheless, our limited empirical knowledge of the relationship between Eastern faiths and suicide among Asian Americans still needs to be addressed.

Depending on individual beliefs, religion can act as a deterrent to suicide, though it can also offer acceptable methods of engaging in suicidal behaviors. In contrast to Western or American religious faiths, Asians often hold religious and spiritual beliefs that consist of multiple faiths. For example, many hold beliefs that are a melding of Confucianism and Buddhism. A very brief overview of the foundational faiths associated with Buddhism, Confucianism, Taoism, and Hinduism will be highlighted here.

Buddhism and Suicide

Buddhism, a common religion among Asians, is based on the teachings and followings of Buddha. Buddha highly recommended that individuals should appreciate life and its basic intricacies. He also stressed that life was impermanent, and to appreciate life and its characteristics, individuals must contemplate factors of death and suffering. According to Buddhism, death is a natural part of both the human cycle and the larger cycle and its natural progression is strongly discouraged. Due to this belief, suicide is strongly discouraged among Buddhists, which probably explains why few empirical studies exist specifically examining suicide and Buddhism. However, according to Kok (1988) no specific or strong sanctions exist against suicide among Buddhists. This fact is further complicated as there are many practical interpretations and practices of Buddhism that can often differ even within the same region. According to Buddhism, death is an inevitable part of our lives and therefore one must spend as much time as possible trying to accept, understand and prepare for death. Suicide therefore, short circuits this preparation for the death process and, as a result, one ends up entering death unprepared, and without the appropriate mindset to enter the next realm of the larger cycle. Additionally, suicide is considered an affront to ancestors. Because suicide can be interpreted in various ways, the practical interpretation of Buddhism allows for multiple views, which can change depending upon the culture, the individual, the region, or the context.

In a recent study, Braun & Nichols (1997) interviewed Buddhist spiritual leaders and other Hawaiian spiritual representatives of Chinese, Japanese, Filipino, and Vietnamese descent. All of the spiritual leaders and representatives considered suicide negatively. There was considerable variability in those beliefs. For example, the Japanese Americans believed that Buddha would be compassionate in such circumstances and that one needed to be nonjudgmental toward both the individual and his or her family. Chinese Americans also viewed suicide as being wrong, though they did allow exceptions under specified and extreme circumstances. Vietnamese Americans indicated that suicide is an act that is equivalent to murder and therefore upsets one's karma. Because a majority of the Filipinos were

Catholic, they considered suicide an affront to the sixth commandment of the Bible (Thou shalt not kill). Overall, Buddhists view suicide negatively because it is considered a selfish act, one that significantly impacts the family and community, and one that disrupts the process or transition from one life to the next. Unfortunately, very little is known about the frequency, ideations, and consequences associated with suicide within Buddhist communities, and clearly more research is needed.

Confucianism, Taoism, and Suicide

Confucianism stresses the importance and significance of relationships, especially with one's elders, parents, and superiors (Range et al., 1999). Five varying relationships need to be stressed: father–son, husband–wife, elder–youth, older brother–younger brother, and ruler–subject. According to Confucianism, a person can attain individuality within each of these relationships, but any conflict affects everyone else. Therefore, suicide would be viewed as being both harmful and disrespectful to all involved in these interpersonal relationships (Range et al., 1999). Taoism also stresses becoming one with Tao, which is viewed as the first cause of the universe. The main tenets of Taoism are compassion, moderation, and humility. According to the teaching of Taoism, life is cyclical and one has to follow Nature's principles. Therefore, an act of suicide would be considered inappropriate and unwise as it conflicts with the teachings of Taoism (Range et al., 1999).

Hinduism and Suicide

Hinduism does not actively deter suicide. As with religions such as Christianity, Hinduism supports the belief that souls are given life by God and exist even after death. However, Hinduism supports the belief of reincarnation, which suggests that there is a cycling process taking place (similar to that found in Buddhism). The goal is that lower life forms cycle to higher forms of life so that in the end the highest form (also known as nirvana) can be achieved. Embedded within reincarnation is a concept known as karma, which is the bond across time concerned with morality and is based on causes and effects. Hinduism is not fatalistic because Hindus believe that people can control their own destinies (Almeida, 1996).

Some holy Hindu men condone suicide as a means to escape suffering, but in general, using suicide in such a way is not condoned within the Hindu faith. These differing points of view are based on how these Hindu religious beliefs are interpreted (Richards & Bergin, 2000). Often a demarcation is made between a "good" and a "bad" death depending on an individual's state of mind at the time of death. A good death is one in which an individual was able to say goodbye and to make peace with others. Suicide is considered a bad death because the individual typically fails to meet this criteria. Some Hindus believe that after one has committed suicide his or her spirit comes back to haunt the living. Others believe that the spirit of one who has completed suicide must suffer greatly, or can even be born as a lower life form through the reincarnation cycle. Suicide rates among Hindus are known to be quite high. For example, in comparison with Christians, Hindu men attempt suicide at a higher rate than Hindu women (Richards & Bergin, 2000). Unlike the majority of completed suicides in the U.S., most Hindus who attempt suicide are not under the influence of alcohol or drugs. The most common method used by Hindus to complete suicide is by household poisons.

Clearly, these conflicting views between the high suicide rates and the negative repercussions from suicide suggested by Hindus indicate that this is a complex relationship and therefore, further in-depth investigation is needed. As with other Asian subgroups and religious faiths, saving face is a strong motivator associated with completing suicide among Hindus. On the other hand, the downfall associated with suicide is often related to the negative social and personal effects that families and communities have to endure after a family member completes suicide. Overall, it is often difficult to delineate the role of religion and spirituality in studies of suicide, yet it is also clear that the understanding of the extent to which religious faith or spirituality are influential in Asian American suicide ideation and completion is still in the infancy stage.

☐ Acculturation and Social Support

As mentioned above, Asian American comprise large, diverse subgroups that have implications for acculturation. Some Asian ethnic groups have a longer history in the U.S. (e.g., Chinese) than others (e.g., Hmong). Most Asian Americans (about 70%) in the United States are foreign-born (U.S. Census Bureau, 2004). It is expected that these foreign-born Asian Americans will experience some period of adjustment from their own culture to the U.S. culture. This consequently has important implications for the subsequent psychological and social well-being of Asian Americans such as in areas of depression and suicide. The following is a brief introduction into this area.

Acculturation is recognized as an important cultural factor in Asian American psychological functioning and well-being (see Liu, Pope-Davis, Nevitt, & Toporek, 1999; Mehta, 1998). It is a complex, multidimensional process associated with negotiating two or more cultures when one enters a new dominant culture after leaving a perceived less valued culture (Berry, 1995). The "national culture" is the culture of origin and is now considered the culture of less value, whereas the dominant culture of contact is referred to as the "host culture" (Ward & Kennedy, 1994). The process and eventually the outcome of acculturation is influenced by how individuals manage the pull between letting go of their original national culture while acquiring the cultural norms and values of the dominant, host and competing culture (Berry, Kim, Minde, & Mok 1987). While numerous studies have investigated Asian American acculturation (e.g., Gim Chung, 2001; Liem, Lim, & Liem, 2000; Yeh, 2003), only a few studies have examined the relationship between suicide and acculturation (Cho, 2003; Lau, Jernewall, Zane, & Myers, 2002). Studies with Asian Americans have shown that acculturation is strongly associated with depression (Chen, Guarnaccia, & Chung, 2003; Jonnalagadda & Diwan, 2005), which, of course, can result in suicidal behaviors. Acculturation has also been strongly documented as a mediating variable and predictor of suicidal behavior, acts, and ideation among Asian Americans (Yang & Clum, 1994). A concern is that too few studies assess individual Asian ethnic groups and instead combine groups into a single sample.

Usually the relationship between acculturation and suicidal acts and ideation among Asians and Asian Americans suggests that individuals are identifying more with their country/culture of origin and are unable to adequately identify or adjust to the new dominant host country/culture (Cho, 2003; Kennedy, Parhar, Samra, & Gorzalka, 2005). This relationship between acculturation and suicide has been demonstrated in a number of studies. For example, Davis (1995) showed that Asian American college students who were more biculturally identified and less Asian identified reported lower levels of suicidal ideation. Similarly in another study, Kennedy et al. (2005) investigated the relationship between acculturation and suicidal ideation in undergraduate students of European, Chinese, and Indo-Asian backgrounds. They found that the more the students identified with their original cultural heritage, the more they were at risk of having suicidal thoughts. Cho (2003) compared international Korean students who had come to the U.S. without their parents with international Korean students who had immigrated with their parents. Cho (2003) reported that those who were without their parents were more likely to experience acculturative stress and therefore were more likely to demonstrate symptoms of depression and suicidal ideation. The Korean students who lived without their parents experienced more transcultural stress than those who lived with their parents and therefore had the benefit of the support and help of their parents.

Yeh (2003) evaluated the relationship between acculturation level and mental health issues in Chinese, Japanese, and Korean immigrant high school students. Yeh (2003) found that the more acculturated students reported fewer mental health issues, which could be attributed to differences in language fluency. This is consistent with previous findings, suggesting that greater and better language abilities lead to better communications and therefore, more positive social interactions (e.g., Salgado de Synder, 1987). There has been some indication of a relationship between age and acculturation (Huang, 1997). Sodowsky and Lai (1997) found that acculturative distress could be associated with lower cultural adjustment in Asian immigrants, especially among the younger age groups.

The relationship between acculturation and suicidal ideation has also been examined among academically gifted Asian Americans. In a study on gifted Asian Indian college students, Jha (2001) used Berry et al.'s (1987) acculturation model to investigate the relationship between acculturation phase and suicidal ideation. Jha found that the "marginalized" (an adaptation strategy when one rejects both one's own and the dominant group's cultural practices) and the "separation" students (acculturation strategy associated with valuing one's cultural norms but rejecting the dominant culture and norms), were more likely to display symptoms of suicidal ideation via acculturative distress and depression. Because both marginalized and separated individuals remain separate from the dominant culture, it underscores the fact that these gifted individuals may experience pressures and cultural isolation within the academic settings. In addition, the pressures from the larger American society reflecting the model minority myth and from the students' parents could contribute to increased suicide rates. Noh (2003) used a narrative approach to study the relationship between suicide and Asian American women, and found that the model minority ideology led to increased social pressures stemming from acts of daily racism and sexism, which in turn could lead to increased suicide rates. However, these findings need confirmation, as there are no known empirical studies linking the model minority myth to suicidal behaviors and thoughts.

Some researchers have also evaluated the relationship between acculturation and suicide within the context of parent–child relationships. Lau et al. (2002) found that acculturation interacted with parent–child conflicts in order to affect suicidality in a sample of 285 outpatient Asian American adolescents. Specifically, high parent–child conflicts and low acculturated Asians were identified as being at greater risk for suicidal behavior than the highly acculturated Asians. Such parent–child conflict was found to be a better predictor of suicidality than were other moderating factors. This research clearly illustrates the immense amount of stress associated with intergenerational family conflict and parent–child relationships in influencing Asian American psychopathology and well-being.

The above studies have demonstrated a certain relationship between acculturation and suicide. However, further research needs to be conducted beyond that of simply reporting the effects of acculturation on a particular variable. Mediation models may help delineate factors that allow for further refinement in our understanding. It is well known that acculturation is a critical issue among Asian Americans, especially given the current shifts in demographics due to continued immigration (Chun, Organista, & Marin 2003).

Familial and Social Integration

Familial and social integration are known to influence well-being and to determine suicidality in various ethnic groups. This is especially true for Asian Americans because of the wide influence of traditional Confucian beliefs among many Asians and Asian Americans. Confucianism, as it places a significant emphasis on family cohesion and collectivism over individualism (Mingzhao, Congpei, Jueiji, & Enyu, 1992), highlights familial and social integration.

Heikkinen, Aro, & Lonnqvist (1993) demonstrated how a supportive social network can help prevent suicide by offering life meaning and providing a buffer against adverse experiences. These authors also stressed that those individuals who had completed suicide had deteriorated social networks and deficient social supports. Similarly, Yang & Clum (1994) examined suicidal behaviors and thoughts among Asian international students in the U.S. They found that higher levels of depression and hopelessness were closely correlated to suicidal ideation, whereas, on the other hand, high levels of problem-solving skills and social support helped mediate symptoms of life stress, depression, hopelessness, and suicidal ideation.

Rudd (1989) tried to demonstrate the link between intact families and suicide in college students by developing a suicidal ideation scale. This study consisted of a sample of 737 students, 53 (7.2%) of whom were Asian American. A large number of the participants had reported experiencing some level of suicidal ideation during the previous year; 14.9% of those students acted in some way on those thoughts and 5.5% actually made attempts on their lives. Rudd found that individuals from disrupted families experienced higher levels of suicidal ideation than did those individuals who came from intact families (defined as those in which both of the participant's biological parents were married and lived together). Even though ethnicity was not found to be a mediating variable in determining suicidal ideation, this could be attributed to insufficient ethnic participants (e.g., only 7.2% of the participants were Asian American). This study does offer some insight into the effects of intact families on suicidal ideation, especially as Asians are a collectivist society and do display a stigma against divorce. This is very different when comparing Asians with European Americans.

☐ Gay/Lesbian/Bisexual Issues and the Asian Community

Most of the information available linking Gay/Lesbian/Bisexual, Transgender, and Questioning (GLBTQ) issues with suicidality are based on a European American and middle-class worldview. Currently, limited information associates GLBTQ issues with suicidality among ethnic groups, and this gap is even wider for Asian Americans. A few empirical studies are summarized in this chapter, though the majority of information is derived from anecdotal evidence. Morris, Waldon, & Rothblum (2001) examined issues of psychological distress and suicidality among lesbians across multiple ethnic groups and found that the degree of "outness" was inversely related to psychological distress, including suicidality. Pinhey & Millman (2004) demonstrated how being a GLBTQ Asian/Pacific Islander adolescent in Guam was highly associated with high suicidal behaviors. Coming out for many GLBTQ individuals is difficult. Greene (1994, 1997) stresses how this process of "coming out" to family and the community in Asian Americans is plagued with feelings of shame and therefore many try to ignore or hide their sexual identity.

Asian cultures vary in their degrees of acceptance toward GLBTQ issues and individuals. For example, the Philippines, Thailand, and Vietnam are more accepting, or at least tolerant, than other countries such as Korea, Japan, China, and India. Some authors have mentioned that being gay in Korea is tantamount to being hidden (Nakajima, Chan, & Lee, 1996; Sohng & Icard, 1996). Even though Asian cultures for centuries have recognized and even documented homosexual behavior, it has in general not been positively accepted (Hinsch, 1990; Nakajima, Chan, & Lee, 1996). Usually being gay is not discussed or even disclosed in Asian families or communities.

Given the paucity of research on GLBTQ issues among Asians and how it influences suicidality, there is an over-reliance on non-empirical research to draw conclusions about the relationship between GLBTQ issues and suicidality. The GLBTQ community in the U.S. is dominated politically and socially by European Americans, meaning that ethnic minority GLBTQ individuals have difficulty finding the necessary and appropriate social or intimate support systems. The Asian American GLBTQ community is complex and often consists of mixed ethnic relationships because they are a small, hidden, and less organized community than the European American GLBTQ community. These mixed ethnic relationships usually occur across Asian ethnic groups (e.g., Filipino and Chinese), or across broader ethnic groups (e.g., Filipino and European American). This makes it even more difficult to be comfortable with one's own sexual and ethnic identity and to be able to come out socially. Support systems such as counseling and social networks for the Asian American GLBTQ community are extremely rare. The few support systems that do exist are available in limited locations such as in big and modern cities. Cultural norms associated with keeping things within the family prevent GLBTQ individuals from seeking the necessary outside help that they may need (Sue & Sue, 2003). A conflict exists between personal identity and alienation because Asian American GLBTQ individuals often believe they have to choose between the Asian community and the GLBTQ community because these individuals are often not accepted by both.

□ Future Directions for Research

Currently, there is a dearth of clinical and empirical literature to guide clinicians in identifying and treating the unique factors associated with Asian American suicide. Some information on general cultural variables exists, but clinicians would be assisted greatly if researchers would highlight both the culture-specific and culture-general factors associated with suicide among Asian Americans. This would be especially beneficial in helping clinicians determine appropriate treatments and also help clinicians keep in mind the factors that need to be considered over the course of therapy (e.g., acculturation, family generational issues, religious and spiritual background).

These variables also need to be examined within the context of the various ethnic groups and contexts within the larger heterogeneous Asian population. For instance, Asians in Hawaii are different from Asians on the mainland, or immigrant/refugee Asians experience issues that differ from other Asians'. Suicidal behaviors, thoughts, and acts among Asians can also be compared in greater detail with other ethnic groups. This will help separate the effects of ethnic minority status such as alienation or social isolation, from the unique characteristics of being Asian American. The literature has investigated to some degree suicide among subgroups of Asians in other parts of the world such as India, Pakistan, China, and Japan. If professionals can begin to understand the differences in suicidality and suicide risk factors for the various Asian groups, research will need to be expanded and compared with those research efforts that have been done abroad. This will help professionals gain a more precise grasp of the variables that are involved in suicidality among Asian Americans.

Research on suicidality among Asian Americans is subject to many of the same difficulties as research on any other aspect of Asian American psychology. For example, although it may be difficult to obtain the sample sizes needed to examine within-group differences, it is very important to look at different Asian ethnic groups separately because the suicide rates and other issues such as suicide acceptableness often differ according to the Asian ethnic subgroup (Lester, 1992; Lester & Walker, 2006). This is especially true with regard to the large amount of diversity that exists within the larger Asian group. Therefore, differences in factors such as language, culture, values, or religion need to be addressed and accounted for. Future research in this area should seek to continue to produce sound epidemiological data, as well as move toward more theoretical understanding of suicide for Asian Americans.

The similarities and differences between suicidal acts or thoughts and completed acts of suicide also need to be investigated with reference to ethnicity among Asian Americans. This means that more sophisticated and exact methodologies will need to be used in the future when conducting research that distinguishes and compares the characteristics of suicide attempters versus suicide completers. Both groups are very distinct and different, making conclusions about one group less generalizable to the other. Some of the initial studies that have been conducted need to be cross-validated, because many of the hypotheses introduced have not been examined or addressed before. Future research can focus on comparison trends between completed suicides versus suicidal attempts between men and women. These issues need to be examined because there could be significant findings related to cultural and gender influences. Future research should also be examined in a nonpatient population for comparison and validation purposes. Often professionals use cross-sectional correlational studies to study suicidality because they are easier and less costly. Future efforts may need to use longitudinal designs in order to gain more information about the likelihood of future suicide behaviors such as attempts and completions.

A program of research on suicide among Asian Americans could be based on the existing knowledge of suicide among White European Americans using the known parameters. As data is accumulated using this framework, it could be compared with the data for White European Americans to determine where similar prevention and treatment approaches would be effective. At the same time, divergence in the pattern of results using this comparative framework could also help identify where culturally accommodated approaches may be needed for Asian Americans (see, e.g., Leong & Lee, 2006).

Consistent with this framework, research needs to be conducted using epidemiological methods to determine the true prevalence rates of suicide among Asian Americans. Such epidemiological surveys could also help identify which are the subgroups of Asian Americans that are at higher risk of suicide. At present, information on high-risk groups are arrived at via isolated studies that have not been conducted using rigorous epidemiological methods. Hence, the first major research question is whether Asian Americans exhibit a higher or lower rate of suicide than

European Americans using community-level epidemiological surveys. Second, which Asian American subgroups are at particular high risk? Third, do Asian Americans exhibit a higher or lower rate of suicide than other racial and ethnic minority groups? Fourth, using a comparative triangulation method recommended by Leong & Zhang (2006), suicide rates of specific Asian American groups should be compared with the suicide rates of that cultural group back in Asia (e.g., comparing suicide rates of Chinese Americans in the U.S. with those of Chinese in China) and referencing both groups back to the European American groups. Using such a triangulation method would help us identify key factors related to suicide that are associated with the immigration or ethnic minority variance (e.g., difference between Chinese Americans and European Americans) versus the culture or nationality variance (difference between Chinese Americans and Chinese). For example, if it is found that suicide rates among Chinese Americans are higher than those of European Americans and yet the rates for Chinese in China are significantly lower than those of European Americans, it may be useful to explore what aspects of Chinese Americans' experiences in the U.S. is contributing to the higher than normal rates found in their country of origin.

Using the comparative framework, research is also needed to determine if the same risk factors for European Americans also hold true for Asian Americans. For example, research has consistently found that clinical depression is a risk factor for suicide for European Americans. Is this relationship also true for Asian Americans? Similarly, alcohol or substance use disorders, history of trauma and abuse, and major physical illnesses have proven to be important risk factors for European Americans. Are these risk factors culture-general and apply to Asian Americans as well? Do media factors also facilitate cluster suicide among Asian Americans? Do major losses and separation serve as a common pathway to suicide for Asian Americans as they do for European Americans?

Understanding suicidality among Asian Americans is only one side of the coin. The other side involves investigating protective factors associated with suicide among Asian Americans. This means broadening the scope of research to include more theoretical, conceptual, and integrative work focused on the effective and culturally sound conceptualization and intervention implementation for suicidality issues among Asian Americans. For example, the diathesis-stress model of suicide, which states that cognitively rigid individuals can become overwhelmed and incapable of coming up with appropriate solutions, has yet to be studied among ethnic groups—let alone Asian Americans specifically.

Additionally, future research targeted at investigating protective factors against suicide among Asian Americans needs to specifically look at cultural variables as important mediating factors in the intervention and prevention process. These protective and cultural factors need to be examined as to whether they are specific and unique to Asian Americans or whether they apply to other ethnic groups. It is not enough to simply correlate these cultural and protective factors with lowered suicide risk among Asians. This research needs to be taken further in order to develop culturally effective and sensitive theories. These theories will then need to be empirically tested and validated on how and why these cultural protective factors buffer suicide risk in Asian Americans.

The current studies on suicidality among Asian Americans have investigated and discovered some common and robust findings (e.g., the finding of the opposite trends for males and females in completed suicide attempts versus completed suicides). These findings need to be replicated and examined in both patient and nonpatient populations. Often, suicide research has targeted solely high-risk populations. Therefore, future research efforts can be targeted at less vulnerable groups, comparing them with the high-risk populations (e.g., middle-aged Asian Americans to elderly or adolescent Asian Americans).

At the same time, it would be important to examine the impact of more macrolevel phenomena on suicide among Asian Americans. For example, in an intriguing study, Mullen & Smyth (2004) found that the suicide rates for ethnic immigrant groups in the U.S. were significantly predicted by the negativity of the ethnophaulisms (slurs) used to refer to those ethnic immigrant groups. Moreover, the authors found that this pattern was obtained even after taking into account the suicide rates for those ethnic immigrant groups in their countries of origin. It is proposed that a fuller understanding of suicide among Asian Americans require that research examine causal and contributing factors along multiple levels of analysis that extend from the microperspective of an individual's mental state to the interpersonal dynamics of marriage and parent–child relationships as well as social and cultural groupings. Evidence for cluster suicides as well as the findings from Mullen & Smyth's (2004) study caution against viewing suicide mainly as a problem of individual psychopathology.

Throughout the chapter it has been highlighted that cultural factors are imperative to understanding and also preventing suicide among Asian Americans. Some of these factors have included issues such as acculturation; family ties, obligations and loyalty; and religiosity. For example, future research can be used to investigate acculturation as a confounding variable on suicide, especially as acculturation is an important cultural identity and moderator variable among Asian American samples. The dynamics and influence of Asian American family ties are high in this population and so future research can investigate the effects of emotional scares or psychological pressures associated with parental/family expectations on suicidality. These cultural factors can help explain the risks associated with suicidality, as well as the protective influences buffering against suicide risk among Asian Americans. Another example involves examining religiosity as a protective factor against suicide, especially as many Asian Americans consider religion an important part of their Asian values and cultures.

□ Conclusion

This chapter has reviewed several areas within the field of suicide research among Asian Americans and even Pacific Islanders. Unfortunately, a limited amount of information is available on this subject for this population, so a review of any available information will prove beneficial in improving our understanding of this phenomenon. With more understating, professionals can be better able to develop and implement effective and appropriate interventions and treatments. One finding that stands out is that there are potentially significant differences among the Asian American ethnic communities. This may be explained in part by the nature of inquiry in this area, as some of the data on suicide among Asian Americans examined in this chapter has come from epidemiological studies. One problem with epidemiological studies of suicide is that they often yield divergent findings, and Moscicki (1989) suggests several reasons for this: (1) underlying populations surveyed may differ from one another in terms of ethnicity, urbanity, or sociodemographics and (2) differences in methodology, such as sampling techniques, instrumentation, and secular trends or cohort effects.

Ultimately, the importance of research on suicide among Asian Americans lies in the end product of helping practitioners intervene and treat suicidal behaviors and thoughts among Asian American clients. Takahashi (1989) found that those clients seeking treatment from mental-health workers as a result of racial identity and discrimination issues were significantly more suicidal than those individuals not experiencing these issues. Only four of 28 items on a problem checklist in the study were significantly related to high degrees of suicidality: racial identity; experiencing discrimination; anxiety, fears, or worries; and depression. Takahashi made several recommendations regarding treatment of Asian Americans that stress the importance of Asian cultural practices and suicidal symptomatology.

Akutsu & Chu (2006) investigated and explained the clinical problems associated with Asian Americans overcoming both cultural and institutional barriers in order to seek professional help associated with suicidal issues. This was investigated across seven different Asian groups (Chinese, Japanese, Filipino, Korean, Vietnamese, and Cambodian) and the authors found both similarities and differences with regard to help-seeking behaviors. These attitudes were found to be dependent on level of acculturation or familiarity with Western concepts of mental health constructs. The implications of this study are clear, especially with regard to providing culturally appropriate and effective treatments and interventions. The authors suggest the following, just to name a few: developing culturally competent skills to meet the needs of Asian Americans regardless of their acculturation level, improving outreach efforts and education programs targeted specifically for Asian ethnic groups, improving the quality of the initial contact with the Asian client so that restricted or underreported clinical symptoms can be probed and revealed, and increasing epidemiological data-driven research (Akutsu & Chu, 2006).

□ Case Study

Introduction

To serve as an illustration of the some of the key variables related to our understanding of suicide among Asian Americans, the chapter will end with a composite case study. The description of the clinical case will be followed by a discussion of some of these variables that clinicians should attend to in dealing with suicide assessment, treatment and prevention among Asian Americans.

Description of Case Study

Ming is a 15-year-old, Buddhist, first-generation Chinese American who moved to the U.S. with her family about 4 years ago. Ming comes from a close-knit family and is the oldest of three girls. Although she has been in the country for 4 years, Ming is experiencing culture shock and is struggling between the conflicts associated with both cultures. She has recently found out that she is attracted to other women and so feels torn about these feelings as a result of both religious and cultural expectations. She struggles with coming out and fears about how this will affect her family and community—especially as it will bring shame to her and those close to her. She is feeling overwhelmed with school and with everything else around her. She can't seem to function and fears that her failure will bring added shame and disgrace to her family. She is at a loss, and she does not know what to do. She feels alone and that no one is able to understand her—including her family, as they are unaware of her struggles. She also feels as if she cannot let her family know as they would be disappointed. As a result, she has become depressed, lonely, and feels guilty for having these issues. Her only way out seems to be suicide and this is something she has contemplated often.

Discussion of Case Study

A search of the literature has suggested that age and gender are important variables to consider for suicide among Asian Americans. Ming is a 15-year-old female adolescent, which puts her in the high-risk category. She is clearly depressed, unmotivated, and experiencing acculturation stress. She just moved to the U.S. with her immediate family so she misses her extended family and country of origin. She is trying to adjust to her new life yet she is also confused as she feels conflicted between the two ethnic and cultural identities. This changing individual and community identity, social isolation, and familial misunderstandings all lead to a state of her experiencing psychological distress and depression.

Depression and these added cultural stresses compound the usual stresses associated with Ming's adolescent growth and development, and these can ultimately result in her having low self-esteem or self-dislike, self-blame, and self-criticism. Also seen from the above literature review, is the fact that Asian Americans have it worse as they are considered the model minority group. This will only add further stress beyond that associated with family expectations, cultural values, guilt, shame, embarrassment, and disappointment experienced by Ming.

Religion and spirituality are important tenets of the Asian culture. Ming is Buddhist and so even contemplating suicide would mean that she would have to flout the teachings and practices of her religion, which is against suicide as it disrupts the cycle of life. Ming is also experiencing distress with regard to her sexual orientation. Clearly, she admits being attracted to other women, which could add more pressure for her as, in general, the Asian community is less tolerant of GLBTQ issues. In addition, this coming-out process would bring further shame and disappointment to her family.

☐ Conclusion

This chapter ends with the following quote from a young Asian American with regard to her sister's suicide:

> I knew of the pressure … as a child of parents whose cultures and expectations were alien to ours. I know of the difficulty in trying to assimilate in a culture that rejects minorities, of the guilt in feeling I've

let down the most important people in my life because I did not accept their value system entirely, of trying to find my place in the world as a young Asian American and a human being. All I can say is, I survived. Lots of us did. My little sister didn't (Cubarrubia, 1994, p. 5).

These are painful words, ones filled with turmoil, guilt and loss. This simple, short, but poignant statement demonstrates some of the cultural issues associated with suicide among Asian Americans described above; such as acculturation/assimilation, loss of face, family obligations and loyalty, and social pressures such as discrimination and prejudice. The review of the literature suggests that some answers are present, but there are still many more to investigate and conceptualize, especially if professionals can begin to help individuals like this girl, her family, her sister who committed suicide, and her community.

☐ References

Akutsu, P. D. & Chu, J. P. (2006). Clinical problems that initiate professional help-seeking behaviors from Asian Americans. *Professional Psychology: Research and Practice, 37*(4), 407–415.

Almeida, R. (1996). Hindu, Christian, and Muslim families. In McGoldrick & J. Giordano (Eds.), *Ethnicity and family therapy* (2nd ed.) (pp. 395–423). New York: Guilford Press.

Bartels, S. J., Coakley, E., & Oxman, T. E. (2002). Suicidal and death ideation in older primary care patients with depression, anxiety, and at-risk alcohol use. *American Journal of Geriatric Psychiatry, Vol 10*(4), 417–427, Special issue: Suicidal behaviors in older adults.

Baruth, L. G., & Manning, M. L. (2003). *Multicultural counseling and psychotherapy* (3rd ed.). Upper Saddle River, NJ: Merrill Prentice Hall.

Beautrais, A. L. (2006). Suicide in Asia. *Crisis 27*(2), 55–57.

Berry, J. W. (1995). Psychology of acculturation. In N. R. Goldberger & J. B. Veroff (Eds.), *The culture and psychology reader* (pp. 457–488). New York: New York University Press.

Berry, J. W., Kim, U., Minde, T., & Mok, D. (1987). Comparative studies of acculturative stress. *International Migration Review, 21*, 491–511.

Bhugra, D. (2002). Suicidal behavior in South Asians in the UK. *Crisis, 23*(3), 108–113.

Braun, K. L., & Nichols, R. (1997). Death and dying in four Asian American cultures: A descriptive study. *Death Studies, 21*, 327–359.

Burr, J. (2002). Cultural stereotypes of women from South Asian communities: Mental health care professional's explanations for patterns of suicide and depression. *Social Science and Medicine, 55*, 835–845.

Chun, K. M., Organista, P. B., & Marin, G. (2003). Acculturation: Advances in theory, measurement and applied research. Washington, D.C.: American Psychological Association.

Cubarrubia, N. (1994, Winter). If we look out for each other, we can make it through. *The Asian American Voice*, pp. 4–5.

Chen, H., Guarnaccia, P. J., & Chung, H. (2003). Self-attention as a mediator of cultural influences on depression. *International Journal of Social Psychiatry, 49*, 192–203.

Cho, Y-B. (2003). Suicidal ideation, acculturative stress and perceived social support among Korean adolescents. *Dissertation Abstracts International: Section B: The Sciences and Engineering, 63* (8–B), pp. 3907.

Diego, A. T., Yamamoto, J., Nguyen, L. H., & Hifumi, S. S. (1994). Suicide in the elderly: Profiles of Asians and Whites. *Asian American and Pacific Islander Journal of Health, 2*, 49–57.

Fugita, S.S. (1990). Asian/Pacific-American mental health: Some needed research in epidemiology and service utilization. In F. C. Serafica, A. I. Schwebel, R. K. Russell, P. D. Isaac, & L. B. Myers (Eds.), *Mental health of ethic minorities* (pp. 66–83). New York: Praeger.

Gim Chung, R. H. (2001). Gender, ethnicity, and acculturation in intergenerational conflict of Asian American college students. *Cultural Diversity and Ethnic Minority Psychology, 7*, 376–386.

Greene, B. (1994). Lesbian women of color: Triple jeopardy. In L. Comas-Diaz (Ed.), *Women of color: Integrating ethnic and gender identities in psychotherapy* (pp. 389–427). New York: Guilford Press.

Greene, B. (1997). Ethnic minority lesbians and gay men: Mental health and treatment issues. In B. Greene (Ed.), *Ethnic and cultural diversity among lesbians and gay men* (pp. 216–239). Thousand Oaks, CA: Sage.

Gregersen, A. T., Nebeker, R. S., Seely, K. L., & Lambert, M. J. (2004). Social validation of the Outcome Questionnaire–45: An assessment of Asian and Pacific Islander College students. *Journal of Multicultural Counseling and Development, 32*, 194–205.

Grunbaum, J. A., Lowry, R., Kann, L., & Pateman, B. (2000). Prevalence of health risk behaviors among Asian American/Pacific Islander high school students. *Journal of Adolescent Health, 27*, 322–330.

Heikkinen, M., Aro, H., & Lonnqvist, J. (1993). Life events and social support in suicide. *Suicide and Life-Threatening Behavior, 23*, 343–358.

Hinsch, B. (1990). *Passions of the cut sleeve: The male homosexual tradition in China.* Berkeley: University of California Press.

Huang, L. N. (1997). Asian American adolescents. In E. Lee (Ed.) *Working with Asian Americans: A guide for clinicians* (pp. 175–195). New York: The Guilford Press.

Jha, A. (2001). Depression and suicidality in Asian Indian students. Dissertation Abstracts International: Section B: The Sciences and Engineering. Vol 62(3–B), pp. 1311.

Jonnalagadda, S. S., & Diwan, S. (2005). Health Behaviors, Chronic Disease Prevalence and Self-Rated Health of Older Asian Indian Immigrants in the U.S. *Journal of Immigrant Health, 7*, 75–83.

Kalish, R. A. (1968). Suicide: An ethnic comparison in Hawaii: *Bulletin of Suicidology*, December, 37–43.

Kearney, L. L., Draper, M., & Baron, A. (2005). Counseling utilization by ethnic minority college students. *Cultural Diversity and Ethnic Minority Psychology, 11*, 272–285.

Kennedy, M. A., Parhar, K. K., Samra, J., & Gorzalka, B. (2005). Suicide Ideation in Different Generations of Immigrants. *Canadian Journal of Psychiatry, 50*, 353–356.

Kisch, J., Leino, E. Vi., & Silverman, M. M.; (2005). Aspects of suicidal behavior, depression, and treatment in college students: Results from the Spring 2000 National College Health Assessment Survey, *Suicide and Life-Threatening Behavior 35*, 3–13.

Kok, Lee-peng (1988). Race, religion, and suicide attempters in Singapore. *Social Psychiatry & Psychiatric Epidemiology, 23*, 236–239.

Lau, A. S., Jernewall, N. M., Zane, N., & Myers, H. F. (2002). Correlates of suicidal behaviors among Asian American outpatient youths. *Cultural Diversity & Ethnic Minority Psychology, 8*, 199–213.

Leach, M. M. (2006). *Cultural diversity and suicide: Ethnic, religious, gender, and sexual orientation perspectives*. Binghamton, NY: Haworth Press.

Leong, F. T. L. & Zhang (2006). Role of cultural contexts in help-seeking attitudes: A comparison of Asians and Asian Americans. Colloquium presented in the Department of Psychology, Michigan State University, East Lansing, MI, February, 2006.

Lester, D. (1992). Suicide among Asian Americans and social deviancy. *Perceptual and Motor Skills, 75*, 1134.

Lester, D. (1994). Differences in the epidemiology of suicide in Asian Americans by nation of origin. *Omega: Journal of Death & Dying, 29*, 89–93.

Lester, D. & Walker, R. L. (2006). The stigma of attempting suicide and the loss to suicide prevention efforts. *The Journal of Crisis Intervention and Suicide Prevention, 27*(3), 147–148.

Liem, R., Lim, B. A., & Liem, J. H. (2000). Acculturation and emotion among Asian Americans. *Cultural Diversity and Ethnic Minority Psychology, 6*, 13–31.

Liu, W. M., Pope-Davis, D. B., Nevitt, J., & Toporek, R. L. (1999). Understanding the function of acculturation and predjudicial attitudes among Asian Americans. *Cultural Diversity and Ethnic Minority Psychology, 5*, 317–328.

Liu, W. T., Yu, E. S. H., Chang, C. F, & Fernandez, M. (1990). The mental health of Asian American teenagers: A research challenge. In A. Rubin, & L. Davis (Eds.), *Ethnic issues in adolescent mental health* (pp. 92–112). Thousand Oaks, CA: Sage Publications.

Mayer, P. & Ziaian, T. (2002). Suicide, gender, and age variations in India: Are women in Indian society protected from suicide? *Crisis, 23*(3), 98–103.

McKenzie, K., Serfaty, M., & Crawford, M. (2003). Suicide in ethnic minority groups. *British Journal of Psychiatry, 183*, 100–101.

Mehta, S. (1998). Relationship between acculturation and mental health for Asian Indian immigrants in the U.S. *Genetic, Social, & General Psychology Monographs, 124*, 61–78.

Mingzhao, F., Congpei, L, Jueiji, W., & Enyu, Z. (1992). Suicidal behaviour in China. In K. L. Peng & W–S. Tseng (Eds.), *Suicidal behaviour in the Asia-Pacific region* (pp. 58–68). Singapore: Singapore University Press.

Morrison, L. L., & Downey, D. L. (2000). Racial differences in self-disclosure of suicide ideation and reasons for living: Implications for training. *Cultural Diversity and Ethnic Minority Psychology, 6*, 374–386.

Morris, J. F., Waldon, C. R., & Rothblum, E. D. (2001). A model of predictors and outcomes of outness among lesbian and bisexual women. *American Orthopsychiatric Association, Inc, 71*, 61–71.

Moscicki, E. K. (1989). Epidemiologic surveys as tools for studying suicidal behavior: A review. *Suicide and Life-Threatening Behavior, 9*, 131–146.

Muehlenkamp, J. J., Gutierrez, P. M., Osman, A., & Barrios, F. X. (2005). Validation of the Positive and Negative Suicide Ideation (PANSI) inventory in a diverse sample of young adults. *Journal of Clinical Psychology, 61*(4), 431–445.

Mullen, B. & Smyth, J. (2004). Immigrant suicide rates as a function of ethnophaulisms: Hate speech predicts death. *Psychosomatic Medicine, 66*, 343–348.

Nakajima, G. A., Chan, Y. H., & Lee, K. (1996). Mental health issues for gay and lesbian Asian Americans. In R. P. Cabaj & T. S. Stein (Eds.), *Textbook of homosexuality and mental health* (pp. 563–581). Washington, D.C.: American Psychiatric Association.

Nishimura, S. T., Goebert, D. A., Ramisetty-Mikler, S., & Caetano, A. (2005). Adolescent alcohol use and suicide indicators among adolescents in Hawaii. *Cultural Diversity and Ethnic Minority Psychology, 11*(4), 309–320.

Noh, E. S. (2003). Suicide among Asian American women: Influences of racism and sexism on suicide subjectification. *Dissertation Abstracts International Section A: Humanities and Social Sciences*, 64(2–A), 2003, pp. 675.

Paniagua, F. A. (2005). Some thoughts on the "staircase to terrorism." *American Psychologist, 60*, 1038–1039.

Pinhey, T. K., & Millman, S. R. (2004). Asian/Pacific Islander adolescent sexual orientation and suicide risk in Guam. *American Journal of Public Health, 94*, 1204–1206.

Range, L. M., Leach, M. M., McIntyre, D., Posey-Deters, P. B., Marion, M. S., Kovac, S. H., Banos, J. H., & Vigil, J. (1999). Multicultural perspectives on suicide. *Aggression and Violent Behavior, 4*(4), 413–430.

Richards, P. S., & Bergin, A. E. (2000). *Handbook of psychotherapy and religious diversity*. Washington, D.C.: American Psychological Association.

Rudd, M. D. (1989). The prevalence of suicidal ideation among college students. *Suicide and Life-Threatening Behavior, 19*, 173–183.

Salgado de Snyder, V. N. (1987). Factors associated with acculturative stress and depressive symptomatology among married Mexican immigrant women. *Psychology of Women Quarterly, 11*, 475–488.

Shiang, J., Blinn, R., & Bonger, B., Stephens, B., Allison, D., & Schatzberg, A. (1997). Suicide in San Francisco, CA: A comparison of Caucasian and Asian groups, 1987–1994. *Suicide and Life Threatening Behavior, 27*, 80–91.

Sodowsky, G. R. & Lai, E. W. M. (1997). Asian immigrant variables and structural models of cross-cultural distress. In A. Booth (Ed.). *International migration and family change: The experience of U. S. immigrants.* Mahwah, New Jersey: Lawrence Erlbaum Associates.

Sohng, S. & Icard, L. D. (1996). A Korean gay man in the U.S.: Toward a Cultural context for social service. In J. F. Longres (Ed.), *Men of Color: A context for service to homosexually active men* (pp. 115–137). New York, England: Harrington Park Press, Haworth Press.

Sue, D. W., & Sue, D. (2003). *Counseling the culturally diverse: Theory and practice* (4th ed.). New York: John Wiley & Sons, Inc.

Takahashi, Y. (1989). Suicidal Asian patients: Recommendations for treatment. *Suicide and Life Threatening Behavior, 19,* 305–313.

U.S. Bureau of the Census. (2004). *We the people: Asians in the U.S.* http://www.census.gov/prod/2004pubs/censr–17.pdf. Last accessed December 28, 2004.

Ward, C., & Kennedy, A. (1994). Acculturation strategies, psychological adjustment, and sociocultural competence during cross-cultural transitions. *International Journal of Intercultural Relations, 18,* 329–343.

Wyche, K. F. & Rotheram-Borus, M. J. (1990). Suicidal behavior among minority youth in the U.S. In A. R. Stiffman & L. E. Davis (Eds.), *Ethnic issues in adolescent mental health* (pp. 323–338). Newbury Park, CA: Sage Publications.

Yamamoto, J. (1976). Japanese American suicides in Los Angeles. In J. Westermeyer (Ed.), *Anthropology and mental health* (pp. 29–35). Chicago: Mouton Publishers.

Yang, B. & Clum, G. A. (1994). Life stress, social support, and problem-solving skills predictive of depressive symptoms, hopelessness, and suicide ideation in an Asian student population: A test of a model. *Suicide and Life-Threatening Behavior. 24*, 127–139.

Yeh, C. J., (2003). Age, acculturation, cultural adjustment, and mental health symptoms of Chinese, Korean, and Japanese immigrant youth. *Cultural Diversity and Ethnic Minority Psychology Journal, 9,* 34–48.

Suicide Among Indigenous Pacific Islanders in the United States

A Historical Perspective

Iwalani R.N. Else and Naleen N. Andrade

□ Introduction

In Hawai'i, someone dies from suicide every three days (Galanis, 2006). Suicide is the final, irreversible act that is sudden and devastating to those left behind. Scientists, clinicians, and lay people see suicide as a symptom, an end result, or a choice that emerges out of malfunctioning social systems, overwhelming psychosocial adversity, or unrelieved mental and behavioral health problems. Determining the epidemiology, along with the biological, psychological, social, developmental and cultural factors that underpin suicide is needed in order to reduce and hopefully eliminate suicide morbidity and mortality.

Suicide remains a serious public health concern in the U.S. In 2003, the suicide rates were 10.73 per 100,000, (Centers for Disease Control, 2006a) which is three times higher than homicides and twice as high as deaths from HIV/AIDS (National Institute of Mental Health [NIMH], 2004). Males have higher rates of completed suicide (4:1) while females have higher rates for attempts (3:1) (NIMH, 2003). Clinical anecdotes from those who survive a suicide attempt reveal that they are unable to see a way to escape their current situation, making suicide seem like the only option to relieve their pain.

Given the above knowledge and findings, why, and more importantly, how is it, that over the past six decades suicide has become the fastest growing cause of death facing youth in America (U.S. Public Health Service, 1999)? Youth suicide in the U.S. has nearly tripled from 1952–1996 alone, and from 1980–1996, suicide rates among 15–19-year-olds increased by 14% and for 10–14-year-olds increased 100% (U.S. Public Health Service, 1999). Similar patterns and trends exist among some indigenous Pacific Islander populations. For example, data comparing age patterns reveals a shift to younger suicides in Western Samoa and Micronesia (Booth, 1999) and in Hawai 'i (Galanis, 2006).

Purpose of this Chapter

This chapter has five main aims. First, it provides a brief history of U.S. colonial history in the Pacific and the resulting effects of that colonization. Second, it reviews the existing literature on the epidemiology of completed and attempted suicides, as well as common patterns associated with gender and age for indigenous Pacific Islanders living within the U.S. and its affiliated Pacific territories and nations. Third, it presents archival data on completed and attempted suicide for Native Hawaiians compared with other major ethnic groups in the State of Hawai'i. Fourth, it summarizes and highlights the findings of two epidemiological studies that assess suicidal behaviors and related psychosocial factors, and measures of psychopathology among two large (Study #1 N = 4,182, from 1992–1996 and Study #2 N = 1,172, from 2000–2004) community samples of youth in Hawai'i. Finally, the authors present social-historical factors to explain suicide phenomenology among Pacific Islanders who—while small in numbers when compared with the total U.S. population—possess striking health disparities when compared with other populations within the U.S. and in their island homelands.

Suicide among U.S. Pacific Islanders

Epidemiological studies conducted among indigenous populations in Hawai'i and the Pacific show pronounced spikes in completed suicide rates among youth, followed by declining rates through middle age and the elderly, without the bimodal second spike among the elderly that is commonly seen in the general U.S. population (Booth, 1999; Hunter and Harvey, 2002; State of Hawai'i Department of Health [DOH], 2004; Tsuang et al., 1992; Yuen, Yahata and Nahulu, 1999). Unfortunately, much of the U.S. suicide data for Pacific Islanders are aggregated into the broad category of "Asian Americans and Pacific Islanders," consequently losing important differences *between* the two groups. A literature search revealed that disaggregate suicide data on U.S. Pacific Islander populations are very limited. Where data are disaggregated, Asian groups have been found to have substantially lower rates of completed suicide than those of Whites (DHHS, 1999), while rates of completed suicide among Pacific Island populations are some of the highest in the world (Booth, 1999).

Pacific Islander Ethnic Groups, Populations, and Social Histories

The term "Pacific Islander" is part of the "Asian and Pacific Islander" racial category established in 1977 by the U.S. Office of Management, Directive 15. White, Black, American Indian or Alaskan Native, and Hispanic are the other four federal racial categories. For this paper, Pacific Islanders refers to descendants of the original peoples of lands claimed by the U.S., which include Hawai'i, Guam, American Samoa, the Commonwealth of the Northern Marianas and the Pacific Island nations of Micronesia, which include: the Federated States of Micronesia, the Republic of Belau (Palau), and the Republic of the Marshall Islands. Pacific Islander groups within the U.S., whose origins come from the original people of lands not claimed by the U.S. (e.g., Tonga, Tahiti, Tokelau, Fiji, Papua New Guinea, Solomon Islands, Vanuatu, etc.), will not be discussed here. The U.S. 2000 Census showed that within the U.S. there are 874,414 (0.3% of the total U.S. population of 281.4 million) Pacific Islanders, of which 401,162 (45.9%) are Native Hawaiian, 133,281 (15.2%) are Samoan, and 115,582 (13.2%) are from Micronesia (92,611 Chamorro; 616 Northern Marianas; 2,121 Federated States of Micronesia; 6,650 Marshallese, 3,469 Belauan; and 9,940 nonspecified Micronesian). While grouped in a federal racial/ethnic category with Asians, Pacific Islanders within the U.S. face a commonly overlooked but salient distinction that affects their social, political, economic, and cultural development within American society. Unlike Asians who share a common history of immigration to America, Pacific Islanders are not immigrants, but indigenous peoples whose health disparities, including suicide rates, mirror American Indians and Alaskan Natives (DHHS, 2001).

Native Hawaiians

Native Hawaiians (hereafter called Hawaiians) settled in Hawai'i as early as the 8th century from the Marquesas and the Society Islands, and later from Tahiti in the 12th and 13th centuries (Daws, 1968, pp. xii–xiii). Hawai'i has eight main islands located in the middle of the northern Pacific Ocean, over 2,300 miles from the nearest land mass, and is described as one of the most remote places on earth. Hawai'i was accidentally discovered in 1778 by British Captain James Cook while he sought a faster Northwest Passage to outrace the Portuguese, Dutch, and Spanish in ocean trade routes. The population of the state of Hawai'i is 1.3 million, with 19.8% (257,400) identifying as Hawaiian. Of the 401,162 Hawaiians in the U.S., 64% live in Hawai'i. Like other indigenous populations in the U.S.—since first contact with Europeans, followed by American traders, whalers, missionaries, and bankers during the 18th and 19th centuries—Hawaiians have sustained devastating loss of their population from infectious diseases, and loss of their lands and sovereignty rights when their monarchy was overthrown. Accompanying these losses was the disintegration of their social, cultural, and healing systems (Andrade, 2006). Following the overthrow of the Hawaiian monarchy, Hawai'i became a U.S. territory in 1898. When the Japanese Empire attacked Pearl Harbor on December 7th, 1941, Hawai'i fell under U.S. military rule when martial law was declared for most of World War II (1941–1944). In 1959, Hawai'i was admitted into the Union and became America's 50th state.

Indigenous Peoples of the Pacific Island Territories and Nations

The indigenous peoples living within the U.S. Pacific territories and nations are U.S. nationals or citizens, depending on the compacts and free association agreements between their governments and the U.S. These include American Samoans, the Chamorro of Guam, and peoples of the Federated States of Micronesia, the Commonwealth of the Northern Marianas, the Republic of the Marshall Islands, and the Republic of Belau. Each territory and nation has its own distinct, yet similar social history of foreign colonization beginning with Europeans (Spanish, Portuguese, British, and German), followed by Japanese, and finally Americans. Their history is punctuated during much of the 20th century by global warfare with World War I (1914–1918), World War II (1941–1945), and a four-decades-old Cold War struggle (1946–1991), particularly military presence, occupation, and subsequent weapons testing and land destruction (Cowan, 2004; Henningham, 1992; Keegan, 1998; Larcy, 1994; Simon, 1997).

American Samoans

Migrating from the islands of east Melanesia, Samoans settled in Samoa in 1000 B.C. First contact with Europeans occurred in 1722, after which followed a series of international acquisitions by the U.S., Germany, and Great Britain. The western Samoan islands went to Germany, and the five eastern islands were annexed to the U.S. beginning in 1900. The eastern islands became the U.S. territory of American Samoa. During World War II, U.S. Marines stationed in American Samoa outnumbered the Samoan population, resulting in profound effects on the indigenous population and society. The U.S. Navy administered American Samoa until 1951, when administrative oversight was transferred to the U.S. Department of the Interior until 1977, when Samoans elected their first governor. An estimated 57,291 Samoans live in American Samoa, where the official languages are Samoan and English. American Samoans living in Hawai'i and the continental U.S. are not U.S. citizens, but U.S. nationals who can freely enter the U.S. and return to their homeland. They settle predominantly in Hawai'i and California. They travel between the U.S. and American Samoa with relative ease, living within large extended family enclaves that maintain their language, traditional foods, and cultural traditions and practices within U.S. Urban centers are often clustered closely around a Samoan church. U.S. Census 2000 data on Samoans include both Western and American Samoans who reside in the U.S., but not Samoans residing in American Samoa (U.S. Census, 2005).

Micronesians

Spread across the East Central Pacific in a geographic area roughly the size of the continental U.S. is a myriad of volcanic islands and coral atolls formerly called Micronesia ("many small islands"). Micronesia shares a common history of U.S. military occupation during and after World War II through the United Nations Trust Territory of the Pacific Islands (Trust Territories), shown in Figure 7.1.

Migrating from Southeast Asia in successive waves, the first Micronesians began settling in this vast expanse of islands from about 1500 B.C., beginning with the islands of Belau and continuing across the eastern Pacific from A.D. 500–1200. The term "Micronesian" is used as a generic racial/ethnic category that may include: Chamorro, Saipanese, Kiribati, Marshallese, Polynesians such as the Kapingamarangi, and Carolinians, named for the Caroline Islands, who comprise Belauans, Pohnpaeans, Chuukese, Kosraeans, and Yapese. The official languages of all these Pacific island nations are their respective native language and English.

Micronesians, like Samoans, settle predominantly in Hawai'i and California, living primarily in urban centers. They travel between the U.S. and Micronesia with relative ease, constrained mostly by sparse economic resources. Major reasons for traveling to the U.S. are tertiary healthcare needs and university education. The oral or written history of Micronesia before European contact is sparse due to a combination of factors. These include foreign colonizers who brought deadly epidemics of infectious diseases and who imposed foreign social and political systems that disre-

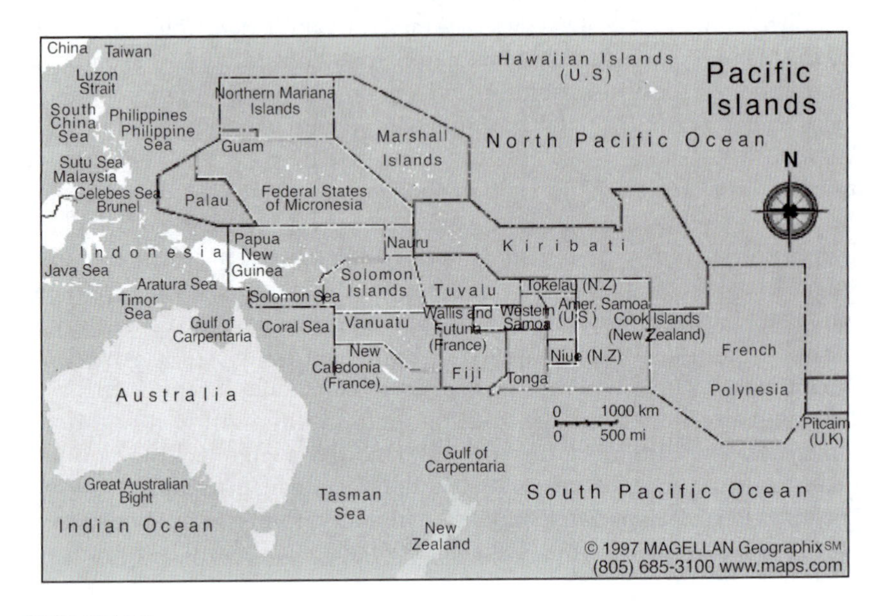

FIGURE 7.1

garded and eroded the indigenous lifestyles, as well as the insular effects of geographic remoteness within the world's largest ocean.

Archeological evidence, such as the canal system and complex of megalithic basalt structures at Nan Madol, Pohnpei, indicate a relatively sophisticated society established in the 12th or 13th century. Oral traditions say Nan Madol was a sacred place—inaccessible to the common populace—from which Sandeleur rulers governed, conducted religious and funerary practices, resided, and were buried after death in elaborate basalt tombs (Andrade, personal communication with Pohnpean elder on Nan Madol field trip, 1982). Geographically, Guam is situated within the Northern Mariana Island Chain, but is not part of the Commonwealth.

Guam—Chamorro

Guam was controlled by Spain from 1668–1898, after which Spain ceded it to the U.S. following the Spanish-American War. The Spanish influence still pervades Guam society, where the majority of the populace is Catholic. On December 8, 1941, the day after the attack on Pearl Harbor, Guam was attacked and seized by the Japanese and was recaptured by the U.S. military in 1944. From 1945 through 1950 Guam was under U.S. military control, with the military taking over one third of the island. In 1950, the U.S. made Guam a territory and transferred its oversight from the Navy to the U.S. Department of the Interior. The people of Guam are U.S. citizens.

Guam's indigenous people are the Chamorro, who make up 42.2% (65,243) of Guam's population of 154,805.

Commonwealth of the Northern Mariana Islands—Chamorro and Carolineans

Like Guam, Spain and its Jesuit missionaries occupied the Northern Marianas until 1899 when Spain sold the islands to Germany. Germany ruled the Northern Marianas until 1914, after which the islands were ceded to Japan at the end of World War I. During World War II, Japan stationed 30,000 troops, along with hundreds of settlers from Japan, on the main island of Saipan to halt the advance of U.S. troops. On June 15, 1944, the U.S. Marines and Army infantry landed on the island, and after 25 days of fierce fighting in the Battle of Saipan, seized the island from Japan on July 9, 1944. The Battle of Saipan is notorious for two mass suicide events that stunned American soldiers. On July 7th, without ammunition and facing defeat at the hands of the Americans, the commander of the Japanese forces ordered his remaining 3,000 soldiers on a suicide night charge, and then killed himself. Armed with swords, knifes, sticks, and bayonets, nearly all of the Japanese soldiers were killed. During the remaining two days of the battle an estimated 1,000 civilians—Japanese, Okinawans, Korean slave laborers, as well as indigenous Saipanese (Chamorro and Carolineans)—jumped off the sea cliffs of Marpi and drowned themselves in the ocean in a mass suicide rather than surrender to the Americans. In 1947 the U.S. began administering the islands as part of the Trust Territories. In 1986, following an 11-year transition; the Northern Marianas became a self-governing U.S. Commonwealth. The population of the Northern Marianas is 69,221, of which Chamorro make up about 27.6% (19,132), and Carolinians represent 5% (3,461).

The Federated States of Micronesia (FSM) and the Republic of Belau—Carolineans

These two Pacific nations are part of the Caroline Islands archipelago. Like the Northern Marianas, the Spanish, Germans, and Japanese occupied these two nations in succession. Beginning in September 1944, the U.S. military seized these islands as part of its Pacific advance during World War II. In 1947 both island groups became part of the Trust Territories administered by the U.S. In 1986, the FSM was granted independence under a Compact of Free Association and is self-governing with the U.S. providing defense and economic assistance.

During World War II, Belau was Japan's center of occupation in Micronesia, and the Japanese quickly outnumbered the indigenous population.

The Battle of Belau was supposed to have ended in three days, but lasted three months (September 15–November 25, 1944). Despite its being the center of Japanese occupation, there were no mass suicides by the civilians at Belau. The Japanese commanding general did not commit suicide, and at the end of World War II in 1945, the Japanese returned to Japan. In 1947 Belau also became a part of the Trust Territories. In 1994, Belau became a self-governing republic in free association with the U.S. and is a member of the United Nations. Carolinians, who are the indigenous ethnic population of FSM and Belau, number about 137,000 and are located on more than 930 islands that make up the five large island states within FSM (Kosrae, Pohnpei, Chuuk, and Yap) and the Republic of Belau.

The Republic of the Marshall Islands—Marshallese

Named for the British explorer John Marshall who visited in 1799, the Marshall Islands' colonial history, like other Micronesian nations, began with Spain and was followed by Germany in the late 19th century. Japan's occupation began in 1914 with World War I and continued until World War II, when U.S. Marine and Army forces won major battles at Kwajalein and Enewetak. In 1947 the U.S. began administering the Marshall Islands as part of the Trust Territories. From 1946–1958 the Marshall Islands was the test center for the U.S. military's emerging nuclear weapons program. Forced relocations of entire island populations on the Bikini and Enewetak atolls were followed by nuclear bomb testing that vaporized entire islands and left others uninhabitable from radiation exposure. Military weapons testing continue till the present day at the Kwajalein atoll's missile testing range. In 1986 the Marshall Islands became self-governing as a republic, with the U.S. continuing to provide defense and economic aid. Indigenous Marshallese number approximately 60,000, most of whom live within the Majuro and Kwajalein atolls.

The Effects of Foreign Colonization and Suicide

All U.S. Pacific Islanders share a common history of colonization. Hawaiians' first foreign contact with the British seamen was followed by expanded commerce and trading with other parts of the world (e.g., sandalwood to China, whale oil to Europe and America). This was followed by the iconoclastic rending of the *kapu* system (the Hawaiian spiritual-religious laws and codes of conduct that provided the social structures that ordered Hawaiian society). Deadly infectious disease epidemics brought in on foreign ships—for which traditional native healers had no effective treatments—decimated the native population. Into this sociopolitical, cultural, and clinical vacuum the first company of American Congregational missionaries and physicians entered and provided an alternative way of life, social order, and healing. Along with the pecuniary goals of the American free market, expanding foreign land use and ownership, via large scale sugar cane and pineapple agriculture, set the steps that inevitably led to the overthrow of the Hawaiian monarchy and full expression of American manifest destiny, capitalism, and militarism.

European commerce and trade during the 16th, 17th, and 18th centuries, followed by Japanese—then American—militarism and global dominance during the 19th and 20th centuries were the most powerful catalysts that impacted American Samoa and Micronesia. The fall of the Soviet Union in 1991 ended the Cold War, and left the U.S. (and China) as world super powers. America's new role as a global super power for social democracy facilitated the U.S. to replace its policy of utilitarian and collateral militarism within the Pacific Trust Territories. The U.S. wanted to implement an executive policy to develop an American model of indigenous sovereignty that restored a muted form of self-determination and self-governance within the islands.

An examination of these indigenous populations who are separated by an expanse of ocean, as well as unique languages and customs, will determine how they relate to, conceptualize, and describe the phenomenology of suicide given their resonating histories of foreign occupation and global warfare. In addition, these factors may yield salient social-cultural insights related to suicide and suicidal behaviors. What were the effects—past, present, and future—upon indigenous people whose communal social and economic structures were eliminated by forced military occupation and martial law? How is it that the Japanese cultural belief and practice of ritualized suicide as a sacrifice for honor (e.g., kamikaze pilots, seppuku) motivated the Saipan Japanese commander to kill himself, and the Chamorro and Carolineans of Saipan to jump to their deaths in a mass suicide rather than be taken as American prisoners? Yet, just three months later in the Battle of Belau, neither the Japanese general nor the Carolineans in Belau (the center of Japanese influence with as many Japanese on island as Saipan) resorted to suicide when faced with a three-month American military invasion and subsequent occupation. How has American culture, with its social ideals of individualism, power (having the most advanced military and nuclear arsenal) and dominating economic global markets, affected these indigenous groups, each of whom is trying to develop its unique process and form of self-determination and self-governance? What are the effects given that these groups are no longer able to depend on a communal subsistence economy, are largely dependent on U.S. economic support, and lacking adequate community infrastructure to develop self-sustaining market economies?

Operational Definition of Completed and Attempted Suicide and Self-Harm

According to the Institute of Medicine (2002), a *completed suicide*, or death by suicide, is defined as a self-inflicted injury resulting in death where there is evidence that the act was intentional. *Suicide attempt* is a self-injurious behavior where there is evidence of an intent to kill oneself that does not result in death, which sometimes, but not always, results in injury. Suicide completions and intent are distinct from *deliberate self-harm* (also called *parasuicidal behaviors*), which refers to intentional self-injurious behavior with no intent to die. The self-inflicted injuries run the gamut of lethality from self-mutilation like cutting or battering to taking overdoses, or deliberate acts of recklessness.

☐ Results of Literature Review

The data presented provide a comprehensive review of suicide and suicide-related data on Hawaiian, Samoan and Micronesian populations and includes information on suicide rates and patterns; phenomenology and epidemiology.

Hawai'i–Completed Suicides among Hawaiians

Suicide is the leading cause of injury related death in Hawai'i (Galanis, 2006) and the 11th (9.6 per 100,000, in 2002) leading cause of death in Hawai'i among all deaths (State of Hawai'i Department of Health [DOH], 2002). Suicide rates on the neighbor islands (when compared with O'ahu residents) are 28% higher, with Maui and Hawai'i residents having the highest rates (DOH, 2004). Hanging or suffocation was the most common mechanism (45%), followed by firearm use (24%). From those autopsied on O'ahu from 1997–1999, 64% had at least one negative life event documented, experienced a serious illness (28%), and had a relationship end (27%). One third (31%) tested positive at autopsy for alcohol use, with heavy use more common in youth. One quarter (26%) tested positive for illicit drugs. Most common were methamphetamine (14%), marijuana, (8%), and cocaine (6%). The majority (62%) had a documented history of mental illness and 22% had a previous suicide attempt. The overall rates for completed suicide in Hawai'i have been equal to or greater than the U.S. national average with rates differing by age, gender, and ethnicity.

Suicide in Hawai'i is high among youth and young adults. Among fatal injuries, suicide was the leading cause of death for 25–34-year-olds, 35–44-year-olds, 45–64-year-olds, and the second leading cause of death for 15–24-year-olds (DOH, 2004). Males in Hawai'i complete suicide more often than females at a rate of approximately three to one.

Since 1908, when Hawai'i began collecting suicide statistics, completed-suicide rates for Hawaiians have been increasing (Kalish, 1968; Ryals, 1970). While the overall suicide rate for Hawai'i is comparable to the U.S. average, data from 2000–2004, disaggregated by age and ethnicity, revealed higher rates for younger Hawaiians (ages 15–44) while Caucasians had the highest rates of those 45 years and older (Galanis, 2007).

Completed suicides by Hawaiians exhibit a distinctly different age distribution compared with the bimodal distribution in the U.S. and most Western nations where there is a peak in young adults, leveling out, then another peak in the elderly. By contrast, data from 2000–2004 show that Hawaiians display a sharp increase in suicide rates from adolescence to young adulthood from 16.8/100,000 for 15–24-year-olds, 18.8/100,000 for 25–44-year-olds then 22.2/100,000 for 35–44-year-olds, approximately twice the U.S. national average (Galanis, 2007). Rates drop sharply starting from the mid-40s, and continue to drop in the middle with a small increase in the elderly. Completed suicide in Hawaiians is clearly a phenomenon associated with adolescents and young adults. In the 10–14-year-old group, Hawaiians account for 27% of the population in Hawai'i, but account for 50% of the completed suicides (Yuen, Yahata, and Nahulu, 1999).

Suicide in Pre-Contact Hawai'i

In pre-European-contact Hawai'i, completed suicide rates were rare, but three forms (two ritualistic and one as mythic metaphor) of suicide have been documented through oral and written traditions. Ritual suicide during warfare took two forms. The first involved an *ali'i* (ruling chief) who chooses to submit himself to be killed and offered up as a sacrifice in order to curse and metaphysically attack the enemy who kills you. An example of this involves the consecration of the *heiau* or temple Pu'ukohola, built by Kamehameha I and dedicated to the god of war, *Kū*. The sacrificial offering was his cousin and rival, Keouakūahu'ula, who knew and accepted that he was to be the sacrifice to consecrate this temple that was to give Kamehameha the *mana* (spiritual power) of *Kū* to defeat his enemies and unite the islands into one kingdom. On the morning of his death Keouakūahu'ula bathed then did *'ōmu'o* (to circumcise). He then dressed himself in finery befitting his high rank, removed all weapons from his fleet of double-hulled canoes and went to his death. The offering of his foreskin was to *Uli*, the goddess of sorcerers, who would give him the means to curse and strike down Kamehameha's rule and dynasty (Kamakau, 1992). The second form of ritual suicide, called *moe hoa, moe pūlua,* or *moe pu'u,* occurred when faithful companions accompanied the *ali'i* in death. This form of suicide is recorded by Kamakau (1992, p. 156–157), described as the weaponless warriors of Keouakūahu'ula who died along side their chief.

Aside from these forms of militaristic suicide, legends, folklore, and oral traditions before Western contact in 1778, suicide was uncommon. Epic mythologies that depicted suicide, (e.g., *Holo Mai Pele* [Kanahele, 2001] and *Halemano*), used them as symbolic or metaphorical devices to teach of the ill effects of obsessive, individualistic, and unrequited love, accompanied by the death of self and rebirth through the power of familial love. In *Holo Mai Pele,* Lohiau dies on the island of Kauai as he pines for Pele, who lives five islands away on Hawai'i, and whom he meets and falls in love with in a dream. He is resurrected by the healing powers of Hi'iaka, (Pele's sister) who takes him to Pele.

In another story, much like Lohiau, Halemano dreams of the perfect woman, pines for her and starves himself to death twice (first because he cannot find her, second because he finds her and she rejects him) and is restored to life by his sister (Pukui et al., 1972, 117). In both these myths suicide is not the major theme, but the destructive end result or consequence of love turned inward runs amok. The major social-cultural theme or mythic truths and lessons in these stories are that: (a) obsessive, individualistic love is not *aloha* (the selfless giving of oneself and resources without the expectation of reciprocity), it is an infatuation, a need to possess the image, rather than share the reality of a person; and, (b) it is the selfless giving of *aloha* by one's siblings or family that restores life and health (what Hawaiians called *lōkahi*) by being a distinct, yet complementary part of one's family. These social-cultural mythic truths, along with ritualized suicide in Hawai'i, suggest that for Hawaiians the fundamental expression of health was to establish and maintain healthy, balanced and reciprocal relationships, even beyond death. Where the relationships were broken beyond repair as in warfare, the only recourse was to *'oki* (to sever) the relationship and strike your enemy (through sorcery in the case of Keoua) even after death.

The Pacific—Completed Suicides among Samoans, Micronesians, Marshallese, and Others

In a study examining available data for 13 Pacific Island nations (not including Hawai'i), Booth (1999) examined characteristics of completed suicides including age and gender for the years 1960–1993. Completed suicides in the Pacific, Micronesia (Chuuk in particular), have some of the highest rates in the world (Booth, 1999; Rubinstein, 2002). Booth (1999) reports standardized suicide completion rates for: Western Samoa (34/100,000); Guam (15/100,000); Chuuk State (30/100,000); and Micronesia (20/100,000). The differences in rates increase dramatically when youth (15–24-year-olds) are disaggregated and examined by gender for: Western Samoa (males: 64/100,000 and females: 70/100,000); Guam (males: 49/100,000 and females: 10/100,000); Chuuk State (males: 182/100,000 and females: 12/100,000); and Micronesia (males: 91/100,000 and females: 8/100,000). In Micronesia, the most common method (80%) was hanging from a standing or seated position and leaning into the noose until the oxygen supply was cut off (Hezel, 1989). The second was ingestion of paraquat (a toxic herbicide), most common in Western Samoa (Booth, 1999). Paraquat poison has no known antidote; a fact that many suicide attempters, particularly women and youth, do not know.

Data also show that, like Hawaiians, indigenous Pacific Islanders from Micronesia, Guam, and Western Samoa have rates of completed suicide that increase sharply from adolescence to young adulthood, with rates dropping from the 30-year age group, continuing to drop for the middle aged and elderly (Booth, 1999; Rubinstein, 2002). Rubinstein (1983) compared the distribution of completed suicides for Belau, Yap, Chuuk, Pohnpei, and the Marshall Islands from 1960–1980 and found that male suicide rates rose sharply in adolescence and peaked at ages 15–24. At older ages, the distribution of male suicide rates differed for each island group. Belau, Yap, and Pohnpei showed a sharp decrease after age 39, while Chuuk and the Marshalls showed a second smaller increase in suicide at age 55–60. Through survey research in Micronesia, Rubinstein (1983) suggests that the epidemic increase in adolescent male suicide starting in the 1960s is a cohort effect among youth of the first post-war generation and reflects a breakdown of pre-war Micronesian village subsistence activities, which were organized around communal lineage-houses. Extended networks of intergenerational families have disintegrated, with socialization falling to the immediate family. Intergenerational discord appears to be a trigger for adolescent suicide in Micronesia.

In a series of suicide autopsies with family members of these Micronesian males, Rubinstein (1983) found that family members used the word "anger" toward the family to describe the emotions that immediately led up to the suicide act. Upon further interview, the families' definition of "anger" was similar to the way Americans describe "depression." In addition, the suicide act had the connotation of an appeal to—rather than an angry retaliation toward—older family members (both siblings and parents). Similarly, Nahulu and Yuen (Andrade, 1998, personal communication) noted similar cultural meanings, i.e., "anger" used to describe "depression" and an appeal rather than retaliation, among Hawaiian youth suicide autopsies.

In addition to the social structure changes noted above, Rubinstein (1983) also described a 12-year pattern of 25 suicides by hanging in the Marshall Islands that he hypothesized to be a process of modeling behavior. The original dramatic suicide hanging and burial of a socially prominent young man caught in an ambivalent love triangle between two women, followed 3 days later by a second man's suicide due to marital problems, catalyzed the community to infuse a new meaning into the act of suicide as a culturally patterned solution to intimate relationship dilemmas.

Comparison of Pacific Islanders to Other Indigenous Populations

Suicide patterns among Pacific Islanders parallel those among other indigenous populations, specifically Native American, Canadian First Nations, Māori, and Australian aboriginals. According to the Surgeon General's (DHHS, 1999) call to action to prevent suicide, from 1979–1992 the suicide rates for Native Americans was 1.5 times the national rate. A disproportionate number of these suicides were among young Native American males ages 15–24 and accounted for 64% of all suicides among Native Americans.

For Canadian First Peoples, the suicide rate has increased to three times the rate of the general population in Canada. In this population, completed suicides occur disproportionately in youth, especially young males, with increasing rates during the teenage years that peak between ages 23–25 and then decline until 60–65 when there is a second smaller peak (Tsuang, Simpson & Fleming, 1992). After age 70, the completed suicide rate for Canadian First Peoples drops below the general population (Kirmayer, 1994).

Māori are the indigenous people of New Zealand. They have strikingly similar language and strong historical-cultural ties to Hawaiians that are recorded in their oral traditions and migration chants that describe migration from Hawaiki (Hawai'i) to Aotearoa, the Māori traditional name for New Zealand. Māori, like other indigenous populations, have a history of foreign colonization by the British. Māori youth, both males and females, had higher rates of suicide than non-Māori youth from 1996 to 1999, with Māori youth one and a half times more likely to complete suicide (Beautrais, 2003). Among males age 15–24, the suicide rate is 38.9/100,000, compared with 29.2/100,000 for non-Māori males in New Zealand. Like other indigenous groups, Māori male suicide peaks at age 15–24 then steadily drops without a second bimodal increase. After age 60, there are no recorded deaths from suicide in New Zealand (Ferguson et al., 2004). In a review of indigenous suicide in Australia, New Zealand, the U.S. and Canada, Hunter & Harvey (2002), note that indigenous youth populations in these countries have high rates of completed suicides. They hypothesize that these high rates are related to the proportions of youth in the population, i.e., the higher rate of youth in a society, the more problems youth will experience. The authors also discuss how similar experiences with colonization such as loss of identity, pride, Aboriginal rights, language, customs, traditions, and environment, contribute to collective despair, and collective suicide (Hunter & Harvey, 2002).

☐ Results of Attempted Suicide in Hawai'i

State of Hawai'i Archival Data

Documented hospitalizations and emergency room visits for nonfatal suicide attempts vary by age, gender, and ethnic background. Galanis (2006) examined injury data for Hawai'i, and noted that more than half (54%) of the attempted suicides are among those aged 15–34, with the highest rates for 15–19-year-olds (18%). Only 3% of those 65 years and older made a suicide attempt requiring hospitalization or a visit to an emergency room. Based on data from the 1999 Hawai'i Youth Risk Behavior Survey, Hawaiian youth (38.9%) had higher rates of attempted suicide requiring treatment than Caucasians (34.1%) and Other Asian American/Pacific Islanders (29.7%) (Nishimura, Goebert, Ramisetty-Mikler & Caetano, 2005). According to findings from the Youth Risk Behavior Surveillance System (Centers for Disease Control and Prevention, 2006b), attempted suicide rates for Hawai'i youth were higher than the U.S. rates for all years (1993, 12.6% vs. 8.6%; 1995, 12.7% vs. 8.7%; 1997, 11.5% vs. 7.7%; 1999, 10.1% vs. 8.3%; and 2001, 13.4% vs. 8.8%). Hawaiian adolescents had significantly higher attempted suicide rates (12.7% vs. 11.4%) than other ethnic groups and much higher rates (18%) in certain selected geographic areas in Hawai'i (Yuen, Yahata, and Nahulu, 1999).

Hawai'i Youth Community-Based Epidemiological Studies

National Center on Indigenous Hawaiian Behavioral Health (NCIHBH), Department of Psychiatry, John A. Burns School of Medicine, University of Hawai'i at Mānoa has collected two waves (1992–1996 [Study #1, N =

4,182] and 2001–2004 [Study #2, N = 1,172]) of community epidemiological data to examine relationships among mental health, cultural affiliation, and ethnic background in Hawai'i high school students. When examining Study #1 data, Yuen and colleagues (2000) found that Hawaiian youth had significantly higher lifetime prevalence rates of suicide attempts (12.9%) than non-Hawaiian students (9.6%).

In examining risk factors for attempted suicide, socio-economic status (SES) in terms of education and employment functioned differently for Hawaiians than for non-Hawaiian youth. Hawaiian adolescents Where their parents had less than a 9th-grade education and were on welfare, disability, or were unemployed, Hawaiian adolescents reported lifetime suicide prevalence rates of 21.9% and 18.0%, respectively. In contrast, non-Hawaiians whose parents fell into these same categories exhibited only modest increases in suicide attempts (14% and 12.5%, respectively). Hawaiians had higher mean symptom scores on measures of depression, anxiety, aggression, and substance abuse.

Based on multiple logistic regression analyses, different factors predicted suicide attempts for Native Hawaiians as compared with non-Hawaiians. Suicide attempts in Hawaiian youth were best predicted (in descending order) by depression, substance abuse, grade level (with 12th-graders having higher rates), Hawaiian cultural affiliation, and main wage earner's education (i.e., measure of SES). Suicide attempts in non-Hawaiians were best predicted (in descending order) by substance abuse, depression, and aggression. Hawaiian cultural affiliation and SES were not predictive of suicide attempts for non-Hawaiians. Of particular note, the study showed Hawaiian cultural affiliation rather than ethnicity was uniquely predictive of suicide attempts for Hawaiian youth. Yuen and colleagues (2000) hypothesized that key transitions (as measured by grade levels) in adolescence are more difficult for Hawaiians to negotiate, and that Hawaiian youth with high levels of Hawaiian cultural affiliation may be less acculturated to Western culture and may experience increased cultural conflict. Hawaiian adolescents with high levels of family support had lower rates of attempted suicide, suggesting that family support served as a potential protective factor.

From 2001 to 2005, the NCIHBH continued its community epidemiological work in Study #2 with Hawaii youth ages 13–18 by surveying 1,172 students. (Please see Else, Andrade & Nahulu [2007] for a full description of the study.) Overall the sample included 700 (59.73%) Hawaiians and 472 (40.27%) non-Hawaiians. Those making significant lifetime suicide attempts were females ($\chi 2$ [1, N = 1,159] = 14.6, maximum R2 = .029, OR = 2.5, OR 95% CI = 1.5-4.0, p = .0001), 12th-graders ($\chi 2$ [1, N = 1,159] = 14.0, maximum R2 = .028, OR = 1.2, OR 95% CI = 1.1–1.4, p = .0002) and those whose parents' educational level was some college or community college or high school graduate/GED ($\chi 2$ [1, N = 1,109] = 7.6, maximum $R2$ = .016, OR = 1.3 CI = 1.1–1.5 p = .0377).

Risk and Protective Factors for Youth Suicide Attempts

For all youth in the sample, risks for attempted suicide were: being sexually active, having had sex with both males and females, talking with a teacher/counselor, getting professional counseling, experiencing family conflict, witnessing or hearing family violence, and having low family support. Conversely, talking to both mothers and fathers, higher levels of family cohesion, family organization, and parental bonding were related to lower risk of lifetime suicide attempts.

Between-Group Differences for Lifetime Suicide Attempts

Those who made a lifetime suicide attempt were analyzed by gender and ethnicity, resulting in four categories of: (1) Hawaiian female, (2) Hawaiian male, (3) non-Hawaiian female, and (4) non-Hawaiian male, with several significant findings between the four groups for lifetime suicide attempts. Using pair-wise comparisons, Hawaiian females had significantly higher rates of making a lifetime suicide attempt than Hawaiian males and non-Hawaiian males. Non-Hawaiian females had significantly higher rates than non-Hawaiian males. Group differences were also observed through the Hawaiian culture scale and its seven factors. The Hawaiian Culture Scale—Adolescent Version (HCS-A) measures constructs of: (1) the source of learning the Hawaiian way of life, and (2) specific cultural traditions measured by the seven subscales of lifestyles, customs and beliefs, activities and social events, folklore and legends, causes–locations, causes–access, and language proficiency (Hishinuma et al., 2000, p. 144). Hawaiians had higher scores than non-Hawaiians, with variability by gender. Hawaiian females followed by Hawaiian males scored significantly higher on the overall score of Hawaiian culture and factors of customs/beliefs, folklore/legends, and language. Hawaiian males followed by Hawaiian females had significantly higher scores on lifestyles, and causes–access. Hawaiian females scored significantly higher for activities, while Hawaiian males had significantly higher scores for causes–locations.

Within-Group Differences for Lifetime Suicide Attempt

Differences in making or not making a suicide attempt within the four groups (Hawaiian females, Hawaiian males, non-Hawaiian females, and non-Hawaiian males) were also investigated. Females (both Hawaiian and non-Hawaiian) had significantly higher rates of alcohol, marijuana, or cigarette use; depression; aggression; and general substance use, and lower rates of family support. Hawaiian females who made a suicide attempt had significantly higher scores on Hawaiian culture factor scores of lifestyles, folklore/legends, causes–locations, and causes–access. Hawaiian males had higher rates of cigarette use, depression, anxiety, aggression, substance use, and overall scores of Hawaiian culture, causes–access, and lower scores on family support. Non-Hawaiian males had higher rates associated with marijuana use, lifestyles, and language.

Acculturative stresses

Again, similar to the findings of Yuen et al. (2000), high levels of Hawaiian acculturation (i.e., identifying with understanding, identifying or doing Hawaiian cultural practices and beliefs) was a risk factor for Hawaiian youth suicide attempts. Interestingly, two Hawaiian culture factors (lifestyles and language) were associated with attempted suicide for the seven non-Hawaiian males who attempted suicide.

Development and Psychopathology

The transitions to high school (from middle school to high school) and to adulthood (from 12th grade to leaving high school) were associated with higher levels of suicide attempts, which may indicate that these youth perceive fewer opportunities for their future. Youth were at higher risk for suicide attempts if they had higher scores on depression, anxiety, aggression, and substance use (smoking cigarettes, drinking alcohol, or abusing other substances).

Social, developmental and clinical implications in the area of acculturative stress are the most challenging to explain because the results of Study #2 beg the question of the utility of culture. How do culture and acculturation facilitate or hinder the ability of adolescents to coexist and thrive within their Hawaiian and non-Hawaiian (or American) worlds? How do Pacific Island indigenous youth (Hawaiian, Samoan, or Micronesian) achieve the core developmental tasks of individuation and independence valued and expected within the American society that exists outside their homes and neighborhoods, while needing to achieve the developmental tasks of differentiation and collective generational interdependence that is valued and reified within the indigenous societies that exist within their homes, neighborhoods, or communities?

The findings among Hawaiian adolescents suggest that the task of defining what uniquely distinguishes them from non-Hawaiians (i.e., establishing a Hawaiian ethnocultural identity), can be difficult for some. How do they distinguish themselves while trying to succeed in a society that is predominately non-Hawaiian? As Hawaiian youth move through the 12th grade to adulthood, the transition can be mired in frustrating ambivalence and disillusionment, especially if they live within family dysfunction. Do adolescents' Hawaiian cultural beliefs, practices, and traditions paradoxically generate conflicts, ambivalence, and irrelevance between individual American cultural goals (e.g., individual economic affluence, social ascent) and being a participating member within a Hawaiian family hierarchy (i.e., maintaining family wholeness and self-sufficiency, as well as fulfilling the role designated by virtue of one's ancestral lineage, ordinal position at birth, or sacred name)?

The findings show that Hawaiian adolescents who are raised in families that possess high cohesion, organization, parent bonding, and family support, have significantly lower rates of suicide attempts. This finding provides a probable means by which youth are able to negotiate the tensions between developmental tasks, family expectations, and cultural differences within Hawaiian homes and neighborhoods and the larger dominant cultural values in America. That is, these youth, their parents, and their family systems are able to negotiate successfully through the ethical gray zones without violating the moral absolutes demanded of their Hawaiian and non-Hawaiian (American and dominant) cultures and social structures to attain the cultural goals that they deem as measures of success.

□ Overall Discussion

The findings on Hawaiian, Samoan, and Micronesian self-injury, suicide attempts, and completed suicide presented in the previous section span epidemiological data from community populations and cultural-historical descriptions of suicide behavior. A summary of common threads that flow through the findings, along with distinct differences, are presented below.

Epidemiological Patterns

All Pacific Islander populations in this study showed patterns of higher suicide rates, when compared with non-Pacific Island populations, with the highest rates of suicide found among young males aged 15–24. While all populations showed an age distribution where male suicides rose sharply from adolescence and peaked at age 20–25, the age distributions after this peak differed for each population: Hawaiians, Belauan, Pohnpeans, and Yapese showed steady decreases without a bimodal increase among the elders. Chuukese and Marshall Islanders had a dramatic decrease followed by a smaller peak at age 60–65. Pacific Islander suicides rates by age and gender followed similar patterns to indigenous populations in the U.S., Canada, and New Zealand. Again, the highest levels of suicide were found in males aged 15–24, peaking at ages 20–25. Suicide age distribution patterns changed after the peak ages of 20–25 among U.S. and Canada indigenous populations, like Chuukese and Marshallese, showing the bimodal curve seen in their non-indigenous cohorts with a second, smaller increase in suicide at age 60–65. New Zealand Māori, similar to Hawaiians, Belauans, and Pohnpeans, showed a steady decrease without a bimodal curve. The reasons for these differences in older male suicide age distribution may be statistical (e.g., geographic area unit size differences), social (e.g., differences in family and social support networks), or nonsocial (e.g., medical illnesses that cause premature mortality).

Two explanations—one genetic, the other social-cultural—may provide the reasons for the absence of the bimodal suicide distribution among the indigenous populations of Hawai'i, Belau, Pohnpei, and New Zealand. Caspi et al. (2003) suggest that the young men (and women) who commit suicide possess the "short" or stress-sensitive form of the serotonin transporter gene (and are therefore at risk for depression and suicide when they experience stressful life events. Those who survive would be expected to have the "long" version of the gene, and therefore not be vulnerable to stressors. Later, the authors posit a family cultural influence to explain the age distribution of high Hawaiian male youth suicide and the absence of the usual bimodal pattern of suicide among individuals aged 60–65.

Social-Cultural Historical Patterns

All Pacific Island indigenous groups share a history of colonization and military occupation, loss of indigenous social structures, networks and processes, cultural fragmentation, political disenfranchisement, socio-economic deprivation, and higher levels of psychosocial adversity (e.g., incarceration, domestic violence, family dysfunction, etc.) in their homelands. Striking parallels in social histories have occurred among North

American and New Zealand indigenous groups. Using sociological theories and hypotheses of acculturative stress, loss of culture, cultural conflict, historical trauma and the effects of colonization, researchers have attempted to describe and explain the resulting effects of psychosocial adversity, health and mental health disparities, and psychopathology including suicide, between Pacific Islanders and the dominant societies they live within (Berry, 1987, 1997; Brave Heart, 1998; Johnston, 2006; Durkheim, 1951; Echohawk, 1997; E Ola Mau, 1985; Kamehameha Schools, 1983; Kirmayer, 1994; Kirmayer et al., 2000; Lester, 1997; Rubinstein, 1983, 2002; Whitbeck, et al., 2004; Young, 1991).

Social and Cultural Meanings of Suicide—Past and Present

U.S. military historians, as well as Rubenstein (1983), Kamakau (1992), and Else, Andrade, & Nahulu (2007) provided anecdotal evidence that describe specific cultural-patterned meanings and uses of suicide in the 18th–20th (during and after World War II, particularly Japanese and Micronesian mass suicides) and 21st centuries of Micronesian and Hawaiian suicide behaviors, as well as cultural assessments and interventions for suicide-related behaviors. Hawaiian warriors in pre-contact Hawai'i, like the Japanese warriors of the 18th–20th centuries, and even the Jewish Zealots of Masada who rebelled against Roman colonization in 73 A.D., used suicide in war as a means to resist and strike back at one's enemy and die with dignity. This type of suicide, which appears to transcend cultures, was described as altruistic suicide by Durkheim (1951) and suggests an extraordinarily high social integration.

Not found among Pacific Islander populations is the phenomenon of suicide terrorism, which rose dramatically in the 1990s and reached its height on September 11, 2001 with the suicide crashes using hijacked commercial airliners into the U.S. World Trade Center and Pentagon. The critical difference of these suicides from those examined here is that suicide terrorism is strategically designed to coerce and control a government to concede to political conditions (Pape, 2003). People sacrifice themselves not in a final noble warrior stance against a formidable enemy, but as a means to direct the actions of the targeted enemy.

The mass suicides of the Japanese and Micronesians in Saipan during World War II, as well as the 12-year pattern of 25 male suicides in the Marshall Islands after World War II, suggest the power of the community or ethnic group to infuse new meaning into a self-destructive act as a viable culturally patterned solution to escape U.S. capture on Saipan, and the distress of ambivalent love, respectively. The Hawaiian pre-contact myths of suicide are used to teach the lesson of the evils of obsessive or unrequited love that is healed by the love of one's siblings and family.

Family and Group Influences on the Individual

The final common thread that runs through all Pacific Island populations studied were the influences—both positive and negative—that families, friends, ethnic groups, and the overall community and society have upon the individual's cognitions, emotions, and behaviors. The Hawaiian youth epidemiology studies showed that talking with parents, parental bonding, family cohesion or support lowered suicide attempts (Else, Andrade & Nahulu, 2007; Yuen, 2000). These findings, along with the other Pacific Islander data we have presented, provide evidence that family—and in the case of Pacific Islanders, extended family—networks act upon the individual in a number of important ways that influence behaviors, including suicide.

First, family networks are an essential tempering and orienting influence in helping individuals throughout their lifespan to sort out the often conflicting cultural goals and expectations that measure success of the larger community and society. In addition, they help individuals navigate through developmental transitions (adolescence to adulthood) that are particularly challenging.

Second, the family—and in its absence, surrogate systems of significant others—is the core or intimate social network through which the culture, or more specifically the collective social meanings (cognitions, emotions, and behaviors), of one's identified ethnic group are communicated, reified, modified, and perpetuated. When family or the core social networks that an individual bonds to is unavailable or dysfunctional, the individual's psychosocial development is hindered along with his or her ability to navigate the environmental challenges.

Third, Pacific Islander families, like many Native American groups, are role-oriented societies (Echohawk, 1997) where the indigenous or sacred name given to a child places upon the child (and the family) the responsibility to live up to that name. The concept of role designation may also explain the high youth (age 15–25) suicide rates among Hawaiian males without the bimodal elderly spike at age 60–65.

Suicide Lifespan Distribution for Hawaiian Males

Hawaiian (as well as Maori, Pohnpean, and Belauan) males commit suicide most often during the ages of 15–24 with a peak at age 20. Following this spike, there is a decrease without the second smaller peak between ages 60–65 (i.e., the bimodal suicide distribution) found in the U.S. and Canada. In addition, Hawaiian men who live to age 40–45 have a sharp decline in their suicide rates. One possible explanation for this finding is the roles that are designated within the traditional Hawaiian family and community system for *keiki* or *mo'opuna* (infants and children or grandchildren, up to the age of 14), *'ōpio* (youth ages 15–35), *mākua* (parent generation ages 35–60) and *kūpuna* (elders or grandparents, aged 60 and older). Having clear role designations in families and communities may be protective against suicide behaviors. In the Hawaiian family system chronological age is not as important as the social role that a person plays within his or her *'ohana*—the extended multigenerational group bonded by blood and *aloha*—who live within neighborhoods and communities that are typically located within an hour of each other.

Role designations for each stage within the life span carry implicit and explicit psychosocial roles. The two extremes of the life span, i.e., *keiki* and *kūpuna*, are cherished by Hawaiian society because *keiki* or *mo'opuna* (which literally translates as the generational wellspring or source) are the future generations that assure the continuity of the people, while *kūpuna* (which translates as the start of the source) assure continuity of the cultural and historical traditions, knowledge, skills, and traditions. The *mākua* generation has the primary responsibility of supporting, nurturing, and protecting children and elders while acquiring the knowledge and developing the skills and mastery to become *kūpuna*.

There is a special role designation for adolescents and young adults or *'ōpio* in Hawaiian society. The term *'ōpio* which means "young, juvenile, immature," connotes a person, male or female, between the ages of 14–35, who has not yet "joined the world of the grown-ups" and is thus not ready to take on significant responsibilities within the family. From about the mid-twentieth century and earlier, *'ōpio* were given the freedom to develop within the structured framework of their *'ohana*. This freedom allowed them to discover—and their elders to observe—their innate talents, interests, and preferences that would then be honed by the apprenticeship and mentoring of *mākua* and *kūpuna*. The motivation, ability, and speed of knowledge and skill acquisition and mastery determined how rapidly an *'ōpio* would advance through to the next level of development within the *'ohana*. The advent of urbanization and the movement of rural Hawaiians into cities separated them from both their families and their family lands. Without the orienting social structures and framework of the *'ohana*, Hawaiian families living in large towns and cities, often without their family elders, had only partially understood social structures and meanings to guide *'ōpio* and their family networks. Into this vacuum of Hawaiian social-cultural orientation *'ōpio* and their families were left to pursue the cultural goals of American society without the means or equal playing field and access to do so.

Since the 1940s, a Hawaiian man who is an *'ōpio* does not have a structured role beyond the expectation that he master the skills to acquire sustenance for himself and his *'ohana*. Male *'ōpio* commonly live at home, and if married, will often move into the wife's home, where he will be treated more as another son who contributes to the family from his employment or by subsistence farming, fishing, and hunting, rather than as the head of a household. For *'ōpio*, acquiring the social and economic power (the critical tasks of the psychosocial developmental stage of identity vs. role confusion) needed to control and protect one's environment is heavily dependent on whether or not there are older males and females within the family home. Male *'ōpio* who are gainfully employed are expected to turn over a significant part of their income (some sign over their entire paycheck and are given an "allowance" till the next pay day) to their mothers, fathers, or grandparents. In the presence of *mākua* and *kūpuna*, an *'ōpio* remains part of the younger members of the family who do not have a leadership voice in the family, until he or she establishes a set of special talents or capabilities that redefine his or her role designation within the *'ohana*.

Usually between the ages 40–45, Hawaiian men and women move from being *'ōpio* to being *mākua*, and are called "Uncle and Aunty," which are terms of respect in the Hawaiian community. For Hawaiian men, the term "Uncle" signifies that one has entered the world of the grownups and has been given increasing levels of responsibility that focus on the mentoring and care for younger members of the family (*keiki* or children and *'ōpio*). During the *mākua* phase of life men and women become experts in their area of work, talents, and interest, and commonly take on roles that assure family history continuity, e.g., learning the family genealogy or oral traditions.

Finally, after the age of 60, Hawaiian men and women become recognized by the *'ohana*, neighborhood and community as a *kūpuna* and are treated with reverence and respect for their unique levels of expertise. They are also given an enormous measure of personal and social standing and power. In summary, the Hawaiian family system in the 20th and 21st centuries has had clear designated roles for *keiki, mākua*, and *kūpuna*. For the *'ōpio* generation, however, the implicit and explicit transition role between being a child vs. not-yet-an-adult, along with the lack of social structures to guide their development, is absent. This places adolescents and younger adult males who are developmentally age-appropriate within social environments that do not help them negotiate and succeed in their Hawaiian worlds. In addition, their current subordinate roles within their extended families hinder their ability to progress to achieve the dominant societal goals of independent socioeconomic self-sufficiency and acquire the symbol of American success for a young man by age 25, which is to be the head of his own household.

We hypothesize that the aforementioned Hawaiian family influences underpin the high suicide rates for young males that peak at ages 20–25.

The steady decline after age 40 may be the result of more structured role designations that occur for men, who after age 40 become *mākua*, followed by becoming *kūpuna* at age 60.

Several limitations of this chapter need to be noted. For suicide rate descriptions, completed suicide and attempted suicide data in the U.S. for Pacific Islanders are rarely disaggregated from Asian Americans, which obscures important differences in the two populations. Instead, rates for Pacific Islanders in the Pacific were reported here. There are no published studies of suicide among American Samoans. Suicide statistics are often based on death and hospitalization reports where there is clear evidence of intent to harm oneself, potentially underestimating rates of completed and attempted suicides. For the study data presented, there is a sample bias for non-participants who are particularly at risk due to absenteeism from school, suspensions, dropouts, and expulsions. It is likely that rates of attempted suicide and other related behaviors of substance use and psychopathology have been underreported.

Summary and Conclusions

We presented information on Hawaiians, Samoans, and Micronesians that included the historical backgrounds of their nations, a literature review on suicide patterns among these populations and other comparable indigenous groups, comprehensive sets of epidemiological data from community samples, and social-cultural information on suicide among these societies before and after contact with foreigners. This chapter makes several first-time contributions that enhance the current scientific knowledge base on these Pacific Islander populations.

First, Pacific Islanders are not Asians, nor are they immigrants or the descendants of American immigrants. They are indigenous peoples who have lived in homelands that were seized or colonized by the U.S. through historical events that parallel those that impacted Native Americans. Similar to Native Americans and other indigenous peoples in Canada and New Zealand, Hawaiians, Samoans and Micronesians have suicide rates and patterns, along with their associated measures of psychosocial adversity and psychopathology, that are strikingly similar.

Second, militaristic altruistic suicides transcend cultures and geographies—whether Japanese in feudal Japan or Saipan in World War II, Hawaiians in pre-contact Hawai'i, or Jewish rebels in Roman-occupied Judea millennia ago—occur in nearly every historical time period where great wars between empires and pockets of all-consuming group resistance occurs. Unlike the present terrorism suicides that strategically aim to coerce governments, altruistic suicide is infused with the defiant nobility of a group's or society's warriors—men, women and children—to carry a message of resistance and a curse to an enemy they perceive as impossible to defeat physically; an enemy they will strive to defeat metaphysically.

Third, all indigenous Pacific Islander populations, (like U.S. and New Zealand indigenous peoples) showed patterns of higher suicide rates with highest rates for males ages 15–25 and with a peak at ages 20–25. The authors suggest that for Hawaiians, and perhaps other Pacific Islanders, differences in age distribution may be due to social and cultural influences in the traditional family systems and role designations for youth, adults, and elders.

Fourth, groups of people within communities give the act of suicide culturally relevant meanings that maintain and strengthen the cohesion of their group and assure conformity to their social mores and ethics. Militaristic or suicide acts of resistance reassert the group's immutable values; mythic lessons of suicide among pre-contact Hawaiians showed the power of family love to restore *lōkahi* (health and harmony in all relationships) and Marshallese redefined suicidal hangings as an acceptable means to settle an irreconcilable dilemma in love. These recurrent themes show the power of a community to completely and artificially create the meaningfulness of suicide and its relationship to behaviors—both pathological and healthy.

Fifth, the findings of this study show that among indigenous Pacific Islander populations—and likely for other indigenous peoples—culture is not lost or taken away from a people by colonization, expanding commerce, or military occupation. Culture is in its entirety a product of humankind's imagination, vision, hopes, fears, and need to live well together. Culture, with its collective social meanings—of cognitions, emotions, and behaviors—along with effective and well-integrated social structures, must be renewed by the members of these unique ethnic groups and societies. Finally, culture provides a group or society with the cognitive, emotional and behavioral agility required to negotiate successfully through the ethical gray zones—without violating their culture's moral absolutes—within which specific dilemmas spawned out of the crucible of real life adversity and deprivation occur.

☐ Acknowledgments

This manuscript was supported by the National Center for Indigenous Hawaiian Behavioral Health (NCIHBH) [National Institute of Mental Health (NIMH; R24 MH5015-01, R24 MH57079-A1), and The Queen Emma Foundation], Asian/Pacific Islander Youth Violence Prevention Center (CDC; R49/CCR918619-05; 1 U49/CE000749-01), the National Institute on Alcohol Abuse and Alcoholism (NIAAA; UO1AA014289-01) and National

Center on Minority Health and Health Disparities (NCMHD). The authors would like to express their appreciation to researchers and administrative support staff of the NCIHBH.

☐ References

Andrade, N. N., Hishinuma, E. S., McDermott, Jr., J. F., Johnson, R. C., Goebert, D. A., Makini, Jr., G. K., Nahulu, L. B., Yuen, N. Y. C., McArdle, J. J., Bell, C. K., Carlton, B. S., Miyamoto, R. H., Nishimura, S. T., Else, I. R. N., Guerrero, A., Darmal, A., Yates, A., & Waldron, J. A. (2006). The National Center on Indigenous Hawaiian Behavioral Health Study of Prevalence of Psychiatric Disorders in Native Hawaiian Adolescents. *Journal of the American Academy of Child and Adolescent Psychiatry, 45*(1), 26–36.

Beautrais, A. (2003). Suicide in New Zealand I: Time trends and epidemiology. *The New Zealand Medical Journal, 116*(1175). Available from http://www.nzma.org.nz/jounal/116-1175/460.

Berry, J. W. (1997). Immigration, acculturation, and adaptation. *Applied Psychology: An International Review, 46*(1), 5–68.

Berry, J. W., Kim, U., Minde, T., & Mok, D. (1987). Comparative studies of acculturative stress. *International Migration Review, 21*, 491–511.

Booth, H. (1999). Pacific Island suicide in comparative perspective. *Journal of Biosocial Science, 31*(4), 433–48.

Brave Heart, M. Y. H. & DeBruyn, L. M. (1998). The American Indian Holocaust: Healing Historical Unresolved Grief. *American Indian and Alaskan Native Mental Health Research, 8*(2), 60–82.

Caspi, A., Sugden, K., Moffitt, T. E., Taylor, A., Craig, I. W., Harrington, H., McClay, J., Mill, J., Martin, J., Braithwaite, A., & Poulton, R. (2003). *Science, 301*(5631), 386–389.

Centers for Disease Control. WISCARS. (2006a). *WISQARS Injury Mortality Reports, 1999–2003.* Retrieved March 4, 2006, from: http://webappa.cdc.gov/sasweb/ncipc/mortrate.html.

Centers for Disease Control. (2006b). YRBSS: *Youth Risk Behavior Surveillance System, Youth Online: Comprehensive Results.* Retrieved from March 6, 2006, from: http://apps.nccd.cdc.gov/yrbss/.

Cowan, J. (2004). *The Maoris in the Great War: A history of the New Zealand native contingent and pioneer battalion, Gallipoli, 1915, France and Flanders, 1916–1918.* London: Naval & Military Press.

Daws, G. (1968). *Shoal of time: A history of the Hawaiian Islands.* Honolulu, HI: University of Hawai'i Press.

Department of Health and Human Services [DHHS] (2001). *Mental Health: Culture, Race, and Ethnicity—A Supplement to Mental Health: A Report of the Surgeon General.* Rockville, MD: U.S. Department of Health and Human Services, Public Health Service, Office of the Surgeon General.

Department of Health and Human Services [DHHS] (1999). *Mental Health: A Report of the Surgeon General.* Rockville, MD: U.S. Department of Health and Human Services, Substance Abuse and Mental Health Services Administration, Center for Mental Health Services, National Institutes of Health, National Institute of Mental Health.

Durkheim, E. (1951). *Suicide.* New York: The Free Press. (The English translation of Durkheim's *Le Suicide* (1897) Paris: Felix Alcan).

Echohawk, M. (1997). Suicide: The scourge of Native American people. *Suicide and Life-Threatening Behavior, 27*(1), 60–67.

Else, I. R. N., Andrade, N. N. & Nahulu, L. B. (2007). Suicide and Suicidal-Related Behaviors among Indigenous Pacific Islanders in the United States. *Death Studies, 31*(5), 479–501.

E Ola Mau: Native Hawaiian Health Needs Study. (1985), Honolulu: Alu Like.

Ferguson, S., Blakely, T., Allan, B., & Collings, S. (2004). *Suicide rates in New Zealand. Public Health Monograph Series No. 10.* Wellington: Department of Public Health Wellington School of Medicine and Health Sciences.

Galanis, D. (2006). *Overview of Suicides in Hawai'i.* Honolulu, HI: Hawai'i Department of Health, Injury Prevention and Control Program.

Galanis, D. (2007). *Suicide rates in Hawai'i, 2000–2004.* Honolulu, HI: Hawai'i Department of Health, Injury Prevention and Control Program.

Goldsmith, S. K., Pellmar, T. C., Kleinman, A. M., & Bunney, W. E. (Eds.) (2002). *Reducing Suicide: A National Imperative.* Washington, D.C: The National Academies Press.

Henningham, S. (1992). *France and the South Pacific: A Contemporary History.* University of Hawaii Press: Honolulu, Hawaii.

Hezel, F. (1989). Suicide in the Micronesian Family. *The Contemporary Pacific, 1*, 43–74.

Hishinuma, E. S., Andrade, N. N., Johnson, R. C., McArdle, J. J., Miyamoto, R. H., Nahulu, L. B., Makini, J., G. K., Yuen, N. Y. C., Nishimura, S. T., McDermott, J. F., Waldron, J. A., Luke, K. N., & Yates, A. (2000). Psychometric properties of the Hawaiian Culture Scale—Adolescent version. *Psychological Assessment, 12*(2), 140–157.

Hunter, E. & Harvey D. (2002). Indigenous suicide in Australia, New Zealand, Canada and the United States. *Emergency Medicine, 14*, 14–23.

Johnston, M. (2006, January 23). Identity loss tied to Maori suicide. *The New Zealand Herald.*

Kalish, R. A. (1968). Suicide: An Ethnic Comparison in Hawai'i. *Bulletin of Suicidology*, Dec., 37–43.

Kamakau, S. M. (1992) *Ruling chiefs of Hawaii* (Rev. ed.). Honolulu: Kamehameha Schools Press.

Kamehameha Schools. (1983). *Native Hawaiian Education Assessment Project (NHEAP).* Honolulu: Kamehameha Schools/Bernice Pauahi Bishop Estate.

Kanahele, P. K. (2001). *Holo Mai Pele.* Honolulu, HI: Pacific Islanders in Communications and the Edith Kanaka'ole Foundation.

Keegan, J. (1998). *World War One.* New York, NY: Vintage Books.

Kirmayer, L. J., Brass, G. M. & Tait, C. L. (2000). The mental health of aboriginal peoples: Transformations of identity and community. *Canadian Journal of Psychiatry, 45*, 607–616.

Kirmayer, L. (1994). Suicide among Canadian Aboriginal People. *Transcultural Psychiatric Research Review, 31*, 3–58.

Larcy, H. (1994). World War Two. In Howe, K. R., Kiste, R. C., & Lal, B. V. *Tides of history: The Pacific Islands in the twentieth century*. University of Hawaii Press: Honolulu, Hawaii.

Lester, D. (1997). Suicide in America: a nation of immigrants. *Suicide and Life-Threatening Behavior, 27*(1), 50–59.

National Institute of Mental Health. (2004). *Suicide Facts and Statistics*. Retrieved March 4, 2006, from: http:www.nimh.nih.gov/suicideprevention/suifact.cfm.

National Institute of Mental Health. (2003). *In Harm's Way: Suicide in America*. Retrieved March 4, 2006, from: http://www.nimh.nih.gov/publicat/harmaway.cfm.

Nishimura, S. T., Goebert, D. A., Ramisetty-Mikler, S., & Caetano, R. (2005). Adolescent Alcohol Use and Suicide Indicators among Adolescents in Hawai'i. *Cultural Diversity and Ethnic Minority Psychology, 11*(4), 309–320.

Pape, R. A. (2003). The strategic logic of suicide terrorism. *American Political Science Review*, 97(3), 1–19.

Pukui, M. K., Haertig, E. W., & Lee, C. A. (1972). *Nana I Ke Kumu: Look to the source* (Vol. II). Honolulu: Hawai'i: Hui Hanai, Queen Lili'uokalani Children's Center.

Rubinstein, D. H. (2002). *Youth suicide and social change in Micronesia*. Occasional Paper, Kagoshima University Research Center for the Pacific Islands, 36, 33–41.

Rubinstein, D. H. (1983). Epidemic suicide among Micronesian adolescents. *Social Science and Medicine, 17*(10), 657–665.

Ryals, J. D., Kinzie, J. D., Cottington, F. & McDermott, J. F. (1970). *A Cross-Cultural Study of Suicide in Hawai'i*. Honolulu: Department of Psychiatry: University of Hawai'i John A. Burns School of Medicine.

Simon, S. L. (1997). A brief history of people and events related to atomic weapons testing in the Marshall Islands. *Health Physics, 73*(1), 5–20.

State of Hawai'i Department of Health [DOH]. Office of Health Status Monitoring. *Vital Statistics Annual Report Hawai'i 2002*.Retrieved January 19, 2006, from: http://www.state.hi.us/health/statistics/vital–statistics/vr_02/index.html.

State of Hawai'i Department of Health [DOH]. (2004). *Fatal injuries in Hawai'i: 1996–2000*. Honolulu, Hawai'i: Injury and Prevention Control Program.

Tsuang, M. T., Simpson, J. C., & Fleming, J. A. (1992). Epidemiology of suicide. *International Review of Psychiatry, 4*, 117–129.

U.S. Census Bureau (2005, August). *We the People: Pacific Islanders in the United States. Census 2000 Special Reports*. U.S. Department of Commerce, Economics and Statistics Administration. Report No. CENSR–26.

U.S. Public Health Service. (1999). *The Surgeon General's call to action to prevent suicide*. Washington, D.C: Department of Health and Human Services.

Whitbeck, L. B., Adams, G. W., Hoyt, D. R., & Chen, X. (2004). Conceptualizing and measuring historical trauma among American Indian people. *American Journal of Community Psychology, 33*(3/4), 119–130.

Young, T. J. (1991). Suicide and homicide among Native Americans: Anomie or social learning? *Psychological Reports, 68*(3), 1137–1138.

Yuen N. Y. C., Nahulu L. B., Hishinuma E. S., & Miyamoto, R. H. (2000). Cultural identification and attempted suicide in native Hawaiian adolescents. *Journal of the American Academy of Child and Adolescent Psychiatry, 39*, 360–367.

Yuen, N. Y. C., Yahata, D., & Nahulu, A. (1999). *Native Hawaiian youth suicide prevention project: A manual for gatekeeper trainees.* Honolulu, Hawaii: Hawai'i Department of Health, Injury Prevention and Control, Emergency Medical Services Systems, Material and Child Health.

Suicide in Native American Communities

A Transactional-Ecological Formulation of the Problem

Carmela Alcántara and Joseph P. Gone

> There is nothing more significant going on in your community than this [suicide] crisis. Defending treaty rights, fighting for sovereignty—none of that matters if we're not dealing with these problems, and I tell you these problems are not just here on Standing Rock.
>
> **—Kevin Gover, Assistant Secretary for Indian Affairs (Olson, 1998)**

For the residents of the Standing Rock Sioux reservation along the North Dakota–South Dakota border, the winter months in 1997 and 1998 were plagued with disbelief, anger, and fear stemming from a suicide epidemic that culminated in 37 attempts among adolescent youth and 5 completed suicides by adolescent males. At the height of this epidemic, an estimated 150 at-risk adolescents were monitored by mental health professionals, relatives, and other tribal members. Additional risks stemming from the unknown influence of suicide pacts and contagion effects were also difficult to manage. In the aftermath of these teen suicides, the Standing Rock Sioux community—along with tribal leaders and federal officials—conferred to strategize suicide prevention measures, including but not limited to the opening of youth recreation centers and the tailoring of mental health services for depression and substance use, as well as a more general rebuilding of reservation life.

The suicide crisis and subsequent prevention efforts at Standing Rock are but one example of many similar instances throughout "Indian Country." This situation, along with the recent international conference entitled Indigenous Suicide Prevention Research and Programs in Canada and the U.S.: Setting a Collaborative Agenda held in Albuquerque, New Mexico (February 2006), illustrate the growing concern regarding the alarming prevalence of suicidal behaviors among American Indian and Alaska Native (AI/AN) communities in the U.S., Canada, and the U.S. territories. Great efforts are being made to summarize the current state of knowledge about suicide in indigenous communities and to set a collaborative agenda between researchers, providers, policy-makers, and tribal members. The resounding desire for action is evident.

Suicide is also a serious public health concern in the U.S. more broadly, with current statistics indicating that it is the eighth leading cause of death in American society (U.S. Public Health Service, 2001). Given the significant personal and societal toll of death by suicide, the 21st century has already witnessed a considerable rise in national attention aimed toward the prevention of suicide. Federal efforts such as the U.S. Surgeon General's Call to Action and the National Strategy for Suicide Prevention served as catalysts for the mobilization of suicide prevention programs nation-wide (U.S. Department of Health and Human Services, 1999, 2001). Suicide is no longer being perceived as the concern of just individuals and their families, but also of the public at large, with increasing prioritization of suicide research and prevention programming. Nonetheless, this newfound emphasis on suicide prevention efforts has been slow to reach the Native American communities at highest risk, and hopeful outcomes, though anticipated, are not ensured. Echoing the statement at the outset of this chapter by former head of the Bureau of Indian Affairs and esteemed Native judiciary figure and law professor Kevin Gover, it is time that suicidality in Indian Country is addressed by research, prevention programming, treatment, and outcome evaluation. To move beyond the specter of untimely death toward more inclusive healing, Native American suicide can no longer remain a neglected phenomenon.

□ Predicting Suicide: Implications for Treatment

The expectation that trained mental health professionals can predict an individual suicide is a common but erroneous perception that has endured among clinicians and clients alike. The probabilities for accurately predicting extremely low base-rate occurrences or statistically rare phenomena such as suicide are remarkably low (Rudd, Joiner, & Rajab, 2000). Essentially, any discussion of suicide must occur in tandem with this more general understanding of low-probability incidents. As explicitly stated by Rudd et al.:

> Low base-rate phenomena such as suicide are impossible to predict with any reliability in the individual case, simply by nature of the statistical problem presented. Actually, we would be correct more often than not simply to predict that a patient *would not* commit suicide, regardless of the clinical presentation. (p. 127)

In sum, appreciation of a statistical approach to suicide highlights the limited ability of clinicians to accurately predict suicide. This limitation underscores the importance of intervention efforts that include reliable risk assessments. These types of assessment strategies identify salient risk factors that place individuals or communities within "suicide zones" (as coined by Litman, 1990, in Rudd et al.) or elevated periods of suicide risk, as well as corresponding theaters of intervention (clinical treatment, management, etc). According to Litman, the severity of the suicide risk zone is dependent on the presence or absence of psychiatric conditions, type and intent of suicidal behavior (ideation, plan, or gesture), risk factors, and identifiable protective factors, which converge to acutely raise the risk for suicide.

Paradoxically, any "treatment" for suicide must necessarily occur before the act itself. Postmortem intervention efforts are obviously impossible, since suicide cannot be prevented in the deceased. It is fundamental then to locate opportunities for prevention along developmental pathways that lead individuals to heightened suicide risk zones. In this light, identifying risk and protective factors within a biopsychosocial frame of reference is one way to determine points of preventive intervention and understand an individual's potential for suicide.

Drawing upon the most current empirical reports on suicidal behaviors and preventive interventions, this chapter offers a brief review of the epidemiological profile of suicide in AI/AN communities, while situating relevant biopsychosocial risk and protective factors within a transactional-ecological framework. Implications for future research and practice are also discussed.

□ Epidemiology of Suicidal Behaviors among American Indians and Alaska Natives

The latest U.S. Census Bureau report estimates that 4.1 million AI/ANs live in the U.S., composing approximately 1.5% of the U.S. population (U.S.

Census Bureau, 2002). Furthermore, according to census reports, there are more than 561 federally recognized tribes speaking over 220 indigenous languages with various dialects. The marked heterogeneity within the AI/AN population contradicts common misperceptions of homogeneity across Native American communities and renders the making of generalizations problematic (Gone, 2003, 2004b). Thus, the cultural heterogeneity of AI/ANs should remain at the forefront of any consideration of suicide intervention programs targeting these populations (Gone, 2004a).

Although a detailed account of the epidemiology of suicide among indigenous persons in the U.S. is beyond the scope of this chapter (see Olson & Wahab, 2006, for a thorough synthesis of the epidemiological profile and relevant risk factors correlated with AI/AN suicide), a brief discussion of the demography of suicidality in Indian Country is presented to provide the necessary context. Current mortality statistics reveal that suicide is the second leading cause of death for AI/AN populations aged 15–24 years of age, the third leading cause of death for ages 5–14 and 25–44 years of age, and the eighth leading cause of death for decedents of all ages (Centers for Disease Control, 2003; Indian Health Service [IHS], 2000–2001a, 2000–2001b). Additionally, the age-adjusted suicide death rate for AI/ANs is 20.2 per 100,000, approximately twice as high as the U.S. all-races rate of 10.6 per 100,000, with males accounting for the majority of suicide decedents (IHS, 2000–2001a, 2000–2001b). Regional variations among the Indian Health Service administrative areas have also emerged. The highest suicide death rates (ranging 5 to 7 times higher than the overall U.S. rates) are documented in the Tucson, Aberdeen, and Alaska service areas. Contrastingly, the lowest suicide rates were found in the California, Nashville, and Oklahoma service areas (Centers for Disease Control, 2003; IHS, 2000–2001a, 2000–2001b). The leading method of suicide among the AI/AN youth was death by firearms, followed by hanging. Of interest, suicide death rates remained relatively unchanged during the 1989–1998 year period examined within the Centers for Disease Control Report (2003). Already apparent from this brief review of the epidemiological landscape of AI/AN suicide is the regional variation in suicide death rates for indigenous peoples in the U.S. Consequently, determining suicide risk zones and appropriate points of intervention is likely to change in relation to the specific suicidality profile of the region.

A detailed portrait of the epidemiology of suicidality in AI/AN communities also needs to take into account the entire spectrum of suicidal behaviors such as suicide ideation and suicidal attempts. Generally, the ratio of suicide ideation and attempts to suicide completion is overwhelmingly high, with far more cases of suicide ideation and attempts occurring in contrast to completed suicides. Although there are few authoritative population-based studies of the prevalence of suicide attempts and suicidal ideation for AI/AN communities (for a brief review of education studies refer to LeMaster, Beals, Novins, Manson, and the AI-SUPER-PFP Team, 2004), a high prevalence of suicidal behaviors has been documented among AI/AN adolescents and young adults, with higher rates found among AI/AN females. Specifically, LeMaster and colleagues found that within a Northern Plains community-based AI reservation sample, females and younger respondents endorsed significantly higher prevalence of suicidal thoughts, plans, and attempts during their lifetime. However, no significant differences emerged between genders for past-year suicidal behaviors. Males reported utilizing violent methods of attempt such as hanging or shooting significantly more, whereas females were more likely to use nonviolent methods of attempt such as overdose. Of note, cutting and stabbing emerged as the common method endorsed across genders.

Moreover, results from LeMaster et al. (2004) also indicate that a greater percentage of the sample had attempted suicide in their lifetime than had engaged in suicidal ideation or planning. LeMaster and colleagues (in line with May, 1987) suggest that such paradoxical results provide evidence for conceptualizing suicide attempts as impulsive acts more so than previously theorized within the suicide risk continuum model (in which ideation is suggested as a preliminary behavior to a suicide attempt). In these cases, intent may vary drastically such that those attempting suicide may be trying to modify interpersonal relationships rather than merely achieving death. This implies that in attempts to restore or mitigate interpersonal conflict, full deliberation of the consequences of untimely death may not have occurred. In this study, AIs were also less likely to disclose their intent to commit suicide to others, with interesting age trends emerging in disclosure preferences. More specifically, those aged 25 and above were more likely to confide in a family member, in comparison to 15–24-year-olds, who were more likely to confide in their friends. Females were also more likely than males to report ever disclosing thoughts about committing suicide in their entire lifetime and within the past year. These results suggest that suicide preventive interventions may need to be tailored to accommodate for differences found between specific age cohorts.

The epidemiology of indigenous suicidality is additionally complicated when one considers that the majority of investigations of suicidal behaviors within AI/AN communities draw upon reservation- or near-reservation-based samples, thereby excluding urban populations. In one of the first empirical inquiries of its kind, Freedenthal and Stiffman (2004) examined the prevalence and correlates of suicidal behaviors for urban-reared versus reservation-reared AI adolescents from a Southwestern state. Results revealed that those having spent two thirds of their lives within an urban setting (urban-reared) endorsed significantly lower rates of suicidal ideation than those having spent two thirds of their lives on a reservation (reservation-reared). Despite the difference in suicidal ideation, equal rates of lifetime-attempted suicide were found.

Notably, the impact of regional and tribal factors on rates of suicide and suicide ideation further convolute this discussion. For example, in a provocative study exploring factors correlated with suicide ideation among American Indian adolescents from three distinct tribes, Novins, Beals, Roberts, and Manson (1999) found that local culture does indeed matter. The authors suggest that the range of factors associated with suicide ideation is reflective of the cultural heterogeneity among the tribal groups. Although no significant differences in the prevalence of suicide ideation among the three tribal groups were found, the other results have important implications for thinking about tribal-specific risk factors. The findings and implications of this study will be examined in a subsequent section.

Several limitations to the demographic information are presented above. First, the data regarding prevalence of suicide completion and suicidal behaviors are overwhelmingly biased toward reservation-based samples, as few studies have investigated suicidality in AI/AN individuals living in urban settings. The samples studied are also predominantly drawn from school-based settings, thereby excluding the frequently absent and those having dropped out of school, presumably the populations most at risk. Second, a dearth of research concerning the prevalence of specific suicidal behaviors such as suicide attempts in AI/AN communities exists, and even fewer studies have been aimed at examining nuances in suicidality as related to tribal heterogeneity. Last, reports on the epidemiology of suicide in AI/ANs are typically limited by potential and frequent misclassification of race and ethnicity on death certificates. Instances of misclassification are estimated to range from 1% to 30% depending on IHS region (Indian Health Service, 1996 in Centers for Disease Control, 2003). Limitations aside, the prevalence of suicide and related behaviors in Indian Country seems overwhelmingly high and undeniably problematic. Although many more questions about the epidemiology of indigenous suicidality remain unanswered, the overarching need for concentrated efforts to prevent suicide is evident.

A review of the relevant biological, psychological, and social risk factors is essential for a comprehensive understanding of suicidality in indigenous communities. Therefore, offered below is a concise description of the relevant risk factors within a biopsychosocial frame of reference that have special importance for Native American communities (readers are encouraged to view Olson & Wahab, 2006, and Strickland, 1997, for more extensive reviews of identified risk factors for AI/AN communities).

Risk Factors within a Biopsychosocial Frame of Reference

At the Biological Level of Analysis

Serotonergic hypofunction has been implicated in suicide since the late 20th century. A surge of studies continue to examine the role of serotonin in anxiety and depressive disorders, with growing attention devoted to its role in antisocial and impulsive behaviors. In one study published by Zhou and colleagues (2005), the genetic linkages between tryptophan hydroxylase 2 (TPH2), an enzyme involved in the biosynthesis of serotonin within the brain, was examined in four diverse ethnic community samples: Finnish Whites, U.S. American Whites, African Americans, and Southwestern AIs respectively. Notably, results from this investigation point to significant differences among the ethnic group samples in the allele frequencies of specified markers. In particular, no individual single marker or TPH2 linkages associated with anxious/depressive or suicidal behaviors were found in the Southwestern AI samples (in contrast to the other three ethnic groups). Moreover, the yin haplotype was more prevalent in African Americans and Finnish Whites with a history of suicidality and impulsive behavior in comparison with controls free of psychopathology. Additionally, the yang haplotype (identified as a protective factor within the other samples) was absent in the Southwestern AI sample, but present in both White populations. Interestingly, the authors attribute some of the findings to the low rates of admixture in the Finnish White and Southwestern AI population. Overall, the work of Zhou and colleagues contributes further to burgeoning evidence on the role of TPH2 haplotype linkage to anxiety, depression, and suicidality, specifically in the Finish White and African American population.

Before interpretations of the intriguing findings by Zhou et al. (2005) can be made however, a cautionary note is in order. Given the nascent field of bioengineering, stating implications about the consequences of the presence or absence of particular genes or genetic linkages is premature. Above all, the findings of the aforementioned study highlight the need for further specialized research that examines the interplay among genetic predispositions, general antecedent conditions, and environmental contexts in ethnic group populations.

At the Psychological Level of Analysis

Considerable research has been devoted to the study of psychological risk factors predisposing individuals to heightened suicide risk zones. The psychological risk factors for suicidality are generally similar across populations and broadly include comorbidity with psychiatric and substance use disorders, family and personal history of suicidality, history of abuse (sexual or physical abuse), general distress, and interpersonal conflict.

Numerous studies examining suicidality in AI/ANs highlight the associations between depression, hopelessness, post-traumatic stress disorder (PTSD), substance abuse/dependence, violent ideation/aggression and lifetime history of suicide attempt and suicide ideation, with suicide attempters reporting higher levels of depressive symptomatology and global distress (see Borowsky, Resnick, Ireland, & Blum, 1999; Dinges & Duong-Tran, 1994; Howard-Pitney, LaFromboise, Basil, September, & Johnson, 1992; LeMaster et al., 2004 for thorough reviews). History of attempted AI suicide has also been associated with higher endorsement of somatic symptoms such as headaches and stomach problems, generalized health concerns, history of sexual or physical abuse, familial history of suicide, and frequent alcohol or marijuana use (Bohn, 2003; Borowsky et al.). For adolescent AI youth, having attempted suicide has also been associated with greater reporting of unintentional injury and violence, sexually risky activities, tobacco, alcohol, and other drug use (Shaughnessy, Doshi, & Everett Jones, 2004). Borowsky et al. also found noteworthy differences in risk factors for adolescent AI males and females. Participation in a gang and a history of psychiatric treatment were associated with past suicide attempts in males, whereas knowing where to access a firearm and attendance in special education classes were associated with suicide attempts in females. The strongest risk factor associated with a history of attempted suicide among both male and female respondents was having a friend or peer attempt or complete suicide.

Further differences have been found between genders in relation to alcohol use prior to completed suicides. May et al. (2002) found that alcohol-involved AI suicides were more prevalent in males, and overwhelmingly high blood alcohol content levels were found in all the AI tribal groups examined. Moreover, alcohol involvement in completed suicides did not distribute along any age or regional trends, and was not associated with any particular method of suicide or residential setting (living on or off reservation). Intimate-partner violence and interpersonal conflict are also important risk factors for AI women, particularly for young adult females (Olson et al., 1999). Interesting age trends within suicide attempter profiles have also been documented. Specifically, significant differences between AI adolescents and adults emerged in reported number of attempts, time of attempt, behavior at time of admission to hospital, types of stressors prior to attempt, and rated motivation at time of attempt (Zitzow & Desjarlait, 1994).

Freedenthal and Stiffman (2004) found intriguing differences concerning psychological risk factors for urban- versus reservation-based samples of AI/ANs. History of physical abuse, a friend attempting or completing suicide, and family history of suicidality, were associated with history of attempted suicide in the urban-reared sample, whereas depression, conduct disorder, cigarette smoking, family history of substance abuse, and perceived discrimination were correlated with history of attempted suicide only within the reservation-reared sample. Urban-reared youth also had lower rates of psychosocial and environmental problems, such as conduct disorder, substance abuse or dependence, perceived discrimination, and gang involvement, in comparison with their reservation-reared youth counterparts. No significant differences emerged in levels of protective factors, abuse history, mental health and behavioral problems, and friends/family suicide history. Notably, higher levels of social support dramatically lessened the odds of suicide attempt only in urban-reared AI youth, whereas depression increased the odds for reservation youth only. Although few studies examined—with Freedenthal and Stiffman being one exception—perceived discrimination as it relates to suicidal behaviors, racism and general stress have been previously referenced as risk factors in suicidal behaviors for AI/ANs (Johnson, 1994).

A handful of researchers interested in the interplay between AI/AN identity and suicidality have found that heightened risk of suicidal behaviors in adolescence has also been attributed to failed attempts to make identity-preserving linkages between the past, present, and future. Thus, failure to identify instances of personal persistence or self-continuity by adolescents was associated with suicidality (Chandler & Lalonde, 1998; Chandler, Lalonde, Sokol, & Hallet, 2003). Chandler and colleagues also found that the ability to identify coherence through time within respondents' life stories served to discriminate suicidal and non-suicidal adolescent participants. However, a perceived sense of self-continuity is presumably one of many psychologically mediated factors that modulate suicidality. For instance, sexual minority status has also been suggested as yet another factor involved in elevated suicide risk zones (Conchran, 2001, in Balsam, Huang, Fieland, Simoni, & Walters, 2004). Results indicate that two-spirit people (those with varied sexual or gender identities) endorse higher rates of childhood physical abuse, historical trauma, anxiety, depression and PTSD symptoms (with reported greater severity) in comparison with their heterosexual Native counterparts (Balsam et al., 2004). These experiences have been previously identified as risk factors for elevated suicidality. It is thus unsurprising that two-spirit participants report significantly more suicide attempts and suicidal ideation (Barney, 2003).

At the Social Level of Analysis

Biopsychosocial models also acknowledge broader sociological risk factors. Therefore, given the historical context of current-day post-colonial relations between AI/ANs and the federal government, recognizing the influence of historical context on contemporary conditions is essential to identifying social risk factors pertinent to AI/AN communities.

The legacy of colonization (referred to as historical trauma, soul wound, intergenerational trauma, historical legacy, American Indian holocaust, and historical unresolved grief) has been offered as a paradigm for understanding and explaining the alarming prevalence rates of mental disorders and social problems—with much attention devoted to its role in suicide—that have beleaguered AI/AN populations for generations both past and present (Brave Heart & DeBruyn 1998; Duran, Duran, & Brave Heart, 1998; Gone, in press c). The "clash between cultures" (also referred to as acculturative stress) or the psychological sequelae and global distress resulting from the acculturation process that has affected tribal structure, religious practices, and personal and community identity, to name but a few domains, has been suggested as a potent precursor to suicidality and psychiatric conditions in general (Alcántara & Gone, 2007; EchoHawk, 1997; Gone, 2006b, in press b; Kirmayer, Brass, & Tait, 2000; Lester, 1997; Strickland, Walsh, & Cooper, 2006). Moreover, the legacy of colonization has been thought to affect the AI/AN psyche through a "colonization of the life world" wherein colonizers impeded and disrupted the mechanisms facilitating the reproduction of Native cultural and social practices (Duran et al., 1998). This rupture or disintegration of AI/AN daily lifeways (conceptualized as cultural discontinuity) is key to transformations of individual and collective identity, and therefore proposed as a mediating mechanism in pathways to pathology (Gone, 1999, 2004a, 2007, 2006, 2006c, in press c; Kirmayer et al., 2000).

Considering the abundant tribal diversity characteristic of AI/ANs, the influence of tribal culture on suicidality must not be overlooked. In Novins et al. (1999) the heterogeneity of psychological risk factors associated with suicidal ideation was explored in each of a Southwest, Northern Plains, and Pueblo tribe. No single variable was significantly associated with suicide ideation across the three tribes, rather, distinct tribal variations emerged in relation to risk factors. For example, a friend attempting or completing suicide in the past 6 months, lower perceived social support, and depressive symptomatology were correlated with history of suicide ideation in the Pueblo tribe. Single-parent households, higher prevalence of reported life events within the past 6 months, and antisocial behavior were linked to suicidal ideation in the Southwest tribe. Finally, low self-esteem in addition to greater endorsement of depressive symptoms was associated with suicide ideation in the Northern Plains tribe.

Novins and colleagues (1999) reasoned that the cultural characteristics of each of the tribes can be used to understand the unique ways in which the factors correlated with suicide ideation varied by tribe. For example, the Pueblo tribe in question is characterized as a close community with a strong emphasis on social support networks, thus the lack of interpersonal support was associated with levels of suicide ideation. The Southwest tribe is characterized by a strong emphasis on the quality of interpersonal relationships (family, community, and peer associations), and therefore those reporting greater interpersonal distress and single-parent households were more likely to endorse suicide ideation. Novins and colleagues also argue that the strong cultural proscriptions against thinking about death in the Southwest tribe may underlie the associations between antisocial behavior and suicide ideation. Last, the Northern Plains tribe is characterized by its emphasis on individual achievement and a more individualistic conception of self. Consequently, negative perceptions of themselves and their own abilities played a significant role in the extent to which Northern Plains adolescents experienced suicide ideation. Interesting gender-by-culture interactions also emerged, such that for the matrilineal Southwest tribe, a more externalized locus of control was associated with suicide ideation in females but not males. For male adolescents from the Northern Plains tribe, reported life events within the past 6 months was associated with suicide ideation; however, this was not found for females. These findings highlight the role of tribal configurations and gender roles in the experience of suicidality.

On a more "macro" level of analysis, socioeconomic conditions such as unemployment and lack of social capital, as well as ecological conditions such as poverty have been proposed as predisposing risk factors for negative mental health outcomes. More recently, Tondo, Albert and Baldessarini (2006) found associations between indices of access to health care and suicide rates in the U.S. Correlated indices include federal aid for mental health services, number of uninsured persons, and availability of psychiatrists or physicians. These findings underscore the importance of ecological factors such as access to and use of appropriate mental health services in mitigating suicide risk. Settings characterized by lower socioeconomic status conditions and rural areas have also been found to be associated with suicidality in AI/ANs (Lester, 1995; Mignone & O'Neil, 2005). Moreover, mounting evidence has called into question the influence of regional and clustering trends on suicidal behaviors. Results indicate that research targeting suicide prevention in AI/AN communities should explore the local cultures of the specific tribal group in addition to the milieu shared with non-indigenous communities (Wissow, Walkup, Barlow, Reid, & Kane, 2001).

Summary of Biopsychosocial Risk Factors

This review of the biological, psychological, and social risk factors for suicide in Native American communities demonstrates that the factors predisposing indigenous persons to heightened suicide risk zones are multifaceted and complex. Single risk factors for suicide are not operating in isolation, but are likely interacting with other risk factors at multiple levels of analysis, evident by the numerous studies that regularly find a combination of risk factors rather than just one associated with suicidal behaviors. It is this interactive network that culminates in pathways to pathological outcomes and increases the possibility for suicidal behaviors. As demonstrated above, genetic linkages, psychiatric conditions, Native identity, social support networks, attitudes toward education, cultural continuity, spirituality, and socioeconomic factors (to list a few) are correlated with suicidality in AI/ANs.

Until now, the discussion has centered on identifying relevant risk factors (biological, psychological, and social) as indicated or suggested in the literature, with practically no attention devoted to examining the protective factors that buffer AI/ANs from engaging in suicidal behaviors. Equally important to knowing the factors leading to heightened suicidality is the formulation of a deeper understanding of the agents as well as the intervention strategies that have aided in preventing suicide among Native peoples. To actively overcome suicide, interventions must establish and reinforce these protective factors.

Protective Factors

Spirituality has been continually suggested as a potential buffer against suicidality for indigenous peoples. A recent study by Garoutte et al. (2003) indicates that a commitment to spirituality in the form of high endorsement of cultural spiritual orientations is associated with a decrease in the number of AI-reported suicide attempts. Alternatively, neither commitment to Christianity nor to cultural spirituality, in the form of high rating of importance of beliefs, was associated with suicide attempts. None of the associations between spiritual commitment and suicidality differed by sex. According to Garoutte and colleagues, these findings suggest that incorporation of indicators of cultural spiritual orientations may be of importance in studies of psychological well-being, because spiritual commitments may provide a means through which to make sense of and structure life. Although a protective association between suicidal behaviors and spirituality has been found, the results are inconclusive regarding the protective effect of indigenous identity (loosely construed) on suicidality. Mixed results concerning the association between connection and engagement with indigenous cultural practices and suicidality have been documented (Dexheimer Pharris, Resnick, & Blum, 1997; Freedenthal & Stiffman, 2004; Howard-Pitney et al., 1992).

Perceived strong family connectedness, social support, and affective relationships with tribal leaders have also been demonstrated to have a protective effect in the reduction of suicidal behaviors (Borowsky et al., 1999; Dexheimer et al., 1997; Howard-Pitney et al., 1992). Interestingly, positive attitudes toward education, perceived interpersonal communication skills, as well as habitual discussion of problems with friends or family members, were also correlated with fewer reporting of suicidal behaviors in the aforementioned studies. Notably, the presence of a nurse or clinic in the school setting also emerged as a correlate of decreased suicidal behaviors in adolescent females. The role of protective factors in the reduction of suicide attempts was highlighted by the findings of Borowsky and associates, wherein the addition of protective factors dramatically reduced suicide risk. In particular, the likelihood of engaging in a suicide attempt increased sharply (up to 14-fold) when all three risk factors were present (friend or family attempted or completed suicide, history of physical or sexual abuse, and weekly substance use). Increasing the number of protective factors generally proved more effective at reducing the likelihood of suicide attempts than reducing the quantity of risk factors. These quantitative findings are corroborated further by a recent qualitative study in which parents and elders expressed the need for suicide-preventive interventions that focus on bolstering protective factors through the strengthening of family, community, and cultural values (Strickland, Walsh, & Cooper, 2006). Thus, greater attention needs to be devoted to increasing the number and types of protective factors present in AI/AN communities.

Moving away from examining individual protective factors to community and societal factors, cultural continuity is emerging as a useful construct in understanding AI/AN youth suicide. The presence of cultural continuity was associated with reduced and in some cases nonexistent rates of suicide in certain AI/AN communities (Chandler & Lalonde, 1998; Chandler et al., 2003). In these studies, cultural continuity was measured by the existence of the following markers: land claims, self-government, police and fire protection services, health services, education, cultural facilities—in essence, these indicators reflect community effectiveness in the preservation and promotion of cultural integrity over time.

A Transactional-Ecological Framework for Understanding Suicidality

From a biopsychosocial framework, an examination of risk and protective factors at the biological, psychological, and social levels of analysis becomes central to any prevention venture. Most suicide-risk assessments and interventions typically begin with the identification of relevant risk and protective factors from a biopsychosocial perspective. Configuring suicidality within a biopsychosocial model, however, harbors the potential (whether intentional or unintentional) to invoke the politics of "person blame" (Albee, 1981; Caplan & Nelson, 1973). If risk factors are identified within a framework that focuses on individual or group "characteristics" or dispositions, then the possibility of person blaming or group blaming for the existence of such characteristics is heightened. Needed instead is a framework that recognizes the interactions between levels of risk and their contexts but circumvents any possibility for engaging with the politics of person or victim blaming. The transactional-ecological framework is an advancement over a strictly biopsychosocial framework because it emphasizes systemic and transactional points of intervention; its political and ethical commitment to examining and targeting systemic factors mitigates against the "tendency to hold individuals responsible for their problems" (Caplan & Nelson, 1973, p. 199).

The transactional-ecological framework proposed by Felner and Felner (1989) is an approach to prevention that targets the interactions between individuals and their environments along developmental trajectories toward negative outcomes. That is, this approach to prevention explicitly disavows person-focused interventions as "blaming the victim" (Ryan, 1971) and instead targets problematic transactions between people and their environments. Moreover, this approach rejects a disease-prevention model of intervention in favor of efforts that target broad-based antecedent conditions that might lead to any number of undesirable outcomes (e.g., school failure, teenage pregnancy, substance abuse) over time without necessarily yielding any specific developmental outcome (e.g., suicide) in reliable ways.

Borrowing from the transactional-ecological framework formulated by Felner and Felner (1989) for prevention efforts in educational contexts, what follows is an elaboration of postulates that are useful when attempting to understand and contextualize suicidality and suicide prevention. The postulates are paraphrased from Felner and Felner (pp. 20–22):

1. Disorder results from deviations in normal developmental pathways and processes. The central objective of prevention programs is to hamper such deviations and reinstate more typical normative pathways.
2. Behavior of concern may be typical and adaptive responses to *disordered* circumstances. Important is the understanding of the contexts in which targeted behavior arose and is maintained. In this way, the target population is not pathologized but understood within disordered contexts.
3. Contextual effects are important. Understanding the contexts in which behavior occurs is essential to effective prevention. Hence, the interaction between children and their environments as well as the effect of settings are the focus of prevention programs.
4. Pathology often originates in factors or conditions outside the person. Appropriate points of intervention are the processes and contexts rather than the person himself or herself.
5. Intervention from a transactional-ecological framework emphasizes prevention of broad-based antecedent factors and processes rather than targeted disorders.

In this conceptual framework, elevated suicide-risk zones are one result of deviations in normative developmental trajectories that lead to negative outcomes. The aim of prevention programs is thus to restore the individual to normative and developmentally appropriate trajectories without "blaming the victim" in the process. As a result, only those biological, psychological, and social risk factors that can be addressed in transactional terms are targeted for preventive interventions. Keeping these postulates in mind, the role of developmental pathways and the interaction between individuals and their contexts is at the core of understanding suicidality. Within this transactional-ecological approach, identifying antecedent conditions that predispose individuals to generic distress and dysfunction is necessary before addressing the interactions between individuals and their contexts. Reinstating normative trajectories (rather than treating individual disorders) is then the first line of defense against dysfunction and pathology.

□ Points of Intervention within a Transactional-Ecological Framework

In a transactional-ecological model, prevention programs vary regarding the designated points of intervention and the targeted risk factors. The points of intervention within this framework are determined by the mechanisms and processes leading to impairment and resiliency, rather than end-states that are relatively unpredictable by nature. As a result, intervening in suicidality is conceptualized within a broad-based "antecedent conditions" prevention model, where in contrast to the specific disease model, the individual is understood and treated as inseparable from his or her environment. Transaction-focused programs are differentiated on account of their intentional and explicit focus on person–environment interactions that predispose individuals to increased risk for dysfunction (Felner & Felner, 1989). Specifically:

> In these approaches, a set of characteristics of the person as well a set of characteristics of the environment must be identified, such that *only when they combine* do they increase risk and distort normal developmental growth patterns. (p. 31)

Essentially, the source of risk is conceptualized as resulting from the combination of persons with specific characteristics developing in compromised contexts. It is important to highlight that the specific focus of prevention programs can be "on one or the other side of the transaction, or both [person and environmental conditions] simultaneously" (p. 23). In general, models of intervention might be crafted along a transactional continuum targeting either the individual (through "person-focused" interventions such as enhancing coping skills of youth with heightened genetic risk for clinical depression), the transaction of the individual and the environment (through "transaction-focused" interventions such as enhancing assertiveness skills for women entering a male-dominated profession), or the environment (through "environmentally focused" interventions such as eradicating impoverished living conditions) respectively. Strictly speaking, however, owing to ethical concerns and political commitments, the transactional-ecological approach to prevention avoids person-focused interventions altogether, emphasizing transaction-focused and even environmentally focused interventions.

Healing: Moving Beyond Suicide

Two reviews of suicide programs in Native communities (May, Serna, Hurt, & DeBruyn, 2005; Middlebrook, LeMaster, Beals, Novins, & Manson, 2001) demonstrate the need for and effectiveness of using community-based models. Although suicide-prevention programs targeting AI/AN communities have frequently addressed broad antecedent conditions with an emphasis on the role of context on the individual, few studies have scrupulously reviewed and evaluated such intervention efforts (see Middlebrook et al., 2001 for a critical review of suicide interventions and recommendations).

According to Middlebrook and colleagues, in cases where outcome evaluations have been conducted, the analyses have been far from rigorous, with results described as "impressionistic" and limited, especially when assessing generalizability to other AI/AN communities. Therefore, information about the effectiveness of the implemented suicide-prevention strategies in designated communities remains largely unknown.

In one study, however, May et al. (2005) evaluated the outcome of prevention efforts within a small AI/AN community over a 15-year period. This prevention effort specifically targeted 10- to 19-year-olds, and incorporated re-education and awareness-raising activities for 20- to 24-year-olds. The prevention program sought to: (1) identify relevant suicide-risk factors for a Western Athabaskan Tribal Nation; (2) identify specific individuals and families at highest risk for suicide, psychopathology, and violent behaviors and implementation of prevention activities; (3) provide mental health services to individuals and families at highest risk; and (4) bolster community awareness through the involvement of tribal leaders, health care providers, parents, elders, youth, and clients. Initial program development and planning included interactive community focus groups centered on identifying problems, barriers, and potential solutions.

Notably, the members of the community identified problems leading to suicide, rather than suicide alone, as areas of concern and emphasized the importance of treating issues of alcoholism, domestic violence, child abuse, and unemployment, rather than just suicide. The results from these focus groups informed the creation of the Adolescent Suicide Prevention Project. Specific components included: surveillance, screening, provision of clinical interventions through outreach services at both health care facilities and popular settings for adolescents (community functions), provision of social services, integration of school-based prevention programs on life-skills development, and community education for adults and adolescents. Professional mental health staff also worked in conjunction with "natural helpers" or adolescent peers who were trained to refer clients to mental health services or to provide counseling to these individuals. May and associates (2005) found a dramatic downward trend in the number and frequency of suicidal attempts and suicidal gestures since the implementation of this community-based intervention model (the program accounted for approximately 60% of the variance), with rates in suicide completion remaining the same.

The study by May et al. (2005) highlights the importance of using community-based and community-run models of suicide interventions in Native American communities. For the New Mexico tribe in this study, the public-health/community-based approach to suicide intervention was effective, and likely remains effective. However, the study did not employ randomization or control techniques, and thus did not directly assess causal linkages; therefore, it remains possible that the reductions in suicide rates can be attributed to other factors. Moreover, one of the objectives of the prevention program described above was to identify specific individuals and families at highest risk by identifying biopsychosocial risk factors. In this way, the prevention program, though community-based, was also person-centered. By locating risk within individuals or families, this approach is vulnerable to the allegations of person- or victim-blaming described earlier. A transactional ecological model would bypass risk identification at the individual or family level and instead target trajectories and transactions generally leading to negative outcomes or dysfunction, such as the general availability of alcohol to minors or the difficult transition of all community adolescents into high school.

Emphasis then needs to be placed on establishing research programs committed to developing interventions that examine and treat individuals *and* communities within a larger transactional-ecological context. In this light, pathology does not reside within the individual, but in the culminating interactions between individual and contexts (stressors, environment, sociocultural factors, etc). Individual acts such as suicide and suicidal behaviors are examined within the context of ecological influences. Moreover, community involvement throughout the program development (from the initial to final stages) is necessary. Similarly, if we are to translate these research findings to clinical practice, great efforts must be made toward the creation of culturally sensitive and culturally competent mental health services. Brief recommendations for future research and clinical practice follow.

☐ Recommendations for Future Research and Clinical Practice

Research

In a recent review of suicide in Native American communities, Olson and Wahab (2006) made several recommendations for clinicians and researchers in the field of suicide. Some of the strategies offered for future research include the utilization of mixed methods (qualitative and quantitative methodologies) and community participatory methods to study suicide, serious consideration of tribal differences, exploration of urban versus reservation contextual influences, and the examination of acculturation effects. Furthermore, Olson and Wahab strongly encourage the incorporation of traditional healers and indigenous practices in research that seeks to learn about and treat suicide in Native American communities. Other recommendations include the exploration of intergenerational effects of historical trauma on conceptualizations of suicide and suicidal behaviors, and the evaluation of suicide interventions. Notably, the recommendation to conduct in-depth studies within and across tribal communities along with the recommendation to incorporate traditional healing in suicide preventive interventions are particularly relevant in Indian Country and will be elaborated further below.

Examining tribal-specific experiences or local culture is an important avenue wherein to address the heterogeneity of American Indian populations. This type of approach can be thought of as *emic* in its design because such approaches emphasize the study of a specific culture's distinctive psychology, cultural practices, folk models, and ways of life as distinctive constructs rather than sources of comparison and generalization (Gone, 2004a, 2007, in press a; Shweder, 1990). As applied to suicide research, emic approaches allow researchers a nuanced lens for examining the meanings and subjective experiences of mental distress without the imposition of etic or universally accepted biomedical conditions or psychiatric disorders. For example, O'Nell's (1996) ethnographic field work about the meanings of depressive like affect among the Flathead provides valuable insight regarding the cultural meaning of loneliness and collective depression in this community. Loneliness was much more than an individual experience, rather, loneliness was inherently tied to an awareness of the self as interdependent. Expressions of loneliness through acts such as gift-giving, visiting, and proper manners were reflections of the connectedness of human life and the need for compassion. Furthermore, Flathead loneliness was a response to current and historical tribal losses, as well as relational and individual disruptions. Moreover, Grossman, Putsch, and Inui's (1993) study of the meaning of death among adolescents in a Salish American Indian community revealed that personal exposure to death, alcohol, and drugs, and Spirit Sickness (English translation of popular illness of distress among the Salish) emerged as key themes in the participant narratives. O'Nell's work coupled with Grossman, Putsch, and Inui's poignantly reflect the need for culturally circumscribed understandings of mental distress and in particular suicide, as a first step in the creation of suicide-prevention efforts.

The recent attention to indigenous or traditional healing approaches to suicide intervention in Native American communities marks a shift in the zeitgeist concerning the use of alternative or complementary approaches to helping people in distress. At a recent conference on indigenous suicide prevention, community representatives advocated the integration of traditional healing practices and tribal leaders in suicide prevention efforts (Gone & Alcántara, 2006). Incorporation of traditional healing practices was deemed central to the acceptance and use of any prevention venture. However, integration is not without consequence. Before any systematic efforts at integration are made, serious dialogue about the implications of the integration of traditional healing practices must occur. Gone and Alcántara (2006) have begun such a dialogue by highlighting some of the challenges that may arise in any attempt to integrate traditional healing and contemporary health care practices. The unique challenges are centered on the description, translation, integration, and evaluation of traditional healing practices. Underlying these challenges are the cultural divergences in epistemology, discourse, and practice between indigenous healing traditions and contemporary health care (Gone, 2003, 2004b, in press a, in press c; Gone & Alcántara, in press). Traditional healers may oppose the articulation, surveillance, regulation, and evaluation of traditional healing practices. Fundamentally, integration of traditional healing practices and contemporary health care practices is not a simple endeavor, and further deliberation is in order.

Clinical Practice

Although death by suicide is a statistically rare occurrence, knowledge of the relevant risk factors and protective factors can be crucial to determining treatment plans and treatment settings. Key to effective treatment planning is the estimation and management of suicide risk. The latest authoritative text on suicide, entitled *Textbook of Suicide Assessment and Management* (Simon & Hales, 2006), is a comprehensive clinical textbook for mental health practitioners. The main objective of the text is to aid clinicians in the clinical assessment and management of *all* patients in suicide-risk zones. Although limited research exists on suicide and suicide intervention in Native American communities, this chapter uses the guidelines provided in the aforementioned text as a springboard from which to make recommendations for clinical practice in AI/AN communities.

Based on the American Psychiatric Association executive committee's practice guidelines for the assessment and treatment of patients with suicidal behaviors, state-of-the-art psychiatric assessment must include an evaluation of current presentation of suicidality, psychiatric illnesses, medical and family history, psychosocial circumstances, and individual strengths and vulnerabilities (Jacobs et al., 2003). Readers are encouraged to review Jacobs and colleagues for a listing of questions that may be helpful in inquiring about specific aspects of suicidal thoughts, plans, and behaviors (pp. 583–585). Of note, "emergency department or crisis situation, intake evaluation, abrupt change in clinical presentation, lack of improvement or gradual worsening despite treatment, anticipation of experience of interpersonal loss or psychosocial stressor, and onset of physical illness" are listed as situations in which suicide assessment may be clinically indicated. The presence of suicidal ideation and behaviors, psychiatric conditions, physical illnesses, psychosocial circumstances such as childhood trauma, family history, presence of impulsivity, aggression, hopelessness, cognitive features (dichotomous thinking, tunnel vision), demographic features like male sex, and access to firearms, to name a few, are discussed as factors generally associated with increased risk. A few of the protective factors listed include children in the home, religiosity, positive social support, and life satisfaction. Determining either the presence or absence of these factors, their severity, and interaction effects are of importance in determining which factors are modifiable. To decrease suicide risk, attention must be devoted to lessen or bolster those risk and protective factors that are modifiable (Jacobs et al.).

Aside from the estimation of suicide risk, its management and mitigation are continual goals in the treatment of patients at risk for suicide. Psychiatric management constitutes "determining a setting for treatment and supervision, attending to patient safety, and working to establish a cooperative and collaborative physician [clinician]–patient relationship" (Jacobs et al., 2003, p. 590). According to these authors, selection of treatment setting is dependent on the estimation of current suicide risk and potential for threat or harm to others, and other indices of a patient's current functioning, including comorbid medical and psychiatric conditions, access and extent of psychosocial support networks, demonstration of appropriate self-care, and cooperation with clinician and treatment. Suicide prevention contracts or "no-harm contracts" should also be used in the context of an established clinician–patient therapeutic relationship. Readers are again encouraged to peruse Jacobs and colleagues for a list of guidelines for the selection of treatment for patients at risk for suicidality (pp. 591–592).

The summary above represents the latest state-of-the-art practice guidelines for the assessment and treatment of patients with suicidal behaviors. However, a major limitation is clear: the guidelines are general and not specific to AI/AN communities. Calls to create culturally sensitive and culturally competent mental health services are common in Indian Country, and mere transposing of state-of-the-art guidelines undermines the unique cultural and historical context of Native communities. To this end, recommendations include the following: (1) increase the availability and access of indigenous interventions and practitioners as well as contemporary health care practices for Native peoples on and off the reservations; (2) recruit and train mental health providers (in particular Native clinicians) who work with Native communities; (3) increase number of psychiatrists specializing in children and adolescents; (4) implement cultural competence in suicide-risk assessment through the exploration of cultural meanings of suicide, help-seeking behavior, and culturally sanctioned versus pathological suicidality, along with the examination of the impact of degree of acculturation and religious views (Olson & Wahab, 2006; Wendler & Matthews, 2006). The fourth recommendation listed can be conceptualized as an extension of an emic approach to suicide intervention. Remembering that emic approaches privilege a specific cultural community's distinctive psychology, folk models, and understandings—essentially its worldview—culturally competent clinical assessment is one venue where emic approaches to clinical practice can be incorporated (e.g., through the incorporation of the diagnostic practices of the community itself). Moreover, situating the individual within a cultural context while recognizing unique individual differences is central to establishing and maintaining a therapeutic alliance (Wendler & Matthews); a strong therapeutic alliance has been linked to better treatment outcomes.

Culturally competent clinical practice with Native clients at risk for suicide should take into account the relevant risk and protective factors on suicidality in Indian Country as documented in the literature. Furthermore, historical and regional factors, tribal differences, acculturation effects, setting effects (urban versus reservation), and gender effects, along with cultural meanings of suicide and suicidal behaviors should be explored in depth.

Of note, our review of the advantages of a transactional ecological framework for conceptualizing suicidality and corresponding forms of intervention underscores the importance of transactional and systemic influences. A transactional-ecological framework excludes person-focused clinical approaches, most of which by design (or in practice) target the individual as the source of difficulty and remediation. Instead, this framework advocates for interventions that focus on "broad-based antecedent conditions" and community-based prevention efforts. Although considerations for person-focused clinical practice were presented above because most mental health services are delivered within the context of a therapeutic dyad, these recommendations deviate from the transactional-ecological framework. Needed are community-based and transaction-focused prevention alternatives. Ultimately, a transactional-ecological framework for conducting research and clinical practice reminds us that the individual must be understood within a specific context in which individual factors combine and interact with the environment.

☐ Conclusion

At the outset of this chapter, Kevin Gover was quoted as urging us to remember that general healing will commence once the issue of suicidality in American Indian and Alaska Native populations is addressed by both indigenous and non-indigenous peoples. Recent outcome evaluations confirm that suicide-intervention programs (especially in AI/AN communities) accounting for the transactional-ecological contexts in which suicide prevention occurs are indeed effective. Hence, situating biopsychosocial risk and protective factors according to Felner and Felner's (1989) transactional-ecological framework is imperative for developing interventions that actually reduce suicide-risk zones. A transactional-ecological framework reminds us that risk and protective factors are operating within an interactive network or transactional system, where an individual's potential for suicide is not independently determined by the presence or absence of particular intrapersonal factors (i.e., within a disease model framework), but is instead dependent on the aggregate interactions among broad-based antecedent conditions and individual variables that unfold within specific contexts over time.

Lessons from both research and clinical practice teach us that upholding an emic approach to both research and practice is a means to ensuring that suicidality in Native communities is studied and treated within an approach that situates individual conceptions, understandings, and experiences of suicide within a cultural context. Cultural competence in suicide intervention research and practice is a consequence of adopting an emic approach. The studies summarized in this chapter indicate that the profile of suicidality is influenced by cultural and regional variability. This proscribes the mere transposing of conventional clinical wisdom into AI/AN communities. Instead, clinical practitioners working with AI/ANs should question the extent to which conventional clinical wisdom (as presented in Simon & Hales, 2006) should be appropriated, tailored, or discarded when working with these communities. Moreover, the added effects of bolstering protective factors versus reducing risk factors is a key research finding that should be accounted for in determining appropriate points of intervention. The current state of affairs indicates that monumental strides are being taken so that suicide in American Indian/Alaska Native communities is no longer a neglected phenomenon. The recent collaborations and dialogues across indigenous and non-indigenous communities, researchers, and clinicians are stepping stones toward Kevin Gover's suggested path to healing.

☐ References

Albee, G.W. (1981). Politics, power, prevention and social change. In J. M. Joffe and G.W. Albee (Eds.), *Prevention through political action and social change*. University Press of New England.

Alcántara, C. & Gone, J.P. (2007). Reviewing suicide in Native American communities: Situating risk and protective factors within a transactional-ecological framework. *Death Studies, 31*, 457–477.

Balsam, K.F., Huang, B., Fieland, K.C., Simoni, J.M., & Walters, K. (2004). Culture, trauma and wellness: A comparison of heterosexual and lesbian, gay, bisexual, and two-spirit Native Americans. *Cultural Diversity and Ethnic Minority Psychology, 10*(3), 287–301.

Barney, D.D. (2003). Health risk factors for gay American Indian and Alaska Native adolescent males. *Journal of Homosexuality, 46,* 137–157.

Bohn, D.K. (2003). Lifetime physical and sexual abuse, substance abuse, depression, and suicide attempts among Native American women. *Issues in Mental Health Nursing, 24,* 333–353.

Borowsky, I.W., Resnick, M.D., Ireland, M., & Blum, R.W. (1999). Suicide attempts among American Indian and Alaska Native youth: Risk and protective factors. *Archives of Pediatric and Adolescent Medicine, 153,* 573–580.

Brave Heart, M., & DeBruyn, L.M. (1998). The American Indian holocaust: Healing historical unresolved grief. *Journal of the National Center, 8*(2), pp. 60–82.

Caplan, N., & Nelson, S.D. (1973). On being useful: The nature and consequences of psychological research on social problems. *American Psychologist, 28,* 199–211.

Chandler, M.J., & Lalonde, C. (1998). Continuity as a hedge against suicide in Canada's First Nations. *Transcultural Psychiatry, 35*(2), 191–219.

Chandler, M.J., Lalonde, C.E., Sokol, B.W., & Hallet, D. (2003). Personal persistence, identity development, and suicide: A study of Native and non-Native North American adolescents. *Monographs of the Society for Research in Child Development, 68*(2), 50–76.

Centers for Disease Control and Prevention. (2003). Injury mortality among American Indian and Alaska Native children and youth. *Morbidity and Mortality Weekly Report, 52*(30), 697–701.

Dexheimer-Pharris, M., Resnick, M.D., & Blum, R.W. (1997). Protecting against hopelessness and suicidality in sexually abused American Indian adolescents. *Journal of Adolescent Health, 21,* 400–406.

Dinges, N.G., & Duong-Tran, Q. (1994). Suicide ideation and suicide attempt among American Indian and Alaska Native boarding school adolescents. *American Indian and Alaska Native Mental Health Research Monograph Series, 4,* 167–188.

Duran, B., Duran, E., & Brave Heart, M. (1998). Native Americans and the trauma of history. In R. Thorton, (Ed.) *Studying native America: Problems and prospects* (pp. 60–76), Wisconsin: University of Wisconsin.

EchoHawk, M. (1997). Suicide: The scourge of Native American people. *Suicide and Life-Threatening Behavior, 27,* 60–67.

Felner, R.D. & Felner, T.Y. (1989). Primary prevention programs in the educational context: A transactional-ecological framework and analysis. In L.A. Bond & B.E. Compas (Eds.), *Primary prevention and promotion in the schools,* (pp. 13–49). Newbury, Park, California: Sage.

Freedenthal, S. & Stiffman, A.R. (2004). Suicidal behavior in urban American Indian adolescents: A comparison with reservation youth in a southwestern state. *Suicide and Life-Threatening Behavior, 34*(2), 160–71.

Garoutte, E.M., Goldberg, J., Beals, J., Herrell, R., Manson, S.M., & the AI-SUPERPFP Team. (2003). Spirituality and attempted suicide among American Indians. *Social Science and Medicine, 56,* 1571–1579.

Gone, J.P. (1999). "We were through as Keepers of it": The "Missing Pipe Narrative" and Gros Ventre cultural identity. *Ethos, 27*(4), 415–440.

Gone, J.P. (2003). American Indian mental health service delivery: Persistent challenges and future prospects. In J.S. Mio & G.Y. Iwamasa (Eds.). *Culturally diverse mental health: The challenges of research and resistance* (pp. 211–229). New York: Brunner-Routledge.

Gone, J.P. (2004a). Keeping culture in mind: Transforming academic training in professional psychology for Indian country. In D. A. Mihesuah & A. Cavender Wilson (Eds.), *Indigenizing the academy: Transforming scholarship and empowering communities* (pp. 124–142). Lincoln, NE: University of Nebraska.

Gone, J.P. (2004b). Mental health services for Native Americans in the 21st century U.S. *Professional Psychology: Research and Practice, 35*(1), 10–18.

Gone, J. P. (2007). "I came to tell you of my life": Narrative expositions of "mental health" in an American Indian community. *Culture and Psychology.*

Gone, J.P. (2006). Mental health, wellness, and the quest for an authentic American Indian identity. In T. Witko (Ed.), *Mental health care for urban Indians: Clinical insights from Native practitioners* (pp. 55–80). Washington, DC: American Psychological Association.

Gone, J.P. (in press b). "So I can be like a Whiteman": The ethnopsychology of space and place in American Indian mental health service delivery. *Culture and Psychology.*

Gone, J.P. (in press a). Encountering professional psychology: Re-envisioning mental health services for Native North America. In L. J. Kirmayer & G. Valaskakis (Eds.), *Healing traditions: The mental health of Aboriginal peoples.* Vancouver: University of British Columbia.

Gone, J.P. (in press c). "We never was happy living like a Whiteman": Mental health disparities and the postcolonial predicament in American Indian communities. *American Journal of Community Psychology.*

Gone, J.P. & Alcántara, C. (2006). *Traditional healing and suicide prevention in Native American communities: Research and policy considerations.* Unpublished report contracted by the Office of Behavioral and Social Sciences Research, National Institutes of Health (Contract No. MI–60823).

Gone, J.P. & Alcántara, C. (in press). Identifying effective mental health interventions for American Indians and Alaska natives. In E. H. Hawkins & R. D. Walker (Eds.), *Best practices in behavioral health services for American Indians and Alaska Natives.* Portland, OR: One Sky National Resource Center for American Indian and Alaska Native Substance Abuse Prevention and Treatment Services.

Grossman, D.C., Putsch, R.W., & Inui, T.S. (1993). The meaning of death to adolescents in an American Indian community. *Family Medicine, 25*(9), 593–597.

Howard-Pitney, B., LaFromboise, T.D., Basil, M., September, B., & Johnson, M. (1992). Psychological and social indicators of suicide ideation and suicide attempts in Zuni adolescents. *Journal of Consulting and Clinical Psychology, 60*(3), 473–476.

Indian Health Service. (2000–2001a). *Regional differences in Indian health.* Rockville, MD: Public Health Service, U.S. Department of Health and Human Services.

Indian Health Service. (2000–2001b). *Trends in Indian health.* Rockville, MD: Public Health Service, U.S. Department of Health and Human Services.

Jacobs, D.G., & Baldessarini, R.J., Conwell, Y., Fawcett, J.A., Horton, L., Meltzer, H., Pfeffer, C.R., & Simon, R.I. (2003). Practice guideline for the assessment and treatment of patients with suicidal behaviors: Part A: Assessment, treatment, and risk management recommendations. In R.I. Simon, & R.E. Hales (Eds.), *The American Psychiatric publishing textbook of suicide assessment and management,* Appendix, (pp. 577–597). Arlington, VA: American Psychiatric Publishing. (Reprinted from *American Journal of Psychiatry,* 2003, *160* (suppl.), 1–60.

Johnson, D. (1994). Stress, depression, substance abuse, and racism. *American Indian and Alaska Native mental health research, 6*(1), 29–33.

Kirmayer, L.J., Brass, G.M., & Tait, C.L. (2000). The mental health of aboriginal peoples: Transformations of identity and community. *The Canadian Journal of Psychiatry, 45,* 607–616.

LeMaster, P.L., Beals, J., Novins, D.K., Manson, S.M., & the AI–SUPERPFP Team. (2004). The prevalence of suicidal behaviors among Northern Plains American Indians. *Suicide and Life-Threatening Behavior, 34*(3), 242–254.

Lester, D. (1995). Social correlates of American Indian suicide and homicide rates. *American Indian and Alaska Native Mental Health Research, 6*(3), 46–55.

Lester, D. (1997). Suicide in America: A nation of immigrants. *Suicide and Life-Threatening Behavior, 27*(1), 50–59.

May, P.A. (1987). Suicide and self-destruction among American Indian youths. *American Indian and Alaska Native Mental Health Research, 1,* 52–69.

May, P.A., Van Winkle, N.W., Williams, M.B., McFeeley, P.J., DeBruyn, L.M., & Serna, P. (2002). Alcohol and suicide death among American Indians of New Mexico: 1980–1998. *Suicide and Life-Threatening Behavior, 32*(3), 240–255.

May, P.A., Serna, P., Hurt, L., & DeBruyn, L.M. (2005). Outcome evaluation of a public health approach to suicide prevention in an American Indian tribal nation. *Research and Practice, 95*(7), 1238–1244.

Middlebrook, D.L., LeMaster, P.L., Beals, J., Novins, D.K., & Manson, S.M. (2001). Suicide prevention in American Indian and Alaska Native communities: A critical review of programs. *Suicide & Life-Threatening Behavior, 31* (suppl.), 132–149.

Mignone, J., & O'Neil, J. (2005). Social capital and youth suicide risk factors in First Nations communities. *Canadian Journal of Public Health, 96,* S51–S54.

Novins, D.K., Beals, J., Roberts, R.E., & Manson, S.M. (1999). Factors associated with suicide ideation among American Indian adolescents: Does culture matter? *Suicide and Life-Threatening Behavior, 29*(4), 332–346.

Olson, J. (1998, January 22). Teen suicides leave Standing Rock reeling—Reservation residents look for answers, assistance after five youths die and 37 more attempt to kill themselves. *The Bismarck Tribune,* p. 01A.

Olson, L., Huyler, F., Lynch, A.W., Fullerton, L., Werenko, D., Sklar, D., & Zumwalt, R. (1999). Guns, alcohol, and intimate partner violence: The epidemiology of female suicide in New Mexico. *Crisis, 20*(3), 121–126.

Olson, L.M., & Wahab, S. (2006). American Indians and suicide. A neglected area of research. *Trauma, Violence, and Abuse, 7*(1), 19–33.

O'Nell, T.D. (1996). *Disciplined hearts: History, identity, and depression in an American Indian community.* Berkeley: University of California Press.

Rudd, M.D., Joiner, T., & Rajab, M.H. (2000). Assessing suicide risk. In D. Barlow (Ed.), *Treatment Manuals for Practitioners. Treating suicidal behavior. An effective, time-limited approach* (pp. 126–147). New York: Guilford.

Shaughnessy, L., Doshi, S.R., & Everett Jones, S. (2004). Attempted suicide and associated health risk behaviors among Native American high school students. *Journal of School Health, 74*(5), 177–182.

Shweder, R.A. (1990). Cultural psychology—what is it? In J.W. Stingler, R.A. Shweder, & G. Herdt. (Eds.), *Essays on Comparative Human Development*, (pp. 1–43). Cambridge, U.K.: Cambridge University Press.

Simon, R.I. & Hales, R.E. (Eds.). (2006). *The American Psychiatric publishing textbook of suicide assessment and management* (pp. 159–176). Arlington, VA: American Psychiatric Publishing.

Strickland, C.J. (1997). Suicide among American Indian, Alaskan Native, and Canadian Aboriginal youth: Advancing the research agenda. *International Journal of Mental Health, 25*(4), 11–32.

Strickland, C.J., Walsh, E., & Cooper, M. (2006). Healing fractured families: Parents' and elders' perspectives on the impact of colonization and youth suicide prevention in a Pacific Northwest American Indian tribe. *Journal of Transcultural Nursing, 17*(1), 5–12.

Tondo, L., Albert, M.J., & Baldessarini, R.J. (2006). Suicide rates in relation to health care access in the U.S.: An ecological study. *Journal of Clinical Psychiatry, 67*(4), 517–523.

U. S. Census Bureau. (2002). The American Indian and Alaska Native population: 2000. (Census 2000 Brief). Washington DC: Author.

U. S. Department of Health & Human Services. (1999). The Surgeon General's call to action to prevent suicide. Washington, DC: Public Health Service, U.S. Department of Health and Human Services.

U. S. Department of Health & Human Services. (2001). National strategy for suicide prevention: Goals and objectives for action. Rockville, MD: Public Health Service, U.S. Department of Health and Human Services.

Wendler, S., & Matthews, D. (2006). Cultural competence in suicide risk assessment. In R.I. Simon & R.E. Hales (Eds.), *The American Psychiatric Publishing textbook of suicide assessment and management* (pp. 159–176). Arlington, VA: American Psychiatric Publishing.

Wissow, L.S., Walkup, J., Barlow, A., Reid, R., & Kane, S. (2001). Cluster and regional influences on suicide in a Southwestern American Indian tribe. *Social Science and Medicine, 53*, 1115–1124.

Zhou, Z., Roy, A., Lipsky, R., Kuchipudi, K., Guanshan, Z., Taubman, J., Enoch, M.E., Virkkunen, M., & Goldman, D. (2005). Haplotype-based linkage of tryptophan hydroxylase 2 to suicide attempt, major depression, and cerebrospinal fluid 5-hydroxyindoleacetic acid in 4 populations. *Archives of General Psychiatry, 62*, 1109–1118.

Zitzow, D., & Desjarlait, F. (1994). A study of suicide attempts comparing adolescents to adults on a Northern Plains American Indian reservation. *American Indian and Alaska native mental health research monograph series, 4*, 35–69.

Prevention, Assessment, Treatment, Training and Research

Suicide Prevention in U.S. Ethnic Minority Populations

Rheeda L. Walker, Gregory E. Townley, and David Dei Asiamah

Intellectuals solve problems; geniuses prevent them.

—Albert Einstein

Suicide is a global phenomenon in which thousands of individuals die daily. In the U.S., these potentially preventable deaths include 3,000 people of color (Leong, Leach, Yeh, & Chou, 2007). Since suicide is often misclassified (cf. Rockett, Samora, & Cobin, 2006), we suggest that the necessity of suicide prevention for people of color is even more urgent than is currently reflected in the scientific literature. The associated burden of suicide involves billions of dollars in medical costs and the profound emotional distress of family and friends (U.S. Public Health Service, 2001). A model of suicide that delineates the unique needs of underrepresented groups such as American Indian, African American, Asian American, and Latinos enlightens suicide prevention efforts for these and other ethnic minority groups in the U.S. The unwavering reality is that people of color are often on the receiving end of marginal health services in the U.S. and worldwide. Suicide prevention efforts must keep the pace of an increasingly diverse world in which non-majority adults and youth demonstrate ever more needs for culturally relevant interventions.

Though sound suicide prevention presupposes adequate suicide *prediction,* some have questioned whether we know enough to predict or prevent suicide (Paris, 2006). In part, prediction is complex because of low base rates, difficulties in surveillance, stigma associated with suicide, and failure of medical reporters to agree upon definitions. In addition to misclassification of possible suicide deaths, risk factors vary. These variations are particularly salient among people of color. Despite the available research, efforts in suicide assessment are lagging. A handful of studies have tested the use of suicide measures with American Indian (Osman, Barrios, Grittman & Osman, 1993) and African American (Westefeld, Badura, Kiel, & Scheel, 1996) samples. Though other studies include ethnic minority individuals in the samples studied, few delineate norms or other useful psychometric insights. These issues are not uncommon in assessment research with ethnic minority group samples (Okazaki & Sue, 1995).

In some cases, prevention efforts are ongoing but have not been evaluated. Thus, the utility of these programs is unknown. The best efforts (though not systematic) toward suicide prevention have been observed for American Indians. Unfortunately, culturally specific suicide prevention programs have not been identified for African Americans or Asian American groups and, to our knowledge, very few have been developed for Hispanics in the U.S.. Nevertheless, there are clues that suicide (and thus, suicide prevention) for these groups differs from that of European Americans.

We have evidence that suicide has different cultural meanings across ethnocultural groups. Nevertheless, there exists a crude approach to clinical practice and research for underrepresented groups in the U.S. that dismisses the heterogeneity of peoples and embraces hegemonic practice. According to Utsey, Walker, and Kwate (2005), culturally sensitive researchers should generate research questions that "consider alternate possibilities, namely, those that are culture-specific" (p. 264). Mishara (2006), president of the International Association for Suicide Prevention astutely poses, "how much of our general understanding of suicide is applicable across cultures and when culture factors may have a predominant influence" (p. 1). Though we know that suicide is a cultural phenomenon, studies have failed to articulate firm research and suicide-prevention strategies that are culturally appropriate. Though suicide prevention is in its infancy in many ways, the dismissal of cultural variation has been disturbing.

In this chapter, we will begin with an overview of risk and protective factors associated with suicide in American Indian, African American, Latino, and Asian American populations. Because prevention efforts should target common risk factors, consideration of these factors is expected to inform culturally relevant prevention and postvention (intervention after a suicide has occurred). We will discuss identified suicide-prevention programs tailored to these groups and suggest a model for suicide prevention that is oriented to the unique experiences of people of color in the U.S.

☐ Overview of Suicide

American Indian suicide

Epidemiology

American Indians experience the highest rates of suicide of all ethnic groups in the U.S. (Olsen & Wahab, 2006). The most recent data show that the suicide rate among American Indians is 1.7 times higher than the rate of the nation as a whole (Indian Health Service, 2000–2001). Suicide is particularly problematic among youth and adult males.

Common risk factors

Many of the same risk factors for suicide in other populations exist among American Indians, including psychological disorders, substance abuse, and environmental stressors (Middlebrook, D.L., LeMaster, P.L., Beals, J., Novins, D.K., & Manson, S.M., 2001; Olson & Wahab, 2006). Major depression and anxiety appear to be the most common mental health problems among American Indians. These problems may arise from racial discrimination, loss of traditional identity, family problems, poverty, inadequate employment, and lack of educational opportunities (Olson & Wahab, 2006). Alcohol consumption appears to be a particularly high suicide-risk factor, and it is more frequently related to suicidal deaths among American Indians than in the general public (Yates, 1987; May et al., 2002). Adverse living conditions on reservations, most notably high homicide rates and economic deprivation, are risk factors that may also help to account for differences in suicide rates across tribes. For example, in a study of 120 counties that are partially or totally located on reservation land, Bachman (1992) found strong correlations between homicide and suicide rates.

Sociocultural factors

Centuries of westward expansion, colonization, and annihilation have forced American Indians from their traditional lands and caused widespread cultural disruption (Crofoot Graham, 2002). An unfortunate consequence of this history that may also contribute to high rates of suicide is the damaging influence of acculturation on tribal unity (Range et al., 1999). In a study of the Apache, Navajo, and Pueblo in New Mexico, Van Winkle and May (1986) found that the Apache had the highest rates of suicide (43.4 per 100,000) and attributed this to their higher levels of acculturation and lower levels of social integration (e.g., religion, cohesive government, and traditional structure). The Navajo had the lowest suicide rates (12.0

per 100,000), and this was credited to strong integrating forces and less acculturation (Van Winkle & May, 1986). Similarly, Lester (1999) reported that suicide rates among 18 tribes were positively associated with acculturative stress and negatively associated with traditional social integration. Acculturative stress may also exacerbate social and environmental stressors that would not alone result in suicide (Lester, 1997).

Despite the probable role of acculturation in suicide, elements of traditional American Indian culture may also contribute to suicide risk. Suicide has been historically present in American Indian societies to prevent capture in warfare and to atone for wrongdoings. American Indian youth may hear stories told by elders of these honorable deaths, and they may commit suicide in order to gain acceptance or honor (Lester, 1997). Additionally, many American Indian cultures believe in reincarnation and reciprocity between the human and spirit worlds; death is simply part of the natural balance of life (Range et al., 1999). Chief Seattle's famous words, as cited by EchoHawk (1997), poignantly illustrate this cultural belief: "For the dead are not powerless. Dead, did I say? There is no death. Only a change of worlds" (p. 66).

African American Suicide

Epidemiology

Crosby and Molock's (2006) summary of African American suicide indicates that it is the sixteenth leading cause of death overall for African Americans but the third leading cause of death for those age 15–19 years and fourth among those age 20–29 years. Several studies assert that suicide is likely underreported in the African American community (Rockett, et al., 2006, Joe & Kaplan, 2001).

Common factors

In a representative sample, African American suicide decedents were found to have been emotionally distressed as indicated by proxy report that mental health services had been sought. Marijuana use, excessive alcohol consumption, and firearm access were more likely associated with suicide decedents than those who died of natural causes (Kung, Pearson, & Wei, 2005). Of note, depression did not differentiate African American suicide decedents from African Americans who died by natural causes or from European American suicide decedents. Factors said to be associated with suicide attempts in low-income African American adults are psychological distress, aggressive tendencies, substance use, poor coping strategies, and poor religious well-being (Kaslow et al., 2004). When present, hopelessness has been observed as a stronger predictor of suicide for African American than European American youth (Durant et al., 2006). Firearms are said to account for a higher rate of suicide deaths in African Americans than for other ethnic groups (cf. Joe et al., 2001; Willis et al., 2003). Joe and colleagues (2001) speculated that residence in a resource-deficient neighborhood may lead to seemingly unregulated access to guns and to increased suicide fatalities.

Despite common assertions that suicide deaths occur more frequently in rural settings than in urban centers (Hirsch, 2006), this finding has been challenged (Willis, 2003). We also know that African American suicide deaths are likely to peak at age 25–34 years (Lester, 1998), are less likely than White suicide deaths to have a family history of suicide (Roy, 2003), and are less likely to be preceded by financial problems, chronic health problems, or substance abuse (Abe, Mertz, Powell, & Hanzlick, 2004).

Sociocultural factors

Religious activities, spirituality, and family support and cohesion have been suggested as key factors in African American suicide resilience (O'Donnell et al., 2004; Gibbs, 1997). Kaslow et al. (2004) noted that low-income suicide attempters demonstrate poor religious well-being and ethnic identification relative to non-attempters. Compton, Thompson, and Kaslow (2005) observed that familial and social supports were also influential in mitigating suicide risk. Interestingly, Walker and Bishop (2005) did not find religiosity to be a better buffer for suicidal thoughts in Black college students. Assertions of the unique protective capacities may be premature (Stack, 1998) in the absence of a convincing body of empirical literature. Alternatively, the disintegration of communalism among African Americans is potentially related to suicidal behavior among African Americans. Some support the notion that the lack of social integration and increasing isolation in a non-supportive society is associated with increased suicide rates (Singh et al., 2002; Wilkinson et al., 1984).

Asian American suicide

Epidemiology

U.S. suicide rates for Asian Americans are approximately 5.5/100,000 (McIntosh, 2006). Even so, epidemiological studies sometimes obscure within-group variability of Asian American populations, which include persons of Chinese, Filipino, Asian Indian, Korean, Vietnamese, and Japanese descent (Census, 2001). Chinese Americans represent the largest of the more than 10 million Asian Americans identified in the most recent

U.S. Census. Though Japanese Americans are relatively well represented in the available suicide literature, Japanese Americans are the smallest Asian American ethnic group in the U.S. This may be because the Japanese American suicide death rates are higher than those of Chinese Americans (Range, 1999). Similar to European Americans, Chinese American suicide rates are said to increase with age (Shiang, 1997) with East Asian women demonstrating the highest rate of suicide across all U.S. ethnic and racial groups (McKenzie, Serfaty, & Crawford, 2003). Most studies have been epidemiological in nature. For the purpose of this discussion, we will highlight specific Asian American groups where appropriate.

Common Factors

Investigations in depression, a common pathway toward developing suicide-risk models, have yielded conflicting results for Asian Americans. These differences in outcomes may be a result of sample differences in acculturation level, generation, and religious beliefs. According to Leong, Leach, Yeh, and Chou (in press), depression, hopelessness, and recent loss contribute to suicide risk for Asian American similarly to other U.S. ethnic groups.

Sociocultural Factors

Though religious teachings vary (Leong et al., in press), religious-inspired beliefs assert profound cultural underpinnings for acceptance or rejection of suicidal behavior. Thus, believers are socialized to shun selfish ideology and protect family or prepare for the next life after proper farewell (see Leong et al., in press). In this way, religious value systems and collectivist worldview are interrelated.

When addressed, suicide in Chinese Americans is often attributed to experiences of marginalization and acculturative stress. In cross-cultural studies, Asian American youth experience higher levels of social and psychological distress and familial conflict than European American peers (Choi, 2006). Lower self esteem than all peers (including Hispanic American and African American) and higher somatic symptoms were also reported. Hence, an additional predictor in Asian American suicide, particularly for youth, is familial level of cohesiveness, which can be challenged by differences in acculturative strategies. Multidimensional studies of Asian American suicide risk are needed to unravel the poorly understood nature of suicide in Asian Americans.

In a study of college students' self-injurious behavior, Asian Americans reported the fewest number of incidents (Whitlock, Eckenrode, & Silverman, 2006). However, Muehlencamp and Gutierrez (2005) posited that young Asian American adults may consider suicide, although these thoughts may not translate to fatal suicide attempts. Liu (2005) explored the effect of parent closeness on suicidal ideation in a multi-ethnic sample and concluded that parental influence was a better indicator of suicide resilience in Asian American than in other ethnic groups. Together, these studies provide some insight to suicide risk for Asian American youth.

Hispanic American Suicide

Epidemiology

Suicide is the seventh leading cause of death among Hispanics in the U.S. Rates for youth mimic those of African American and European American youth as the third leading cause of death in the 10–24-year age group. Suicide deaths are most frequently the result of firearms, followed by suffocation and poisoning (Centers for Disease Control, CDC, 2004a). Men are much more likely to die by suicide, with a ratio of approximately 6:1. The highest rate of suicide among males is said to occur for those over age 85. Hispanic suicide death rates occur at much younger ages for women, peaking at 50–54 years. Mexican Americans are said to account for the majority of Hispanic suicides while Cubans have been least likely to die by suicide relative to Central and South American and Puerto Ricans in the U.S. (National Center for Health Statistics, 2001).

According to the recent Youth Risk Behavior Survey (YRBS), Latina girls demonstrate suicide attempt rates higher than those of other ethnic groups with 21% of Latina youth age 14–17 years having self-reported suicide attempts (CDC, 2004b). Further, foreign-born girls have been said to surmount sociocultural and emotional challenges more so than those girls born in the U.S. (SAMHSA, 2003). This observation is consistent with Hovey and King's (1997) assertion that adjustments to cultural shifts plague Hispanics and particularly Mexicans in the U.S.

Sociocultural Factors

As is the case for other ethnic minority groups, the usual constellation of suicide risk does not always hold for Hispanics in the U.S. Though psychiatric problems, substance use, and life stressors may underlie suicidality, studies show that, relative to European Americans, suicide rates have not reflected rates of depression. For example, even in the face of economic or marital strain and unemployment for most Mexican and Cuban Americans and also for African Americans, major depression does not automatically confer risk for suicide (Oquendo, Ellis, Greenwald, Malone, Weissman, & Mann, 2001). One epidemiological study demonstrated that Puerto Ricans reported significantly higher rates of major depressive episodes than European Americans but surprisingly low suicide attempt rates (Oquendo, Lizardi, Greenwald, Weissman, & Mann, 2004).

☐ Suicide Prevention Efforts

Despite what we know about suicide risk in American Indian, African American, Hispanic, and Asian American groups, relatively little has been done to address this public health problem. Here, we will review ongoing prevention efforts with the most successful being culturally relevant efforts that involve communities and utilize traditional cultural practices and belief systems.

American Indian Suicide Prevention

The finding that American Indian suicide prevention efforts have had some success is echoed in the literature alongside the call for more empirically validated and published suicide-prevention programs (Middlebrook et al., 2001; May et al., 2005; Olson & Wahab, 2006). Suicide-prevention programs among American Indians have ranged from broad public health-based interventions aimed at enhancing self-esteem and decreasing substance abuse among young people to targeted preventions designed to identify at-risk individuals (Olson & Wahab, 2006). Interventions intended to limit access to both alcohol and means of suicide (e.g., ropes, guns, drugs, and knives) have also been suggested (May, Serna, Hurt, & DeBruyn, 2005). Unfortunately, relatively few of the suicide-prevention programs have been reported in the literature, so their overall effectiveness is unclear (Olson & Wahab, 2006).

One successful prevention program was implemented in response to alarming rates of suicide among a New Mexico Athabaskan tribe. The IHS provided funding for an initial small model adolescent suicide prevention project that evolved to a broad-focused program with a $1 million annual budget. The prevention program focused on the 10–24-year-old age group and sought to: (1) identify suicide risk factors among individuals and families, (2) implement prevention activities and provide direct mental health services to high-risk individuals and families, and (3) implement a communitywide systems approach to enhance community knowledge of suicide (May et al., 2005). Integrated program components included continuous data- and information-gathering, clinical interventions, social services, school-based approaches, and neighborhood "natural helper" groups that engaged in peer training, client referral, and counseling (May et al., 2005).

Over 15 years of the intervention's being in place, a substantial drop (61.1%) in suicidal gestures and attempts was observed. The suicide death rate did not significantly decrease, but neither did it increase, which is heartening given the significant increases that had historically occurred in 6- to 8-year cycles (May et al., 2005). The success of this suicide-prevention project was due primarily to a concerted effort to involve the community in every aspect of the program—from planning to implementation to continuous evaluation and feedback. The importance of community life for most American Indians cannot be overstated, and the long-term sustainability of prevention efforts demands that researchers and practitioners work closely with tribes in a fully collaborative capacity.

Another empirically supported suicide prevention effort evolved in response to rising rates of suicide among youth and young adults in a Southwestern Zuni tribe. The intervention used a life skills training approach modeled primarily after Bandura's social cognitive theory (2004). Multiple methods, including self-reports, behavioral observations, and peer ratings, were utilized to combat individual-, peer-, and environmentally influenced suicidal behaviors. Results confirmed that the students who received the intervention scored significantly lower on suicidal probability and hopelessness than students in a control group (LaFromboise & Howard-Pitney, 1995). It is unclear whether the results can generalize to other American Indian tribes, but the social cognitive approach provides a compelling framework for future preventive efforts.

Loss of cultural identity has been reported as a major risk factor for American Indian suicide (Duran & Duran, 1995). Some prevention efforts have utilized traditional cultural practices to reduce self-destructive behaviors and suicide among American Indian youth. The Association of American Indian Affairs in New York City supports a traditional Indian musical group known as "Project Dream." The youth who started the project were former substance abusers who wished to prevent self-destructive behaviors in other teenagers (Johnson & Tomren, 1999). Similarly, the South California Indian Center Education Component involves urban American Indian youth in an intertribal dance workshop to divert them from gang membership and substance abuse (Johnson & Tomren, 1999). These types of youth-based prevention efforts provide a relatively low-cost and easily implemented means of reconnecting American Indian adolescents to a culture that may buffer them from suicide and other self-destructive behaviors.

Suicide-prevention programs aimed at addressing American Indian mental health problems may be quite effective, so it is vital to improve mental health treatment and prevention services among this population. Crofoot Graham (2002) suggests that helping professionals must have a basic understanding of healing traditions and the American Indian relational worldview in order to assist suicidal youth and adults. According to the relational worldview, health and wellness are a balance of four major factors: the spirit, the context, the mind, and the body (Cross, 1998). One way to tap into this worldview is to use Linehan's Reasons for Living Inventory (RFL) to determine if individuals are out of balance in any of the four factors (Crofoot Graham, 2002). If they are, clinicians can help them connect with traditional healing approaches to support growth and combat suicidal thoughts and behaviors. Despite the potential utility of assessing balance with the RFL, psychometric properties for American Indians should be assessed to determine its validity and reliability among this population.

There is evidence that American Indians value the role of native healers and traditional healing practices as much as or more so than they do mental health professionals (Johnson & Cameron, 2001). This may be due in part to issues of trust, given the tenuous history between American Indians and the United States government. Traditional healers may also be more adept at interpreting symptoms and complaints. For example, the words "depressed" and "anxious" are absent from the languages of some American Indians. Additionally, American Indians ascribe different meanings and words to their illnesses (Johnson & Cameron, 2001). Clinicians, particularly those who are not aware of these differences, may misdiagnose clients, fail to recognize problems, or rely too closely on stereotypes and biases when interpreting symptoms. To best assist clients, it is vital that practitioners consult with traditional healers or trusted community members at all levels of mental health treatment and prevention (Duran & Duran, 1995).

There remains a great need for future research aimed at understanding the similarities and differences among suicide rates, risk factors, and belief systems within the varied American Indian tribes. This can be achieved through both quantitative and qualitative data-collection methods. One suggestion is to collect suicide rates and risk-factor data from tribes throughout the U.S. and use multilevel statistical modeling to determine the influence of reservation location or type of neighborhood (e.g., rural versus urban) on the results. Another suggestion is to conduct focus groups on reservations to establish tribe-specific definitions of suicide and encourage open dialogue among community members. Although the current reality of suicide in American Indian communities is a grim one, enhanced research techniques and suicide-prevention efforts may hold the key to abating what has been called "the scourge of Native American people" (EchoHawk, 1997, p. 60).

African American Suicide Prevention

Limitations to suicide prevention in African Americans may be due in part to stigma associated with suicidal behavior and also alternative beliefs about what constitutes suicide. Widely held beliefs hold that suicide, as it is currently defined, does not occur in the Black community. African American adults are not believed to commit suicide in the face of overwhelming life problems (Walker, Lester, & Joe, 2006). Early and Akers (1993) noted that drug use has been conceptualized as a "slow suicide" that is understandable in light of social and economic conditions. Otherwise, suicide is believed to be contrary to Black identity.

Preventive efforts are not advised to be implemented in isolation, as individuals do not exist in isolation. An effect preventive effort should involve a community-level approach that targets local gathering areas, schools, and work places as well as religious institutions. Doing so promotes an understanding that prevention occurs at the individual level, taking into consideration the dynamic social and environmental factors.

Asian American Suicide Prevention

To our knowledge, no known suicide prevention programs have been developed specifically for Asian American populations. The dearth of such prevention programs may be a result of the relatively low death rates. In the case of Asian American youth or adults who have attempted suicide, Takahashi (1989) detected that "treatment for suicidal patients is conducted in terms of the basic tenets of Western culture" (p. 305). Given the ubiquitous shame-avoidance in Asian American cultures, clinicians should be particularly sensitive to pervasive cultural ideology. Given the need for more rigorous assessment, a social-cognitive investigation of Japanese American suicide might pursue interactive effects of perceived shame, self-appraisal, and somatic depression in predicting suicide.

Hispanic American Suicide Prevention

Attending to Hovey and King's (1997) poignant assessment of the dismal Latino suicide literature, it is not surprising that Latino suicide-prevention efforts are even more scarce. Empirically evaluated youth suicide-prevention programs have targeted adolescents only (Donnell, Sueve, Wardlaw, &, O'Donnell, 2003). Even so, prevention efforts might be best served by more global violence prevention. Though suicide deaths typically outrank homicide deaths, this is not true for either Latino or African American populations. The Center for Hispanic Youth Violence Prevention (2003) promotes community-based programming and holistically attacks youth violence. Unfortunately, the challenge for prevention is to demonstrate efficacy. Even more, inclusive cross-cultural models of suicide are gravely needed.

□ A Culturally Relevant Model for Suicide Prevention

Suicide prevention is inherently complicated by insufficient understanding of proximal and distal factors. Vulnerability to psychiatric symptomatology and suicide proneness that are overridden by cultural buffers such as ethnic identity is important to realize in culturally germane models of suicide. Social and environmental circumstances that lead to suicide in underrepresented U.S. groups are more complicated than those that appear in current models for suicide (cf. Maris, 2002). Mainstream definitions of suicide should address suicide-risk profiles and definitions that are informed by the respective communities.

We insist on a model of suicide prevention that emphasizes cultural resilience and social realities in determining suicide risk for underrepresented groups (see Figure 9.1). In doing so, we will revisit the primary culprits in suicide vulnerability and also cultural milieus that seemingly protect certain groups and individuals who identify with those groups. Despite the overwhelming dearth of literature, a pattern emerges that suggests that prevention efforts target three key domains for people of color. These areas are (1) *accurate* assessment and treatment of psychiatric symptoms, which includes (2) the impact of race-related stressors and acculturative vulnerability, and (3) ethnocultural resilience.

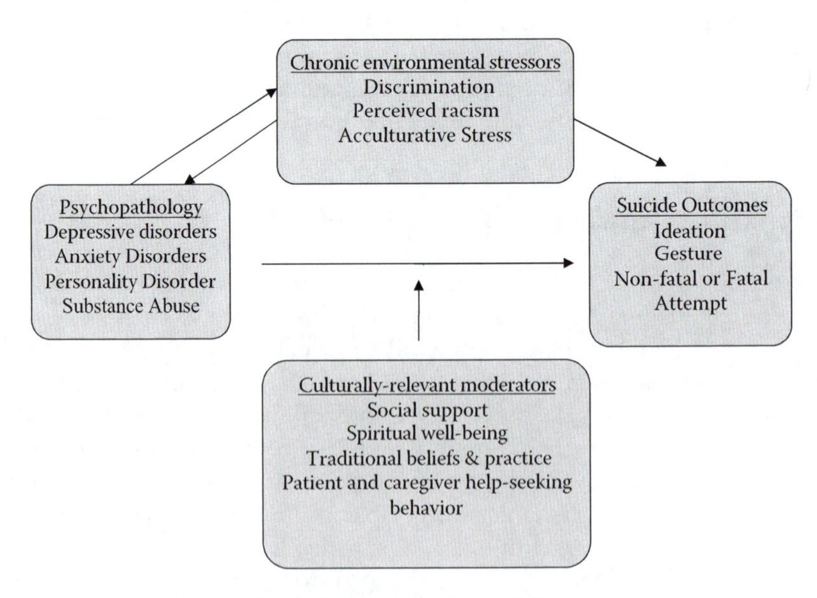

FIGURE 9.1 Pathways to ethnic minority suicide outcomes.

Assessment and Treatment of Axis I problems

In the model, we acknowledge that risk factors such as mood and personality disorders, as well as substance-use problems, are related to suicide risk. Most research findings indicate that depressive symptomatology and presence of a mood disorder, Axis I clinical problems, often precede suicide thoughts and suicidal behavior. Primary prevention efforts that address problems of undiagnosed and untreated Axis I mental health problems are believed to trigger suicidal thoughts and behavior at least in American Indian and Asian American groups. Primary prevention efforts, characterized as those that enlist broad environmental changes and circumvent suicidogenic factors (Maris, 2002, p. 321) are warranted. Such changes would affect incidence of anxiety and emotional effects of unemployment, racism, and other factors that potentially contribute to African American suicide risk. Primary prevention is akin to universal prevention efforts, which are implemented regardless of individuals' projected risk. Selective and indicated prevention programs target the intervention to those with most immediate needs (i.e., present with one or more suicide-risk factors or who have attempted suicide).

Universal prevention efforts are potentially most strategic since risk factors have been poorly identified for people of color. As an example, very few studies have examined suicide risk among ethnocultural individuals diagnosed with borderline personality disorder (BPD) a psychological condition characterized by extreme emotional dysregulation, implusivity, and self-harm behavior. Interestingly, Latino men have been said to demonstrate higher rates of BPD than both European American and African American men (Castaneda, & Franco, 1985; Chavira et al., 2003). Even more, Latinos diagnosed with BPD are more likely than African American and European Americans to attempt suicide (Chavira et al., 2003).

Race-Related Stressors and Acculturative Vulnerability

Internalized experiences of mistreatment and eroded cultural identity must be rigorously tested in people of color. Psychological distress is often caused by chronic race-related stressors and daily life hassles (e.g., Hwang, Myers, & Takeuchi, 2000). This has important implications for prevention such that coping mechanisms might be enacted to buffer potentially suicidogenic experiences, including familial conflict and acculturation-related stress. In a college student sample, Walker, Wingate, Obasi, and Joiner (in press) found that symptoms of depression were related to suicide ideation for African American college students only if self-reported ethnic identity was low, emphasizing the importance of a positive cultural identity.

Prevention models for people of color should be compelled to address pervasive environmental stressors. Institutional racism such that Black men report more job and legal discrimination than Black women (Broman, Mavaddat, & Hsu, 2000) is a potential target for primary efforts. Even more, this discrimination is particularly salient for young Black adults who are most at risk for suicide death. Even in an increasingly liberal society, subtle racism affects people of color in employment, healthcare, and even mental health service settings (Constantine, 2007; Dovidio & Gaertner, 2000).

For youth, acculturation level and conflict with parents has been found to increase vulnerability to suicide. Though these challenges commonly contribute to suicide risk, depression, and adjustment difficulties, culturally laden interventions can ameliorate these problems. As an example, Asian clients who experience a worldview-match with their therapists have reported a stronger working alliance (Kim, Ng, & Ahn, 2005).

Ethnocultural Resilience

Attention to culturally relevant moderators is akin to a positive psychology approach to suicide for underrepresented groups. Wingate et al. (2006) consider "how do the majority of individuals successfully cope with life's stressors?" Positive psychology emphasizes everyday happiness rather than individual vulnerability or psychiatric distress. Given that Hispanics and African Americans in particular suffer an inordinate amount of social and economic strain in the U.S. but demonstrate phenomenally low fatal suicide attempts, studies of how high-functioning people of color cope would be instructive for prevention efforts. Oqendo et al. (2001) observed that Puerto Rican and Mexican American males benefit from suicide protection despite the prevalence of depression. Similar observations have been made for African American women (Nisbet, 1996). The mitigating features of cultural identity and spirituality have been demonstrated in only a few studies and warrant specific exploration to the buffering mechanisms.

It is reasonable to enact treatment and intervention at the societal rather than individual level to be most effective (Lester, 2006). Doing so with a highly stigmatized public health challenge is tricky but worth the effort. Walker and colleagues (2006) found that African Americans were less likely than European Americans to attribute suicide to interpersonal problems. The consequence of this belief is that, even if one expresses suicidal thoughts in response to a recent stressor, those warning signs may go unaddressed. Societal ills such as racism will not be ameliorated in this lifetime, but changing opinions about suicide is feasible.

Activating ecological approaches may have the best outcomes for addressing a myriad of risky behavior. As an example, Henggeler and colleagues and others have found decreased criminal behavior (Borduin et al., 1995; Henggeler et al., 1992), marijuana drug use (Henggeler et al., 2002), decreased psychiatric symptoms (Henggeler et al., 2003), and suicide attempt rates (Huey et al., 2004) associated with multisystemic therapy (MST). MST is a strengths-based approach that involves identifying key determinants for behavioral problems and developing collaborative familial and community networks as well as medical interventions tailored to each youth and implemented in homes or wherever is most accessible for the youth and family.

In all, systematic models of suicide prevention should be tailored to the sociocultural and ethnic reality associated with membership in a specified ethnic group. Though a model that details prevention efforts for each U.S. ethnic minority group is beyond the scope of this chapter, we highlight some considerations for African Americans. One example relates to an insistence on valid strategies for assessment and diagnosis. Legitimate approaches include comprehension that presence of PTSD may be more predictive of suicidal behavior than major depressive disorder in African Americans (Joe et al., 2006). Finely tuned assessment further recognizes both emerging symptoms *and* syndromal levels of depression as African Americans are said to demonstrate psychiatric symptoms that may not reach clinical levels of disorder (see Kessler, Berglund, Zhao, Leaf, & Bruce, 1996; Robins & Regier, 1991). Also, best assessment includes consideration that a strong sense of ethnic identity may dissuade thoughts of suicide even in depressed young adults (Walker et al., in press). We propose a revision of the general suicide-assessment framework (Joiner, Walker, Rudd, & Jobes, 1999) that integrates the domain of racism, ethnic identity, and acculturative stressors.

Potential sites for addressing high-risk suicidal behavior are hospital emergency departments. African Americans receive the majority of healthcare in these departments but are most likely to be underdiagnosed for psychiatric problems (Kunen, Smith, Niederhauser, & Morris, 2005). Trained emergency department personnel have a high probability of offsetting future suicide attempts. Additionally, media attention to suicide in the African American community may have similar effects, as did awareness campaigns to the insidious HIV and AIDS epidemics.

In addition to addressing community-wide beliefs, individual-level prevention efforts may be approached via social cognitive interventions and reinforcing notions of self-efficacy (see Bandura, 2004). Public health campaigns may be instrumental in reducing the stigma associated with African American suicide but also in reinforcing African cultural ideals and sense of fortitude. An important component of increasing self-efficacy is increasing self-knowledge, particularly for African Americans. Additionally, fostering connections to social systems via family therapy and group counseling with individuals who have attempted suicide can be key. The approach not only provides guidance and social supports for those experiencing stressors that might lead to a suicide attempt but also provides a setting for learning new coping strategies and alternative behaviors as well as more adaptive appraisals of stress.

There are multiple potential points of intervention. As an example, African American and other ethnic minority spiritual and religious leaders are contacted for emotional help as frequently as for spiritual and religious need (Young, Griffith, & Williams, 2003). Thus, suicide-prevention efforts might involve these community-resource officers in discussions of prevention and intervention efforts. A very sad reality is that when individuals are identified, very few resources are available; others are not identifiable or provoke fears brought on by stigma. Thus, free mental health clinics advertised as family health centers (Poussaint & Alexander, 2000) may become an important enterprise. These centers may include *anticipatory* objectives that return to African-centered rituals and traditions so that African-centered cultural practice is not lost on younger generations.

Current prevention efforts have had limited utility. Kataoka, Stein, Lieberman, and Wong (2003) noted that ethnic minority youth have been under-identified for prevention programming. It is also notable that, though religious-based efforts have been suggested, the reality is that such efforts may not influence youth suicide, particularly for African Americans. Kunjufu (1994) noted that Black male adults and youth are not strongly socialized toward religious institutions. Thus, Utsey, Hook and Stanard's (2007) promotion of community-based intervention merits additional investigation and research support.

□ Future Directions

In sum, allies in public health promotion ought to be attuned to alternative conceptualizations of suicide that include chronic alcohol and drug use, as well as poor health behavior, as forms of parasuicide in oppressed peoples. Otherwise, conventional definitions will lead to wrongly classified deaths. Serious efforts of prevention cannot begin without even more refined efforts of categorizing self-harm behavior. Gibbs (1997) and recently Rockett and colleagues (2006) brought notice to the paradox of Black suicide—the notion that a group could be so persistently denigrated yet so resilient. Culturally inclusive perspectives might eliminate the paradox.

An Alternative Strategy for Assessing Risk

Recurring themes in ethnic minority suicide have suggested a potent influence of acculturation, familial and social cohesion, and racial or ethnic identity above and beyond the complex underlying psychiatric factors. Given the imprecise nature of suicide-risk prediction and the poorly understood influence of sociocultural factors, innovative strategies for calculating actual risk are needed, particularly for people of color. For better targeted prevention, Modai and colleagues (Modai, Kuperman, Goldberg, Goldish, & Mendel, 2004; Modai et al., 2002) explored the use of fuzzy logic and neural network identification to better predict medically serious suicide attempts. Fuzzy logic calculates nonlinear algorithms for which large numbers of variables can be manipulated in predicting certain outcomes. These methods are suited to classifying complex problems with multiple variables for which influences modulate across clients. Modai and colleagues concluded that (virtual) fuzzy logic can be useful in the identification of high-risk individuals who might otherwise go overlooked by clinical personnel. The nonlinear neural networks are trained to determine suicide risk as a function of a predetermined variable set. However, this methodology has not been pursued by social scientists and speaks to the need for cross-disciplinary approaches to suicidology. Smithson (1987) noted that fuzzy logic mirrors "people's natural tendencies," which are often unclear, but that the theoretical approach may be actualized by probability techniques that social scientists already utilize.

Clinical and community efforts in suicide prevention would be suited to broad emphasis on protective factors. For some groups, suicide prevalence is much lower where the cultural milieu is stronger (see Lester, 1997). For others, suicide is said to have been much lower before major sociocultural shifts (Gibbs, 1988; Walker, under review). Thus, strategies that invest in a positive psychology approach to suicide prevention in which suicide protection is enhanced may be most promising toward primary prevention efforts.

In generating prevention programming, prevention strategists are cautioned to attend to basic needs (O'Donnnell et al., 2004) and perhaps also stigmas. In doing so, social factors and challenges with anxiety and depression may be allayed, thereby minimizing risk for people of color. Stigma associated with mental health care exacerbated by poor cultural competence also undermines prevention efforts. Brown, Abe-Kim, and Barrio (2003) asserted that help-seeking is often associated with character weakness in lay people. Walker, Lester, and Joe (2006) suggested that African American caregivers may not seek help for potentially suicidal family and friends because struggle is *expected*; suicide is not believed to be a legitimate problem-solver among lay persons. Thus, efforts to prevent suicide should also include increased community awareness of risk and resiliency factors. Given that risk profiles vary across age groups—rates are higher among African American youth and elder Asian American women—ongoing efforts for suicide prevention across the lifespan are also gravely needed.

Diekstra (1989) insisted on "the assembly of scientifically sound information on the causation of suicidal behavior, on efficacy of intervention and prevention schemes and on effective methodologies for implementing such schemes in a variety of cultural and socioeconomic situations" (p. 19) in addition to improving services and information to the general public. Unfortunately, research methods in psychology are enmeshed in a western worldview for which changes are far to come. Thus, new methods that include virtual and qualitative inquiry will perhaps inform suicide prevention efforts.

□ Conclusion

Suicide is one of several premature-death outcomes for which appropriate primary interventions could be efficacious in minimizing death. Knox (2004) asked that if we know that suicide is a public health problem, why are we not doing anything about it. We might add, if we know that ethnic groups that have traditionally been "protected" are no longer so, then how do we invest in replenishing important psychological buffers.

The Surgeon General's (U.S. Public Health Service, 1999) initial proposal for suicide prevention recommended awareness, intervention, and methodology (AIM) as the framework for suicide prevention. Later, the National Strategy for Suicide Prevention (USDHHS, 2001) established objectives for reducing suicide in the U.S. The objectives included promoting awareness, reducing access to lethal means, promoting effective clinical practice, supporting suicide research, and expanding surveillance. However, the stated plans understated the explicit need for culturally appropriate prevention efforts, and suicide prevention for ethnically diverse groups remains relatively nonexistent.

Despite the determination to treat all groups as if they were the same, the need to develop culturally appropriate suicide prevention and postvention is critical. The primary strength of the model is its attention to ethnocultural realities (e.g., acculturative distress) and adaptive cultural deculturation norms that preceded. Better research into the multidimensional interactive risk factors will yield effective prevention. Further, efforts toward suicide prevention for underrepresented persons in the U.S. may have international implications. As an example, Black Caribbean, Bangladeshi, and South Asian adults born in England reported more suicidal ideation than those who relocated to England as adults (Crawford,

Nur, McKenzie, & Tyrer, 2005). Similar to treatment observations for those in the U.S., ethnic minority persons in London were also less likely to receive psychiatric services than White individuals post-suicide attempt. Research findings consistently espouse the toxic nature of cultural transition. Yet, few resources have been invested in the unique needs of people of color. Applications that promote daily strength, hope, creativity, and meaningful connections to others will forge a new dimension in suicide prevention.

☐ References

American Psychiatric Association (1994). *Diagnostic and statistical manual of mental disorders*, 4th ed. Washington, D.C. Author.

Anderson, M.L. & Taylor, H.F. (2000). *Sociology: Understanding a diverse society*. Belmont, California: Wadsworth/Thomson Learning.

Bachman, R. (1992). *Death and violence on the reservation: Homicide, family violence, and suicide in American Indian populations*. New York: Auburn House.

Bandura, A. (2004). Health promotion by social cognitive means. *Health Education & Behavior, 31*(2), 143–164.

Berrios, G.E. & Chen, E.Y. (1994). Recognizing psychiatric symptoms. Relevance to the diagnostic process. *British Journal of Psychiatry, 163*, 308–314.

Bohn, D.K. (2003). Lifetime physical and sexual abuse, substance abuse, depression, and suicide attempts among Native American women. *Issues in Mental Health Nursing, 24*, 333–352.

Borduin, C.M., Mann, B.J., Cone, L.T., Henggeler, S.W., Fucci, B.R., & Blaske, D.M., et al. (1995). Multisystemic treatment of serious juvenile offenders: Long-term prevention of criminality and violence. *Journal of Consulting and Clinical Psychology, 63*, 569–578.

Broman, C.L., Mavaddat, R., & Hsu, S. (2000). The experience and consequences of perceived racial discrimination: A study of African Americans. *Journal of Black Psychology, 26*(2), 165–180.

Canetto, S.S. & Lester, D. (1998). Gender, culture, and suicidal behavior. *Transcultural Psychiatry, 35*(2), 163–190.

Castaneda, R., Franco, H. (1985). Sex and ethnic distributions of borderline personality disorder. *American Journal of Psychiatry, 142*, 1202–1203.

Centers for Disease Control and Prevention. (2004a). Suicide among Hispanics—United States, 1997–2001. *MMWR, 53*, 478–481.

Centers for Disease Control and Prevention. (2004b). Youth risk behavior surveillance—United States, 2003. *Morbidity and Mortality Weekly Report, 53(SS–2)*, 1–96.

Chance, S.E., Kaslow, N.J., Summerville, M.B., and Wood, K. (1998). Suicidal behavior in African American individuals: Current status and future directions. *Cultural Diversity and Mental Health, 4*(1), 19–37.

Chavira, D.A., Grilo, C.M., Shea, T., Yen, S., Gunderson, J.G., Morey, L.C., Skodol, A.E., Stout, R.L., Zanarini, M.C., & Mcglashan, T.H. (2003). Ethnicity and four personality disorders. *Comprehensive Psychiatry, 44*(6), 483–491.

Chen, E.Y. (1994). A neural network model of cortical information processing in schizophrenia: Interaction between biological and social factors in symptom formation. *Canadian Journal of Psychiatry, 39,* 362–367.

Choi, H., Meininger, J.C. Roberts, R.E. (2006). Ethnic differences in adolescents' mental distress, social stress, and resources. *Adolescence, 41,* 263–283.

Compton, M.T., Thompson, N.J., & Kaslow, N.J. (2005). Social environment factors associated with suicide attempt among low-income African Americans: The protective role of family relationships and social support. *Social Psychiatry and Psychiatric Epidemiology, 40,* 175–185.

Crawford, M.J., Nur, U., McKenzie, K., & Tyrer, P. (2005). Suicidal ideation and suicide attempts among ethnic minority groups in England: Results of a national household study. *Psychological Medicine, 35,* 1369–1377.

Crofoot Graham, T.L. (2002). Using reasons for living to connect to American Indian healing traditions. *Journal of Sociology and Social Welfare, 29*(1): 55–75.

Cross, T.L. (1998). Understanding family resiliency from a relational worldview. In H.I. McCubbin, E.A. Thompson, A.I. Thompson, and J.E. Fromer. *Resiliency in Native American and immigrant families.* Thousand Oaks, CA: Sage.

Davenport, J.A. & Davenport, J. (1987). Native American suicide: A Durkheimian analysis. *Social Casework, 68*(9): 533–539.

Diekstra, R.F. (1989). Suicide and Attempted Suicide: An international perspective. *Acta Psychiatrica Scandinavica 80*(354, Suppl.) 1–24.

Dovidio, J.F. & Gaertner, S.L. (2000). Aversive racism and selection decisions: 1989 and 1999. *Psychological Science, 11*(4), 315–319.

Duran, E., & Duran, B. (1995). *Native American postcolonial psychology,* Albany, NY: State University of New York Press.

Durant, T., Mercy, J., Kresnow, M., Simon, T., Potter, L, & Hammond, W.R. (2006). Racial differences in hopelessness as a risk factor for a nearly lethal suicide attempt. *Journal of Black Psychology, 32*(3), 285–302.

Early, K. E. & Akers, R. L. (1993). "It's a white thing": An exploration of beliefs about suicide in the African American community. *Deviant Behavior: An Interdisciplinary Journal, 14,* 277–296.

EchoHawk, M. (1997). Suicide: The scourge of Native American people. *Suicide and Life Threatening Behavior, 27*(1): 60–67.

Feldman, M., and Wilson, A. (1997). Adolescent suicidality in urban minorities and its relationship to conduct disorders, depression, and separation anxiety. *Journal of the American Academy of Child and Adolescent Psychiatry, 36,* 75–84.

Firestone, R. (1997). Suicide and the inner voice. Thousand Oaks, CA: Sage.

Garrett, M.T., & Carroll, J.J. (2000). Mending the broken circle: Treatment of substance dependence among Native Americans. *Journal of Counseling and Development, 78*(4), 379–388.

Gibbs, J.T. (1988). *Young, Black and male in America: An endangered species.* Westport, CT: Greenwood.

Gibbs, J.T. (1997). African American suicide: A cultural paradox. *Suicide and Life-Threatening Behavior, 27,* 68–79.

Henggeler, S.W., Clingempeel, W.G., Brondino, M.J., & Pickrel, S.G. (2002). Four-year follow-up of multisystemic therapy with substance abusing and substance dependent juvenile offenders. *Journal of the American Academy of Child and Adolescent Psychiatry, 41,* 868–874.

Henggeler, S.W., Melton, G.B., & Smith, L.A. (1992). Family preservation using multisystemic therapy: An effective alternative to incarcerating serious juvenile offenders. *Journal of Consulting and Clinical Psychology, 60*, 953–961.

Henggeler, S.W., Rowland, M.D., Halliday-Boykins, C.A., Scheidow, A.J., Ward, D.M., Randall, J., et al. (2003). One-year follow-up of multisystemic therapy as an alternative to the hospitalization of youths in psychiatric crisis. *Journal of the American Academy of Child and Adolescent Psychiatry, 42*, 543–551.

Henry, A.F. and Short, J.F. (1954). *Suicide and homicide: Some economic, sociological, and psychological aspects of aggression*. New York: Free Press.

Hirch, J. (2006). A review of the literature on rural suicide: Risk and protective factors, incidence, and prevention. *Crisis, 27*(4), 189–199.

Hovey, J.D. & King, C.A. (1997). Suicidality among acculturating Mexican Americans: Current knowledge and directions for research. *Suicide and Life-Threatening Behavior, 27*, 92–103.

Howard-Pitney, B., LaFromboise, T.D., Basil, M., September, B., Johnson, M. (1992). psychological and social indicators of suicide ideation and suicide attempts in Zuni adolescents. *Journal of Consulting and Clinical Psychology, 60*(3): 473–476.

Huey, S.J., Henggeler, S.W., Rowland, M.D., Halliday-Boykins, C.A., Cunningham, P.B., Pickrel, S.G., et al. (2004). Multisystemic therapy effects on attempted suicide by youth presenting psychiatric emergencies. *Journal of the American Academy of Child and Adolescent Psychiatry, 43*, 183–190.

Hwang, W.C., Myers, H.F., Takeuchi, D.T. (2000). Psychosocial predictors of first-onset depression in Chinese Americans. *Social Psychiatry and Psychiatric Epidemiology, 35*, 133–145.

Ialongo, N., McCreary, B.K., Pearson, J.L., Koeing, A.L., Wagner, B.M., Schmidt, N.B., Poduska, J., and Kellam, S.G. (2002). Suicidal behavior among urban African American young adults. *Suicide and Life-Threatening behavior, 32*(3), 256–271.

Indian Health Service. (2000–2001). *Trends in Indian health*. Rockville, MD: Public Health Service, U.S. Department of Health and Human Services.

Joe, S., Baser, E., Breeden, G., Neighbors, H.W., & Jackson, J.S. (2006). Prevalence of and risk factors for lifetime suicide attempts among Blacks in the United States. *Journal of the American Medical Association, 296*, 2112–2123.

Joe, S. and Kaplan, M.S. (2001). Suicide among African American Men. *Suicide and Life-Threatening Behavior, 31*, 106–121.

Johnson, J.L. & Cameron, M.C. (2001). Barriers to providing effective mental health services to American Indians. *Mental Health Services Research, 3*(4), 215–223.

Johnson, T. & Tomren, H. (1999). Helplessness, hopelessness, and despair: Identifying the precursors to Indian youth suicide. *American Indian Culture and Research Journal, 23*(3): 287–301.

Joiner, Jr., T.E, Walker, R.L., Rudd, M.D., & Jobes, D.A. (1999). Scientizing and routinizing the assessment of suicidality in outpatient practice. *Professional Psychology: Research and Practice, 30*, 447–453.

Kaslow, N.J., Price, A.W., Wyckoff, S., Grall, M.G., Sherry, A., Young, S., et al. (2004). Person factors associated with suicidal behavior among African American women and men. *Cultural Diversity and Ethnic Minority Psychology, 10*(1), 5–22.

Kataoka, S.H., Stein, B.D., Lieberman, R., & Wong, M. (2003). Suicide prevention in schools: Are we reaching minority youths? *Psychiatric Services, 54,* 1444.

Kessler, R.C., Berglund, P.A., Zhao, S., Leaf, P.J., & Bruce, J.L. (1996). The 12-month prevalence and correlates of serious mental illness. In R. W. Manderscheid & M. A. Sonnenschein (Eds.). *Mental health, United States, 1996* (DHHS Pub. No. [SMA] 96–3098). Washington, D.C. Government Printing Office.

Kim, B.S., Ng, G.F., & Ahn, A.J. (2005). Effects of client expectation for counseling success, client-counselor worldview match, and client adherence to Asian and European American cultural values on counseling process with Asian Americans. *Journal of Counseling Psychology, 52,* 67–76.

Knox, K.L., Conwell, Y., & Caine, E.D. (2004). If suicide is a public health problem, what are we doing to prevent it? *American Journal of Public Health, 94,* 37–45.

Kunen, S., Smith, P.O., Niederhauser, R., & Morris, J.A. (2005). Race disparities in psychiatric rates in emergency departments. *Journal of Consulting and Clinical Psychology, 73*(1), 116–126.

Kung, H., Pearson, J.L., & Wei, R. (2005). Substance abuse, firearm availability, depressive symptoms, and mental health service utilization among White and African American suicide decedents aged 15 to 64 years. *Annals of Epidemiology, 15,* 614–621.

Kunjufu, J. (1994). *Adam, where art you? Why most Black men don't go to church.* Chicago, IL: African American Images.

LaFromboise, T.D., & Howard-Pitney, B. (1995). The Zuni life skills development curriculum: Description and evaluation of a suicide prevention program. *Journal of Counseling Psychology, 42*: 479–486.

Leong, F.L. and Leach, M. (2007). Ethnicity and suicide in the United States. *Death Studies.*

Lester, D. (1997). Suicide in America: A nation of immigrants. *Suicide and Life-Threatening Behavior, 27*(1): 50–59.

Lester, D. (1999). Native American suicide rates, acculturation, stress, and traditional integration. *Psychological Reports, 84,* 398.

Lester, D. & Yang, B. (2006). Should suicide prevention programs target individuals or society as a whole? *Crisis, 27*(4), 200–201.

Linehan, M.M., Goodstein, J.L., Nielsen, S.L., & Chiles, J.A. (1983). Reasons for staying alive when you are thinking of killing yourself: The Reasons for Living Inventory. *Journal of Consulting and Clinical Psychology. 51*(2), 276–286.

Liu, R.X. (2005). Parent–youth closeness and youth's suicidal ideation: The moderating effects of gender, stages of adolescence, and race or ethnicity. *Youth and Society, 37,* 145–175.

Maris, R.W. (2002). Suicide. *The Lancet. 360,* 319–326.

Maris, R.W., Berman, A.L., & Silverman, M.M. (2000). *Comprehensive textbook of suicidology.* New York, NY: Guilford Press.

May, P.A., & Moran, J.R. (1995). Prevention of alcohol misuse: A review of health promotion efforts among American Indians. *American Journal of Health Promotion, 9*(4), 288–299.

May, P.A., Serna, P., Hurt, L., DeBruyn, L.M. (2005). Outcome evaluation of a public health approach to suicide prevention in an American Indian tribal nation. *American Journal of Public Health, 95*(7), 1238–1244.

May, P.A., Van Winkle, N.W., Williams, M.B., McFeeley, P.J., DeBruyn, L.M., & Serna, P. (2002). Alcohol and suicide death among American Indians of New Mexico: 1980–1988. *Suicide and Life-Threatening Behavior, 32*(2), 240–255.

McIntosh, J.L. (2006). Retrieved November 2, 2006, from http://www.suicidology.org/associations/1045/files/2003datapgb.pdf.

McKenzie, K., Serfaty, M., & Crawford, M. (2003). Suicide in ethnic minority groups. *British Journal of Psychiatry, 183,* 100–101.

Middlebrook, D.L., LeMaster, P.L., Beals, J., Novins, D.K., & Manson, S.M. (2001). Suicide prevention in American Indian and Alaska Native communities: A critical review of programs. *Suicide and Life-Threatening behavior, 31* (Suppl.): 132–149.

Mirabal-Colón, B. (2003). Developing a center for Hispanic youth violence prevention. *Puerto Rico Health Sciences Journal, 22,* 89–91.

Mishara, B.L. (2006). Cultural specificity and universality of suicide. *Crisis, 27,* 1–3.

Modai, I., Kuperman, J., Goldberg, I., Goldish, M., & Mendel, S. (2004). Fuzzy logic detection of medically serious suicide attempt records in major psychiatric disorder. *Journal of Nervous and Mental Disease, 192,* 708–710.

Modai, I., Kurs, R., Ritsner, M., Oklander, S., Silver, H., Segal, A., et al., (2000). Neural network identification of high-risk suicide patients. *Medical Informatics and the Internet in Medicine, 27,* 39–47.

Muehlenkamp, J. & Gutierrez, P.M. (2005). Validation of the Positive and Negative Suicide Ideation (PANSI) Inventory in a diverse sample of young adults. *Journal of Clinical Psychology, 61,* 431–445.

National Center for Health Statistics. (2001). Vital statistics mortality data, underlying cause of death, 1997–2001. Hyattsville, Maryland: U.S. Department of Health and Human Services, Public Health Service, CDC.

Nisbet, P. A. (1996). Protective factors for suicidal Black females. *Suicide and Life-Threatening Behavior, 26,* 325–341.

O'Carroll, P.W., Berman, A.L., Maris, R.W., Moscicki, E.K., Tanney, B.L., & Silverman, M.M. (1996). Beyond the Tower of Babel: A nomenclature for suicidology. *Suicide and Life-Threatening Behavior, 26*(3), 237–252.

O'Donnell, L., O'Donnell, C., Wardlaw, D. M., Stueve, A. (2004). Risk and resiliency factors influencing suicidality among urban African American and Latino youth. *American Journal of Community Psychology, 33*(1/2), 37–49.

O'Donnell, L., Stueve, A. Wardlaw, D. M., & O'Donnell, C. (2003). Adolescent suicidality and adult support: The Reach for Health Study of Urban Youth. *American Journal of Health Behavior, 27,* 633–644.

Okazaki, S. & Sue, S. (1995). Methodological issues in assessment research with ethnic minorities. *Psychological Assessment, 7*(3), 367–375.

Olson, L.M. & Wahab, S. (2006). American Indians and Suicide: A neglected area of research. *Trauma, Violence, & Abuse, 7*(1): 19–33.

Oquendo, M.A., Ellis, P., Greenwald, S., Malone, K.M., Weissman, M.M., & Mann, J.J. (2001). Ethnic and sex differences in suicide rates relative to major depression in the United States. *American Journal of Psychiatry, 158,* 1652–1795.

Oquendo, M.A., Lizardi, D., Greenwald, M.M., & Weissman, J.J. (2004). Rates of lifetime suicide attempt and rates of lifetime major depression in different ethnic groups in the United States. *Acta Psychiatrica Scandinavica, 110,* 446–451.

Osman, A., Barrios, F.X., Grittman, L.R., & Osman, J.R. (1993). The Multi-Attitude Suicide Tendency Scale: Psychometric characteristics in an American Indian sample. *Journal of Clinical Psychology, 49,* 701–708.

Paris, J. (2006). Predicting and preventing suicide: Do we know enough to do either? *Harvard Review of Psychiatry, 14,* 233–240.

Poussaint, A.F. & Alexander, A. (2000). *Lay my burden down: Unraveling suicide and the mental health crisis among African Americans.* Boston: Beacon Press.

Range, L.M., Leach, M.M., McIntyre, D., Posey-Deters, P.B., Marion, M., Kovac, S.H., Banos, J.H., & Vigil, J. (1999). Multicultural perspectives on suicide. *Aggression and Violent Behavior, 4*(4): 413–430.

Robins, L. & Regier, D. (1991). *Psychiatric disorders in America: The epidemiologic catchment area study.* New York: Free Press.

Rockett, I.R., Samora, J.B. Coben, J.H. (2006). The black–white suicide paradox: Possible effects of misclassification. *Social Science and Medicine, 63,* 2165–2175.

Sainsbury, P. & Barraclough, B.M. (1968). Differences between suicide rates. *Nature, 220,* 1252.

Seiden, R.H., and Freitas, R.P. (1972). Why are suicides of young blacks increasing? *HSMSH Health Reports, 87,* 3–8.

Selkin, J. (1983). The legacy of Emile Durkheim. *Suicide and Life-Threatening Behavior, 13,* 3–14.

Shiang, J., Blinn, R., Bongar, B., Stephens, B., Allison, D., & Schatzberg, A. (1997). Suicide in San Francisco, CA: A comparison of Caucasian and Asian groups, 1987–1994. *Suicide and Life-Threatening Behavior, 27,* 80–91.

Singh G. K., Siahpush, M. (2002). Increasing rural–urban gradients in U.S. suicide mortality, 1970–1997. *American Journal of Public Health, 92*(7), 1161–1167.

Smithson, M. (1987). *Fuzzy set analysis for behavioral and social sciences.* New York: Springer-Verlag.

Stack, S. (1998). The relationship between culture and suicide: An analysis of African Americans. *Transcultural Psychiatry, 35,* 253–269.

Substance Abuse and Mental Health Services Administration. (2003). Summary of findings from the 2000 National Household Survey on Drug Abuse (DHHS Publication No. SMA 01–3549, NHSDA Series H–13). Rockville, MD.

Takahashi, Y. (1989). Suicidal Asian patients: Recommendations for treatment. *Suicide and Life-Threatening Behavior, 19,* 305–313.

Taylor, R.J., Chatters, L.M., Jayakody, R., Levin, J. S. (1996). Black and white differences in religious participation: A multi-sample comparison. *Journal for the Scientific Study of Religion, 35*(4), 403–411.

U.S. Department of Health and Human Services. (2001). National strategy for suicide prevention: Goals and objectives for action. Rockville, MD: Author.

U.S. Public Health Service. The Surgeon General's call to action to prevent suicide. Washington, DC: U.S. Department of Health and Human Services, 1999.

Utsey, S.O., Adams, E.P., & Bolden, M. (2000). Development and initial validation of the Africultural Coping Systems Inventory. *Journal of Black Psychology, 26,* 194–215.

Utsey, S.O., Hook, J.N., & Stanard, P. (2007). A reexamination of cultural factors that mitigate risk and promote resilience in relation to African American suicide: A review of the literature and recommendations for future research. *Death Studies 31*(5), 399–416.

Utsey, S.O., Walker, R.L., & Kwate, N.O. (2005). Conducting quantitative research in a cultural context: Practical applications to conducting research with ethnic minorities. In M. G. Constantine & D. W. Sue, (Eds.), *Strategies for building multicultural competence in mental health and educational settings*. Washington, D.C.: American Psychological Association.

Van Winkle, N.W. & May, P.A. (1986). Native American suicide in New Mexico, 1959–1979. *Human Organization, 45*, 296–309.

Walker, R.L., Lester, D., & Joe, S. (2006). Lay theories of suicide: An examination of culturally relevant suicide beliefs and attributions among African American and European Americans. *Journal of Black Psychology, 32*(3), 320–334.

Walker, R.L., Wingate, L.R., Obasi, E.M., & Joiner, T.E. (in press). An empirical investigation of acculturative stress and ethnic identity as moderators for depression and suicidal ideation in African American and European American college students.

Westefeld, J.S., Badura, A., Kiel, J., & Scheel, K. (1996). Development of the College Student Reasons for Living Inventory with African Americans. *Journal of College Student Psychotherapy, 10*, 61–65.

Whitlock, J., Eckenrode, J., & Silverman, D. (2006). Self-injurious behavior in a college population. *Pediatrics, 117*, 1939–48.

Wilkinson, K.P. & Israel, G.D. (1984). Suicide and rurality in urban society. *Suicide and Life-Threatening Behavior, 14*, 187–200.

Willis, L.A., Coombs, D.W., Drentea, P., and Cockerham, W.C. (2003). Uncovering the mystery: Factors of African American suicide. *Suicide and Life-Threatening Behavior, 33*(4), 412–429.

Wingate, L.R., Burns, A.B., Gordon, K.H., Perez, M., Walker, R.L., Williams, F.M. et al. (2006). Suicide and positive cognitions: Positive psychology applied to the understanding and treatment of suicidal behavior. In T.E. Ellis. *Cognition and suicide: Theory, research, and therapy*. Washington, D.C.: American Psychological Association.

World Health Organization. (2006). Retrieved October 31, 2006, from http://www.who.int/mental_health/prevention/suicide/suicideprevent/en/.

Yates, A. (1987). Current status and future directions of research on the American Indian child. *American Journal of Psychiatry, 144*(9), 1135–1142.

Young, T.K. (1997). Recent health trends in the Native American population. *Population Research and Policy Review, 16*, 147–167.

Young, J., Griffith, E., & Williams, D. (2003). The integral role of pastoral counseling by African-American clergy in mental health. *Psychiatric Services, 54*, 688–692.

Testing and Assessment

John S. Westefeld, Lillian Range,
Jay M. Greenfeld,* and Julie Jenks Kettman*

> ... most clinicians want to be ethically responsible and thorough in their assessments of culturally different clients. Unfortunately, they all too often are at a loss as to how to achieve this end. Out of frustration ... some clinicians meander through the process or simply give up. Neither practice is acceptable.... (Ridley, Li, & Hill, 1998, p. 897).

We agree that multicultural assessment, generally, is a complex and multifaceted task, and that there are many differences of opinion as to how best to accomplish the task effectively. The task is exacerbated when we are dealing with the issue of the assessment of suicidal risk, because of the many as yet unanswered issues vis-a-vis the specifics of suicide assessment. Nevertheless, in this chapter we will attempt to examine the issue of assessment as it relates to the assessment of suicidal risk among ethnically diverse persons.

Suicide is the 13th leading cause of death worldwide, and the 11th leading cause of death in the U.S. Further, among those aged 10–24 in the U.S., suicide is the 3rd leading cause of death. Also, in 2002, suicide and self harm resulted in almost 125,000 emergency room visits (Centers for Disease Control and Prevention [CDC], 2004). In view of this disturbing information, assessment of suicide risk is critical.

Groups of different ethnic backgrounds vary in their suicide rates. For example, African Americans are unlikely to die by suicide. African American women are at particularly low risk. In 1996, for every 100,000 people,

* Third authorship shared equally.

African American women died from suicide at the rate of 1.90, compared with the national average of 11.41 for women and men, and 4.42 for women of all ethnic groups (CDC, 1999). African American students also reported less self-harm than Hispanic and European American students (Blum et al., 2004). Given that ethnicity enters into suicide risk, it is important to make sure that risk assessment is culturally sensitive.

Cultural sensitivity in suicide-risk assessment has at least four facets. One, cultural sensitivity should entail ensuring that ethnic minority individuals are included in the development and standardization of suicide-assessment instruments. Two, cultural sensitivity should include awareness that ethnic minority individuals may be less likely to disclose suicidal information than majority individuals. Three, there needs to be knowledge of different minority groups. Four, cultural sensitivity should involve careful attention to cultural issues when assessing for suicidal thoughts and actions. These facets of cultural sensitivity are the focus of the present chapter.

Ethnic Inclusiveness and Suicide Instruments

Screening is only one component of an overall, comprehensive, multistep process of suicide assessment. Nevertheless, some of the tools available may enlighten this endeavor. Suicide-assessment questionnaires have advantages and disadvantages. Advantages include speed and the concomitant possibility of reaching a large number of people, access to information that may be difficult to obtain by observations and verbal interaction, ease of completion for those familiar with questionnaires, availability of established norms for some instruments, offering points that can be good starters for discussion, and indirect information provided by questionnaire responding. Disadvantages are the temptation to accept responses uncritically; the possibility that therapists or clients view the questionnaires as superseding the therapeutic relationship; the implication that suicide tendencies are static; and for some questionnaires, the issue of cost (Range, 2005). A further disadvantage is that ethnic minority individuals may have fewer chances to be included in the development and standardization of the questionnaire than majority individuals.

One review of 20 widely used inventories (Range & Knott, 1997) recommended most highly Beck's Scale for Suicide Ideation series (SSI) (Beck & Steer, 1991), Cole's (1988) self-administered adaptation of Linehan's structured interview called the Suicidal Behaviors Questionnaire (SBQ) (Linehan, 1981), and Linehan's Reasons for Living Inventory series (RFL)

(Linehan, Goodstein, Nielson, & Chiles, 1983). These instruments vary in the diversity of their development and standardization samples.

The SSI in its various iterations is arguably the most researched suicide-assessment instrument. It has been termed a classic questionnaire (Range, 2005). Originally developed for in- and outpatients, the SSI in paper-and-pencil form is adapted from a clinical rating scale (Beck, Steer, & Weissman, 1979). The 19 items ask patients to rate the severity of each symptom (e.g., wish to die) on a 3-point scale from 0 to 2, with total scores ranging from 0 to 38. The original standardization sample was 60 adult inpatients diagnosed with mixed psychiatric disorders (Beck et al.). A subsequent follow-up study included adolescent psychiatric inpatients (70 girls, 38 boys) from a suburban, middle- to upper-middle-class community near Philadelphia. Of these, 71 (65.7%) were European American, 22 (20.4%) were African American, and 15 (13.9%) were Hispanic American (Steer, Kuman, & Beck, 1993). Although this standardization sample included information about ethnicity and some diversity in ethnic background, the diversity was limited, as was socioeconomic status, a factor often linked to ethnicity.

Clinicians administered and scored the original SSI, but alternatives are now available. A modified SSI for paraprofessionals (Miller, Norman, Bishop, & Dow, 1986) added five new prompt questions. A self-report version (Beck, Steer, & Ranieri, 1988) is in paper-and-pencil format. A further improvement of the SSI is to ask people about their suicidal thoughts at the worst point in their lives (SSI-W) (Beck, Brown, Steer, Dahlsgaard, & Grisham, 1999). Among almost 4,000 outpatients (mostly educated European Americans) evaluated over 19 years at an outpatient clinic, scores of 16 or higher indicated high risk of suicide. Those at high risk were 14 times more likely to eventually die by suicide than those at low risk (Beck et al., 1999). This version of the SSI is promising in sensitivity and specificity of predicting eventual suicide. Further, the sample size in development was large, but the sample was limited in diversity. Nevertheless, its developers called for research on its most promising version, the SSI-W, with ethnic minority populations and those with varying educational levels.

In contrast, the SBQ is a short screening questionnaire. Originally, it was a seven-page questionnaire designed to be administered as a structured interview (Linehan, 1981). Cole (1988) used factor analysis to pare these questions to four. For example, one question is "Have you ever thought about or attempted to kill yourself," with answers from 1 (No) to 6 (I attempted to kill myself and I think I really hoped to die). The four questions are anchored differently, reflecting the original instrument and how people actually responded. Designed for adults, the SBQ is widely used and can be completed in less than five minutes. Because of its brevity and ease of scoring, it is recommended as a screening tool in research or clinical settings (Range & Knott, 1997). However, information about the initial development of the SBQ has not been published.

The original long SBQ has been used with psychiatric inpatients, shoppers (Linehan et al., 1983), and college students (e.g., Neyra, Range, & Goggin, 1990); the shortened four-question version has been used with college students (e.g., Cole, 1988), adult outpatients (e.g., Cotton, Peters, & Range, 1995) and in simplified form with children (e.g., Cotton & Range, 1993). Thus, this brief screening form is used in studies involving a variety of populations, but no information about its differential impact on persons of diverse cultures is available.

The SSI and SBQ are similar in focusing on the negative. In contrast, the RFL focuses on the positive. The RFL is 48 reasons for not killing oneself, rated on a 6-point scale from 1 (not important at all) to 6 (very important). The reasons cluster into six factors: survival and coping beliefs, responsibility to family, child concerns, fear of suicide, fear of social disapproval, and moral objections. This inventory requires no self-disclosure of past or present suicidal ideation. Rather, respondents imagine the factors that would prevent them from killing themselves if they ever felt suicidal (Linehan et al., 1983). The emphasis on life-affirming ideas common among non-suicidal people, and potentially lacking in suicidal people, is unique in suicide-assessment instruments (Graham, 2002).

The original standardization sample for the RFL included students at a Catholic university, senior citizens, middle-aged adults, and workers in a congressional office. Confirmatory samples included adults from a congressional office, graduate classes in psychology, people waiting in line at a King Tut exhibit, factory workers, people in the waiting room at a train station, and adults at a shopping center (Linehan et al., 1983). Researchers described them as having a variety of ages, marital statuses, educational levels, and ethnic backgrounds, but no specific information about ethnicity is reported. This sample is the most diverse in initial development reported by any of the major suicide-assessment inventories. However, reporting ethnic backgrounds of participants would have added to our understanding of the diversity of the sample.

The RFL has been adapted for U.S. college students (Westefeld, Cardin, & Deaton, 1992), U.S. adolescents (Gutierrez, Osman, Kopper, & Barrios, 2000), U.S. men prison inmates (Ivanoff, Jang, Smyth, & Linehan, 1994), Italian university students (Innamorati et al., 2006), and Swedish adults (Dobrov, & Thorell, 2004). Across many groups, the RFL has wide appeal.

Ethnic background makes a difference in people's reasons for living. For example, among U.S. undergraduates, African American students scored significantly higher on coping strategies to buffer against suicide and on moral objections against suicide than their European American counterparts (Ellis & Range, 1991; Morrison & Downey, 2000). Also, among inpatients in New York state, those with Latino ethnic background reported significantly higher survival and coping beliefs, responsibility to family, and moral objections to suicide (Oquendo et al., 2005). Reasons for living link to a relational worldview common to most American Indian people (Graham, 2002). Different ethnic minority groups may emphasize different reasons for living. For example, some ethnic groups may emphasize the immorality of suicide, whereas others emphasize responsibility to family or children.

Differences in reasons for living extend to countries outside the U.S. as well. In the United Kingdom, Jews reported significantly stronger moral-religious objections to suicide than Protestants (Loewenthal, MacLeod, Cook, Lee, & Goldblatt, 2003), and Muslims endorsed moral, total, and (marginally) survival-and-coping reasons for living more strongly than did Hindus (Kamal, & Loewenthal, 2002). Rural residents in Australia reported significantly more reasons to live than their urban counterparts (McLaren & Hopes, 2002). Individuals in some ethnic groups endorse stronger reasons for living than individuals in other ethnic groups.

When devising a suicide-assessment battery for a specific individual, it is important to take advantage of the varied instruments by assessing both negative and positive characteristics (Range, 2005). Of the three widely used suicide assessment instruments, the RFL involved the most diverse U.S. sample in its initial development, and has a positive focus that appeals to many individuals across ethnically diverse communities. Suicide questionnaires may supplement the information provided by an interview or provide directions for further probing, but it is important to keep in mind their possible bias.

☐ Ethnicity and Disclosure of Suicidal Thoughts and Actions

Intake forms ask people to disclose suicidal thoughts and actions. However, people of different ethnic backgrounds may answer these questions differently due to cultural ideas about suicide or ideas about disclosing suicide. Although no research to date has examined ethnic differences in self-disclosure of suicidal ideation, most research reports ethnic minority differences in self-disclosure in general (Morrison & Downey, 2000). Furthermore, minority individuals, specifically African Americans (Vontress, 1981), Hispanic Americans (Laval, Gomez, & Ruiz, 1983), Asian Americans (Sue & Sue, 1990), and Native Americans (Everett, Proctor, & Cortmell, 1983), are particularly reluctant to self-disclose to Caucasian counselors because of the hardships they have experienced as a result of racism. Thus, difficulties arise due to cultural norms prohibiting disclosure of personal information, particularly about suicide, and cultural barriers across different groups.

Indeed, lack of self-disclosure concerning suicidal feelings may contribute to the differential rates of suicidal thinking, attempts, and completions in a variety of ethnic minority groups. One examination of 355 files of a large Midwestern university counseling center's intake data for the 1990–1991 year included 22 clients who reported on intake questionnaires that they had been suicidal, and 333 clients who reported that they had not been suicidal. However, in a clinical assessment of 157 of these individuals, 49 of these supposedly non-suicidal clients disclosed that they were suicidal, and 98 did not (Morrison & Downey, 2000). The reasons these individuals were queried further on the issue of suicide varied, but included responses on the intake form, situational factors, and demographics. In a comparison of European American students to all ethnic minority students, significantly more ethnic minority clients indicated no suicidality on the intake form when they were, in fact, contemplating suicide (Morrison & Downey). Thus, some individuals reported no suicidality on questionnaires, but did reveal some suicidal thoughts or actions in person when probed verbally about suicidality. These individuals who revealed hidden suicidal thoughts were more likely to be minorities than those who revealed no hidden suicidal thoughts. This research supports the idea that ethnic minority individuals report suicidal thoughts and actions on intake forms less frequently than majority individuals.

Also, clients who indicated on the intake form that they wished to speak to a counselor for racial identity and discrimination issues were significantly more suicidal than those who indicated no ethnicity or discrimination concerns (Morrison & Downey, 2000). Both findings indicate that in a relatively homogeneous sample of college students at a university outpatient clinic, ethnic background was a consideration in whether they were suicidal and disclosed their suicidality.

Morrison and Downey's research was unique in examining ethnic background in whether a person reveals suicidality on an intake form. Their findings highlight the limitations of intake forms. It could be that the standard suicide questions on intake forms fail to capture the full extent of people's suicidal thoughts and actions.

An important limitation of Morrison and Downey (2000), however, is the homogeneity of the sample. As might be expected from a counseling center population, the sample was two thirds women, and slightly more than half were within the traditional college age. Ethnic backgrounds included more than 80% Caucasian, with the remaining clients reporting being African American (7%), Asian American (5%), Hispanic American (3%), and international (1%). Although it would have been methodologically desirable to analyze this information for students of different ethnic backgrounds, the sample distribution by race was insufficient for a more sophisticated statistical treatment. This type of limitation, typical of real world research, combines people with heterogeneous ethnic backgrounds. Nevertheless, an implication of this research is that suicide questions on intake forms may be insensitive to suicidality, particularly for ethnic minority groups.

Alternatively, it could be argued that following any standardized questions leads an interviewer to miss important suicidal thoughts and actions. Thus, structured interviews may miss suicidality. For example, one study compared paper-and-pencil and computer-scored SSIs among a group of 105 in- and outpatients being treated at a suburban general hospital in New Jersey. They typically reported more suicidality on the computer-scored version than on the clinician-rated version (Beck, Steer, & Ranieri, 1988). In that this study involved over 90% European American individuals, it is limited in sample diversity, but suggests that professionals following a structured interview format elicited less information about suicidality than a computer asking the same questions. Interviewing individuals about possible suicidal thoughts and actions or depressed, unhappy feelings requires sensitivity to cultural factors that influence responses. Cultural factors might include the inability to label feelings as depressed, the unwillingness to disclose distress to someone from a different culture, or the belief of having no control over important aspects of life.

□ Sensitivity to Ethnic Minority Issues when Assessing for Suicidal Thoughts and Actions

Counseling potentially suicidal ethnic minority individuals requires that the counselor realize that explanations of suicidal behavior may be culture-bound and potentially limited in applicability to an increasingly diverse population. Sensitivity to ethnic diversity issues means realizing that the knowledge base comes from only one perspective and that there is a great need to develop a truly multicultural psychology that recognizes important dimensions of the human condition such as race, culture, ethnicity, gender, religion, sexual orientation, and other sociodemographic variables (Sue, 2004). We now turn to an examination of suicide risk assessment in four ethnic minority populations.

Assessment and African Americans

In recent decades, suicidologists have been very concerned about the increasing African American suicide rate, especially among youth, as it increased by 114% for 10–19-year-olds between 1980–1995 (Centers for Disease Control [CDC], 1998). Although African Americans still have a lower suicide rate than all other Americans, these increases suggest that clinicians need better suicide risk assessment methods for African Americans. In addition, since African Americans are less likely than others to endorse direct questions about suicidal ideation (Morrison & Downey, 2000), culturally competent assessments are particularly important.

Certain demographic groups within the African American population are at higher risk than others. For example, African American adolescent girls think about suicide more often than African American boys (Spann, Molock, Barksdale, Matlin, & Puri, 2006). Homeless African Americans have consistently been found to be at higher risk for suicidal behavior and repeat suicide attempts than African Americans who are not homeless (Anglin, Gabriel, & Kaslow, 2005; Kaslow, Jacobs, Young, & Cook, 2006), thereby indicating that it is important to ask about the stability of a client's living situation in a clinical interview to help determine the level of suicide risk.

African Americans share a number of risk factors with other ethnic groups. For example, a history of prior suicide attempts has been found to be a major risk factor (Compton, Thompson, & Kaslow, 2005). In low-income African Americans, higher levels of suicidal intent, planning, and lethality are more likely to occur with repeat suicide attempters. In addition, a history of psychiatric treatment or substance abuse has also been more common in African Americans who are repeat suicide attempters (Kaslow et al., 2006). Attitudes toward suicide or a personal attempt history have also been found to be associated with suicide-risk level, and those at risk for multiple attempts also experience significantly more regret for surviving a past attempt than single attempters (Kaslow et al., 2006).

As is true for other groups, hopelessness and depression increase suicide risk in African Americans. When measuring hopelessness, the Beck Hopelessness Scale (Beck, Weissman, Lester, & Trexler, 1974) has been found to have excellent internal consistency reliability within African American groups (e.g., Kaslow et al., 2006).

Depression is arguably the biggest predictor of suicidal behaviors in African Americans (Compton et al., 2005) and has been linked to suicidal ideation as well (Molock, Puri, Matlin, & Barksdale, 2006). In addition to using some traditional measures discussed earlier to assess depressive symptoms, it is important to assess for specific cultural issues affecting African Americans that can contribute to depression and hopelessness. For example, racial and ethnic discrimination has been shown to lead to mental health difficulties, including depression in African Americans (Klonoff, Landrine, & Ullman, 1999; Sellers, Copeland-Linder, Martin, & Lewis, 2006). In addition to interviewing African American clients about the extent to which they have experienced racial discrimination, measures such as the Schedule of Racist Events (Landrine & Klonoff, 1996) can be used to assess the extent to which clients are experiencing discrimination. Discussing the results of this inventory with the client can lead to better understanding about how social experiences are contributing to depression and thereby might be increasing suicide risk.

Religiosity has also been studied frequently in the African American population, in particular as it relates to suicide. African Americans who have attempted suicide have been more likely to have no religious affiliation than non-attempters within the African American population (Anglin et al., 2005). Therefore, asking about the extent to which clients ascribe to a particular religious affiliation provides important information about a risk factor for suicide attempts in this population. Some have theorized that strong religious beliefs or affiliation lead to African Americans believing suicide is immoral and therefore suicide is less of an option for them. However, attitude about the acceptability of suicide does not explain the relationship between religious well-being and whether an individual has attempted suicide. Rather, there appears to be a larger protective component of religiosity, which has been identified as a sense of personal and spiritual purpose (Anglin et al., 2005).

Religiosity and spirituality levels can be measured by a variety of inventories, but when assessing spirituality with African Americans, in particular, a specific assessment referred to as "spiritual ecomaps" has been recommended. Similar to a family genogram, a spiritual ecomap allows the client to diagram the relevant spiritual systems at play in his or her life, including the relationship with God and a faith community (Hodge & Williams, 2002). Using a spiritual ecomap in session with clients can open dialogue about the ways in which they feel a spiritual purpose in life because of their connection to faith communities or higher powers. However, research that specifically correlates suicide risk to certain outcomes on a spiritual ecomap is still necessary.

Some conflict exists in the literature concerning what role interpersonal or relationship issues play in contributing to suicide risk in African Americans. Some studies demonstrate that repeat suicide attempters are more likely to have experienced divorce, separation, or death of a partner (Kaslow et al., 2006). Repeat suicide attempters have also experienced more interpersonal traumas (abuse, physical attack, etc.) and non-interpersonal traumas (natural disasters, car accident, etc.) during childhood than first-time attempters (Kaslow et al., 2006). For African American women, experiencing domestic violence increases suicidal risk (Kaslow, et al., 1998). Therefore, clinicians must ask specifically about relationship status and history of violence during a comprehensive suicide-risk assessment and recognize cultural variables that may make domestic violence more of a problem in some African American families as compared with Caucasian families, because of socioeconomic differences. Among African American couples, partner violence has been shown to increase as neighborhood poverty increases (Cunradi, Caetano, Clark & Schafer, 2000). Therefore, cultural issues such as socioeconomic disparity can contribute to risk for domestic violence and therefore suicidality.

Lower family cohesion and family adaptability as well as lower levels of perceived social support increase suicide risk in African Americans (Compton et al., 2005). Clinicians should consider using the Medical Outcomes Study (MOS) Social Support Survey (Sherbourne & Stewart, 1991), a well-known measure used in research with a number of African American groups, as one paper-and-pencil tool for assessing perceived social support in African Americans if clinical interview questions have not been sufficient.

African Americans' locus of control, or beliefs about their ability to impact change in their lives, has also been linked to suicide risk. For example, in African American high school students, increased suicide risk is associated with external and fatalistic locus of control (Spann et al., 2006). Considering the social discrimination that African Americans continue to face, it is not surprising that some may lack an internal locus of control because they may feel little control over their environment. As a result, assessing for clients' sense of empowerment in the world and their locus of control to effect change in their life can inform suicide-risk assessments.

Multiple protective factors have been identified for African Americans. Level of religiosity can serve as a potential risk factor, as discussed previously, but this variable can also be viewed as a protective factor. African Americans consistently participate in more public and private religious practices than other racial/ethnic groups (Molock et al., 2006) and religiosity has been shown to lower risk for African American adults (Greening & Stoppelbein, 2002; Kaslow, Thompson, Brooks, & Twomey, 2000). The probability of African Americans' attempting suicide also decreases with higher endorsement of religious well-being (Anglin et al., 2005). When assessing for protective factors, the College Student Reasons for Living Inventory has been found to be effective with African American college students, in particular (Westefeld, Badura, Kiel, & Scheel, 1996).

Internal locus of control has been found to be among the most important protective factors against suicidal behavior in African American adolescents (Spann et al., 2006). Also, a religious coping style consistent with believing that the individual and spiritual being solve problems together is linked to African Americans' having more reasons for living (Molock et al., 2006). In addition, social support has been identified as an important protective factor for African Americans (Kaslow et al., 2000; Kaslow, Sherry, Bethea, Wyckoff, Compton, Grall et al., 2005). For African American men, protective factors include positive social support and living in an area where there is little difference between income and occupational status for African Americans versus Caucasians (Burr, Hartman, & Matteson, 1999).

The variety of suicide risk and protective factors that have been identified for African Americans in the literature offers clinicians guidance when assessing suicidal risk. Although it is important to ask African American clients whether they have thought about harming themselves or completing suicide, research suggests that African Americans are less likely to admit suicidality when asked directly (Morrison & Downey, 2000). As a result, clinicians must be familiar with other important variables to assess when determining suicidal risk. Some information about risk level can be gleaned by considering whether African American clients fit particular demographic characteristics that place them at higher risk of suicidal ideation or behaviors. Homelessness, for example, is a major risk factor (Anglin et al., 2005; Kaslow et al., 2006).

Overall, in addition to asking directly about suicidal thoughts, intent, and plans, clinicians should assess a number of demographic variables, symptoms of depression, level of hopelessness, religiosity, coping styles, psychological treatment history and prior substance abuse in African Americans as part of a comprehensive assessment for suicide risk. As compared with other groups in the United States, African Americans have one of the longest histories of being discriminated against and the societal implications of this discrimination have been documented to have an impact on African Americans' mental health (Klonoff et al., 1999; Sellers et al., 2006). As a result, inquiring about the extent to which African Americans have experienced discrimination is important to consider because it has been linked to depression. Also, assessing clients' sense of empowerment or how strongly they believe that they can create change in their lives and their environment is an additional component to assess when considering suicide risk in this population.

Assessment and Asian Americans

According to the census of 2000, persons who identify as Asian Americans make up 3.6% of the population in the United States, or about 10 million people. In 2002, suicide was the eighth leading cause of death for Asian Americans and Pacific Islanders (CDC, 2007). In addition, although Japanese and Chinese American elders have the highest suicide rate among elderly persons in the U.S. (Baker, 1994; Lester, 1994), they have received little attention from researchers. In fact, there has also been a lack of research on suicide within the Asian American community among all age groups.

In a variety of Asian cultures, suicide is regarded as morally wrong and disrespectful toward family (Chen, Chen, & Chung, 2002), thereby making suicidality more difficult to assess among some Asian American clients. Furthermore, a number of Asian American clients with depression may express passive suicidal thoughts or strong indicators of suicidality when questioned, but because of the shame about suicide, they find it difficult to directly acknowledge past attempts, ideation, intent, or plan (Chen et al., 2002). As a result, it is important to assess for passive suicidal thoughts, such as clients' acknowledgment that they have given up on life or wish that an event would happen that would cause death.

Among Asian Americans, the most common symptoms that contribute to mental distress that may lead to suicidal ideation include authoritative parenting styles (Blair & Qian, 1998), lack of physical attention and affection from family members (Juang & Tucker, 1991), academic failure, performance anxiety, feelings of isolation (Lorenzo, Pakiz, Reinherz & Frost, 1995), and low self-esteem (Mintz & Kashubeck, 1999). Some paper–pencil measures may provide additional information about the level of suicide risk in some Asian Americans. Specifically, the Suicide Assessment Checklist (SAC; Rogers, Alexander & Subich, 1994) is a measure comprising 21 items completed by the counselor that focus on demographic, historical, psychological, psychosocial, and clinical factors known to be associated with higher suicidal risk. For example, historical questions assess the level of lethality of any past suicide attempt (Rogers et al., 1994) and add to information about the level of risk for Asian American clients. Psychological, psychosocial, and clinical questions allow the clinician to rate the client's level of feelings of worthlessness, hopelessness, social isolation, depression, impulsivity, hostility, intent to die, environmental distress, and future perspective (Rogers, Lewis, & Subich, 2002). Clinicians must be aware of other culture-specific values for many Asians, including focus on perfectionism (Chang, 1998), academic achievement, and honoring the family (Chung, 2003), that should guide questions in a clinical interview for assessing suicide risk. In youth or young adults, emotional distress is often presented in the form of concern about academic performance versus distress about a family or romantic relationship (Cheng, Leone, & Geist, 1993) as this tends to feel more culturally appropriate. However, it is still important for clinicians to ask Asian American clients about their relationship with family because strained family relationships can contribute to high levels of hopelessness and helplessness than would not necessarily be expected in non-Asian American youth and young adults (Chung, 2003).

High perfectionism has been found to predict suicidality and hopelessness in Asian American college students (Chang, 1998), which suggests that clinicians could assess perfectionism to enhance their understanding of client risk. Chang (1998) and others have used the Multidimensional Perfectionism Scale (Frost, Marten, Lahart, & Rosenblate, 1990) as a brief multidimensional measure of perfectionism with Asian Americans.

Recent evidence has also suggested that Asian Americans' social problem-solving style, or the way they cope cognitively, affectively, and behaviorally predicts suicidality above and beyond perfectionism (Chang, 1998). When there is concern about a potentially suicidal Asian American client, to more clearly understand the level of risk it is recommended that clinicians assess the extent to which the client engages in negative, avoidant, or impulsive problem-solving versus a more positive, rational style.

When assessing for previous suicidal behavior, Asian clients and their families may refute any previous suicidal attempt(s) in order to avoid shame or guilt. Thus, the focus of the assessment should be on asking questions about the occurrence of any unusual injuries or accidents that have transpired within the family, or the individual in question, to learn about past suicidal behavior (Chen et al., 2002).

Elderly Asian Americans are usually without support systems and resources; they rarely see their children and are sometimes neglected (Shiang, 1986). Therefore, assessing different life patterns, life stages, expectations, and access to methods of completing the act of suicide is essential to comprehensive assessment with this population.

When working with a Southeast Asian client who identifies as a Muslim, several unique factors should be considered when assessing suicide risk. When assessing for depression, it is not enough to ask if the client is feeling sad, as this will typically be denied. Instead, it is important to ask about somatic symptoms, as it is typically more common to express distress through these physical complaints (Hedayat-Diba, 2000). Also, many Muslims will not directly endorse suicidality if asked a question that is typical in assessing risk, such as "Are you feeling like harming yourself?" Instead, assess suicidality in part by phrasing the question less directly and inquiring if they wish that God would let them die (Dubovsky, 1983). Although completed suicides are less frequent in Muslims around the world compared with other religious peoples, Muslims still attempt suicide at a rate comparable to other religious groups (Lester, 2006) and must be assessed in ways that are sensitive to their unique culture.

Assessment and Hispanic Americans

By the year 2020, Hispanics are expected to make up 17% of the U.S. population (Cheesman, 1996). In 2001, suicide was the third leading cause of death among Hispanics aged 10–24. The age-adjusted suicide rate for all Hispanics in 2001 was 5.6/100,000—lower than the national rate of 10.7/100,000 (National Center for Health Statistics, 2001).

According to Hovey (2000), approximately one quarter of Latino American adolescents experience significant levels of suicidal ideation. This phenomenon may be explained by the fact that some adolescent Latino

Americans may be experiencing high-intensity acculturative stress, which accounts for high levels of depressive symptoms and suicidality.

With respect to assessment and what clinicians should be aware of, educational, occupational, economic and acculturation status need to be evaluated among Hispanic Americans (Ungemack & Guanaccia, 1998). Exploration of the motivation behind suicide is an essential element in this assessment, as differences in the meanings, motivation, and acceptance of suicide within some Hispanic American families may be viewed quite differently depending on the family of origin and the individual's ethnic background (Ungemack & Guanaccia, 1998). Thus, clinicians should be aware of culturally sensitive preventions and tendencies (Rew, Thomas, Horner, Resnick & Beuhring, 2001).

Effective assessment involves a number of key parameters. For example, Catholicism and frequent church attendance have been associated with a diminishing rate of suicide and suicide attempts (Sorenson & Golding, 1988). Moreover, as is the case with some Native Americans, establishment of a strong familial connection and social support may help protect those at risk of suicide (Ungemack & Guanaccia, 1998). Gutierrez, Rodriguez, and Garcia (2001) suggest that for Hispanic Americans an effective assessment technique is the utilization of a specific packet of questionnaires (e.g. the Beck Depression Inventory, Adult Suicidal Ideation Questionnaire, and Multi-Attitude Suicide Tendency Scale). Furthermore, providing information on the suicidality history and exposure to suicidal tendencies and behaviors within the culture and community may be of utility in some cases. According to *Catallozzi, Pletcher, and Schwarz (2001),* it is important for clinicians to recognize risk factors for suicide, but it is even more important to screen all adolescents for suicidal thoughts and feelings. Last, if the focal point of progress post-assessment and research can focus on educational attainment, mending familial ties and understanding and becoming more comfortable with the acculturation process, suicidal ideation may diminish (Hovey & King, 1997).

When assessing Hispanic Americans for suicidality, context and method are important, as is accounting for acculturative stress and factors related to socioeconomic status (SES), because those in lower SES groups are more vulnerable (Smith, Marcy, & Warren 1985; Canino & Roberts, 2001). Moreover, researchers need to attend to the community-based samples of high-risk children by creating more longitudinal studies. Researchers also need to attend to implementing studies on effective intervention programs within communities, organizations, and leaders at all levels within the Hispanic culture. These are all protective factors that need to be strongly considered for both clinicians and researchers in the hope of enhancing awareness and diminishing the frequency of suicidality.

Assessment and Native Americans

Of the numerous ethnic groups within the U.S., American Indians and Alaska Natives have the highest proportional rates of suicide (Barowsky, Resnick, Irelan, & Blum, 1999) and this has been a concern of suicidologists for many years. According to Barowsky et al. (1999) the suicide rate for American Indian and Alaska Native youth from 1991 to 1993 was 31.7 per 100,000, which was more than twice the national average for all youth. As a result, suicide is the second leading cause of death for American Indian and Alaska Native youth (Indian Health Service, 1996).

When considering suicide assessment in this population, clinicians should be aware that attempted suicide among the Native American population is strongly associated with depression (Howard-Pitney, LaFromboise, Basil, September, & Johnson, 1992; Hollis, 1996; Shaffer, et al., 1996), substance use, (Woods, Lin, Middleman, Beckford, Chase. & DuRant, 1997), loss of a family member or friend to suicide, (Brent et al., 1993; Brent, Bridge, & Johnson, 1996), availability of firearms (Brent, Perper, Moritz, Baugher. & Allman, 1993), and a history of physical or sexual abuse. (Chandy, Blum, & Resnick, 1996; Garnefeski & Diekstra, 1997).

When testing and assessing for the risk of suicide among Native Americans, a significant number of factors need to be considered. First and foremost, one has to consider the history of attempted suicide within the family and any current familial conflicts, because a history of family suicide may contribute to suicidal ideation (Manson et al., 1989). It is also important to assess the verbal response from the individual because some Native Americans may describe their depressive symptoms and conceal their suicidal thoughts by expressing somatic complaints (Barowsky et al., 1999).

Additional assessment should include alcohol or drug use and abuse and potential access to firearms. May et al. (2002) found that American Indian and Alaska Native youth suicide attempts, especially among female adolescents, were directly associated with accessibility to firearms. Much of the suicidal ideation among Native Americans has a direct association with substance abuse (Gattrell et al., 1993). May et al. (2002) found, however, that among American Indian suicide attempts, alcohol involvement was lower for attempts than for completions. The age of the individual needs to be considered when assessing for substance use, as age is linked to more frequent suicidal ideation. According to Brent et al., (1993) the alcohol use in younger adult populations of Native Americans contributed to more successful and unsuccessful suicide attempts than was the case for non-Native Americans.

Following assessment, one must consider what factors need to be considered and attended to in order to prevent a further increase in the already high rates of suicide among this population. May et al. (2002) found that those who attempted suicide less often, or not at all, within the Native American and Alaska Native community had a stronger connection to their families, and verbally expressed their concerns or distress with close friends and family members, thus increasing their emotional sense of empowerment. This was especially true among adolescents. Therefore, these protective factors need to be strongly considered when examining suicide risk in this population.

□ The Multicultural Assessment Procedure

Thus far in this chapter we have examined the issues related to suicide assessment among ethnic minority groups in terms of specific paper-and-pencil measures. We have also explored some of the unique assessment issues related to the four major ethnic groups. In this final section, we will briefly describe what we believe to be an excellent example of a model for conducting multicultural assessment. This model was developed by Ridley, Li, and Hill (1998) and is called the Multicultural Assessment Procedure (MAP). The model is generic and deals with the general issue of multicultural psychological assessment. However, we believe the model has excellent applicability to the specific issue of suicidal assessment. Thus, we will briefly describe the model as well as discuss its applicability to the assessment of suicidal risk. The authors describe the MAP as pragmatic, flexible, and cyclical. We will describe each of its four phases, as well as discuss its potential applicability to the assessment of suicidal risk among ethnic minorities.

Phase 1 is called "Identifying Cultural Data." In this phase, the clinical interview, among other techniques, is stressed. As a part of the clinical interview, the authors emphasize the importance of exploring the client's cultural background as a part of this interview because "... culture is always relevant to psychological assessment. ..." (p. 870).

The authors stress that cultural data is that which might be typical for a person from that culture as well as individual idiosyncrasies (i.e., unique to the individual, and not necessarily expected to be found among members of the client's group). In terms of assessing for suicide, the major implication of this stage is accounting for the client's culture in terms of risk. In other words, there might be cultural information that may in turn relate to the client's degree of depression, hopelessness, or a variety of other generic risk factors, though such factors may be exacerbated when examined in light of cultural variables. However, it is also very important not to assume that there are necessarily cultural variables that come directly into play in terms of suicidal risk. Such variables may, or may not, exist.

Phase 2, "Interpret Cultural Data," relates to interpreting the overt and covert cultural data in a manner that allows the clinician to form an assessment, in this case of suicidal risk. The examination of base rates is particularly relevant here. The authors state: "Base rates about particular psychological disorders, comorbid conditions, medical conditions that present as psychological symptom patterns, and suicide rates in various populations are probably the most important about which to know" (p. 875). In terms of suicide, knowledge of base rates among various ethnic groups (as discussed elsewhere in this text) provides us with at least some initial assessment of potential risk. The authors also believe that it is very important in this phase to determine which stressors are dispositional and which are environmental; this in turn can assist in determining the potential degree of suicidal risk.

In Phase 3, we "Incorporate Cultural Data." In this phase, we test the hypotheses that were generated during phase 2. So, for example, if we determine that there may be some element of suicidal risk, and we are trying to determine how MUCH risk—an issue that often confronts clinicians and researchers—then in this phase we attempt to test our hypotheses via three primary mechanisms: Ruling out medical explanations, the utilization of psychological testing, and comparing data with Diagnostic and Statistical Manual of Mental Disorders (DSM IV) criteria (APA, 2000). Concerning DSM IV specifically, there are clearly some multicultural limitations. If for example, we arrive at a depressive diagnosis in terms of DSM IV that has implications for the assessment of suicidal risk, it is very important to be aware of the fact that this diagnosis, and its implications for suicidal risk, are subject to potential cultural limitations. Quoting Ridley, Li, and Hill (1998):

> "... it is important that practitioners are cognizant of problems that exist with the DSM IV in relation to multicultural assessment ... Therefore, although we recognize the necessity and utility of applying working hypotheses to DSM IV criteria, we list this activity as only one of several methods useful in clinical hypotheses testing. In addition, diagnosis is only one part of a comprehensive assessment. ... (p. 882)

In Phase 4, "Arrive at a Sound Assessment Decision," we take the previous three steps and make a determination (i.e., is this client at risk for suicide, and if so, how MUCH risk?). Therefore, what we are really doing here is combining the cultural variables/history, the base rates, the direct assessment data, and the clinical interview in order to determine risk. At best, as has been pointed out repeatedly (e.g., Westefeld et al., 2000), it is still very difficult to predict suicidal risk for any individual—or for any group. However, this model incorporates a variety of analyses/data, including cultural variables, and will raise the odds of our making an accurate prediction. The MAP is one way we believe that clinicians can generically and specifically apply the principles of multicultural assessment to the assessment of suicidal risk.

Conclusion

The key conclusion to be derived from this chapter is the fact that suicidal assessment among under-represented groups has both a generic and a specific component. That is to say, on the one hand there are certain universals about the assessment of suicidal risk among all persons, (e.g., depression, hopelessness, helplessness, history of attempting, and having a plan). On the other hand, some risk factors/assessment issues are unique to a variety of populations, as outlined in this chapter. The key is a blending of the two in order to conduct the most valid risk assessment possible. This blending is a difficult and complex task; however, we believe it is the most effective means of assessing suicidal risk. It is also very important to note that there are often more individual differences within groups than between groups, thus, generalizing about any group and suicidal risk may be suspect (Westefeld et al., 2000).

Future researchers need to do even more to identify the unique assessment issues for a wide variety of populations while not ignoring the universal generic assessment phenomena. This will involve empirical investigations within a variety of ethnic groups as well as people in general.

References

Anglin, D.M., Gabriel, K.O.S., & Kaslow, N.J. (2005). Suicide acceptability and religious well-being: A comparative analysis in African American suicide attempters and non-attempters. *Journal of Psychology and Theology, 33,* 140–150.

Baker, F. M. (1994). Suicide among ethnic minority elderly: A statistical and psychosocial perspective. *Journal of Geriatric Psychiatry, 27,* 241–264.

Barowsky, I.W., Resnick, M.D., Ireland, M., & Blum, R.W. (1999). Suicide attempts among American Indian and Alaskan native youth: Risk and protective factors. *Archives of Pediatrics and Adolescent Medicine, 153,* 573–580.

Beck, A. T., Brown, G.K., Steer, R.A., Dahlsgaard, K.K., & Grisham, J.R. (1999). Suicide ideation at its worst point: A predictor of eventual suicide in psychiatric outpatients. *Suicide and Life-Threatening Behavior, 29,* 1–9.

Beck, A.T., Kovacs, M., & Weissman, A. (1979). Assessment of suicidal intention: The Scale for Suicidal Ideation. *Journal of Consulting and Clinical Psychology, 47,* 343–352.

Beck, A., Steer, R., & Ranieri, W. (1988). Scale for Suicide Ideation: Psychometric properties of a self-report version. *Journal of Clinical Psychology, 44,* 499–505.

Beck, A.T., Weissman, A., Lester, D., & Trexler, L. (1974). The measurement of pessimism: The Hopelessness Scale. *Journal of Consulting and Clinical Psychology, 42,* 861–865.

Blair, S.L. & Qian, Z. (1998). Family and Asian students' educational performance. *Journal of Family Issues, 19,* 335–374.

Blum, R.W., Beuhring, T., Shew, M.L., Bearinger, L.H., Sieving, R.E., & Resnick, M.D. (2004). The effects of race/ethnicity, income, and family structure on adolescent risk behaviors. *American Journal of Public Health, 90,* 1879–1884.

Bongar, B. (2002). *The suicidal patient: clinical and legal standards of care.* Washington, D.C. American Psychological Association.

Bradford, J., Ryan, C., & Rothblum, E.D. (1994). National health care survey: Implications for mental health care. *Journal of Consulting and Clinical Psychology, 62,* 228–242.

Brent, D.A., Bridge, J., Johnson, B.A., & Connolly, J. (1996). Suicidal behavior runs in families: A controlled family study of adolescent suicide victims, *Archives of General Psychiatry, 53,* 11455–1152.

Brent, D.A., Perper, J.A., Moritz, G, Allman, C., Schweers, J., Roth, C., Balach, L., Canobbio, R., & Liotus, L. (1993). Psychiatric sequelae to the loss of an adolescent peer suicide. *Journal of American Academy of Child and Adolescent Psychiatry, 32,* 509–517.

Brent, D.A., Perper, J., Moritz, G., Buagher, M., & Allman, C. (1993). Suicide in adolescents with no apparent psychopathology. *Journal of American Academy of Child and Adolescent Psychiatry, 32,* 494–500.

Brent, D.A., Perper, J., Moritz, G., Buagher, M., & Schweers, J.C. (1993). Firearms and adolescent suicide: A community case-control study. *American Journal of Diseases of Children, 147,* 1066–1071.

Burr, J.A., Hartman, J.T., & Matteson, D.W. (1999). Black suicide in U.S. metropolitan areas: An examination of the racial inequality and social integration–regulation hypotheses. *Social Forces, 77,* 1049–1081.

Canino, G. & Roberts, R.E. (2001). Suicidal behavior among Latino youth. In M.M. Silverman, L. Davidson, & L. Potter (Eds.), National Suicide Prevention Conference background papers special supplement. *Suicide and Life-Threatening Behaviors,* 31, 66–78.

Catallozzi, M., Pletcher, J.R. & Schwarz, D.F. (2001). Prevention of suicide in adolescents. General pediatrics. *Current Opinion in Pediatrics. 13,* 417–422.

Centers for Disease Control [CDC]. (2007). Asian American Populations. Retrieved January 9, 2007 from http://www.cdc.gov/omh/Populations/NHOPI/NHOPI.htm.

Centers for Disease Control [CDC]. (2006). Asian American Populations. Retrieved January 9, 2007 from http://www.cdc.gov/omh/populations/AsianAm/AsianAm/htm.

Centers for Disease Control [CDC]. (2004). Suicide and attempted suicide. *Morbidity and Mortality Weekly Report, 53*(22), 471–498.

Centers for Disease Control [CDC]. (2002). CDC surveillance summaries: Youth risk behavior survey. *Morbidity and Mortality Weekly Report, 51,* 1–68.

Centers for Disease Control [CDC]. (1999). Suicide deaths and rates per 100,000. Retrieved December 1, 2006 from http://www.cdd.gov/ ncipe/data/us9794/suic.html.

Centers for Disease Control [CDC]. (1998). Suicide Among Black Youths—United States, 1980–1995. Retrieved December 1, 2006 from http://www.cdc.gov/mmwr/preview/mmwrhtml/00051591.htm.

Chandy, J.M., Blum, R.W., Resnick, M.D. (1996). Gender-specific outcomes for sexually abused adolescents. *Child Abuse and Neglect, 20,* 1219–1231.

Chang, E.C. (1998). Cultural differences, perfectionism, and suicidal risk in a college population: Does social problem solving still matter? *Cognitive Therapy and Research, 22,* 237–254.

Chase, B.W., Cornille, T.A., & English, R.W. (2000). Life satisfaction among persons with spinal cord injuries. *Journal of Rehabilitation, 66,* 14–20.

Cheeseman, Day J. U.S. Census Bureau, Population Projections of the United States by Age, Sex, Race, and Hispanic origin: 1995 to 2050, *Current Population reports,* P25–1130, Washington, DC: U.S. Government Printing Office, 1996.

Chen, J.-P., Chen, H., & Chung, H. (2002). Depressive disorders in Asian American Adults, *Western Journal of Medicine, 176,* 239–244.

Cheng, D., Leong, F.T.L., & Geist, R. (1993). Cultural differences in psychological distress between Asian and Caucasian American college students. *Journal of Multicultural Counseling and Development, 21,* 182–190.

Chung, I.W. (2003). Examining suicidal behavior of Asian American female college students: Implications for practice. *Journal of College Student Psychotherapy, 18,* 31–47.

Cole, D.A. (1988). Hopelessness, social desirability, depression, and parasuicide in two college student samples. *Journal of Consulting and Clinical Psychology, 56,* 131–136.

Compton, M.T., Thompson, N.J., & Kaslow, N.J. (2005). Social environment factors associated with suicide attempt among low-income African Americans: The protective role of family relationships and social support. *Social Psychiatry Epidemiology, 40,* 175–185.

Cotton, C.R., Peters, D.K., & Range, L.M. (1995). Psychometric properties of the Suicidal Behaviors Questionnaire. *Death Studies, 19,* 391–396.

Cotton, C.R., & Range, L.M. (1993). Suicidality, hopelessness and attitudes toward life and death in children. *Death Studies, 17,* 185–191.

Cunradi. C.B., Caetano, R., Clark, C., & Schafer, J. (2000). Neighborhood poverty as a predictor of intimate partner violence among Caucasian, African American, and Hispanic couples in the United States: A multilevel analysis. *Annals of Epidemiology, 10,* 297–308.

Currier, J.M., Holland, J.M., & Neimeyer, R.A. (2006). Sense-making, grief, and the experience of violent loss: Toward a mediational model. *Death Studies, 30,* 403–428.

Dobrov, E. & Thorell, L.H. (2004). "Reasons For Living"—Translation, psychometric evaluation and relationships to suicidal behaviour in a Swedish random sample *Nordic Journal of Psychiatry, 58,* 277–285.

Dubovsky, S. (1983). Psychiatry in Saudi Arabia. *American Journal of Psychiatry, 140,* 1455–1459.

Ellis, J.B. & Range, L.M. (1991). Differences between blacks and whites, women and men in reasons for living. *Journal of Black Studies, 21,* 341–347.

Everett, F., Proctor, N., & Cortmell, B. (1983). Providing psychological services to American Indian children and families. *Professional Psychology, 14,* 588–603.

Fletcher, J.M. (1989). Nonverbal learning disabilities and suicide: Classification leads to prevention. *Journal of Learning Disabilities, 22,* 176, 179.

Frost, R.O., Marten, P., Lahart, C., & Rosenblate, R. (1990). The dimensions of perfectionism. *Cognitive Therapy and Research, 14,* 449–468.

Gatrell, J.W., Jarvis, G.K., & Derkensen, L. (1993). Suicidality among adolescent Alberta Indians. *Suicide and Life-Threatening Behavior, 23,* 366–373.

Graham, T.L.C. (2002). Using reasons for living to connect to American Indian healing traditions. *Journal of Sociology and Social Welfare, 29,* 55–75.

Greening, L. & Stoppelbein, L. (2002). Religiosity, attributional style, and social support as psychosocial buffers for African American and White adolescents' perceived risk for suicide. *Suicide and Life-Threatening Behavior, 32,* 404–417.

Gutierrez, P.M., Osman, A., Kopper, B.A., & Barrios, F.X. (2000). Why young people do not kill themselves: The Reasons for Living Inventory for adolescents. *Journal of Clinical Child Psychology, 29,* 177–187.

Gutierrez, P.M., Rodriguez, P.J., & Garcia, P. (2001). Suicide risk factors for young adults: testing a model across ethnicities. *Death Studies, 25,* 319–340.

Hedayat-Diba, Z. (2000). Psychotherapy with Muslims. In P.S. Richards & A.E. Bergin (Eds.). *Handbook of Psychotherapy and Religious Diversity.* Washington DC: American Psychological Association.

Hodge, D.R. & Williams, T.R. (2002). Assessing African American spirituality with spiritual ecomaps. *Families in Society: The Journal of Contemporary Human Services, 83,* 585–595.

Hollis, C. (1996). Depression, family environment, and adolescent suicidal behavior. *Journal of American Academy Child Adolescent Psychiatry, 35,* 622–630.

Hovey, J.D. (2000). Acculturative stress, depression and suicidal ideation in Mexican immigrants. *Cultural Diversity and Ethnic Minority Psychology, 6,* 134–151.

Hovey, J.D. & King, C.A. (1997). Suicidality among Acculturating Mexican Americans: Current knowledge and directions for research. *Suicide and Life-Threatening Behavior, 27,* 92–103.

Howard-Pitney, B., LaFromboise, T.D., Basil, M., September, B., & Johnson, M. (1992). Psychological and social indicators of suicide ideation and suicide attempts in Zuni adolescents. *Journal of Consulting and Clinical Psychology, 60,* 473–476.

Indian Health Service (1996). *Trends in Indian Health,* 1996. Rockville, MD.: U.S. Department of Health and Human Services.

Innamorati, M., Pompili, M., Ferrari, V., Cavedon, G., Soccorsi, R., Aiello, S., et al. (2006). Psychometric properties of the Reasons for Living Inventory in Italian university students. *Individual Differences Research, 4,* 51–56.

Ivanoff, A., Jang, S.J., Smyth, N., & Linehan, M.M. (1994). Fewer reasons for staying alive when you are thinking of killing yourself: The Brief Reasons for Living Inventory. *Journal of Psychopathology and Behavioral Assessment, 16,* 1–13.

James, A., Lai, F.H., & Dahl, C. (2004). Attention deficit hyperactivity disorder and suicide: A review of possible associations. *Acta Psychiatrica Scandinavica, 110,* 408–415.

Juang, S.-H. & Tucker, C.M. (1991). Factors in marital adjustment and their interrelationships: A comparison of Taiwanese couples in America and Caucasian American couples. *Journal of Multicultural Counseling and Development, 19,* 23–31.

Kamal, Z. & Loewenthal, K.M. (2002). Suicide beliefs and behaviour among young Muslims and Hindus in the UK. *Mental Health, Religion and Culture, 5,* 111–118.

Kaslow, N. J., Jacobs, C.H., Young, S.L., and Cook, S. (2006). Suicidal behavior among low-income African American women: A comparison of first-time and repeat suicide attempters. *Journal of Black Psychology, 32,* 349–365.

Kaslow, N. J., Sherry, A., Bethea, K., Wyckoff, S., Compton, M.T., Grall, M. B., et al. (2005). Social risk and protective factors for suicide attempts in low income African American men and women. *Suicide and Life-Threatening Behavior, 35,* 400–412.

Kaslow, N.J., Thompson, M.P., Brooks, A.E., & Twomey, H.B. (2000). Ratings of family functioning of suicidal and nonsuicidal African American women. *Journal of Family Psychology, 14,* 585–599.

Kaslow, N.J., Thompson, M.P., Meadows, L.A., Jacobs, D., Chance, S., Gibb, B., et al. (1998). Factors that mediate and moderate the link between partner abuse and suicidal behavior in African American women. *Journal of Consulting and Clinical Psychology, 66,* 533–540.

Klonoff, E. A., Landrine, H., & Ullman J. B. (1999). Racial discrimination and psychiatric symptoms among Blacks. *Cultural Diversity and Ethnic Minority Psychology, 5,* 329–339.

Kowalchuk, B. & King, J.D. (1989). Adult suicide versus coping with nonverbal learning disorder. *Journal of Learning Disabilities, 22,* 177–179.

Landrine, H. & Klonoff, E.A. (1996). The Schedule of Racist Events: A measure of racial discrimination and a study of its negative physical and mental health consequences. *Journal of Black Psychology, 22,* 144–168.

Laval, R.A., Gomez, E.A., & Ruiz, P. (1983). A language minority: Hispanics and mental health care. *American Journal of Social Psychiatry, 3,* 42–49.

Lester, D. (2006). Suicide and Islam. *Archives of Suicide Research, 10,* 77–97.

Lester, D. (1994). Differences in the epidemiology of suicide in Asian Americans by nation of origin. *Omega: Journal of Death and Dying, 29,* 89–93.

Lester, D. & Abde-Khalek, A.M. (1998). Suicidality and personality in American and Kuwaiti students. *International Journal of Social Psychiatry, 44,* 280–283.

Linehan, M.M. (1981). *Suicidal behaviors questionnaire.* Unpublished inventory, University of Washington, Seattle, Washington.

Linehan, M., Goodstein, J., Nielsen, S., & Chiles, J. (1983). Reasons for staying alive when you are thinking of killing yourself: The Reasons for Living Inventory. *Journal of Consulting and Clinical Psychology, 51,* 276–286.

Loewenthal, K.M., MacLeod, A.K., Cook, S., Lee, M., & Goldblatt, V. (2003). The suicide beliefs of Jews and Protestants in the UK: How do they differ? *Israel Journal of Psychiatry and Related Sciences, 40,* 174–181.

Lorenzo, M.K., Pakiz, B., Reinherz, H.Z., & Frost, A. (1995). Emotional and behavioral problems of Asian American adolescents: A comparative study. *Child and Adolescent Social Work Journal, 12*, 197–212.

Manson, S.M., Beals, J., Dick, R.W. & Duclos, C. (1989). Risk factors for suicide among Indian adolescents at a boarding school. *Public Health Reports, 104,* 609–614.

Maris, R.W., Berman, A.L., & Silverman, M.M. (2000). *Comprehensive textbook of suicidology.* New York: Guilford.

May, P.A., Van Winkle, N.W., Williams, M.B., McFeeley, P.J., DeBruyn, L.M. & Serna, P. (2002). Alcohol and suicide death among American Indians of New Mexico: 1980–1998. *Suicide and Life-Threatening Behavior, 32,* 240–255.

McCullough, M.E., Weaver, A.J., Larson, D.B., & Aay, K.R. (2000). Psychotherapy with mainline Protestants: Lutheran, Presbyterian, Episcopal/Anglican, and Methodist. In P. S. Richards & A.E. Bergin (Eds.). *Handbook of Psychotherapy and Religious Diversity.* Washington DC: American Psychological Association.

McDaniel, J.S., Purcell, D., & D'Augelli, R. (2001). The relationship between sexual orientation and risk for suicide: Research findings and future directions for research and preventing suicide. *Suicide and Life Threatening Behavior, 31,* 84–105.

McLaren, S. & Hopes, L.M. (2002). Rural–urban differences in reasons for living. Australian and *New Zealand Journal of Psychiatry, 36,* 688–692.

Middlebrook, D.L., LeMaster, P.L., Beals, J., Novins, D.K. & Manson, M. (2001). Suicide prevention in American Indian and Alaskan Native communities: A critical review of programs. In M.M. Silverman, L. Davidson, & L. Potter (Eds.), National Suicide Prevention Conference background papers special supplement. *Suicide and Life-Threatening Behavior, 31,* 66–78.

Mintz, L.B., & Kashubeck, S. (1999). Body image and disordered eating among Asian American and Caucasian college students: An examination of race and gender differences. *Psychology of Women Quarterly, 23,* 781–796.

Molock, S.D., Puri, R., Matlin, S., & Barksdale, C. (2006). Relationship between religious coping and suicidal behaviors among African American adolescents. *Journal of Black Psychology, 32,* 366–389.

Morrison, L.L. & Downey, D.L. (2000). Racial differences in self-disclosure of suicidal ideation and reasons for living implications for training. *Cultural Diversity and Ethnic Minority Psychology, 6,* 372–386.

National Center for Health Statistics. Vital statistics mortality data, underlying cause of death, 1997–2001. Hyattsville, Maryland: U.S. Department of Health and Human Services, Public Health Service, CDC, 2001.

National Center for Injury Prevention and Control (NCIPC). Retrieved January 5, 2007 from http://www.cdc.gov/ncipc/.

Neyra, C., Range, L.M., & Goggin, W.C. (1990). Reasons for living following success and failure in suicidal and nonsuicidal college students. *Journal of Applied Social Psychology, 20,* 861–868.

Oquendo, M.A., Dragatsi, D., Harkavy-Friedman, J., Dervic, K., Currier, D., Burke, A. et al. (2005). Protective factors against suicidal behavior in Latinos. *Journal of Nervous and Mental Disease, 193,* 438–443.

Rabinowitz, A. (2000). Psychotherapy with Orthodox Jews. In P.S. Richards & A.E. Bergin [Eds.]. *Handbook of Psychotherapy and Religious Diversity.* Washington DC: American Psychological Association.

Range, L.M. (2005). The family of instruments that assess suicide risk. *Journal of Psychopathology and Behavioral Assessment, 27,* 133–140.

Range, L. & Knott, E. (1997). Twenty suicide assessment instruments: Evaluation and recommendations. *Death Studies, 21,* 25–58.

Rew, L., Thomas, N., Horner, S.D., Resnick, M.D. & Beuhring, T. (2001). Correlates of Recent Suicide Attempts in a Triethnic Group of Adolescents. *Journal of Nursing Scholarship 33,* 61–367.

Richards, P. S. & Bergin, A. E. (2000). Religious diversity and psychotherapy: Conclusions, recommendations, and future directions. *Handbook of Psychotherapy and Religious Diversity.* Washington DC: American Psychological Association.

Ridley, C.R., Li, L.C., & Hill, C.L. (1998). Multicultural Assessment: Reexamination, reconceptualization, and practical application. *The Counseling Psychologist, 26,* 827–910.

Rogers, J.R., Alexander, R.A., & Subich, L.M. (1994). Development and Psychometric analysis of the Suicide Assessment Checklist. *Journal of Mental Health Counseling, 16,* 352–368.

Rogers, J.R., Lewis, M.M., & Subich, L.M. (2002). Validity of the Suicide Assessment Checklist in an emergency crisis center. *Journal of Counseling & Development, 80,* 493–502.

Rourke, B.P. (1989). Nonverbal learning disabilities, socio-emotional disturbance, and suicide: A reply to Fletcher, Kowalchuk and King, and Bigler. *Journal of Learning Disabilities, 22,* 186–187.

Rourke, B.P., Young, G.C., & Leenaars, A.A. (1989). A childhood learning disability that predisposes those afflicted to adolescent and adult depression and suicide risk. *Journal of Learning Disabilities, 22,* 169–175.

Sagnir, M. & Robins, E. (1984). *Male and female homosexuality: Explorations of a potential relationship.* Paper presented at the annual meeting of the American Association of Suicidology, Anchorage, AK.

Schneider, S.G., Farberow, N.L., & Kruks, G.N. (1989). Suicidal behavior in adolescent and young adult gay men. *Suicide and Life-Threatening Behavior, 19,* 381–394.

Schneider, S.G., Taylor, S.E., & Hammen, C. (1991). Factors influencing suicide intent in gay and bisexual suicide ideators: Differing models for men with and without human immunodeficiency virus. *Journal of Personality and Social Psychology, 61,* 776–788.

Sellers, R., Copeland-Linder, N., Martin, P.P., & Lewis, R.L. (2006). Racial identity matters: The relationship between racial discrimination and psychological functioning in African American adolescents. *Journal of Research on Adolescence, 16,* 187–216.

Shaffer, D., Fisher, P., Hicks, R.H., Povides, M., & Gould, M. (1995). Sexual orientations in adolescents who commit suicide. *Suicide and Life-Threatening Behavior, 25,* 64–71.

Shaffer, D., Gould, M.S., Fisher, P., Trautman, P., Moreau, D., Kleinman, M., & Flory, M. (1996). Psychiatric diagnosis in child and adolescent suicide. *Archives of General Psychiatry, 53,* 339–348.

Shafranske, E.P. (2000). Psychotherapy with Roman Catholics. In P.S. Richards & A.E. Bergin (Eds.). *Handbook of Psychotherapy and Religious Diversity.* Washington DC: American Psychological Association.

Sherbourne, C.D. & Stewart, A.L. (1991). The MOS Social Support Survey. *Social Science Medicine, 32,* 705–714.

Sorenson, S.B. & Golding, J.M. (1988). Suicide ideation and attempts in Hispanics and non-Hispanic whites: Demographic and psychiatric disorder issues. *Suicide and Life-Threatening Behavior, 18,* 205–218.

Spann, M., Molock, S. D., Barksdale, C., Matlin, S., & Puri, R. (2006). Suicide and African American teenagers: Risk factors and coping mechanisms. *Suicide and Life-Threatening Behavior, 36,* 553–568.

Steer, R.A., Kumar, G., & Beck, A.T. (2003). Self-reported suicidal ideation in adolescent psychiatric inpatients. *Journal of Consulting and Clinical Psychology, 61,* 1096–1099.

Sue, D.W. (2004). Whiteness and ethnocentric monoculturalism: Making the "invisible" visible. *American Psychologist, 59,* 761–769.

Sue, D.W. & Sue, D. (1990). Counseling the culturally different: Theory and practice (2nd ed.). New York: Wiley.

Svetaz, M.V., Ireland, M., & Blum, R. (2000). Adolescents with learning disabilities: Risk and protective factors associated with emotional well-being: Findings from the National Longitudinal Study of Adolescent Health. *Journal of Adolescent Health, 27,* 340–348.

Tang, N.K. & Crane, C. (2006). Suicidality in chronic pain: A review of the prevalence, risk factors, and psychological links. *Psychological Medicine, 36,* 575–586.

Trautman, E.C. (1961). The suicidal fit: A psychobiologic study on Puerto Rican immigrants. *Archives of General Psychiatry, 5,* 98–105.

Ungemack, J.A. & Guanaccia, P.J. (1998). Suicidal Ideation and Suicide Attempts Among Mexican Americans, Puerto Rico and Cuban Americans. *Transcultural Psychiatry, 35,* 307–327.

Vontress, C. (1981). *Racial and ethnic barriers in counseling.* In P. Pederson, J.G. Draguns, W.J. Lonner, & J.E. Trimble (Eds.), Counseling across cultures (pp. 87–107). Honolulu: University of Hawaii Press.

Walker, R.L., Lester, D., & Joe, S. (2006). Lay theories of suicide: An examination of culturally relevant suicide beliefs and attributions among African Americans and European Americans. *Journal of Black Psychology, 32,* 320–334.

Westefeld, J.S., Badura, A., Kiel, J.T., & Scheel, K. (1996). Development of the College Student Reasons for Living Inventory with African Americans. *Journal of College Student Psychotherapy, 10,* 61–65.

Westefeld, J.S., Cardin, D., & Deaton, W.L. (1992). Development of the College Student Reasons for Living Inventory. *Suicide and Life-Threatening Behavior, 22,* 442–452.

Westefeld, J.S., Range, L.M., Rogers, J.R., Maples, M.M., Bromley, J. L., & Alcorn, J. (2000). Suicide: An overview. *The Counseling Psychologist, 28,* 445–510.

Woods, E.R., Lin, Y.G., Middleman, A., Beckford, P., Chase, L., DuRant, R.H. (1997). The associations of suicide attempts in adolescents. *Pediatrics, 99,* 791–796.

Ethnic Considerations in Intervention and Treatment with Suicidal People

James R. Rogers and Devon E. Whitehead

Throughout the literature on suicidal individuals in the U.S. are references to the existence of differences in suicidality as a function of diversity-related characteristics (e.g., Westefeld, Range, Rogers, Maples, Bromley, & Alcorn, 2000). For example, in terms of variations in suicidal behaviors as a function of biological sex, there is a fairly consistent sex-related difference reported, with males dying by suicide to a much greater extent than females (Maris, Berman, & Silverman, 2000). Similarly, differences in suicide attempts are consistently reported in the literature with females engaging in suicide attempts to a much greater extent than males as well as relatively stable age-related differences, with suicide rates generally increasing with age. Differences related to identification based on race are also reported. With regard to race, suicide rates are highest for Native American individuals and non-Hispanic Whites, and substantially lower for people of Hispanic origin, non-Hispanic African Americans, and individuals of Asian or Pacific Island backgrounds (American Psychiatric Association [APA], 2003).

More specifically related to a general consideration of ethnicity, culture-related values and beliefs have also been identified as contributors to variability in both suicide and suicide attempts, most specifically, beliefs and values related to death in general and suicide in particular (APA, 2003; Shea, 1999, Westefeld et al., 2000). In addition to views of death and suicide, differences related to acceptable ways of coping with shame, distress, and physical illness, including values related to talking about suicide, have been suggested as important cultural considerations (APA; Choi, Rogers, & Werth, in press).

Nested within ethnicity and culture, differences have also been identified in the literature based on sexual orientation (Westefeld et al., 2000). While there are no solid data linking sexual orientation to increases in death by suicide, data do suggest an increase in suicide attempts for gay, lesbian, and bisexual individuals (McBee-Strayer & Rogers, 2002). In regard to sexual orientation, suggested contributors to a heightened risk for suicidality include stress related to disclosure of one's orientation and the experience of homophobia and homophobia-related harassment (APA, 2003).

Similarly, religious-based differences have also emerged. In terms of affiliation, data suggest a relation between religious denomination and suicide rates as well as attitudes toward suicide. For example, data from the National Center for Health Statistics suggest that mainstream Protestantism is associated with higher rates as compared with a variety of denominations (Pescosolido & Giorgianna, 1989). Similarly, individuals self-identified as Catholic or Methodist have reported less favorable attitudes toward suicide than those identified as agnostic or atheist, with other Protestant, Lutheran, and Jewish individuals falling in between (Rogers, Gueulette, Abbey-Hines, Carney, & Werth, 2001). While differences in attitudes toward suicide as a function of religious affiliation have been identified in the literature, the importance of those differences rests on the existence of a clear link between attitudes and suicidal behaviors; a link that has yet to be even modestly supported in the literature (Rogers, 1996). Beyond simple affiliation, however, Marion and Range (2003), Pescosolido and Giorgianna (1989), and Westefeld et al. (2000) have suggested that religious beliefs, and in particular, the strength of those beliefs, may serve a protective or buffering function to suicidal behavior.

In addition to considering individual characteristics and their relation to suicide under the umbrella of ethnicity and culture, Westefeld et al. (2000) and others have acknowledged the reality that two or more of these factors can be present in the same individual. For example, a degree of risk potentially associated with being a Native American can be exacerbated by the co-occurrence of identification as gay, lesbian, or bisexual. While considering the potential impact of ethnic group membership on suicide attitudes, beliefs, and behaviors, it is also critical to keep in mind that knowledge of group-related similarities and differences may or may not generalize to any one individual case as within-group differences are consistently found to be greater than between-group differences (Range et al., 1999).

Despite a persistent call in the literature to account for and consider ethnic and cultural characteristics in suicide intervention and treatment, little in the way of specific guidance in the extant literature relates to how these characteristics likely impact work with suicidal individuals. In fact, the state of specificity with regard to intervention and treatment with clients based on ethnic characteristics mirrors that of suicide intervention and treatment in general. For example, Rogers and Soyka (2004) have criticized what they termed the "one size fits all" approach to suicidal individuals, and the practice guidelines developed by the APA (2003) state that "the approach to the suicidal patient is common to all individuals *regardless of diagnosis or clinical presentation*" (pp. 7–8, italics added). Thus, the identification of important ethnic and cultural characteristics notwithstanding, standard approaches to working with suicidal individuals are relatively silent with regard to these areas of diversity. The purpose of this chapter, therefore, is to provide an overview of what is and what is not known about intervention, and treatment with suicidal individuals in general and specific to clients from diverse ethnic and cultural backgrounds, offer some practical suggestions in this area based on the Collaborative Assessment and Management of Suicidality (CAMS) model developed by Jobes and his colleagues (Jobes, 2006), and to suggest ideas for future research.

☐ Approaches to Intervention and Treatment

Crisis Intervention

Intervention and treatment activities with suicidal individuals are intimately connected with the suicide-risk assessment process, although they are often presented separately in the literature. In general, assessment and intervention activities are typically discussed in terms of the crisis intervention model and considered as those activities that occur when the client is at a heightened risk for suicidal behavior (Callahan, 1998). For example, the crisis intervention approach is typically employed when a client presents with strong suicidal thoughts, a well developed action plan for suicide, or a recent suicide attempt. As such, an effective initial intervention plan (i.e., treatment) is based on an assessment of the client's risk for engaging in suicidal behaviors with the immediate consideration being whether safety can be maintained in an outpatient versus an inpatient setting. Specific interventions that may be part of this crisis intervention approach are the identification of risk and protective factors, identifying the underlying message, allowing for ventilation, engaging social support, contracting for safety, referral for medication, and referral for psychotherapy (Westefeld et al., 2000).

Despite the reality that the crisis intervention approach provides the basis for suicide assessment and intervention training in most mental health practice programs (Thomas & Leitner, 2005), empirical support for its effectiveness is severely lacking (Rogers & Soyka, 2004). Beyond the mere lack of support for effectiveness, Rogers and Soyka have argued that the crisis intervention model approach has the potential to result in adverse outcomes. For example, they have argued that the application of the model may have distancing and marginalizing effects, may contribute to the stigma of suicide, and can perpetuate the notion of suicide as a taboo subject. Any of these potential outcomes could have a negative impact on the intervention process in general and the quality of the relationship between the client and the clinician, specifically. While Rogers and Soyka have critiqued the crisis intervention model as a rigid template for working with suicidal individuals based upon their understanding of the literature, Thomas and Leitner have provided a somewhat more flexible perspective.

Based on their research, Thomas and Leitner (2005) described three potential response styles of suicide intervention that therapists can use when applying the crisis intervention model: the fight response, the flight response, and the ideal response. The fight response style is the more directive and aggressive of the three approaches and similar to the therapist responsibility approach identified by Ellis (2004). This style involves the therapist's taking primary control of the client's suicidal crisis and unilaterally determining the methods of intervention to be taken (e.g., outpatient therapy, medication, shock treatments, involuntary hospitalization, police involvement, etc.) with minimal input from the client. Although this response may result in a fast reaction to the crisis, it usually comes at the expense of the therapeutic alliance because the therapist and client often become enmeshed in a power struggle over decision-making regarding the client's life.

Contrary to the fight response, an alternative style is described by these authors as the flight response. This style is characterized by therapist detachment and avoidance or minimization of the client's emotional experience. Therapists who respond in this manner may be uncomfortable with working with suicidal individuals and may inadvertently communicate that discomfort through both verbal and non-verbal behavior (Shea, 1999). Thus, they may create or exacerbate barriers to effective communication around the emotionally charged issue of suicide. Outcomes of this approach may include reaffirming clients' perception that no one cares about them, an inadequate assessment of suicidality, or false assurance for the client that everything will be okay.

Finally, the third option is referred to by Thomas and Leitner (2005) as the "ideal" response style. This approach is similar to the collaborative style discussed by Ellis (2004), Jobes (2006), and Rogers and Oney (2005). The ideal response style takes a humanistic approach toward the suicidal crisis in that therapists convey acceptance, understanding, and a genuine desire to perceive the situation from the client's perspective. Additionally, this style provides a safe environment for clients to express their feelings and progress at their own pace. Although, at times, therapists using the ideal style will have to take actions similar to those seen in the fight response style (i.e, involuntary hospitialization), the manner in which these actions are taken is different because the client is involved collaboratively in the decision process. As might be expected, this is the style most preferred by suicidal clients, although the fight style has been identified as the most commonly experienced response by clients (Thomas & Leitner, 2005).

While the ideal response was most commonly preferred in their research, for some clients the fight and flight styles were the preferred modes. Thus, rather than considering the crisis intervention model or the styles suggested by Thomas and Leitner (2005) as either good or bad, the data suggest the possible presence of ethnic, cultural, and individual differences that need to be considered in an attempt to match response styles to clients. Nevertheless, no empirical data currently support the contention that the application of the crisis intervention model to suicide-risk assessment and intervention is effective in general, much less for members of any specific groups based on ethnic and culture-related characteristics.

Treatment Approaches

Beyond the crisis intervention model, Maris et al. (2000) identified a variety of treatment approaches that have been applied to suicidal individuals. These include brief therapy, cognitive-behavioral approaches, dialectical behavior therapy, psychopharmacotherapy, psychoanalytic and psychodynamic therapy, electroconvulsive therapy, family therapy, and group therapy. According to these authors, across the various treatment approaches effectiveness research is rare and the research that does exist has provided inconclusive results.

This sentiment is echoed by Rudd, Joiner, and Rajab (2001) in their review of the limited controlled and randomized studies on the treatment of suicidality. Based on their review of 22 studies, these authors suggested that few conclusions can be drawn related to treatment effectiveness for suicidal clients, much less the identification of which suicide intervention treatment approaches are most appropriate for which clients. Specifically, Rudd et al. have highlighted the need to identify which treatment approaches work for which clients and under what circumstances. In a similar vein, Mishara (2006) stated that the current status of developing guidelines to deal with suicidal clients reflects the underlying assumption that "there are more commonalities in suicide prevention activities around the world than there is diversity" (p. 1). However, given the significant differences in the responses of individuals from diverse ethnic and cultural backgrounds from other therapeutic approaches and interventions (Ponterotto, Casas, Suzuki, & Alexander, 2001), it is reasonable to anticipate that differences would exist in responses to interventions related to suicidal crises. Moreover, the data presented by Thomas and Leitner (2005) have provided some initial empirical support for this expectation as it relates to the application of the crisis intervention model in suicide assessment and intervention.

In summary, ubiquitous application notwithstanding, there is very little empirical support for the effectiveness of the crisis intervention model as a suicide assessment and intervention strategy in the general population. In fact, the crisis intervention approach has been recently criticized for its potential to exacerbate barriers to developing a therapeutic alliance and negatively impact communication related to the sensitive topic of suicidality. In addition, methodologically sound empirical research on treatment approaches applied to working with suicidal individuals has been limited and inconclusive with regard to the effectiveness of those approaches. As limited as research is related to working with suicidal individuals in general, however, knowledge related to working with members of ethnically and culturally diverse groups in this area is exceptionally narrow.

□ Diversity-Sensitive Guidelines

While it is clear that clinical and research efforts need to be directed at evaluating the appropriateness and effectiveness of currently accepted strategies to working with suicidal individuals from ethnically diverse backgrounds, in the absence of empirically supported approaches we next highlight some diversity-sensitive general guidelines for working with suicidal clients. Although our goal is to provide suggestions for working with individuals from ethnically diverse backgrounds, we reiterate the conclusion from Range et al. (1999) and others (Choi, Rogers, & Werth, in press; Sue & Sue, 2003) indicating that within-group differences are consistently greater than between-group differences and caution that by emphasizing differences we may run the risk of increasing prejudice and reinforcing generalizations (Takahashi, 1997).

With this caveat in mind, several general recommendations have been identified in the literature as appropriate for working with individuals from ethnically and culturally diverse backgrounds. These general recommendations are based on issues of language, respect for diversity, and compatibility of beliefs about suicide (Atkinson, Bui, & Mori, 2001; Range et al., 1999). The backdrop for these recommendations is the concept of multicultural competency.

Multicultural Competence

As multicultural competence is generally viewed as the basis for working effectively with individuals from diverse backgrounds across all issues (Ponterotto, et al., 2001), it is also relevant for working with suicidal clients. Despite the lack of empirical evidence linking multicultural competence to treatment outcome (Atkinson et al., 2001) characteristics of competence in this area are theoretically and logically linked to the development of a productive therapeutic relationship in general, and to effective communication related to issues of suicide specifically (Shea, 1999). The core characteristics of multicultural competence include counselor awareness of personal values and biases, awareness of the client's worldview, and counselor knowledge related to multicultural issues (Constantine & Ladany, 2001). Although we have previously identified the lack of empirical evidence for ethnically and culturally appropriate suicide intervention strategies, the need for counselor self-awareness and an understanding of the client's world is critical to addressing suicidal issues with diverse clients (Choi, et al., in press; Shea, 1999).

Counselor Self-Awareness

In terms of the broad literature related to multicultural competence, counselor self-awareness focuses on developing an understanding of one's own cultural and ethnic background and development. The goal of this understanding is to identify the associated values, beliefs, assumptions, and biases that are embedded in the socialization process, but often unexplored. The assumption under the multicultural rubric is that self-aware counselors are less likely to impose their worldviews and related assumptions onto their clients, thereby providing more ethnically and culturally sensitive treatment than might otherwise occur. Beyond the more general self-awareness expected as a function of developing multicultural competence, Shea (1999) has identified the need for value clarification specific to issues of suicide as a basis for effective work in this area.

For example, Shea (1999) identified five potential beliefs about suicide and suicidal individuals that therapists should explore to help clarify their values. According to Shea, one's beliefs related to these areas will impact his or her ability to work effectively with suicidal clients. Therefore, Shea suggests that counselor self-awareness can be explored through a careful consideration of the following questions:

- Is suicide a sign of weakness?
- Is suicide a sin or in some way immoral?
- Does suicide represent a taboo topic (i.e., is it difficult for me to address)?

- Is a consideration of suicide illogical and a sign of being "crazy"?
- What is my understanding of my responsibility, morally, ethically, and legally, when a client is suicidal?

What is first important in considering these issues is answering the questions "How might my beliefs in relation to these questions impact my work with a suicidal client?" and "To what extent are my beliefs a product of my own ethnic and cultural heritage that may differ from folks from other backgrounds?" Most importantly, Shea urges counselors to be aware that clients are very likely to differ on these issues as a function of ethnic and cultural heritage and suggests that unresolved differences in beliefs with regard to suicide are likely to negatively impact intervention and treatment outcomes with suicidal individuals.

Beyond these suicide-specific self-exploration areas, Shea (1999) has also suggested a number of more directly personal issues that counselors need to explore in order to work effectively with suicidal clients, These include:

- What are my experiences with suicide and other suicidal behaviors with family or friends in my personal life?
- Have I ever been suicidal?
- Can I picture myself ever being suicidal and, if so, under what circumstances?
- How would my life be impacted if I lost a loved one to suicide?
- How would I respond to a client's question regarding whether it is okay to kill one's self?

By exploring these questions, Shea suggests that mental health practitioners can guard against inadvertently allowing their biases to negatively impact the intervention and treatment process and avoid the development of countertransference in the therapeutic relationship.

Taken together, both a broad consideration of issues related to multicultural competence with regard to counselor self-awareness and self-understanding, and values clarification specific to suicide and other suicidal behaviors are viewed as important for working with clients (Constantine & Ladany, 2001; Shea, 1999). Equally important is developing an understanding of the client's world, first, based on general knowledge of ethnic and cultural characteristics and second, by avoiding assumptions derived from that general knowledge and exploring the client's phenomenological experience of his or her world.

Understanding the Client's World

In conjunction with counselor self-awareness, developing both a general and specific understanding of the client's world and worldview is a key component of multicultural competence (Constantine & Ladany, 2001). In terms of a general understanding, developing a knowledge base related to ethnic and cultural characteristics provides a basis for initial understanding when working with clients from diverse backgrounds. While identifying specific group characteristics related to suicide risk is beyond our focus, Leach (2006) and a number of authors in this volume have provided overviews of these characteristics (e.g., Alcantara & Gone; Duarte-Velez & Bernal; Leong, Leach, Yeh & Chou; Utsey, Hook, & Stanard). However, as suggested by these and other authors (e.g., Takahashi, 1997), when a general understanding of group characteristics translates into expectations at the individual level, the potential for developing faulty assumptions, inappropriate generalizations, and the perpetuation of stereotypes is great. Thus, while it is important from a multicultural competency perspective to have background knowledge of ethnic and cultural group differences and similarities, only openness and exploration at the individual level can provide the depth of understanding necessary to respond in a diversity-sensitive manner to any particular client.

Beyond general issues of multicultural counseling competency and beliefs and values related specifically to issues of suicide, we offer three general recommendations that diversity-sensitive counselors should consider in their work with suicidal clients. These include attention to potential miscommunication by assuming shared meaning in language, an attitude of respect for diversity, and the compatibility of beliefs between the client and counselor with regard to suicide.

Language

The first recommendation is related to language usage, and while we would argue that the issue is a concern even when English is the first language for both the therapist and client, the potential for misunderstanding may be exacerbated when the therapist and client come from diverse ethnic or cultural backgrounds (Atkinson et al., 2001). For example, Paniagua (2005) has suggested that when the therapist and client are from different cultures, it is imperative that linguistic issues be considered. For instance, within the intervention and treatment process, it is likely that individuals for whom English is a second language may not fully understand the questions the therapist is asking. Rather than asking for clarification, clients may respond to questions out of a very different understanding of the words from what the therapist intended and be reluctant to ask for clarification out of deference to clinicians. This potential for a mismatch in linguistic understanding can negatively impact the process, resulting in inappropriate conclusions and decisions on the part of the counselor regarding risk assessment, intervention, and treatment.

Similarly, English-as-a-second-language clients may not fully understand the ramifications of the assessment process including their rights regarding informed consent. While we would argue that the potential for language to create a barrier to understanding in any therapeutic encounter is substantial, the probability for it to lead to inaccurate suicide assessment, intervention, and treatment when the therapist and client are from diverse backgrounds is considerable.

The concern over language issues is not limited to formal language differences or misunderstandings that may occur when English is a second language, however. Less obvious may be the lack of shared meanings in colloquialisms and local dialects. Thus, even when English is the primary language for the counselor and the client, the counselor's assumption that words convey the same meanings and connotations for the client may be in error. Therefore, it is important for counselors to be aware of potential mismatches in language usage that may occur as a function of diversity-related differences and to work for clarity and shared meaning in their interactions with clients.

Respect for Diversity

Range et al. (1999) cite several culture-specific recommendations related to respect for ethnic and cultural diversity. According to these authors, knowledge of diversity characteristics can allow counselors to understand how these characteristics "*may* interact with individual and familial forces to contribute to, or buffer against, suicidality." (p. 423, italics added). First, they suggest that it is important that clinicians recognize the dignity of every individual while respecting his or her cultural heritage. Second, they state that for all ethnic groups, pride in heritage is an important aspect of personal development and should be encouraged and fostered. Third, for many ethnic groups, engaging in outreach efforts such as community- and school-based clinics are essential in making mental health care available. Fourth, for many ethnic groups, the ties of family are a strength and can be utilized in treatment if used carefully. Finally, for many groups, religious beliefs can also be useful in terms of providing support and serving a protective function against suicidal behavior. The diversity-sensitive attitudes embedded in these recommendations fit most clearly into the "ideal" response (Thomas & Leitner, 2005) and are noticeably aligned with the multicultural competence characteristic of having an awareness of the client's worldview (Constantine & Ladany, 2001).

Compatibility of Beliefs about Suicide

Atkinson et al. (2001) suggest that the most important consideration regarding sensitive treatment in a multicultural or diverse context is the compatibility of the counselor's and client's beliefs related to the cause of the client's presenting problem. Here again, compatibility is a major component of a productive therapeutic alliance and, as it relates to suicide intervention and treatment, requires counselors to negotiate a joint understanding with clients regarding their suicidality. That is, rather than the counselor as the expert, the client should be viewed as the expert in his or her suicidality (Choi et al., in press; Jobes, 2006; Rogers & Soyka, 2004) and areas of compatibility between the counselor's and client's beliefs about suicide, its causes, consequences, and intervention and treatment strategies need to be identified (Atkinson et al., 2001).

Beliefs about Suicide

As indicated in the previous discussion of developing one's self-awareness around beliefs and values related to suicide, Shea (1999) suggests that clients, likewise, have beliefs related to what it means to be suicidal. Beliefs that can lead to difficulty in working with suicidal individuals include viewing a consideration of suicide as a sign of weakness, believing that suicide is a sin or in some way immoral, believing that only "crazy" people become suicidal, and considering a discussion of suicide as taboo. Clients who may believe that suicide is a sign of personal weakness, a sin, or immoral may be reluctant to accurately share their suicidal thoughts, feelings, and behaviors, as to do so would mark them as weak, sinful, or immoral. Similarly, clients who believe that one has to be "crazy" to consider suicide would be risking being viewed as crazy and potentially being "locked up" should they admit to being suicidal. Finally, a belief that a discussion of suicide is socially inappropriate in any situation will clearly have a negative impact on the quality of an assessment of suicide risk and subsequent intervention and treatment planning. Thus, important questions to be addressed include:

- Is suicide a sign of weakness in my client's ethnic group or culture and to what extent has this belief been internalized by my client?
- Is suicide a sin or in some way immoral in my client's ethnic group or culture and to what extent has this belief been internalized by my client?
- Does suicide represent a taboo topic in my client's ethnic group or culture and to what extent has this belief been internalized by my client?

- Is a consideration of suicide illogical and a sign of being "crazy" in my client's ethnic group or culture and to what extent has this belief been internalized by my client?

Based on a clear understanding of client beliefs across these areas, counselors can then work with their clients to find common ground in order to provide an ethnically, culturally, and clinically acceptable focus to intervention and treatment.

An additional area that needs to be explored with clients in terms of compatibility of beliefs about suicide is the idea that individuals have a "right" or even a social responsibility (Choi et al., in press; Rogers, 1996) to take their own lives and the connected issue of "rational" suicide. Just as Werth (1992), Rogers and Britton (1994), and Rogers et al. (2001) have demonstrated that there are significant differences among counselors related to these issues, clients are likely to have beliefs about the acceptability of suicide that can impact intervention and treatment outcomes. For example, a client's belief that suicide can be rational and is a "right" of the individual may result in an adversarial stance between the client and the counselor, with the client reluctant to be forthcoming related to his or her suicidal intent and plans. Overtly exploring these beliefs with clients will likely reduce the potential that differences may lead to therapeutic barriers.

Beliefs about Causes of Suicide

A shared understanding about the causes of suicide between the counselor and client can also be important under the rubric of compatibility of beliefs and those beliefs can differ as a function of ethnic and cultural differences. For example, to the extent that a client believes that suicide and other suicidal behaviors are "caused" by genetics or neurochemical imbalances, he or she is likely to react poorly to a suggestion for interventions grounded in cognitive behavioral conceptualizations of suicide. Alternatively, if suicidal behavior is viewed by a client as a reasonable response to contextual situations, then he or she may be less open to considering a psychopharmacological intervention as part of treatment. Thus, developing areas of consensus with clients regarding diverse beliefs about causes of suicide can enhance the potential that clients will engage in treatment when there is a match between casual beliefs and treatment approaches.

Summary

Working effectively with suicidal clients from ethnically and culturally diverse backgrounds theoretically and logically requires counselors to be multiculturally competent in a general sense, self-aware in terms of values and beliefs about suicide and suicidal individuals, knowledgeable about group-related suicide risk factors, and diversity sensitive with regard to suicide-specific beliefs and values that clients may hold—quite a potentially overwhelming expectation for counselors, especially given the high level of anxiety often experienced by clinicians when working with high-risk clients (Bonner, 1990). However, following the cautions offered by Takahashi (1997), Range et al. (1999) and others that expectations arising from group-specific knowledge can bias clinical judgments at the individual level, we next outline a specific intervention protocol that we believe can be sensitively applied when working with suicidal clients. While we believe that a diversity-sensitive counselor could work effectively from a variety of models focused on the issue of suicide, the CAMS approach developed by Jobes and his colleagues (see Jobes, 2006) seems particularly well suited as a protocol to enhance the diversity sensitivity of clinicians working with suicidal clients.

☐ Diversity-Sensitive Intervention and Treatment Planning Using the CAMS Model

For a number of reasons we believe that the CAMS model is not only adaptable to intervention and treatment in diversity contexts, but actually pulls from an appreciation of differences in its form and content. First, the CAMS model is theoretically grounded and based on Shneidman's (1988, 1993) cubic model of suicide, Beck's formulation of hopelessness (Beck et al., 1979), and Baumeister's (1990) conceptualization of self-loathing or self-hate. Being theoretically driven rather than empirically derived based on general risk-factor models allows a shared understanding of the client to develop more easily during the assessment process. Second, included in the protocol is an assessment of client-identified reasons for living and reasons for dying that facilitate an understanding of the client's view of the world. Third, the application of the CAMS model strongly promotes a collaborative therapeutic relationship with the suicidal client as the "expert" and the reduction of suicidality as the target problem. Viewing suicidal behavior as an effort to cope with unbearable situations, Jobes and Drozd (2004) describe the CAMS approach as one integrating:

> ... a range of behavioral, cognitive, psychodynamic, humanistic, existential, and interpersonal approaches to assessing, understanding, managing, and intervening with suicidality. (p. 75)

While a thorough presentation of the CAMS protocol is beyond the scope of this chapter, we next highlight some components of the model that are specifically relevant to diversity-sensitive work with suicidal individuals. Those components are the theoretically based items, the overall rating of suicide risk, and the identification of reasons for living and reasons for wanting to die.

The first three theoretically based items come from Shneidmans' (1988) cubic model. This model identifies three general psychological dimensions that reflect more or less universal experiences of human beings. For example, *psychological pain* reflects an internal experience of malaise or suffering that is unique to the individual and a function of his or her ethnic, cultural, or other diversity-related characteristics. Similarly, *press* (identified as *stress* in the CAMS), refers to the mostly external stresses and pressures that impact individuals psychologically and can become overwhelming, thereby influencing suicidal behavior. Finally, *perturbation* (identified as *agitation* in the CAMS), refers to being emotionally upset and, as agitation increases, the likelihood of a client taking a suicidal action to escape the psychological pain and stress becomes greater.

Next, based on the work of Beck et al. (1979), clients are asked to rate, again on a subjective scale of distress, their level of hopelessness and identify what aspect of life seems to be most hopeless. The work of Beck and his colleagues (e.g., Beck, 1986; Brown, Beck, Steer, & Grisham, 2000) has consistently found hopelessness to be highly correlated with suicidal behavior and there is evidence that this relationship holds cross-culturally (Leach, 2006). Similarly, drawn from the theoretical work of Baumeister (1990) conceptualizing suicidal behavior as an attempt to escape from oneself, clients are asked to provide a rating of their feelings of self-hate and to identify what they most hate about themselves.

Using the CAMS protocol, clinicians and clients work together to understand and identify the client's status on these dimensions, rate the dimensions using a subjective scale of distress, and then identify, specifically, what are the most painful, stressful, and emotionally urgent aspects of his or her life. Clearly, however, a number of issues related to multicultural competency and diversity sensitivity can come into play using this model. Specifically, while these characteristics are generally considered as "universal," the concepts themselves may not be familiar to clients from different ethnic and cultural backgrounds and the language used to describe them may not convey the intended meanings. For example, the constructs of "psychological pain" and "agitation" may not have the same meaning for clients from different ethnic and cultural backgrounds and the personal meanings of those terms are likely to vary as a function of level of acculturation. Thus, it is important for counselors to work to ensure a shared understanding of the words used in the CAMS—and their connotations.

With a shared conceptual understanding as the backdrop, cultural factors that may play a role in the client's suicide status can be explored. Cultural factors that may be related to one's level of psychological pain may be internalized guilt or shame related to experiences of discrimination as a member of an ethnic minority group or as a function of intergenerational conflict. Similarly, oppression, discrimination, intergenerational conflict, and communication problems related to English as a second language may be impacting one's feelings of being overwhelmed.

Through discussions of pain, stress, agitation, hopelessness, and self-hate, ethnically and culturally sensitive counselors can help clients explore the potential impacts of their minority status on their experience of pain, stress, agitation, hopelessness and self-hate. While clients may or may not identify minority-related experiences as the most pressing issues across the five areas, it is likely that negative experiences or feelings related to acculturation, oppression, discrimination, intergenerational conflict, and communication may serve to exacerbate other more proximal concerns and become treatment topics as immediate risk for suicidal behavior diminishes.

In addition to the five theoretically grounded risk-assessment items described above, clients make an overall rating of their risk for engaging in suicidal behavior and indicate to what degree their suicidality is related to their feelings about themselves versus feelings about others. These latter ratings can clearly lead to discussions that may reveal cultural, spiritual, religious, or other socially grounded beliefs and values, especially those related to suicide and suicidal behaviors that may be impacting, both positively and negatively, the development of suicidal behavior.

Next, clients are prompted to identify and subsequently rank their reasons for living and reasons for wanting to die. This approach is grounded primarily in the theoretical and empirical work of Linehan, Goodstein, Nielson, and Chiles (1983) and subsequent work on the Reasons for Living Inventory developed by these and other authors. As before, an ethnically and culturally sensitive exploration of reasons for living and reasons for dying can serve to enhance the therapeutic relationship and allow the counselor to develop a clearer understanding of the client's worldview, a necessary step in developing a diversity-sensitive relationship. Responses in this section may reveal specific ethnically and culturally related beliefs and values impacting clients. For example, despite significant psychological pain, stress, or hopelessness, clients from a strong communal or group-oriented culture may identify the potential impact of suicide on the family as a reason for living. Alternatively, bringing shame or disgrace on one's family and extended family may be identified as a reason for dying subsequent to a humiliating event. Specific responses notwithstanding, the benefit to the counselors from the reasons for living and dying components of the CAMS is that responses can be used to facilitate a shared understanding of the meanings of suicidality for the client and more directly inform intervention and treatment options.

An additional benefit of using the CAMS protocol beyond its applicability in an ethnically and culturally diverse setting is that the model also prompts for the more typical "standard of care" information that counselors are accustomed to focusing on in their work with suicidal clients. This information includes an assessment of the suicide plan; history; intent; substance abuse; relational, health, and physical problems; loss, isolation; impulsivity; legal problems; and shame. The protocol also prompts for an evaluation of the client's mental status, preliminary diagnostic impressions, and treatment plan. Finally, the CAMS model includes a "Suicide Tracking Form" whereby clients self-evaluate on the original five theoretical items and the overall suicide risk item at each subsequent clinical contact until the client's struggle with suicidality has been successfully resolved.

To conclude, counselors who are sensitive to issues of diversity in general, who have an awareness of their own values and beliefs related to suicide, and are cognizant of the importance of understanding the client's beliefs and values related to suicide are likely to find the CAMS protocol as one that can facilitate suicide intervention and treatment with clients from diverse backgrounds. In addition, the assessment component, (i.e., collaboratively identifying reasons for living and wanting to die, specifics of self-hate, hopelessness, stress, agitation, and pain), can provide valuable insight into the client's world and translate in a straightforward manner into treatment goals and interventions focused on achieving those goals.

Our judgment regarding the value of the CAMS as appropriate for ethnically and culturally sensitive intervention and treatment with suicidal clients is not strongly supported by empirical research. However, as we have indicated previously, neither is the crisis intervention model nor any other model of working with suicidal individuals. Based on what we see as a match between the collaborative, nonjudgmental, supportive, and "client as expert" approach embedded in the CAMS and the general philosophy underlying the multicultural competency movement, we believe that the CAMS holds promise for work in this area. In addition, the extant research on the CAMS has shown positive results (Jobes, 2006), suggesting that similar research focused specifically on work with clients from diverse ethnic, cultural, sexual-orientation, and religious backgrounds is appropriate.

☐ Summary and Suggestions for Future Research

Despite empirically identified differences in the expression of suicidal behaviors as a function of a variety of diversity-related characteristics, traditional assessment, intervention, and treatment models continue to focus on commonalities across suicidal individuals and minimize unique aspects of the suicidal experience. Moreover, theoretical discussions and research linking multicultural counseling competency conceptualizations with assessment, intervention and treatment approaches to working with suicidal clients is severely lacking.

Under the assumption that sensitivity to issues of diversity, including counselor self-awareness, an appreciation of clients' worldviews, beliefs and values, and attention to potential language barriers, is as relevant to working with suicidal individuals as it is to other client concerns, counselors would do well to explore their beliefs and values in this critical area. With multicultural sensitivity and sensitivity to values and beliefs related to suicide as the backdrop, the CAMS model appears to be a very promising protocol to help counselors maintain a diversity-sensitive stance when faced with suicidal clients.

Whether employing the CAMS model or any other approach to working with suicidal clients, there is a great need for research in this area. Specific to differences as a function of diversity characteristics, research needs to move beyond merely identifying that differences do exist, and begin to focus on developing a more in-depth understanding of the antecedents and consequences of those differences. Qualitative designs investigating phenomenological experiences of diverse clients may be especially useful in this regard. In addition, assessment, intervention, and treatment approaches such as reflected in the CAMS protocol need to be evaluated in terms of their effectiveness and relative efficacy. In the absence of research targeted at gaining a more comprehensive understanding of the interface between diversity characteristics and suicidal behavior, the field will continue to focus on common or general approaches, and miss potential opportunities to save lives by promoting diversity-sensitive approaches to assessment, intervention, and treatment with suicidal people.

☐ References

American Psychiatric Association (2003). Practice guideline for the assessment and treatment of patients with suicidal behaviors. Washington, D.C.: Author.

Atkinson, D.R., Bui, U., & Mori, S. (2001). Multiculturally sensitive empirically supported treatments—an oxymoron? In Ponterotto, J.G., Casas, J.M., Suzuki, L.A., Alexander, C.M. (Eds.), *Handbook of multicultural counseling* (2nd ed.) (pp. 552–574). Thousand Oaks, CA: Sage.

Baumeister, R.F. (1990). Suicide as escape from self. *Psychological Review, 97,* 90–113.

Beck, A.T. (1986). Hopelessness as a predictor of eventual suicide. *Annals of New York Academy of Sciences, 487,* 90–96.

Beck, A.T., Rush, A.J., Shaw, B.F., & Emery, G. (1979). *Cognitive therapy of depression.* New York: Guilford Press.

Bonner, R.L. (1990). A "M.A.P." to the clinical assessment of suicide risk. *Journal of Mental Health Counseling, 12*, 232–236.

Brown, G.K., Beck, A.T., Steer, R.A., & Grisham, J.R. (2000). Risk factors for suicide in psychiatric outpatients: A 20-year prospective study. *Journal of Consulting and Clinical Psychology, 68*, 371–377.

Callahan, J. (1998). Crisis in theory and crisis intervention in emergencies. In P.M. Kleepies (Ed.), *Emergencies in mental health practice* (pp. 22–40). New York: Guilford Press.

Choi, J.L., Rogers, J.R., & Werth, J.L., Jr. (in press). Suicide risk assessment with Asian American college students: A culturally informed perspective. *The Counseling Psychologist.*

Constantine, M.G. & Ladany, N. (2001). New visions for defining and assessing multicultural counseling competence. In Ponterotto, J.G., Casas, J.M., Suzuki, L.A., Alexander, C.M. (Eds.), *Handbook of multicultural counseling* (2nd ed.) (pp. 482–498). Thousand Oaks, CA: Sage.

Ellis, T.E. (2004). Collaboration and a self–help orientation in therapy with suicidal clients. *Journal of Contemporary Psychotherapy, 34*, 41–57.

Jobes, D.A. (2006). *Managing suicidal risk: A collaborative approach.* New York: Guilford.

Jobes, D.A. & Drozd, J.F. (2004). The CAMS approach to working with suicidal patients. *Journal of Contemporary Psychotherapy, 34*, 73–85.

Leach, M.M. (2006). *Cultural diversity and suicide: Ethnic, religious, gender, and sexual orientation perspectives.* New York: Haworth Press.

Linehan, M.M., Goodstein, J.L., Nielson, S.L., & Chiles, J.A. (1983). Reasons for staying alive when you are thinking about killing yourself: The Reasons for Living Inventory. *Journal of Consulting and Clinical Psychology, 51*, 276–286.

Marion, M.S. & Range, L.M. (2003). African American college women's suicide buffers. *Suicide and Life-Threatening Behavior, 33*, 33–43.

Maris, R.W., Berman, A.L., Silverman, M.M. (2000). *Comprehensive textbook of suicidology.* New York: Guilford.

McBee-Strayer, S.M. & Rogers, J.R. (2002). Lesbian, gay, and bisexual suicidal behavior: Testing a constructivist model. *Suicide and Life-Threatening Behavior, 32*, 272–283.

Mishara, B.L. (2006). Cultural Specificity and universality of suicide. *Crisis, 27*, 1–3.

Paniagua, F.A. (2005). *Assessing and treating culturally diverse clients.* Thousand Oaks, CA: Sage Publications.

Pescosolido, B.A. & Giorgianna, S. (1989). Durkheim, suicide, and religion: Toward a network theory of suicide. *American Sociological Review, 54*, 33–48.

Ponterotto, J.G., Casas, J.M., Suziki, L.A., & Alexander, C.M. (Eds.) (2001). *Handbook of multicultural counseling* (2nd ed.). Thousand Oaks, CA: Sage.

Range, L.M., Leach, M.M., McIntyre, D., Posey-Deters, P.B., Marion, M.S., Kovac, S.H., Banos, J.H., & Vigil, J. (1999). Multicultural perspectives on suicide. *Aggression and Violent Behavior, 4*, 413–430.

Rogers, J.R. (1996). Assessing right to die attitudes: A conceptually guided measurement model. *Journal of Social Issues, 52*, 63–84.

Rogers, J.R. & Britton, P.J. (1994). AIDS and rational suicide: A counseling psychology perspective or a slide on the slippery slope? *The Counseling Psychologist, 22*, 171–178.

Rogers, J.R., Gueulette, C.M., Abbey-Hines, J., Carney, J.V., & Werth, J.L., Jr. (2001). Rational suicide: An empirical investigation of counselor attitudes. *Journal of Counseling and Development, 79,* 365–372.

Rogers, J.R. & Oney, K.M. (2005). The clinical use of suicide assessment scales: Enhancing reliability and validity through the therapeutic relationship. In R.I. Yufit & D. Lester (Eds.), *Assessment, treatment, and prevention of suicidal behavior* (pp. 7–27). Hoboken, NJ: John Wiley & Sons.

Rogers, J.R. & Soyka, K.M. (2004). "One size fits all": An existential–constructivist perspective on the crisis intervention approach with suicidal individuals. *Journal of Contemporary Psychotherapy, 34,* 7–22.

Rudd, M.D., Joiner, T., & Rajab, M.H. (2001). *Treating suicidal behavior: An effective, time-limited approach.* New York: Guilford.

Shea, S.C. (1999). *The practical art of suicide assessment.* New York: Wiley.

Shneidman, E. (1993). *Suicide as psychache: A clinical approach to self-destructive behavior.* Northvale, NJ: Aronson.

Shneidman, E. (1988). Some reflections of a founder. *Suicide and Life-Threatening Behavior, 18,* 1–12.

Sue, D.W., & Sue, D. (2003). *Counseling the culturally diverse* (4th ed.). New York: John Wiley & Sons.

Takahashi, Y. (1997). Culture and Suicide: From a Japanese Psychiatrist's Perspective. *Suicide and Life-Threatening Behavior, 27,* 137–145.

Thomas, J.C. & Leitner, L.M. (2005). Styles of suicide intervention: Professionals' responses and clients' preferences. *The Humanistic Psychologist, 33,* 145–165.

Wampold, B. (2001). *The great psychotherapy debate: Models, methods, and findings.* Mahwah, NJ: Lawrence Erlbaum Associates.

Werth, J.L., Jr. (1992). Rational suicide and AIDS: Considerations for the psychotherapist. *The Counseling Psychologist, 20,* 645–659.

Westefeld, J.S., Range, L.M., Rogers, J.R., Maples, M.R., Bromley, J. L., & Alcorn, J. (2000). Suicide: An overview. *The Counseling Psychologist, 28,* 445–510.

Clinical and Research Training in Suicidality in Ethnic Communities

Sherry Davis Molock, Samantha Matlin, and Henry Prempeh

□ Introduction

Suicide is currently the 11th leading cause of death for all age groups across all ethnic communities. However, there is considerable variation in the rates of completed suicide within the different ethnic groups. While suicide is in the top 10 leading causes of death across almost all age groups in the non-Hispanic white and Asian American communities, it is a leading cause of death primarily among the young (under the age of 45) in the African American, Hispanic, and Native American communities (National Center for Injury Prevention and Control, 2006).

While suicides represent a major public health problem in the U.S., completed suicides represent only a small fraction of suicidal behaviors. Suicide attempts and other self-injurious behaviors are particularly taxing for youth, with an estimated 124,409 emergency room visits in U.S. hospitals in 2002 (Centers for Disease Control, [CDC], 2004). The Youth Risk Behavior Surveillance System found that the overall prevalence of suicide attempts for Hispanic students grades 9–12 (11.3%) was much higher than both white and black students, 7.6%, and 7.3% respectively (CDC, 2006). Of the students who actually attempted suicide one or more times in the past 12 months, 14.9% were Hispanic females, which was higher than all other students across gender and racial groups including both African

American females (9.8%) and Caucasian American female students (9.3%). While African American females have lower attempt rates than White American or Hispanic females, African American and Hispanic males surpassed White American males in suicide attempts that required medical attention for the first time in 2003 (CDC 2004). The attempt rates for Asian American high schoolers was not reported because there were so few suicides in this group that the coefficients were believed to be unstable.

The epidemiological data suggests that while completed suicides are somewhat rare, many psychologists probably have experience working with clients who have suicidal ideation and make suicide attempts. Research suggests that psychologists report receiving varying degrees of training in suicidality at different junctures in their careers. For example, Ellis and Dickey (1998) reported that 75% of a sample of psychology internship programs offered didactic training in suicidality. Kleespies, Penk, and Forsyth (1993) found that 55% of predoctoral interns reported receiving some training in suicidality in their graduate programs. McAdams and Foster (2000) conducted a national survey of professional counselors and found that nearly one quarter had experienced the suicide of a client they were treating; within this group, 24% were students when the suicide occurred. More recently, Dexter-Mazza and Freeman, (2003) surveyed predoctoral psychology interns who were trained in PhD or PsyD programs in clinical, counseling, or school psychology. They found that 5% had experienced the suicide of a client, 99% had treated at least one suicidal client, but only 50% reported receiving some formal training in suicide risk assessment and/or treatment.

Practicing psychologists also report varying degrees of training in suicidality, with 35–55% reporting they received didactic training in suicidality in graduate school (Bongar & Harmatz, 1991; Dexter-Mazza & Freeman, 2003) and 40–75% reporting they received some training on their predoctoral internship (Dexter-Mazza & Freeman, 2003; Ellis & Dickey, 1998; McAdams & Foster, 2000). While the majority of psychologists are receiving some training in the assessment and treatment of suicidal behaviors, the training experience is often described as limited and is often done informally.

Even fewer training programs address how race and ethnicity influence the assessment, treatment, and development of intervention/prevention programs in suicidality. To date, no formal studies have examined the role that race/ethnicity might play in training professional psychologists in suicidality. The American Psychological Association (APA) guidelines on multicultural competence suggest that in order to work with racially and ethnically diverse groups, psychologists need to develop contextual competence, which can be accomplished via culture-centered training (APA, 2003). Culturally competent psychologists need to understand the myriad of contexts in which people function, as well as how these contexts influence behavior. Culture-centered training should help students recognize that all persons, including themselves, are influenced by different historical, ecological, and sociopolitical contexts. An example of a culturally centered approach to research is the one used by Alegria and her colleagues (2005) in the National Latino and Asian American Study (NLAAS). This innovative study is a nationally representative community household survey designed to get estimates of the prevalence of mental disorders and the rates of mental health service utilization in Latino and Asian American communities. The study not only includes multiple ethnic groups within both communities, but also uses an eco-epidemiological model that posits that the risk for psychiatric illness is associated with a person's social position in the U.S., which is defined by the person's ethnicity, race, education, occupation, income, wealth, and social status.

This chapter will highlight some of the particular barriers to addressing race and ethnicity in suicide training, as well as offer potential solutions to overcome them. It is our hope that identifying some of these barriers will help therapists, researchers, supervisors, and students consider these factors when engaging in this type of work. We also hope that increasing awareness of the difficulties in this area will bring increased appreciation for individuals who focus on the study, prevention, and treatment of suicide. Furthermore, by illustrating potential solutions for overcoming these barriers, we hope to encourage more individuals to want to prevent suicide among racial and ethnic minorities. Finally, we hope that this chapter will help improve the quality and appropriateness of suicide prevention among ethnic minority groups.

☐ Barriers to Addressing Race and Ethnicity in Suicide Training

Several factors make it difficult to address ethnicity in suicide training. Culturally centered psychologists need to receive training on how their own ethnic identities and cultures impact their relationship with a client, how they influence the types of research questions they choose to ask or not ask, and how they influence the types of prevention programs they choose to develop in ethnic communities. This may be particularly difficult for majority-culture trainees and professional psychologists because it requires them to examine their own White privilege and examine the possibility that they harbor prejudiced views of ethnic groups. Sue (2006) argues that "whiteness" is by default the normative standard in American society against which all other communities of color are measured. Because being White is considered to be normative, it automatically confers privilege and dominance on Whites in our society. He argues that White privilege renders communities of color as either deviant or invisible and allows Whites to engage in racial discrimination and maintain racist institutions while simultaneously maintaining their individual and collective advantage and innocence.

One component of developing cultural sensitivity is recognizing that traditional psychological theories and treatments may not be applicable to all populations. For instance, many theories of psychotherapy emphasize the importance of individualism and autonomy in psychological well-being. However, previous chapters in this book have highlighted the importance of family and the larger community on individual well-being for many racial and ethnic groups. Thus, as psychologists, we need to be willing to include culturally centered models that promote and enhance the well-being of clients from communities of color. This means that therapists must be willing to free themselves of their role as the "expert" in order to facilitate positive growth in their clients.

Second, researchers and clinicians often ignore the heterogeneity that occurs within ethnic minority groups. Groups that have different cultures, histories of immigration to the United States, and different experiences with addressing community perspectives on assimilation and acculturation are often grouped together as if there are no intra-ethnic differences within ethnic groups. For example, Joe, Baser, Breeden, Neighbors, and Jackson (2006) recently found an interaction between ethnicity and gender in suicide attempts among blacks living in the U.S., with black Caribbean men reporting the highest rates of lifetime suicide attempts. Other researchers have found regional, socioeconomic, and intra-racial or ethnic group differences in the rates of depression and suicidality in Latino (Oquendo, Ellis, Greenwald, Malone, Weissman, & Mann, 2001) and Asian American groups (Leong, Leach, & Gupta, 2007). For example, secondary analyses on the National Comorbidity Study (NCS) that stratified Latinos and Asians by nativity found that Mexican Americans born in Mexico had lower rates of psychiatric disorder than those born in the U.S. (Vega, Kodoly, Aguilar-Gaxiola, Alderte, Gatalano & Garaveo-Anduaga, 1998).

Third, it is often hard to articulate how race, ethnicity, and culture influence suicidal behaviors because they often operate in the background, out of conscious awareness. Individuals who come from ethnically diverse communities may engage in behaviors that reflect deeply held cultural belief systems but be completely unaware of the cultural significance of the behavior. For example, both Native American and Asian communities emphasize the importance of respecting elders, and youth from these communities are often taught to show deference to adults, particularly in public forums. Similarly, African American youth are often taught that calling adults by their first name is a sign of disrespect, so they may attach the formal title "Mr." or "Miss" to the first name of an adult as a sign of respect. While none of the youth from these communities may understand their behavior as culturally determined, nonetheless, the behaviors reflect cultural values that are central to the particular community.

Fourth, because culture often operates in the background, it is also difficult to operationalize and hence measure. The boundaries of culture are quite fluid, so people often operate in multiple cultural contexts, often at the same time. How a devoutly religious Afro-Caribbean woman understands and expresses suicidal thoughts and behaviors may be simultaneously shaped by cultural scripts about how Christians, Latinas, blacks, and immigrants experience, understand, and express suicidality. A culturally centered psychologist needs to be trained to appreciate how all of these contexts shape the suicidal behavior of this client (Canetto & Lester, 1998).

We often train graduate students in the assessment and treatment of suicide using Eurocentric models with little thought to whether these techniques are appropriate to use in ethnic minority communities. This occurs, in part, because behavioral problems and psychopathology are believed to be universally expressed. It also occurs because most Western models in the social sciences value independence, uniqueness, and orthogonal relationships; therefore, behaviors that are not unique to a particular ethnic group are often dismissed as culturally irrelevant. However, a phenomenon does not have to be unique to a particular ethnic group to be central to the community. For example, spirituality can be considered an important but not necessarily unique component of both Native American and African American culture. The protective role that spirituality plays against suicidal behaviors in these communities may not be unique, but it is still culturally relevant.

Psychology trainees may need particular help in addressing their own potential for ethnic bias because research suggests that students and professional psychologists are often resistant to dealing with issues of race and ethnicity in their work because of feelings of guilt about harboring prejudiced views or fears of being labeled racist (Ancis, & Sanchez-Hucles, 2000; Mckenzie-Mavinga, 2005). Others may choose to de-emphasize group membership by adopting a "We Are the World" approach that discourages discussion of ethnic group differences, thereby minimizing the potential disclosure of prejudiced views and in-group/out-group biases. However, research suggests that using a color-blind approach does not necessarily lead to equitable treatment of different ethnic groups and may lead to increased segregation, employment discrimination, and the negation of cultural identity that may be critical to the psychological well-being of persons of color (Brewer & Brown, 1998; Harrell, 1999; Jones, 1991). It is important to train students and professional psychologists to examine their ethnic identity and the ethnic identity of other groups, as well as to develop comfort in acknowledging differences among individuals and groups.

The minimization of ethnic group differences also occurs because of the underlying assumption of universality in the expression of suicidality and in the intervention models used to treat suicidal clients. Hence, until 1979, ethnic differences in suicide rates were depicted as "White" and "nonWhite." Many suicidologists continue to make no mention of the racial composition of their sample, which implies that ethnic minority group members and Whites experience the same cultural and social reality. This omission of the ethnic composition of the sample in peer reviewed journals is even more puzzling in the context of the requirement that all federally funded research makes a concerted effort to include ethnic minority group participants or justify why they are *not* included in the sample (National Institute of Health, 2001).

Betancourt and Lopez (1993) note that mainstream psychology generally ignores the role of culture in psychological phenomena, and when it does include ethnicity or culture as a variable, it often fails to identify the specific aspect of culture (e.g., values, experiences, identity) that may account for differences in behavior. Thus, graduate students often overlook the importance of culture in their clinical and research endeavors, or are permitted to do simplistic between-group designs where race is the between-group factor and no particular aspect of race, ethnicity, or culture is directly measured. Betancourt and Lopez (1993) note that such between-group comparisons assume the universal expression of behaviors across different cultural groups and minimize the complexity of culture and ignore the diversity that exists within cultural groups. Trainees also need to be taught how to address the stigma often associated with the seeking of mental health treatment in ethnic minority communities (U.S. Department of Health and Human Services, 1999). In the African American community, it may be helpful to develop partnerships with churches that can encourage and give church members "permission" to seek treatment for depression and suicidal behaviors by helping to change treatment-seeking norms in churches. The American Indian Service Utilization, Psychiatric Epidemiology, Risk and Protective Factors Project noted that just as many American Indians sought help for depression and anxiety from a mental health professional as they did from a traditional healer (Beals et al., 2005). It may be important to train students to develop liaisons with traditional healers as important members of treatment teams when designing suicide intervention and prevention programs for Native Americans (Novins et al., 2004).

Our current training models encourage students to use Eurocentric assessment, treatment, and research methods that often view members of ethnic communities as treatment resistant because they are more likely to refuse treatment or drop out of treatment early (Davis & Ford, 2004; Snowden, 1999). Students need to be trained to use models that focus not only on affecting change at the level of the individual, but at the level of the community and institutions as well. For example, the authors have developed a partnership with faith-based institutions in the African American community to develop suicide prevention programs for youth and young adults. In addition to working to develop programs that can reduce risk factors and enhance protective factors for youth at risk for suicide, the program also aims to effect change at the family, community, and institutional levels by partnering with churches to change help-seeking and service utilization norms in the church community.

Admittedly, it is often difficult to develop such programs in ethnic communities because it is difficult to recruit participants and conduct research in ethnic communities. Because of societal discrimination, the history of unethical research conducted in ethnic communities (e.g., the Tuskegee study) and the communities' receiving little known benefit from scientific studies, ethnic minorities often hold suspicions about the conduct of research (Sanders-Thompson, Bazile & Akbar, 2004). Research has demonstrated that community partnerships that are long-lasting, embody the values of the community, and provide community oversight provide a successful model to developing and sustaining research with randomized intervention assignment (Wandersman & Florin, 2003).

Further, many of the tools used in suicide-risk assessment are presumed to be reliable and valid for all ethnic groups, although these presumptions have often not been empirically validated (Molock & Douglas, 1999). This may be particularly important for ethnic communities because there is some limited evidence that there may be cultural differences in the expression of the risk factors associated with suicidal behaviors. Students need to be trained in recognizing that depression and suicide may be expressed differently in some ethnic communities and need to modify or ask additional sets of questions to ensure that they are conducting a valid assessment of suicide risk. For example, Politano, Nelson, Evans, Sorenson & Zeman (1986) found the behavioral component of depression, especially as it pertains to oppositionality, to be more prominently expressed in African American children. As previously noted, Asian Americans are more likely to present with somatic complaints when dealing with depression (Oquendo et al., 2001), and African Americans may be less likely to overtly express feelings of hopelessness during a suicide attempt (Molock, Kimbrough, Blanton, McClure & Williams, 1994). Research also suggests that ethnic clients are less likely to disclose suicide intent during intake interviews in counseling centers (Morrison & Downey, 2000). These findings suggest that suicide-risk assessment tools need to be sensitive to ethnic differences in the presentation of suicidal symptoms and rely more on tools that have been tailored to the cultural context of the client (Sue & Sue, 2003).

□ Solutions

Developing Cultural Sensitivity

Several ways exist in which we can better prepare psychologists to assess, treat, and conduct research on suicidal behaviors in ethnic communities. It is important to reiterate that formal suicide training in graduate programs needs to be strengthened and should be required in all graduate training programs for psychologists (Dexter-Mazza & Freeman, 2003). A key solution to treating ethnic suicidal clients is developing cultural sensitivity. which can be defined as "the ability to adjust one's perceptions, behaviors, and practice styles to effectively meet the needs of different ethnic or racial groups" (Health Resources and Services Administration, 2006).

To develop multicultural competence, students need to be encouraged to utilize a culture-centered approach that acknowledges that all individuals are influenced by sociocultural, ecological, and other contextual factors (APA, 2003). A culture-centered approach differs from a disease-specific model that focuses on the individual as separate from his or her environment. Felner and Felner's (1989) transactional-ecological framework is a valuable model to teach clinicians to consider how an individual's potential for suicide is influenced by interactions among broad-based conditions (e.g., poverty, unsafe living conditions) and individual variables (e.g., depression, hopelessness). Utilizing an ecological framework demands that individuals be understood and treated as inseparable from their environment.

Graduate programs could use this transactional-ecological framework not only to assess suicide risk, but also to develop culturally/ecologically valid suicide interventions. For example, most suicide-risk assessment tools rely heavily on the cognitive behavioral model that focuses on the individual's maladaptive behaviors and beliefs. The use of the transactional-ecological framework would require trainees to learn how to assess cultural values and beliefs that may infer risk or protect members of ethnic minority groups from suicide. To not only assess suicide risk, but to design an ecologically valid intervention that is contextualized to the needs of the client, students could also be trained to do ecological assessments of the environment by actually visiting the community and assessing level of violence in the community, degree of crowdedness, ethnic tensions, level of family and community support, spirituality, access to resources, financial resources, immigrant status of family, cultural beliefs about suicide, and mental health service utilization.

Although no specific standards for multicultural training among graduate programs in clinical and counseling psychology exist, Chae, Foley, and Chae (2006) highlight three types of multicultural training that can help psychologists better address the needs of ethnic minority suicidal clients. These typologies include: (a) separate course, (b) integration or infusion, and (c) area of concentration. In the separate course model, didactic and experiential approaches are emphasized where students are exposed to curriculum that focuses on cultural factors among ethnic groups as well as asked to increase their own awareness of their racial and ethnic identity. The integration or infusion model emphasizes the importance of infusing multicultural issues into all coursework. The area of concentration model allows students to select various didactic and experiential courses and take part in practicum sites that emphasize multicultural training. Each approach has its advantages and disadvantages and a combination of all three approaches, where students are taught about various racial and ethnic groups, encouraged to explore their own identities, and take part in practicum sites that work with racial and ethnic minorities, would likely be most effective in training therapists to become culturally competent. Because it is unlikely that students will receive training specifically focused on suicide among ethnic minority clients, it may be particularly important for programs to decide where this topic can be best addressed.

Graduate programs can begin to address multicultural training and even suicide by providing a rigorous, but safe, training environment in which students can honestly explore how they have been exposed to racist views of ethnic minority groups, as well as how they have directly or indirectly participated in the perpetuation of stereotyping of ethnic groups or engaged in racist and discriminatory behaviors. Students should also explore how larger institutions establish policies that are discriminatory; these topics can be explored in didactic class work but in process groups as well. An important first step in such training might be to have outside trainers come to graduate programs and conduct cultural sensitivity training for faculty, because faculty members not only need to address their own prejudiced views and discriminatory practices, but must feel comfortable enough with the topic to train students in these sensitive areas. Students could also benefit from participating in ethnically diverse process groups in their first year of training. Process groups can provide graduate students with the time and space to explore difficult topics with their peers. It would be beneficial to use outside facilitators for these groups so that students can openly address the myriad of issues around ethnic diversity without being evaluated or judged by faculty.

Graduate programs should also work to identify certain didactic and course opportunities, as well as practicum sites that integrate training on suicide among ethnic minority groups. In addition to offering specific courses dedicated to issues of race and ethnicity, many courses, such as assessment, research methods, and psychopathology can fairly easily integrate topics on suicide among ethnic groups. Graduate programs should also develop community partnerships with organizations that work with ethnic minority and suicidal clients. This will facilitate students to obtain these types of placements that will provide practical opportunities to apply the knowledge gained in coursework.

Training in Assessment and Therapy

Multicultural training in suicide must be extended to all elements of suicide, including assessment and treatment. For instance, although students may receive training in using suicide assessment measures, they must also consider when these measures might not be appropriate among certain ethnic groups. For example, the belief that African Americans do not commit suicide is prevalent in American society, even among African Americans (Early & Akers, 1993). This may affect whether an African American client endorses items such as "I would like to kill myself" (BDI-II; Beck, Steer, & Brown, 1996). Thus, therapists must try to understand how clients from differing ethnic groups talk about death and dying. For example, religiously devout African Americans may use words like "transitioning" and "going on to glory" to describe thoughts about death and dying. Furthermore, many racial and ethnic minorities, such as Native Americans and Asian Americans, adhere to the cultural value of hiding one's feelings or sharing psychological problems only with family members (Sue & Sue, 2003). Thus, it may not be appropriate for therapists to assess the suicidal risk of a client within the first few minutes of meeting. To overcome this barrier, and given the importance of interpersonal relations among many racial and ethnic minority clients, therapists may have to work to establish rapport with clients and gain trust before doing standardized assessments.

A therapist working with an ethnic minority client in ongoing therapy after experiencing suicide ideation or engaging in suicidal behaviors (e.g., making an attempt) must consider how the race or ethnicity of both the client and the therapist may affect treatment. Racial and ethnic differences between clients and therapists are often relevant and have an impact on the therapeutic process; therefore, it is important for psychologists to be able to discuss these topics with their clients as necessary. Cardemil and Battle (2003) offer seven recommendations on how therapists can incorporate issues of race and ethnicity in treatment. They recommend that therapists be willing to: (a) suspend preconceptions about clients' race or ethnicity; (b) recognize that clients may be quite different from other members of their racial or ethnic group; (c) consider how racial or ethnic differences between therapist and client might affect psychotherapy; (d) acknowledge that power, privilege, and racism might affect interactions with client; (e) when in doubt, err on the side of discussing the importance of race and ethnicity in treatment; (f) be willing to take risks with clients; and (g) keep learning about issues of race and ethnicity.

More specifically, it may be helpful for therapists to consider how to incorporate cultural values into the treatment of suicide. A growing body of literature focuses on the protective role of family support and spirituality against suicide among many racial and ethnic minorities, including African Americans, Native Americans, Asian Americans, and Latino Americans (Garoutte et al., 2003; Heikkine, Aro, & Lonnqvist, 1993; Taylor, Chatters, & Levin, 2004). This means that therapists need to be trained to utilize these culturally salient protective factors when appropriate in treatment. For instance, therapists may need to be willing to include family members and even important community members in a client's treatment. Therapists may have to extend the notion of family to include fictive kin and extended family members in the sessions. This may require greater flexibility in a therapist's approach to treatment. It also requires graduate programs to offer therapy courses in topics such as family therapy to teach students how to do work with families and communities in treatment.

Perhaps an even greater challenge for therapists is to adopt a willingness to integrate spirituality into treatment (e.g., Aten & Leach, in press). This does not mean that therapists need to learn theological doctrine to work with religious clients. However, it does mean that therapists are willing to recognize the value of spirituality to a client's well-being and are open to discussing how the client can rely on his or her spiritual beliefs to heal. Therapists can ask their clients about their faith beliefs and traditions and what their faith tradition teaches about suicide. Do their faith beliefs around the topic of suicide make it easier or more difficult to seek help when they are feeling suicidal? Therapists need to ask how these beliefs may enhance or hinder their sense of well-being during times of suicide crisis. For example, self-directed religious coping (i.e., God gives individuals the freedom to resolve their own problems) has been found to be associated with positive self-esteem and a sense of self-efficacy (Phillips et al., 2004), but it has also been related to higher levels of depression and lower levels of spiritual well-being (Hathaway & Pargament 1990; Wong-McDonald & Gorsuch, 2000). Molock and her colleagues (2006) studied the role of religious coping in a sample of African American adolescents and found that self-directed religious coping was a risk factor for fewer reasons for living and for suicide attempts. Thus, students need to be trained in how to understand and incorporate spirituality as appropriate in treatment.

Particular characteristics and behaviors can facilitate therapists' work with clients from various racial and ethnic groups. Overall, therapists need to recognize the limitations of their own worldview. This requires therapists to endorse an open perspective on mental well-being and to be flexible in their therapeutic approaches. For example, it is usually unhelpful if therapists insist that their clients initially adopt a biomedical model in their understanding of depression. Therapists must also be willing to see the world through the client's eyes. How are depression and suicide described and understood in the client's ethnic community? What is the community's response to persons who feel depressed or suicidal? Further, therapists who enjoy learning about people and cultures that are different from themselves will find this challenging work particularly exciting.

Similarly, therapists have to recognize that not all ethnic groups have the same understanding of therapy. This requires therapists to provide psycho-education about the structure and intention of therapy, as well as the process. Therapists working with clients from diverse backgrounds also need to be willing to confront insecurities about asking clients to teach them. Therapists should try to learn the language and metaphors utilized by certain groups and use them in treatment. For example, in the first author's work with African American youth, she has noted that African American males often deny suicidal ideation and intent, but will engage in high-risk behaviors that are similar to victim-precipitated homicide (e.g., taking an unloaded gun to confront a bully with the knowledge that the bully carries a loaded weapon) or extremely dangerous "games" (e.g., Russian roulette). The author has learned that the best way to elicit information about such behaviors is to ask specific questions about the behaviors but to not label them as suicidal.

It is also important for therapists to seek outside help when appropriate from experts in various ethnic and racial groups. This requires therapists to build relationships with both psychologists in the field and community leaders. Therapists can also increase the comfort of clients by creating a "culture-friendly" environment. This may include decorating offices in warmer, more inviting decor than is typical in medical settings, and including artwork, maps, and photographs from a variety of cultures. Finally, therapists must be cognizant that significant heterogeneity exists within ethnic groups and be careful not to assume certain characteristics about a client because he or she belongs to a certain group. Sources of such heterogeneity include immigration history and time frame, language skills, acculturation, ethnic or racial identity, perceived minority status, experiences with discrimination, and socioeconomic status (Cardemil & Battle, 2003). For example, five targeted suicide prevention programs for American Indian/Alaskan Native youth meet the IOM's standard for evidenced-based preventions (e.g., the Zuni Life-Skills Development Curriculum; LaFromboise & Howard-Pitney, 1994, 1995; the Western Athabaskan "Natural Helpers" Program; May, Serna, Hurt, & DeBruyn, 2005). While these programs have made some impressive gains in combating suicidal behaviors in American Indian/Alaskan Native youth, it is important to remember the cultural differences between Native American groups and that some historical enmities between groups makes different tribes resistant to accepting programs that do not acknowledge unique cultural beliefs and practices. So it is important for trainees to realize that even culturally centered programs designed for one group (e.g., Ojibwe reservations) may not generalize to another group (e.g., Lakota people of North Dakota) (Goldston, Molock, Whitbeck, Zayas, Murakami, & Hall, in press).

Increased Research

In addition to training students on how to work with ethnic minority clients who may be suicidal, faculty and supervisors must train students on how to do multicultural research on suicide. Many of the recommended guidelines for doing therapy with clients extend to research. For instance, it is important to recognize that the way in which we often conduct research (e.g., taking an expert role on a problem) may not be appropriate among certain racial groups that have a mistrust for research or who do not believe that suicide is a problem in their ethnic community. For example, the authors conduct workshops and research on suicide in African American churches where congregants are often surprised to hear that African Americans, particularly "saved black folks" would contemplate suicide. We also need to be willing to shift our research paradigms to include collaborative models where researchers partner with individuals or communities to address the needs and goals of the individual or community.

Furthermore, researchers need to consider how certain culturally held values need to be incorporated into the way research is conducted. For example, as discussed previously, given the importance of interpersonal relations among many ethnic minority groups, researchers must also take time to develop relationships with participants before engaging in research. This may require researchers to "hang out" in the community before initiating data collection. Through relationship building, researchers can increase feelings of comfort in both participants and researchers in doing research on difficult topics such as suicide. Furthermore, by spending time with participants, researchers can learn the etiquette or customs of the group (e.g., how leaders or elders are addressed) and how the myriad of groups handle discussions around mental illness and suicidal behaviors. Researchers also learn the metaphors and language used to describe suicidality by spending time in the community. Another illustration of how cultural values may need to be considered is how data is collected. Some cultures, such as African Americans, value verbal communication. Therefore, utilizing paper-and-pencil measures may not yield as valid or comprehensive results as in-person or telephone interviews, particularly with a topic as sensitive as suicide.

It is important to train students that it is legitimate to study suicidality *within* a specific ethnic group, rather than assuming the phenomenon is the same for all groups or finding out how suicidal behaviors in communities of color depart from what occurs for Whites. For example, suicide "contagion" or modeling effects have been reported among both White and American Indian/Alaskan Native youth. However, it is possible that American Indian/Alaskan Native youth may be at particular risk for suicide "contagion" or modeling effects because of the small, but intense social networks in which American Indian youth tend to interact on rural reservations (Bechtold, 1988; Wissow, Walkup, Barlow, Reid, & Kane, 2001). While suicide clusters occur among White youth as well, the reasons for the clusters and the risk factors associated with the clusters may be obviated by using the more traditional between-group designs (Goldston, et al., in press).

Indeed, students need to be trained to understand that the assumption of behavioral universality makes it difficult to conduct cross-cultural and within-group studies on suicide in communities of color because such assumptions eliminate the need for this important research. Without it, psychologists may make faulty assumptions about the expression of suicidality in ethnic communities. For example, while it has been estimated that 50% of all youth suicide attempts involve drug use (Berman & Jobes, 1991), several investigators have found that African American youth are less likely than Whites to use drugs during a suicide attempt (Molock, Kimbrough, Blanton, McClure & Williams, 1994; Willis, Coombs, Drentea, & Cockerham, 2003), and are less likely to express suicide intent during a suicide crisis (Morano, et al., 1993; Summerville, Abbate, Siegel, Serravezza, & Kaslow, 1992).

A previously mentioned course where graduate programs can incorporate training on suicide is in research methods classes. Students in research methods classes can be assigned "case studies" that explore what happens to their understanding of suicidality in communities of color when between- versus within-group studies are designed. For example, would the suicide rates for African American and Latino males appreciably change if "victim-precipitated homicides," where the victim intentionally engages in behavior in a life-threatening context that almost guarantees that another person (e.g., police officer) will kill the victim, were also classified as suicides (Garrison, Jackson, Addy, McKeown, & Waller, 1991; Parent, 1999; Wolfgang, 1958)? While it has been estimated that nearly 30% of urban homicides are victim-precipitated (Van Zandt, 1993), such a death is not formally recognized as a form of suicide. Research also suggests that Asian Americans are more likely to somaticize symptoms of depression and are more likely to attribute depression to social causes (Morrison & Downey, 2000). Graduate programs should be training students to ask different types of questions when screening for depression in ethnic communities. We should also be training students to appreciate that ethnic differences in etiological models of mental illness have implications for the design and implementation of intervention programs in these same communities. It is important for trainees to know that noting ethnic differences in suicidality no way implies that one form of suicide is more "psychologically mature" or "better" than another. It may simply be that cultural factors facilitate the expression of one form of suicide over another.

In a similar vein, culture will also influence the research methodology. One area of research that demonstrates this very clearly is shown in the literature on service utilization for mental health problems in general and suicidality in particular. Pick, Poortinga and Givauden (2003) note that most interventions in psychology that are designed to treat or prevent suicide are aimed at the individual (e.g., the treatment of the symptoms of depression) with little regard to context (e.g., changing norms about treatment seeking). In fact, most suicide intervention/prevention models are predicated on research that is conducted on White, middle-income individuals, who constitute only 5% of the world's population (Stuart, 2004). But health psychologists who study service utilization and help-seeking behaviors are beginning to advocate for a contextual perspective that views help-seeking behaviors as occurring in an ecological niche influenced by contextual factors (e.g., sociocultural, interpersonal, situational, personal, and biological) at multiple levels (Anderson & McNeilly, 1991; Cauce et al., 2002). Current interventions often fail to be adapted by ethnic communities because they use an epidemiological symptoms-based approach rather than the functional impairment paradigm that is used by most families (Leaf, Bruce & Tischer, 1986; Cauce et al., 2002).

Students can be trained to use quantitative and qualitative methods (e.g., focus groups, key informant interviews) so that they can develop suicide interventions that use culturally relevant, current help-seeking behaviors as their starting point in the intervention. Trainees can also learn how to develop community partnerships using community-based participatory research (CBPR) models. CBPR has been recognized as a potentially more suitable approach than traditional "outside expert" perspectives in developing prevention programs, particularly among minority and ethnic groups (Holkup, Tripp-Reimer, Salois, & Weinert, 2004) and has been successfully used to address health disparities among ethnic populations (Burrus, Liburd, & Burroughs, 1998; Campbell et al., 2000; Giachello et al., 2003; Hart & Bowen, 2004). These models assume that organizations and communities contribute unique strengths and shared responsibilities to enhance understanding of a given phenomenon and to integrate this knowledge with action to improve the health and well-being of community members (Israel, Schulz, Parker, & Becker, 1998).

Students can be trained to use CBPR models so they can focus on building upon the strengths and resources within the community, rather than focusing on pathology, such as suicide. Trainees should also be taught that developing collaborative partnerships means involving community partners in all phases of the research; it may be helpful to include community partners on master's and dissertation committees to ensure that this process does not occur in name only. Trainees could also be encouraged to use a cyclical and iterative process in program development and in the dissemination of information, making sure that the information obtained from the project is beneficial to all partners, not just the students and their research advisors (Israel et al., 1998).

Trainees can also be taught to address such problematic issues as selection bias in randomized clinical trials (RCT) (Braver & Bray, 1992; Rothman & Greenland, 1998) by using alternative sampling procedures (e.g., multiplicity sampling) to increase the number of ethnic participants, because the use of probability sampling in RCT has been found to yield the lowest number of participants among African Americans and Latinos (Cabral et al., 2003). The attrition rate in ethnic minorities is also high in these studies because the methods commonly used in such studies may be viewed as exploitative (e.g., no treatment control group) or the informed consent procedures may be seen as removing legal protections for the participants (Corbie-Smith et al., 2003). Multiplicity sampling elicits the help of family or peer networks to recruit participants and has been successfully used in field research to yield hard to reach minority participants (Rothbart, Fine, & Sudman, 1982). Students can also be trained to build up community trust over time and to make sure they develop positive relationships with trusted community stakeholders (e.g., clergy; Ammerman, 2002).

☐ Conclusion

To train psychologists to work with ethnic communities in the area of suicide requires a genuine belief that the cultural context of all people is an important part of who they are and a commitment to treating the whole person. It also requires a paradigm shift away from traditional models of assessment, treatment and research so that students are taught not only to consider the multiple contexts in which clients interact, but also to examine themselves as persons with myriad contexts, and to honestly look for areas in their own backgrounds that might both enhance and hinder their work with suicidal clients from culturally diverse backgrounds. It will also require programs to use different research models to enhance the participation of ethnic communities in research, to engage in community participatory research and to develop true partnerships with communities of color where the need for the research is driven by the community, and not for the career enhancement of the psychologist. Finally, it requires trainees to understand that there are different ways of knowing in the world; psychological and research models are one way to help us understand ourselves and our environment, but that there are ways of understanding people of color that are indigenous to particular communities, and that these are equally valid ways of knowing and understanding ourselves and others.

□ References

Alegria, M., Takeuchi, D., Ganino, G., Duan, N., Shrout, P., Xiao, L., Vega, W., Zane, N., Vila, D., Woo, M., Vera, M., Guarnaggia, P., Aguila-Gaxiola, S., Sue, S., Esgobar, J., Keh-Ming, L., & Gong, E. (2005). Considering context, place and culture: the National Latino and Asian American Study International. *Journal of Methods in Psychiatric Research, 13*(4), 208–219.

American Psychological Association (APA). (2003). Guidelines for providers of psychological services to ethnic, linguistic, and culturally diverse populations. *American Psychologist, 48,* 45–48.

Ammerman, A. (2002). Process evaluation of the church-based PRAISE project: Partnership to reach African Americans to increase smart eating. In A. Steckler, & L. Linnan (Eds.), *Process evaluation for public health interventions and research* (pp. 96–111). San Francisco: Jossey-Bass Publishers.

Ancis, Julie R., Sanchez-Hucles, Janis V. (2000). A preliminary analysis of counseling students' attitudes toward counseling women and women of color: Implications for cultural competency training. *Journal of Multicultural Counseling & Development, 28,* 16–31.

Anderson, N.B. & McNeilly, M. (1991). Age, gender, and ethnicity as variables in psychophysiological assessment sociodemographics in context. *Psychological Assessment, 3,* 376–384.

Aten, J. & Leach, M.M. (Eds.) (in press). *Integrating spirituality across the therapeutic process in counseling and psychotherapy.* Washington, DC: American Psychological Association.

Beals, J., Novins, D., Whitesell, N., Spicer, P., Mitchell, C., & Manson, S. (2005). Prevalence of mental disorders and utilization of mental health services in two American Indian reservation populations: Mental health disparities in a national context. *American Journal of Psychiatry, 162,* 1723–1732.

Bechtold, D. (1988). Cluster suicide in American Indian adolescents. *American Indian and Alaska Native Mental Health Research, 1,* 26–35.

Beck, A.T., Steer, R.A., & Brown, G.K. (1996). *Manual for Beck Depression Inventory–II.* San Antonio, TX: Psychological Corporation.

Berman, A.L. & Jobes, D. (1991). *Adolescent suicide: Assessment and intervention.* Washington, DC: American Psychological Association.

Betancourt, H. & Lopez, S.R. (1993). The study of culture, ethnicity, and race in American psychology. *American Psychologist, 48,* 629–637.

Bongar, B. & Harmatz, M. (1991). Clinical psychology graduate education in the study of suicide: Availability, resources, and importance. *Suicide and Life-Threatening Behavior, 21,* 231–244.

Braver, S.L. & Bay, R.C. (1992). Assessing and compensating for self-selection bias (non-representativeness of the family research sample). *Journal of Marriage and Family, 54*, 925–939.

Brewer, M.B. & Brown, R.J. (1998). Intergroup relations. In D.T. Gilbert & S. T. Fiske (Eds.), *The handbook of social psychology* (4th ed., Vol. 2, pp. 554–594). New York: McGraw-Hill.

Burrus, B.B., Liburd, L.C., & Burroughs, A. (1998). Maximizing participation by black Americans in population–based diabetes research: The Project DIRECT pilot experience. *Journal of Community Health, 23*(1), 15–27.

Cabral, D.N., Napoles-Springer, A.M., Miike, R., McMillan, A., Sison, J.D., Wrensch, M.R., Perez-Stable, E.J., & Wiencke, J.K. (2003). Population and community based recruitment of African American and Latinos: The San Francisco Bay Area Lung Cancer Study. *American Journal of Epidemiology, 158*(9), 272–279.

Campbell M.K., Motsinger B.M., Ingram, A., Jewell, D., Makarushka, C., Beatty, B., Dodds, J., McClelland, J., Demissie, S., & Demark-Wahnefried, W. (2000). The North Carolina Black Churches United for Better Health Project: Intervention and process evaluation. *Health Education and Behavior, 27*(2), 241–53.

Canetto, S. & Lester, D. (1998). Gender, culture, and suicidal behavior. *Transcultural Psychiatry, 35*, 163–190.

Cardemil, E.V. & Battle, C.L. (2003). Guess who's coming to therapy? Getting comfortable with conversations about race and ethnicity in psychotherapy. *Professional Psychology: Research and Practice, 34*(3), 278–286.

Cauce, A.M., Domenech-Rodriguez, M., Paradise, M., Cochran, B., Shea, J.M., Srebnik, D., & Baydar, N. (2002). Cultural and contextual influences in mental health help seeking: A focus on ethnic minority youth. *Journal of Consulting and Clinical Psychology, 70*, 44–55.

Centers for Disease Control and Prevention, National Center for Injury Prevention and Control. (2004). Web-based Injury Statistics Query and Reporting System (WISQARS) [Online]. Retrieved from http://www.cdc.gov/ncipc/wisqars/default.htm February, 02 2006.

Center for Disease Control and Prevention. (2006). Youth Risk Behavior Surveillance–United States. *Morbidity and Mortality Weekly Report, 55*(SS-5), 1–108.

Chae, M.H., Foley, P.F., & Chae, S.Y. (2006). Multicultural competence and training: An ethical responsibility. *Counseling and Clinical Psychology Journal, 3*, 71–80.

Davis, S.D. & Ford, M.E. (2004). A conceptual model of barriers to mental health services among African Americans. *African American Research Perspectives, 10*(1).

Dexter-Mazza, E.T. & Freeman, K.A. (2003). Graduate training and the treatment of suicidal clients: The students' perspective. *Suicide and Life Threatening Behavior, 33*(2), 211–218.

Early, K.E. & Akers, R.L. (1993). "It's a white thing": An exploration of beliefs about suicide in the African American community. *Deviant Behavior, 14*, 277–296.

Ellis, T. & Dickey, T.O. (1998). Procedures surrounding the suicide of a trainee's patient: A national survey of psychology internships and psychiatry residency programs. *Professional Psychology: Research and Practice, 29*, 492–497.

Felner, R.D., & Felner, T.Y. (1989). Primary prevention programs in the educational context: A transactional-ecological framework and analysis. In L.A. Bond & B.E. Compas (Eds.), *Primary prevention and promotion in the schools*, (pp. 13–49). Newbury, Park, California: Sage.

Garoutte, E.M., Goldberg, J., Beals, J., Herrell, R., Manson, S.M., & the AI-SUPER-PFP Team. (2003). Spirituality and attempted suicide among American Indians. *Social Science and Medicine, 56,* 1571–1579.

Garrison, C.Z., Jackson, K.L., Addy, C.L., McKeown, R.E., & Waller, J.L. (1991). Suicidal behaviors in young adolescents. *American Journal of Epidemiology, 133*(10), 1005–1014.

Giachello, A.L., Arrom, J.O., Davis, M., Sayad, J.V., Ramirez, D., Nandi, C., & Ramos, C. (2003). Reducing diabetes health disparities through community-based participatory action research: the Chicago Southeast Diabetes Community Action Coalition. *Public Health Reports, 118*(4), 309–23.

Goldston, D., Molock, S.D., Whitbeck, L., Zayas, L., Murakami, J.L., & Hall, G. (in press). Cultural considerations in adolescent suicide prevention and psychosocial treatment. *American Psychologist.*

Harrell, C.J.P. (1999). *Manichean psychology: Racism and the minds of people of African descent.* Washington, DC: Howard University Press.

Hart, A., & Bowen, D.J. (2004). The feasibility of partnering with African American barbershops to provide prostate cancer education. *Ethnic Discourse, 14,* 269–273.

Hathaway, W.L. & Pargament, K.I. (1990). Intrinsic religiousness, religious coping, and psychosocial competence: A covariance structure analysis. *Journal for the Scientific Study of Religion. 29,* 423–441.

Health Resources and Services Administration (HRSA). Health Careers Opportunity Program Definitions. Retrieved February 1, 2007, http://bhpr.hrsa.gov/diversity/definitions.htm.

Heikkinen, M., Aro, H., & Lonnqvist, J. (1993). Life events and social support in suicide. *Suicide and Life-Threatening Behavior, 23,* 343–358.

Holkup P.A., Tripp-Reimer, T., Salois, E.M., Weinert, C. (2004). Community-based participatory research: An approach to intervention research with a Native American community. *ANS Advances in Nursing Science, 27,* 162–75.

Israel, B.A., Schulz, A.J., Parker, E.A., & Becker, A.B. (1998). Review of community-based research: Assessing partnership approaches to improve public health. *Annual Review of Public Health, 19,* 173–202.

Joe, S., Baser, R.E., Breeden, G., Neighbors, H.W., & Jackson, J. (2006). Prevalence of and risk factors for lifetime suicide attempts among blacks in the United States. *Journal of the American Medical Association, 296,* 2112–2123.

Jones, J.M. (1991). Psychological models of race: What have they been and what should they be? In: J. D. Goodchilds (Ed.). *Psychological perspectives on human diversity in America: Master lectures in psychology* (pp. 3–46). Washington, DC: American Psychological Association.

Kleespies, P.M., Penk, W.E., & Forsyth, J. P. (1993). The stress of patient suicide behavior during clinical training: Incidence, impact, and recovery. *Professional Psychology: Research and Practice, 24,* 293–303.

LaFromboise, T. & Howard-Pitney, B. (1994). The Zuni Life Skills Development curriculum: A collaborative approach to curriculum development. *American Indian and Alaska native mental health research (Monographic series), 4,* 98–121.

Leaf, P.J., Bruce, M.L., & Tischler, G.L. (1986). The differential effect of attitudes on the use of mental health services. *Social Psychiatry, 21,* 187–192.

Leong, F.T.L., Leach, M.M., & Gupta, A. (in press). Asian Americans and suicide. In: F.T.L. Leong., & M.M. Leach, (Eds.), *Suicide among racial and ethnic groups: Theory, research, and practice*. Brunner-Routledge.

May, P., Serna, P., Hurt, L., & DeBruyn, L., (2005). Outcome evaluation of a public health approach to suicide prevention in an American Indian tribal nation: 1988–2002. *American Journal of Public Health, 95,* 1238–1244.

McAdams, C.R. & Foster, V.A. (2000). Client suicide: Its frequency and impact on counselors. *Journal of Mental Health Counseling, 22,* 107–121.

McKenzie-Mavinga, I. (2005). Understanding black issues in postgraduate counselor training. *Counseling and Psychotherapy Research, 5,* 295–300.

Molock, S.D. & Douglas, K.B. (1999). Suicidality in the African American community: A collaborative response from a womanist theologian and a community psychologist. *The Community Psychologist, 3,* 32–35.

Molock, S.D., Kimbrough, R., Blanton, M., McClure, K., Williams, S. (1994). Suicidal ideation and suicide attempts among African American college students. *Journal of Black Psychology, 20,* 138–151.

Molock, S.D., Puri, R., Matlin, S., & Barksdale, C. (2006). Relationship between religious coping and suicidal behaviors among African American adolescents. *Journal of Black Psychology.* 32,(3), 366–389.

Morano, C.D., Cisler, R.A., & Lemerond, J. (1993). Risk factors for adolescent suicidal behavior: Loss, insufficient familial support, and hopelessness. *Adolescence, 28,* 851–865.

Morrison, L.L., & Downey, D.L. (2000). Racial differences in self-disclosure of suicide ideation and reasons for living: Implications for training. *Cultural Diversity and Ethnic Minority Psychology, 6,* 374–386.

National Center for Injury Prevention and Control (NCIPC). 2006. Leading causes of death and fatal injuries: Mortality reports [Online Database]. Retrieved from http://www.cdc.gov/ncipc/wisqars/.

National Institute of Health (2001). Policy and Guidelines on the Inclusion of Women and Minorities in Clinical Research: Amended 2001. Retrieved from http://grants.nih.gov/grants/funding/women_min/guidelines. January 28, 2007.

Novins, D., Beals, J., Moore, L., Spicer, P., & Manson, S. (2004). Use of biomedical services and traditional healing options among American Indians: Sociodemographic correlates, spirituality, and ethnic identity. *Medical Care, 42,* 670–679.

Oquendo, M.A., Ellis, S.P., Greenwald, S., Malone, K.M., Weissman, M.M., & Mann, J.J. (2001). Ethnic and sex differences in suicide rates relative to major depression in the United States. *American Journal of Psychiatry, 158,* 1652–1658.

Parent, R.B. (1999). Victim-precipitated homicide: Police use of deadly force. *American Association of Suicidology Newslink. 25,* 16–17.

Phillips, R.E., Lynn, Q.K., Crossley, C.D., & Pargament, A.I. (2004). Self-directed religious coping: A deistic God, abandoning God, or no God at all? *Journal for the Scientific Study of Religion, 43,* 409–418.

Pick, S., Poortinga, Y.H., & Givauden, M. (2003). Integrating intervention theory and strategy in culture-sensitive health promotion programs. *Professional Psychology: Research and Practice.* 34, 422–429.

Politano, P.M., Nelson, W.M., Evans, H.E., Sorenson, S.B. & Zeman, D.J. (1986). Factor analytic evaluation of differences between Black and Caucasian emotionally disturbed children on the Children's Depression Inventory. *Journal of Psychopathology and Behavioral Assessment, 8,* 1–7.

Rothbart, G.S., Fine, M., & Sudman, S. (1982). On finding and interviewing the needle in the haystack: The use of multiplicity sampling. *Public Opinion Quarterly, 46,* 408–421.

Sanders-Thompson, V.L., Bazile, A., & Akbar, M. (2004). African Americans' perceptions of psychotherapy and psychotherapists. *Professional Psychology: Research and Practice, 35,* 19–26.

Snowden, L.R. (1999). African American service use for mental health problems. *Journal of Community Psychology, 27,* 303–313.

Stuart, R.B. (2004). Twelve practical steps to achieving multicultural competence. *Professional Psychology: Research and Practice, 35,* 3–9.

Sue, D.W. (2006). The invisible whiteness of being: Whiteness, white supremacy, white privilege, and racism. In: M. Constantine & D.W. Sue (Eds.), *Addressing racism: Facilitating cultural competence in mental health and educational settings (pp. 15–30).* Hoboken, NJ: John Wiley & Sons, Inc.

Sue, D.W. & Sue, D. (2003). *Counseling the culturally diverse: Theory and practice (4th ed.).* New York: Wiley.

Summerville, M.B., Abbate, M.F., Siegel, A.M., Serravezza, J., & Kaslow, N.J. (1992). Psychopathology in urban female minority adolescents with suicide attempts. *Journal of the American Academy of Child and Adolescent Psychiatry, 31,* 663–668.

Taylor, R. J., Chatters, L.M., & Levin, J. (2004). *Religion in the lives of African Americans: Social, psychological, and health perspectives.* Thousand Oaks, CA: Sage Publications.

U.S. Department of Health and Human Services (U.S.DHHS) (1999). Mental Health: A Report of the Surgeon General. Rockville, MD, SAMHSA, Center for Mental Health Services.

Van Zandt, C.R. (1993). Suicide by cop. *Police Chief, July,* 24–30.

Vega, W.A., Kodoly, B., Aguilar-Gaxiola, S., Alderte, E., Gatalano, R., Garaveo-Anduaga, H. (1998). Lifetime prevalence of DSM-III-R psychiatric disorders among urban and rural Mexican Americans in California. *Archives of General Psychiatry, 55,* 771–778.

Wandersman, A. & Florin, P. (2003). Community interventions and effective prevention. *American Psychologist, 58,* 441–448.

Willis, L.A., Coombs, D.W., Drentea, P., & Cockerham, W.C. (2003). Uncovering the mystery: factors of African American suicide. *Suicide & Life-Threatening Behavior,* 33, 412–429.

Wissow, L., Walkup, J., Barlow, A., Reid, R., Kane, S. (2001). Cluster and regional influences on suicide in a Southwestern American Indian tribe. *Social Science and Medicine, 53,* 1115–1124.

Wolfgang, M.E. (1958). Victim-precipitated criminal homicide. *Journal of Criminal Law, 48,* 1–11.

Wong-McDonald, A. & Gorsuch, R.L. (2000). Surrender to God: An additional coping style? *Journal of Psychology and Theology, 28,* 149–161.

Challenges for Research on Suicide among Ethnic Minorities

Mark M. Leach and Frederick T. L. Leong

Now that readers have perused their way through the previous chapters we can reflect on the current status of the field and offer some ideas regarding needed research direction over the next decade. We discussed a range of ideas based on the three sections of the book, including theories of suicide and their lack of information regarding ethnic minorities, various ethnic groups in the U.S., and assessment, prevention, intervention, and training issues. Many of the authors in this volume expressed frustration with the small amount of research literature and highlighted the need for more research. This need is especially true given that ethnic minorities are less likely to report distress to mental health professionals and the actual suicidal behavior rates may be significantly under-reported. It is through research that we can begin to alter traditional prevention, intervention, and postvention programs to include contextually relevant approaches. Quite frankly, the research field has woefully under-included ethnic minorities and the research possibilities are almost endless. Most of what is known about suicide stems from the majority culture with the underlying understanding that most assessment, prevention, and interventions are universal. Some areas for future research consideration are presented in this chapter. Some of the ideas are summarized from the authors in this text while others are abridged from Leach (2006).

□ Theory

As both Leenaars (Chapter 2) and Lester (Chapter 3) highlight, no current or past theory development includes ethnic cultural factors. It is our contention that separate theories are unnecessary, though more advanced theory through the inclusion of ethnic variables should be included in future theory development. For example, Walker, Townley, and Asiamah (Chapter 9) include environmental stressors and culturally relevant moderators that have the potential to be incorporated into new theory.

How can we look at suicide from a cultural and ethnic perspective? Leenaars asks, "What new components might be incorporated into existing theories of suicide?" Given the fluidity of culture, can we consider adaptable theories of suicide? In other words, humans are embedded within multiple cultures simultaneously, and the inclusion of cultural identity factors is numerous. For example, an individual may identify primarily as Muslim in a particular context, but in another context the fact that she is Asian and female may be more prominent. The influence of these and other identity factors become unequally important, making culturally sensitive suicide assessments more difficult.

As discussed by multiple authors in this volume, perhaps we must first begin with language. The language of suicide differs across ethnic groups, yet we still assess for suicidal behaviors primarily in a unidimensional fashion. The language of the White middle class can be effective for some persons of color, but we must also recognize that this language is limiting. As Molock, Matlin, and Prempeh (Chapter 12) mention, religiously devout African Americans may speak of "transitioning" rather than suicide or dying. Cultures, including ethnic cultures, define suicidal behaviors differently, yet little is known about how they conceive and perceive suicide. Relationships with shame, precipitated suicide, and assisted suicide are barely touched from a research perspective. It is at the fundamental level of language that we must begin when considering new developments in theory.

African Americans and Suicide

A fundamental component of this book is highlighted in Utsey, Stanard, and Hook's chapter (Chapter 4) when they stated that more research is needed to tease out African American cultural variables from common variables. They noted that African American suicide barrier variables include religion and spirituality, family cohesiveness, social support, and prosocial behaviors, among others. However, they also indicated that many of these factors may be common across all ethnic groups. Irrespective of Boykin (1983), who conducted one of the few studies teasing out African

American cultural variables, few studies have truly assessed ethnic factors particularly salient for a specific ethnic group. Utsey et al. indicated that only two recent articles in a special issue on suicide in the *Journal of Black Psychology* assessed cultural risk and protective factors associated with African American suicide. It is clear that more studies are needed.

One finds these concerns in a variety of ethnically related studies disciplines. For example, shame has been associated with multiple outcomes, including suicide, among Asian Americans, yet shame occurs across cultural groups. Few studies have compared factors across ethnic groups to determine the nuances contained within ethnic cultures. For example, what components of religion and spirituality may buffer suicide more for African Americans than for other ethnic groups? Is it simply the level of intrinsic faith (the level to which individuals "live" their faith), though research indicates that this is unlikely? Is it the quality of the relationship with the church community that is stronger, something that may require answers through qualitative research efforts? Are there generational cultural values that interact with religious variables that strengthen suicide buffers? Similarly, increased social support buffers suicide among many ethnic communities, so how much impact does it have within the African American community when compared with other communities? Among African Americans, women tend to use social support systems more than men, perhaps helping to explain the very low rates of suicide completions (but not attempts) among women. Why is it that social support is not an adequate buffer of suicide attempts? Readers will note that these questions can be asked of any ethnic group. More studies assessing the ethnic facets of religion, social support, and other seemingly universal factors are needed.

Utsey et al. also put forward the need to determine cultural influences of initial versus repeat offenders, as these individuals often show motivational differences. A call was also put forth to enhance methodological sophistication, as many studies are currently limited by correlational designs. Finally, few studies have compared suicidal behaviors across the lifespan. Given that African American suicide rates tend to decrease in the mid-30s age range it may be important to determine what common and culture-specific factors contribute to this change.

Walker et al. (Chapter 9) spoke of the need for more research on the social stigma involved in suicide within the African American community to verbalize suicidal ideation. What does it mean to verbalize suicidal thoughts? Are there differences between verbalizing them to another African American or, for example, a white counselor? What role do sociohistorical factors play (e.g., as one client stated to me (Leach), "My ancestors were slaves and had it a lot worse than I do. I should be able to handle this"). Other questions to consider may be embedded within African

American culture itself. What cultural nuances help explain the large gap between men and women suicide completion rates? Attempt rates?

What role does daily racism play in suicide? Constantine and Sue (2007) and others (e.g., Franklin & Boyd-Franklin, 2000) have recently begun to assess daily racism, and relatedly, microaggressions. Microaggressions are the daily racial stresses that persons of color have to contend with that can tax coping strategies. Pieterse and Carter (2007) recently found that racism-related stress was related to psychological distress. Castle, Duberstein, Meldrum, Conner, and Conwell (2004) called for research to examine the effects of racism and discrimination on suicide. Their argument is that obvious racism stressors may not be sufficient to contribute to suicide, but daily, small, racism behaviors gradually build and may contribute to it. Research in this area, particularly when combined with racial identity and other identity factors (e.g., gay identity), could prove fruitful.

Utsey et al. also called for more autopsy and longitudinal studies instead of simple correlation or cross-sectional designs. While the latter are important, they often fail to include individuals from across the developmental lifespan. Given the early development of the field, qualitative designs could prove important to assess for the cultural nuances discussed above. Current assessment instruments often fail to fully grasp the cultural factors separating one ethnic group from another.

As very little empirical data exists in this area, more research assessing differences between African American attempters and completers is needed. The notion of "hidden ideators" becomes important here; individuals who do not express suicidal ideation on intake forms but are secretly suicidal. African Americans are less likely than Whites to express suicidal intent, so more research into covert exploration methods is needed. We recognize cultural differences in the expression of emotions, but virtually no research has delved into the expression of suicidal behaviors. Experimental studies using videotapes of counselors assessing for suicide using varying levels of severity and cultural sensitivity could be conducted fairly easily. A series of studies including a variety of factors could also be addressed, such as the ethnicity of the counselor, gender, age, religious affiliation, etc. In addition, cultural variables such as racial identity could be assessed. To our knowledge, only a handful of studies (e.g., Kaslow et al., 2004; Sanyika, 1995) have addressed Black racial identity and suicide, with results in the expected direction. African Americans who feel more connected to their communities are less likely to express suicidal ideation than those who feel less connected. Other studies assessing emotional support networks among Mexican Americans have found similar results (e.g., Griffith, 1985). In relation, acculturation could be assessed to determine connection with the community.

Hispanic Americans

As mentioned by Duarte-Velez and Bernal (Chapter 5), individual subgroups based on sociocultural history and country of origin are often combined into a broad term called Hispanic Americans. The majority of suicide research with Latinos have combined a variety of ethnicities into this category, and usually include adolescents. Almost two-thirds of Latinos in the U.S. are of Mexican heritage (followed by Puerto Ricans and Cubans; Paniagua, 2005) and much more research on acculturation, family dynamics, generation status, and the role of religion, for example, would be beneficial with this ethnic group. However, given the diversity within these cultures, it would benefit the field to further delineate ethnic groups, at least by beginning with country-of-origin differences. For example, some evidence indicates that Nicaraguan Americans may have higher rates than Cuban Americans (Vega, Gil, Warheit, Apospori, & Zimmerman, 1993; Vega, Gil, Zimmerman, & Warheit, 1993). From there, researchers can begin to assess nuances within Latino cultures to create a more robust understanding of the field. For example, among lower socioeconomic Puerto Ricans who had previously attempted suicide, Marrero (1998) found many of the usual factors associated with suicide (e.g., unemployment, hopelessness, family history), but also found that depression was not a strong correlate. Other authors (e.g., Gutierrez, Rodriguez, & Garcia, 2001) reported similar findings with depression, indicating that the role of depression in suicide may differ depending on the ethnic group discussed. A large study including a variety of ethnic groups could discern the role of depression in suicide. Follow-up studies examining reasons for the differences could prove fruitful and offer insight into differing prevention and intervention efforts.

An important feature within Latino cultures includes increased study of intergenerational differences both within families and across ethnic cultures as a whole. Studies on attitudes toward suicide based on acculturative changes are in their infancy yet are an important variable for consideration. The role of acculturation in suicide continues to be debated. Rasmussen, Negy, Carlson, and Burns (1997) found that although acculturation contributed to a considerable portion of the variance among Latino adolescents, it did so only in combination with other predictor variables (e.g., depression, self-worth). Determining the degree to which acculturation is a critical variable or whether it is an additive variable is a definite research need within the literature. Immigration status and age may also be important factors. Though their study did not address suicide, Padilla, Alvarez, and Lindholm (1986) found that adolescents arriving in the U.S. after age 14 with resultant acculturative stress contributed to lower self-esteem. Similar immigration-related stress was found by Mena, Padilla, and Maldonado (1987) based on year of arrival into the U.S. Are support systems related to generation status and what is this relationship with suicide? Conducting a similar study today while including suicidal behaviors (e.g., ideation, intent, attempts) would add significantly to our understanding of the role of acculturation with Latino adolescents.

Additionally, concomitant coping strategies could be assessed based on acculturation level, age of arrival, family history, self-esteem, and a variety of other sociocultural variables. The literature on coping mechanisms and styles among Latino Americans is virtually nonexistent. Given the inclusion of religion as a buffer against suicide for Latino Americans it would be interesting to delve further into the role of *fatalismo* and related constructs. Fatalismo, associated with Catholicism, is the belief that a divine providence controls the world. Hispanic cultures differ in their emphasis on fatalism, but one would hypothesize that the greater the belief, the less likely that suicidal behaviors will occur. These studies have implications for prevention and intervention efforts. Currently, no prevention efforts for Latino Americans exist, but these studies highlight differences between ethnic groups that may need to be taken into account.

General questions also need responses. Why are Mexican Americans at greater risk for suicide than other ethnic groups and what explanatory variables may account for these differences? What meaning is given to suicide across ethnic groups? O'Donnell, Stueve, Wardlaw, and O'Donnell (2003) found that half of economically disadvantaged Latino adolescents would not approach a family member if in emotional straits, and were more likely to attempt suicide than those who did approach family members. Similarly, among incarcerated youths, Sanchez-Barker (2003) found that connecting with the Latino culture increases emotional development, leading her to conclude that increasing ethnic identity may help reduce negative outcomes. Duarte-Velez and Bernal mentioned the need for including in-depth interviews from multiple informants to get narratives of family environments and family history of suicide. It is our contention that qualitative research approaches could significantly increase our knowledge of the multiple ethnic populations given the paucity of literature in the field. For example, qualitative approaches may be best to answer some of the questions above such as the meaning placed on suicide by the community. Finally, other within-group identity status models can be studied in relation to suicide. What is the role of sexual identity status as it relates to membership in an ethnic minority group? Does being a double or triple minority add to stress that may have an accumulative effect on suicidal behaviors? Does English-language fluency contribute to suicide? Griffith (1985) found that individuals with greater English-language fluency were more likely to have larger support networks than those with less fluency. Might there be a fluency by country-of-origin interaction effect? Zayas and colleagues (Zayas & Dyche, 1995; Zayas, Kaplan, Turner, Romano, & Gonzales-Ramos, 2000; Zimmerman &

Zayas, 1995) have conducted a number of studies that present important cultural factors associated with suicide, including some of those listed above. These studies are some of the few that attempt to highlight culture-specific factors within a variety of Hispanic communities.

Asian Americans

Suicide is a relatively rare event among Asian Americans, though there is increased interest in examining it among the vast ethnic groups because of increased demographic numbers in the U.S. and more awareness of the ethnic subgroups. Consistent with many of the chapters in this book, the suicide literature with Asian Americans is seriously lacking. Virtually no research has been conducted assessing specific treatment factors as they relate to suicide. As Leong, Leach, and Gupta (Chapter 6) indicated, Asian Americans now compose over four dozen ethnic groups. Unfortunately, much of the literature compiles them into one large category. Chapter 6 was intended to provide a brief overview of a few of the factors to consider within the suicide literature, though readers interested in a broader perspective can consult Leach (2006). Their chapter showed limitations of the suicide literature, as did most of the chapters in the book. Only a handful of studies delineate even a few Asian American subgroups, a significant concern given that even the limited research indicates that rates and methods may differ, perhaps based in part on cultural histories. A need for more research delineating subgroups is clearly needed in order to highlight both culture-general and culture-specific factors. Some of the questions listed above in other sections can be included here.

Because of the paucity of published literature, researchers interested in assessing Asian American suicide are in a position to significantly impact the field. For example, McKenzie, Serfaty, and Crawford (2003) reported that East Asian women over the age of 65 had the highest proportional rate of suicide among all women residing in the U.S. Elderly Chinese- and Japanese American women also have high rates, indicating a need to further determine causes for these alarming rates. Are the rates related to intergenerational acculturation differences? Does life meaning and satisfaction change depending on ethnic group or subgroup? Though longitudinal studies are often recommended they are often costly and, by definition, time-consuming. Cross-sectional designs may offer greater information in a shorter time-frame given needs within the field.

Other research needs abound. Some Asian communities are more accepting of lesbian-gay-bisexual (LGB) issues than others. What role does being LGB play in suicide given that both hiding one's sexuality and coming out often have deleterious effects? What type of intergenerational family concerns arise surrounding issues such as dating behaviors, school pressures, or coping skills expectations? Are there suicide language differences that therapists have to attend to based on subgroup? What types of differences occur between suicide attempters and completers, given that the groups are often considered distinct? Are there consistencies with these types and do gender differences occur across ethnic subgroups? Can we clarify the role of religion and spiritual influences on suicide? For example Buddhism, Confucianism, Hinduism, and Catholicism share certain ideas about suicide yet exhibit differences in the admonition against suicide (see Leach, 2006).

Theoretical and methodological considerations can be advanced, as culturally accommodative approaches may offer the most robust outcomes. Additionally, epidemiological studies that include multiple subgroups are further needed. As discussed in Westefeld et al. (Chapter 10), the suicide testing and assessment field is in its infancy with regard to all persons of color, and Asian Americans are no exception. In essence, there is a scarcity of suicide literature assessing subgroups of Asian Americans, and researchers interested in this area could add significantly to the field.

Hawaiians and Pacific Islanders

As Else, Andrade, and Nahulu (Chapter 7) indicated early in their chapter, Hawaiians and Pacific Islanders are typically combined into a general Asian American category when assessing suicide and a wide variety of other constructs. Their call for separate study of Hawaiians and Pacific Islanders exemplifies the lack of literature for these diverse ethnic groups. A brief perusal of PsycINFO, the Internet source for psychological abstracts, revealed approximately 30 entries on Hawaiians, Pacific Islanders, and suicide. The majority of these articles were non-empirical, leaving only a handful of studies assessing these populations.

Else et al. highlighted some fundamental questions that could be addressed. For example, qualitative studies could assess the influence of socio-cultural histories beset by military occupation and martial law on suicidal behaviors. Other questions raised include how individualism has influenced these groups. What are the intergenerational issues associated with suicidal behaviors, similar to other ethnic groups moving through an acculturation process? Why is the trajectory of suicide different for Hawaiians than for most other ethnic groups? How do culture and acculturation facilitate or hinder adolescent development, particularly for cultures that have ever-increasing intergenerational influences of individualism and collectivism? Does the interface of individualism and collectivism contribute to ambivalence and irrelevance, factors associated with suicide? What are the relative strengths of families, friends, ethnic groups, and communities when considering suicide buffers?

Overall, assessing suicidal behaviors among Hawaiians and Pacific Islanders is in such a state of infancy that only a small number of researchers have even attempted to determine the influences of cultural variables on suicide. We charge suicidologists to collaborate with those conducting research with these populations in order to exponentially increase our knowledge of the field, resulting in better services. This section of this chapter is the smallest for a reason, though it could easily be the largest for the exact same reason: there is such a need for research that the field is wide open. Any of the variables discussed in earlier sections could be included here.

American Indians

Similar to many of the other ethnic groups, there are significant differences among tribe affiliation on a wide variety of cultural variables. More than 500 tribal groups speaking 150 languages, with different histories and cultural nuances, exist in the U.S. American Indians have the highest proportional rate of suicide in the country, almost double the national average. The overwhelming majority of completed suicides occur among adolescents and young adults. However, there is enormous variability among the tribes, with some displaying high rates of suicide while other tribes show virtually none (Leach, 2006; Lester, 2001). Because of this variation, Alcantara and Gone (Chapter 8) highlight the need for research assessing tribal-specific risk factors. Researchers can also begin to assess the relative importance of some risk factors over others based on tribal affiliation. Conversely, utilizing a health approach, the same questions could be assessed from a coping mechanisms perspective. The authors also suggest that more evaluation is needed between urban-reared and reservation-reared individuals, consistent with Freedenthal and Stiffman (2004). Acculturation effects on suicide are not clear, especially when assessing across urban and reservation communities. Particularly when assessing small communities, collective depression, both historical and current, is a virtually untouched research area with implications for definitions of life satisfaction among tribal groups, meaning hope and numerous other variables.

Less access to mental health services has been suggested as one of the reasons for an overall high rate of suicide, and this ecological approach can be applied to a variety of ethnic groups. It is well known that persons of color consistently underutilize mental health services (e.g., Paniagua, 2005), so such services may have to go to them. One way to increase services is through prevention efforts. As Alcantara and Gone indicate, few prevention efforts have been implemented, and these are generally not founded on rigorous research. Consistent with the call by Middlebrook, LeMaster, Beals, Novins, and Manson (2001), more research, especially tribal-specific research, is needed. Suicide prevention should focus on the family, community, and cultural values. While some values may differ across tribes, common themes such as spirituality and collective history can be incorporated across prevention efforts. What fundamental factors should be incorporated regardless of tribal affiliation? What is the role of spirituality in suicide prevention and intervention depending on tribe? Is spirituality more influential for reservation-versus urban-based individuals? Do family and community play differential roles in prevention and intervention? Alcantara and Gone discuss the benefits of incorporating a transactional–ecological model to target differing trajectories based on a variety of sociocultural variables (alcohol availability, transition to high school).

Mixed-methods designs are needed to assess cultural nuances across tribes. Similarly, Chapter 8 discusses the need to include the community as a research member when studying suicide. Communities of all types across the country have experienced the lone researcher going into their neighborhoods, collecting data, and then not give back to the community. Given some of the close-knit American Indian communities it is imperative that community participation be part of the study. Related, prevention and intervention efforts clearly benefit when the community is involved. In fact, traditional healers can be an effective means of assisting with the process (Gone & Alcantara, 2006).

Prevention

Walker, Townley, and Asiamah. (Chapter 9) indicated that the best prevention efforts to date were designed for specific American Indian tribal groups, though these efforts are largely unsystematic. There are a few exceptions, such as an empirically validated prevention program by LaFromboise and Howard-Pitney (1995), using a social-cognitive approach with the Zuni tribe. Among others also mentioned was the Indian Health Services funded Adolescent Suicide Prevention Project. Unfortunately, Walker et al. also indicate that there are no specific prevention programs designed for African Americans and Asian Americans, and very few for Hispanic Americans. However, the authors did make suggestions for those interested in designing prevention programs. For example, parental influences are strong among Asian Americans and should be considered important when designing and assessing programs. Marginalization and acculturation stress, especially among lower SES groups, may contribute to suicide. Inclusion of these factors by means of community and family connections may be especially important to to answer prevention questions. Topics such as cultural and racial identity and family cohesion may be particularly important as part of prevention efforts.

An often overlooked segment of the population is the elderly. Among both Chinese Americans and European Americans, elderly persons have very high rates of suicide. Research into prevention of suicide among the elderly is virtually nonexistent. Many articles discuss the need for elderly suicide prevention but very few attempts have been made, and none directed toward ethnic communities. That said, trajectories differ across ethnic groups, so many researchers perceive little need for such research when compared with the rates of adolescent suicide. For example, elderly African Americans and American Indians have low elderly suicide rates, making prevention efforts difficult.

Walker et al. offer some other insights into possible research agendas. They correctly indicate that researchers must begin to examine meanings and word usage when discussing illnesses within communities. For example, they mention that some American Indian groups do not use words consistent with depression and anxiety, highlighting the need for more research foundation prior to developing prevention efforts. Good qualitatively designed studies assessing how words are used to describe feelings related to suicide are of utmost importance and are necessary prior to prevention development. Other areas in need of research studies include cultural resilience factors, acculturation vulnerability, and racial and ethnic stressors. Many of the prevention efforts currently in use today were developed for adolescents and young adults based on a White, middle-class perspective. Prevention programming with ethnic minority youth has been minimally recognized (Kataoka, Stein, Lieberman, & Wong, 2003).

A particularly interesting assessment method was mentioned in Chapter 9. Multilevel statistical modeling can determine the influence of reservation location or rural versus urban effects on suicide. This method would help determine the strength of variables across multiple domains and might need serious consideration if researchers want to determine specific influential factors in different regions. Alcantara and Gone mentioned the need to delineate individual tribal cultural influences on suicide and this method would assist in making a large leap to achieving this goal. This method could be helpful in furthering the goal of understanding alternative conceptualizations of suicide, because definitions can differ depending on ethnic group and the local community.

Overall, suicide prevention programs developed for communities of color is abysmal and in need of significant development. Unfortunately, until many of the questions in previous chapters of this book are answered it will be difficult to develop these programs. Researchers interested in prevention who are also culturalists may want to initiate discussions regarding cultural factors associated with specific ethnic groups that have potential for inclusion in prevention programs. From there prevention refinements can be determined and implemented.

Measurement and Assessment Issues

In the Westefeld, Range, Greenfeld, and Kettman chapter (Chapter 10) it was noted that, though multiple studies have included ethnic minorities as sample groups, few have systematically assessed suicide with ethnicity as a cultural variable. Additionally, given the available instruments, very few have incorporated ethnicity. Perhaps we should consider measurement from a different perspective. Rather than relying on questionnaires alone we can begin to consider more integrative research designs and statistical procedures. Molock et al. (Chapter 12) propose that social scientists begin to collaborate with other fields familiar with fuzzy logic theory. Fuzzy logic is a means to assess large numbers of variables on multiple outcomes in a nonlinear manner. It has great potential in the suicide literature to determine issues such as whether suicide rates differ nationally with finer distinctions. As Molock et al. indicated, social scientists are generally not familiar with these procedures, leading to a need for increased interdisciplinary collaboration. Other underutilized research designs can be incorporated into the literature, for example multilevel linear growth models (see McCullough & Root, 2005 for an expanded discussion) that can assess individual longitudinal data. These designs allow for multiple measurement times over multiple people, which could be beneficial for those in therapy groups.

Instrument development and validation are two areas in need of significant reexamination. Which components of traditional suicide instruments can be considered universal and which need modification based on ethnic and cultural backgrounds? Westefeld et al. reported that the majority of suicide assessment instruments either have no reported ethnic data or utilized samples in which persons of color were significantly underrepresented. In essence, which suicide-related tests have greater validity among ethnic groups? Do test standardization differences occur among ethnic groups? Is the factor structure of instruments the same? Should wording differences occur for the same general constructs? For example, the authors reported a study indicating that Muslims may endorse an item such as, "Do you wish God would let you die?" more than standard items. Do clients see testing instruments as superseding the therapeutic relationship? What is the role of acculturation in test development given language changes as a result of acculturation?

As discussed in Chapter 9, cultural issues such as discrimination, racial and ethnic identity, and acculturation are in need of further development. Existing models of suicide often include "common" beliefs that negative rumination, various stressors, and impulsivity contribute to suicide. While these may be true, what is minimized is the cultural factors contributing to the rumination and stressors. For example, as mentioned earlier, the impact of daily racial microaggressions (e.g., Constantine & Sue, 2007) on suicidal behaviors may prove fruitful. In essence, what is the cumulative impact on depression and hopelessness of small racial battles that occur on an almost daily basis? Methodologically, what is needed is more mediator models that account for the effects of cultural variables on depression and suicide. For example, research indicates that racism and depression are positively correlated (e.g., Watkins, Green, Rivers, & Rowell, 2006), and research indicates that depression and suicide are positively correlated. To what extent does racism influence suicide (Castle, Duberstein, Meldrum, Conner, & Conwell, 2004)?

Other questions arising from our limited understanding of ethnic testing and assessment include: What differences among ethnic groups occur regarding Reasons for Living (RFL)? In essence, do some ethnic groups endorse RFL items over other items and in which groups is RFL more likely to influence suicide based on racial identity or acculturation status? Are there differences in ethnic self-disclosure of suicide ideation and previous attempts rather than general self-disclosure? African Americans are less likely to endorse suicide items than European Americans. How can the self-disclosure literature be modified to include ethnicity? In Chapter 10, Westefeld et al. reported a study on hidden ideators, with results indicating that the majority of hidden ideators were persons of color. More research assessing these ideators is clearly needed, and intake forms may need to be modified to catch these individuals. Studies assessing the language of intake forms could be completed to create forms that optimize the assessment of ideators. Is hidden ideation based on the level of discrimination experienced, racial identity, spirituality, or family cohesion? What is the role of problem-solving styles on suicide assessment? Further work on religious problem solving and ethnicity may yield fruitful results. Overall, the suicide testing and assessment literature has significantly lacked strategic and rigorous evaluation, with most of what is known based on inadequate samples and little within-group delineation. Questions such as these and many others can be conducted across a variety of ethnic groups, particularly if more collaboration among diverse geographic researchers occurs.

Treatment

As noted in Chapter 2, it becomes difficult to intervene without fully understanding the meaning, beliefs, and values associated with suicide. Different ethnic groups may define and talk about suicide differently, and it is noteworthy that there is not more research in these areas. Is there a relationship between definitions and number and types of attempts? Rogers and Soyka (2004) were critical of the "one size fits all" approach to practice guidelines and suicidal clients. Their notion that alternative and more flexible models (Thomas & Leitner, 2005) are needed captures the spirit of this book. Their "ideal" approach found within the CAMS model (Jobes, 2006), though not specifically designated as cultural, is consistent with a culturally sensitive approach. In this model both client and counselor work together to arrive at solutions, rather than counselors quickly jumping into a general crisis intervention mode. Additionally, their argument could be extended to state that culturally sensitive treatments are needed regardless of type of intervention (prevention, intervention, postvention). The authors stress the need for more research using the CAMS model as a theoretical foundation. Rogers and Whitehead (Chapter 11) also discussed Baumeister's work on self-loathing as it could relate to suicide. Essentially, participants could rate themselves on the degree to which their suicidality is related to their feelings of self and others, followed by ranking reasons for living and dying. It is easy to understand that different ethnic groups may view these differently, especially if considering constructs such as collectivism, family of origin, family cohesion, spirituality, social support systems, and shame and guilt.

As Rogers and Whitehead indicated, more research is needed on values clarification of counselors (Shea, 1999), and they list a number of questions for the counselor to ask himself or herself that could easily be translated into research questions. Consistent with other recommendations in other chapters the authors also suggest that more research on language use, including dialects, is in significant need. For example, does the client fully understand his or her rights and can consent be fully given if the language of the consent form or release form, for example, is the second language of the client?

The literature within the counseling psychology field on ethnic matching (counselor–client) is large and sometimes contradictory (e.g., Atkinson & Lowe, 1995), yet virtually nothing is understood about how matching applies to suicide interventions. Multiple studies using case scenarios or videos could easily be accomplished assessing participant responses to various counselors. What factors are most important for clients based on racial identity, acculturation status, and other within-group cultural variables? Perhaps more importantly, these studies could be modified based on the level of client suicidality. For example, is ethnic matching more important for less suicidal people—perhaps those with fleeting suicidal thoughts rather than active, consistent thoughts? Perhaps clients with a history of suicide but not presently? Does it differ based on ethnic group? Of course, ethical considerations are necessary whenever engaging in this type of research.

Readers can see that, given earlier chapters and even this chapter, until more is understood about ethnicity and suicide it will be difficult to offer culturally appropriate treatments. This area has the potential for explosive growth given that the groundwork has already been laid in areas like ethnic matching. It is through further research efforts that the potential of flexible approaches to suicide interventions can become realized.

Training and Research

Suicide training in graduate programs varies widely, and as Molock, Matlin, and Prempeh (Chapter 12) stated, it is important for us to gain a better understanding of the actual training that occurs nationally, particularly as it relates to competency standards. Along with the type of training, how does the training and student knowledge differ based on level of training? Developmental models of counselor development (e.g., Stoltenberg, McNeill, & Delworth, 1998) are based on the premise that counselors progress through a series of stages from novice counselor to expert. It would be expected that the level of suicide understanding and intervention competency is based on students' respective levels of development. More difficult suicidal client cases would be more easily handled by more advanced students. Thus, studies assessing varying levels of suicide difficulty by level of counselor development could be accomplished using role plays or video vignettes. What strategies can be implemented by trainers to assist counselors (in training) to conduct more effective suicide assessments? How much of their suicide training gets incorporated into actual suicide interventions? Based on developmental level, what level of client difficulty causes the greatest amount of counselor concern? What cultural variables are the more advanced counselors considering compared with the less advanced counselors? Does ethnicity play more of a role if the counselor and client are ethnically dissimilar? Are more advanced counselors more likely to use an "ideal" approach than less advanced counselors?

Molock et al. described the research difficulty in recruiting participants of color, and the need for more community participation. However, she indicated that communities are hesitant to assist in research efforts given that little return benefit is given. It is clear that researchers will have to become more creative with their efforts and include communities of color in order to add validity to their interventions. Joining with local community leaders instead of a "hit and run" approach to community research will be necessary. For example, Molock suggested that asking community leaders to be members of dissertation committees may open doors to the community. It was suggested that researchers revisit Felner and Felner's (1989) transactional–ecological model, which is much more community and culturally focused as a means to theoretically organize the research. Issues such as service utilization are needed, including an understanding of the local norms to seeking mental health treatment rather than the treatment itself. Similarly, Molock et al. indicated that trainees should understand community-based participatory research models, especially when considering developing prevention programs. Overall, it is evident that the field is lacking in suicide training research with respect to students and clients of color.

Common Themes

Readers will notice some common threads interwoven throughout the chapters. First, a number of authors indicated that very little theory is available to guide their research, and some suggested borrowing either from other fields or modifying existing theory to include cultural variables. It is difficult to develop culturally sensitive prevention and intervention programs, for example, when relying on a generic framework based on White, middle-class values. We will return to this very important issue at the end of the chapter.

The amount of incremental validity is related to the second challenge, increasing our knowledge of within-group factors. Cultural within-group variables such as acculturation, racial identity, and perceptions of racism have been assessed to various degrees, although they are low overall when compared with well-established suicide correlates such as depression and diagnosis. What is needed is to continue to reconsider what is known about suicide within a context of culture. For example, few studies have considered whether suicide ideation rates among people with affective disorders differ based on racial identity status. We can continue to assess affective disorders and suicide while including some study participants of color, but unless ethnic and cultural groups are primary considerations, our understanding of the role of culture will be limited. Additionally, we can assess cultural variables across and within groups simultaneously rather than simply individually. For example, degree of acculturation has been assessed to a moderate degree, usually in relation to the Latino population. Significantly fewer studies have been conducted with Asian Americans or other immigrant groups. Does degree of acculturation have similar amounts of influence on suicide across multiple ethnic groups, do they differ, or do they differ in relation to other factors such as family stability, religion, and socioeconomic status? Coping strategies and other barriers to suicide could also be included. Numerous studies have indicated that strong family ties are considered a buffer against suicide, yet it is unclear whether family has equivalent effects across groups.

Each of the five ethnic-specific chapters (African American, Asian American, Hawaiian and Pacific Islander, Latino American, Native American) underscored the need to examine within group differences. Each indicated that their respective ethnic group does not constitute a unitary category given the large variations based on country or tribe of origin, acculturation level, racial identity, family history, religious background, sexual orientation, and a host of other factors. Researchers can begin by examining some of the basics more closely: for example, how do two or more broadly defined Asian ethnic groups differ and maintain commonalities regarding suicidal behaviors? Are there differences within country of origin based on religious attitudes? From there researchers can begin to consider more in-depth cultural nuances. The other authors were equally concerned about the continued potential to conglomerate individuals based on simple ethnic group criteria. Readers can draw their own examples from their own interests but it is clear that the influence of culture in relation to well-established ideas about suicide in the U.S. is lacking.

Third, methodological considerations must be addressed. Some of the authors expressed the need for greater design complexity. For example, cross-sectional designs have been under-utilized within the ethnicity and suicide literature. Both qualitative and mixed-method designs are strongly encouraged given the infancy of the field. Suicide language was mentioned in multiple chapters as an area of needed study. Members of ethnic groups may have a variety of definitions of suicide and may describe it differently in clinical sessions. Qualitative studies can be particularly useful to discern the language nuances associated with suicide. Mixed-methods designs have become more frequently used within the social science literature and its potential with suicide studies is extensive. As discussed in Chapter 10, few research instruments have been designed that remotely included persons of color much less included a contextual theoretical framework, yet through qualitative and mixed-methods designs it is hoped that contextualized instrument development and refinement will occur. Other approaches such as multilevel statistical modeling hold promise in the field. Finally, researchers need to increase the number of mediating models that help explain suicide. For example, depression and suicide ideation may be mediated through hopelessness and loneliness (Chou, 2006).

In sum, each of the areas presented in this text work in tandem, and each much be addressed if the suicide field is to become more inclusive. It is our belief that culture must be considered more fully as a foundation from which to address suicide, though the degree to which it is influential will differ widely based on the type of research project. However, it is through cultural consideration that the field will become more robust, and we will be able to better predict, prevent, and intervene when suicidal behaviors occur. Toward this end, we would like to propose a theoretical framework for guiding research in this arena.

□ Proposed Theoretical Framework for Research on Suicide among Ethnic Minorities

As noted earlier in our review of theory as reflected in the Leenaars and Lester chapters, there is no current or past theory development with regard to suicide among racial and ethnic minority groups in the U.S. Furthermore, one of the common themes running throughout the chapters is the lack of any theoretical framework to guide research. Therefore, a major challenge for researchers will be to identify a culturally relevant and suitable theoretical framework in which to examine culture and suicide.

Following up on Chapter 8's recommendation to examine culture and suicide within an ecological perspective, we would like to propose using Brofenbrenner's (1979) Ecological Systems Theory as a theoretical framework in which to examine and consider culture's impact on suicide among ethnic minorities. In his model, Bronfenbrenner (1977, 1979) identified five major interrelated subsystems influencing human behavior: (a) the microsystem, which consists of the interpersonal relations and settings in which an individual lives including family, peers, school, neighborhood; (b) the mesosystem, which consists of interactions between two or more microsystem environments, such as the relations between an individual's school and family environments and between peers and family, etc; (c) the exosystem, which involves linkages between subsystems that indirectly influence individuals, such as the health care systems and grandparents or between a parent's job stress and child's extramural activities; (d) the macrosystem, which consists of the ideological components of a given society such as norms and values, e.g., Judeo-Christian ethic and democratic ideals that dominate the U.S. culture, and (e) the chronosystem, which integrates the temporal dimension and is concerned with the patterning of environmental events and transitions over the life course, and effects created by time or critical periods in development.

In applying Bronfenbrenner's model to the study of suicide among ethnic minorities, contextual factors can be considered from these multiple systems in order to examine individuals more robustly. This theoretical framework may help begin to answer questions related to which factors maintain "universality" when considered from a contextualist perspective, and which allow for greater predictive validity when added to our current conceptualizations of suicide. These questions can be assessed from a variety of subtexts. For example, depression is generally considered a correlate of suicide, yet authors in this text have presented studies indicating that depression may not be a good predictor of suicide when considering some cultural variables. Shame has been mentioned as a suicide correlate among Asian Americans, yet shame occurs in practically all cultures and the degree to which its importance in suicidal behaviors differs among ethnic groups may be considerable. Researchers need to begin to approach suicide from a cultural framework to a greater degree than it presently does, meaning that cultural theories and variables should be well integrated into studies. It is only then that we can be able to determine the incremental validity associated with cultural factors.

We have chosen Bronfenbrenner's model (1977, 1979) because it recognizes the multiple levels and contextual factors that influence human development. As a model of human development, it is able to capture the positive aspects of development (e.g., positive psychology) as well as the negative aspects of development (e.g., self-harm and self-destructive behaviors). We believe that the use of a model such as Bronfenbrenner's will not only guide us with regard to what contextual factors to study but will also enrich our research directly by including ecologically valid designs and variables in our study of suicide among ethnic minorities. Based on Bronfenbrenner's (1977, 1979) model, we will present four broad propositions for using this theoretical framework to study culture and suicide among ethnic minorities in the U.S.

- **Proposition 1**: Applying Bronfenbrenner's ecological model to the study of culture and suicide will increase our knowledge base with regard to multilevel and contextual influences on suicide among ethnic minorities.
- **Proposition 2**: Bronfenbrenner's articulation of the microsystem, mesosystem, exosystem, macrosystem, and chronosystem is flexible enough to accommodate for cultural influences on suicide within sub-cultural groups of a country (e.g., ethnic minorities in the U.S.) as well as suicide across different cultures (e.g., patterns of suicide in Sweden versus China).
- **Proposition 3**: The study of culture and suicide needs to examine the interactive and cumulative effects of the structures and processes within the microsystem, mesosystem, exosystem, macrosystem, and chronosystem on an individual's risk and protective factors for suicide.
- **Proposition 4**: The elements within the microsystem, mesosystem, exosystem, macrosystem, and chronosystem that may shape and influence suicide will vary across cultures not only within each major systems but also as interactions between systems.

It is important to note that our presentation of this theoretical model is meant to be only a starting point for us in guiding research in this arena. Future theoretical refinements will be needed in order to specify how Bronfenbrenner's model (1977, 1979) will facilitate specific research studies of suicide among ethnic minorities. We hope that this proposal will serve as a stimulus for using Bronfenbrenner's rich and complex model of human development to guide research on suicide among ethnic minorities as well as an impetus to search for other theoretical frameworks.

□ References

Atkinson, D.R. & Lowe, S.M. (1995). The role of ethnicity, cultural knowledge, and conventional techniques in counseling and psychotherapy. In J. Ponterotto, J.M. Casas, L.A. Suzuki, & C.M. Alexander (Eds.), *Handbook of multicultural counseling* (pp. 387–414). Thousand Oaks, CA: Sage.

Boykin, A.W. (1983). The triple quandary and the schooling of Afro-American children. In E. Neisser (Ed.), *The school achievement of minority children* (pp. 57–92). Hillside, NJ: Lawrence Erlbaum Associates.

Bronfenbrenner, U. (1977). Toward an experimental ecology of human development. *American Psychologist, 32*, 513–531.

Brofenbrenner, U. (1979). *The ecology of human development*. Cambridge, MA: Harvard University Press.

Castle, K., Duberstein, P.R., Meldrum, S., Conner, K.R., & Conwell, Y. (2004). Risk factors for suicide in Blacks and Whites: An analysis of data from the 1993 National Mortality Followback Survey. *American Journal of Psychiatry, 161*, 452–458.

Chou, K.L. (2006). Reciprocal relationship between ideation and depression in Hong Kong elderly Chinese. *International Journal of Geriatric Psychiatry, 21*, 594–596.

Constantine, M.G. & Sue, D.W. (2007). Perceptions of racial microaggressions among Black supervisees in cross-racial dyads. *Journal of Counseling Psychology, 54*, 142–153.

Felner, R.D. & Felner, T.Y. (1989). Primary prevention programs in the educational context: A transactional–ecological framework and analysis. In L.A. Bond & B.E. Compas (Eds.), *Primary prevention and promotion in the schools* (pp. 13–49). Newbury-Park, CA: Sage.

Franklin, A.J. & Boyd-Franklin, N. (2000). Invisibility syndrome: A clinical model of racism on African American males. *American Journal of Orthopsychiatry, 70*, 33–41.

Freedenthal, S. & Stiffman, A.R. (2004). Suicidal behavior in urban American Indian adolescents: A comparison with reservation youth in a southwestern state. *Suicide and Life-Threatening Behavior, 34*, 160–171.

Gone, J.P., & Alcantara, C. (2006). *Traditional healing and suicide prevention in Native American communities: Research and policy consideration*. Unpublished report contracted by the Office of Behavioral and Social Sciences Research, National Institutes of Health (Contract No. MI–60823).

Griffith, J.E. (1985). Social support providers: Who are they? Where are they met?—and the relationship of network characteristics to psychological distress. *Basic and Applied Social Psychology, 6*, 41–60.

Gutierrez, P.M., Rodriguez, P.J., & Garcia, P. (2001). Suicide risk factors for young adults: Testing a model across ethnicities. *Death Studies, 25*, 319–340.

Jobes, D.A. (2006). *Managing suicidal risk: A collaborative approach*. New York: Guilford.

Kaslow, N.J., Webb-Price, A., Wyckoff, S., Grall, M.B., Sherry, A., Young, S., Scholl, L., Upshaw, V.M., Rashid, A., Jackson, E.B., & Bethea, K. (2004). Person factors associated with suicidal behavior among African American women and men. *Cultural Diversity and Ethnic Minority Psychology, 10*, 5–22.

Kataoka, S.H., Stein, B.D., Lieberman, R., & Wong, M. (2003). Suicide Prevention in Schools: Are We Reaching Minority Youths? *Psychiatric Services, 54*, 1444.

LaFromboise, T.D. & Howard-Pitney, B. (1995). The Zuni Life Skills Development curriculum: A collaborative approach to curriculum development. *American Indian and Alaska Native Mental Health Research*, 4, 98–121.

Leach, M.M. (2006). *Cultural diversity and suicide: Ethnic, religious, gender, and sexual orientation perspectives*. Binghamton, NY: Haworth Press.

Lester, D. (2001). *Suicide in American Indians*. Hauppauge, NY: Nova Science Publishers.

Marrero, D.N. (1998). Suicide attempts among Puerto Ricans of low socioeconomic status. *Dissertation Abstracts International: Section B: The Sciences and Engineering, 58*(7–B), 3929.

McCullough, M.E. & Root, L.M. (2005). Forgiveness as change. In E.L. Worthington, Jr., *Handbook of forgiveness* (pp. 91–107). New York: Routledge.

McKenzie, K., Serfaty, M., & Crawford, M. (2003). Suicide in ethnic minority groups. *British Journal of Psychiatry, 183*, 100–101.

Middlebrook, D.L., LeMaster, P.L., Beals, J., Novins, D.K., & Manson, S.M. (2001). Suicide prevention in Native American and Asaska Native communities: A critical review of programs. *Suicide and Life-Threatening Behavior, 31*, 132–149.

Mena, F.J., Padilla, A.M., & Maldonado, M. (1987). Accultruative stress and coping strategies among immigrant and later generation college students. *Hispanic Journal of Behavioral Sciences, 9*, 207–225.

O'Donnell, L., Stueve, A., Wardlaw, D., & O'Donnell, C. (2003). Adolescent suicidality and adult support: The reach for health study of urban youth. *American Journal of Health Behavior, 27*, 633–644.

Padilla, A., Alvarez, M., & Lindholm, K.J. (1986). Generational status and personality factors as predictors of stress in students. *Hispanic Journal of Behavioral Sciences, 8*, 275–288.

Paniagua, F.A. (2005). *Assessing and treating culturally diverse clients*. Thousand Oaks, CA: Sage.

Pieterse, A.L. & Carter, R.J. (2007). An examination of the relationship between general life stress, racism-related stress, and psychological health among Black men. *Journal of Counseling Psychology, 54*, 101–109.

Rasmussen, K.M., Negy, C., Carlson, R., & Burns, J.M. (1997). Suicide ideation and acculturation among low socioeconomic status Mexican American adolescents. *Journal of Early Adolescence, 17*, 390–407.

Rogers, J.M. & Soyka, K.M. (2004). "One size fits all": An existential-constructivist perspective on the crisis intervention approach with suicidal individuals. *Journal of Contemporary Psychotherapy, 34*, 7–22.

Stoltenber, C.D., McNeill, B., & Delworth, U. (1998). *IDM supervision*. San Francisco: Jossey-Bass.

Thomas, J.C. & Leitner, L.M. (2005). Styles of suicide intervention: Professionals' responses and clients' preferences. *The Humanistic Psychologist, 33*, 145–165.

Sanchez-Barker, T.N. (2003). Coping with depression: Adapted for use with incarcerated Hispanic youth. Dissertation Abstracts International: Section B: The Sciences and Engineering, 64(5–B), 2403.

Sanyika, A.M. (1995). Distinguishing suicide from parasuicide among African Americans. *Dissertation Abstracts International, 56*, 4–B, 2340.

Shea, S.C. (1999). *The practical art of suicide assessment*. New York: Wiley.

Vega, W.A., Gil, A., Warheit, G., Apospori, E., & Zimmerman, R. (1993). The relationship of drug use to suicide ideation and attempts among African American, Hispanic, and white non-Hispanic male adolescents. *Suicide and Life-Threatening Behavior, 23*, 110–119.

Vega, W.A., Gil, A.G., Zimmerman, R.S., & Warheit, G.J. (1993). Risk factors for suicidal behavior among Hispanic, African-American, and non-Hispanic white boys in early adolescence. *Ethnicity and Disease, 3*, 229–241.

Watkins, D.C., Green, B.L., Rivers, B.M., & Rowell, K.L., (2006). Depression and black men: Implications for future research. *Journal of Men's Health and Gender, 3*, 227–235.

Zayas, L.H. & Dyche, L.A. (1995). Suicide attempts in Puerto Rican adolescent females: A sociocultural perspective and family treatment approach. In J. K. Zimmerman & G.M. Asnis (Eds.), *Treatment approaches with suicidal adolescents*. (pp. 203–218). Oxford, England: John Wiley and Sons.

Zayas, L.H., Kaplan, C., & Turner, S., Romano, K., & Gonzalez-Ramos, G. (2000). Understanding suicide attempts by adolescent Hispanic females. *Social Work, 45*, 53–63.

Zimmerman, J.K. & Zayas, L.H. (1995). Suicidal adolescent Latinas: Culture, female development, and restoring the mother-daughter relationship. In S. S. Canetto & D. Lester (Eds.), *Women and suicidal behavior*. (pp. 120–132). New York: Springer Publishing.

INDEX

A

B

C

D

E

I

J

K

L

M

N

O

P

R

S

T

U

V

W

Y